Our Sovereign State ★

To Lincoln Steffens, George Norris, and Fiorello La Guardia,

great fighters in the cause of good government

★OUR SOVEREIGN STATE

★ EDITED BY ROBERT S. ALLEN
Editor of "Our Fair City," and Co-author of "Washington Merry-Go-Round"

NEW YORK ★

THE VANGUARD PRESS, INC.

CONTENTS ★ ★ ★

INTRODUCTION: *The Shame of the States*
BY ROBERT S. ALLEN

MASSACHUSETTS: *Prisoner of the Past*.   23
WILLIAM V. SHANNON

NEW YORK: *Backslider*   69
ROBERT G. SPIVACK

PENNSYLVANIA: *Bossed Cornucopia*   96
HERMAN A. LOWE

GEORGIA: *Paradise of Oligarchy*   132
TARLETON COLLIER

OHIO: *Oxcart Government!*   166
RICHARD L. MAHER

ILLINOIS: *The "New Look"*   189
DON E. CHAMBERLAIN

WISCONSIN: *A State That Glories in Its Past*   216
WILLIAM T. EVJUE

LOUISIANA: *Beak Too Big For Its Belly*   245
RALPH S. O'LEARY

NEBRASKA: *Norris: In Victory and Defeat*   278
J. E. LAWRENCE

v

Contents

TEXAS: *Owned by Oil and Interlocking Directorates* 314
  HART STILWELL

UTAH: *Contrary State* 345
  ERNEST LINFORD

CALIFORNIA: *The First Hundred Years* 373
  RICHARD V. HYER

Introduction ★ ★ ★

THE SHAME OF THE STATES

ROBERT S. ALLEN

STATE government is the tawdriest, most incompetent, and most stultifying unit of the nation's political structure.

In state government are to be found in their most extreme and vicious forms all the worst evils of misrule in the country. Venality, open domination and manipulation by vested interests, unspeakable callousness in the care of the sick, aged, and unfortunate, criminal negligence in law enforcement, crass deprivation of primary constitutional rights, obfuscation, obsolescence, obstructionism, incompetence, and even outright dictatorship are widespread characteristics.

Further, imbedded between the municipalities at the bottom and the federal system on top, state government is the wellspring of many of the principal poisons that plague both.

"Rotten borough" state government holds in crippling thralldom our greatest cities. It deprives them of equitable legislative representation, of a just weight in the election of state officials, mulcts them, and meddles harassingly in the pettiest details of their household affairs.

The Police Commissioner of Boston * is appointed by the State and not by the Mayor. Boston subways, parks, sewers, water system, and even bathing beaches are ruled by the

---

* Chapter I, Page 23, "Massachusetts: *Prisoner of the Past*"

State and not by the municipality. Mighty New York City,* with a budget several times that of the State, has to go hat-in-hand to the latter for permission to deal with transit problems. Chicago's † transit system is run by a State body, and the pensions the great metropolis pays its police and firemen are fixed by the State. Atlanta,‡ with a population greater than the combined total of fifty-five Georgia counties, still has only six "unit" votes as against their one hundred and ten in the nomination of State officers. And when Atlanta wants to dispose of an abandoned water plant, the city must go to the State for permission.

At the same time, behind the phony cloak of "states' rights," state government is the ready tool of every monopolistic and reactionary interest seeking to block and hamstring national liberal measures.

The whining wail of "states' rights" is to be heard in the attempted steal by the big oil giants of the oil tidelands, the nation's last great oil reserves; in the multi-million-dollar jeremiad of the American Medical Association against national health insurance; in the racist filibusters against civil rights; in the huge lobbying and pressure drives of the utilities against TVA, MVA, CVA, and other vital conservation and power developments; in the fusillades against extending social-security benefits, against strengthening child-labor laws, against low-cost housing, federal aid to education, federal regulation of the stupendous insurance monopoly, etc., etc., etc.

It is a rare liberal measure or project of national import that is not challenged by the shabby ghost of "states' rights." The years of the New Deal and Fair Deal have reverberated with the hoarse croaks and groans of this bedraggled specter.

* Chapter II, Page 69, "New York: *Backslider*"
† Chapter VI, Page 189, "Illinois: *The New Look*"
‡ Chapter IV, Page 132, "Georgia: *Paradise of Oligarchy*"

Yet, while invoking it furiously and incessantly, state government never fails to rush clamorously to Washington the instant the going gets rough.

The 1949 Nebraska Legislature self-righteously adopted a resolution demanding federal economy. But when severe blizzards struck the State, it immediately raised a hue and cry for federal aid. Washington responded immediately and generously, spending millions of dollars to save Nebraska meat and dairy herds. The State, officially on record both for federal economy and for federal relief for its cattle, expended the grand total of $100,000 for that purpose.

Numerous other instances of such blatant inconsistency are to be found on the records of virtually every state in the Union.

The arrant speciousness of the "states' rights" cry was forcefully summed up by Professor T. V. Smith, University of Chicago, and a former Illinois Congressman. In " 'States' Rights' and the Rights of the States," published in the magazine of the Council of State Governments, he declared:

"When New England long ago talked big about 'states' rights,' the talk was, as we now see, a confession of weakness. Tall talk was trying to substitute for inefficient competition. When the talk migrated to the South and crystallized as a sacred dogma, it betokened, as we now see, an inferior labor system and a state of mind closely approaching self-pity. Whatever power states have lost, or do lose, has its cause obscured rather than clarified by reassertions of such dogma.

"What rights the states have lost have been compensated for in privileges gained. That accounts for the willingness with which the states have lost what they have lost, especially during the depression years. There certainly has been no snatching of power from them; there has, to the contrary, been much beseeching on their part for the privilege of participating in the numerous benefits offered by the federal government.

"We can say this for the federal government in recent years: What it has done has been done not to destroy the states but to save their solvency, to preserve their dignity, to further their integrity. Federal solicitude for the sovereignty of the states is no new thing. Alexander Hamilton was the first New Dealer in this regard.

"Instead of passing by on the other side of the impoverished original states, Hamilton boldly proposed that the new federal government, itself in debt some fifty-five millions, should assume the debt burden of the thirteen states, some twenty-five millions more (millions then looked like billions now). It was ruin for the government, shouted all those who made it their business to fear their own fears. So today. Strangely enough, there was not much complaint of the loss of 'states' rights' then, and not much now, from the shuffling of debts off shoulders that could not bear them to shoulders that could.

"Solvency of states saved in recent years, the federal government has continued its older policy of helping the states maintain their dignity. To extend the power of the states beyond the state boundaries is no help to the dignity of the state-idea in our system. And it is precisely this sort of trial which we inflict when we leave to the states the matter of controlling corporations that outrun the state in scope, if not also in power. By federal control over interstate commerce in general and by a growing disposition federally to regulate specifically the great corporations, the national government has been doing its share to keep intact the dignity of the states. By such methods, culminating in the Wage and Hour Law, we have raised a friendly ceiling over the states and laid a solid floor under state standards of industrial decency.

"And, faith, it has not been done a day too soon for the dignity of the states. They are quite helpless before the great interstate monopolies that can migrate from state to state like birds of passage, and can even secede from the nation, as the states are unable to do. Moreover, in dealing with these giants, the states are at a great disadvantage in being required by the Constitution to maintain a democratic form of government. The corporations can be feudalistic or even totalitarian, so far as state power is concerned to say nay to their will to power. They can, and do, as the La Follette committee revealed, maintain private police forces and stock their arsenals not only with guns and revolvers but with other weapons such as gases.

"Although they are never fully sovereign nor are they yet

wholly subsidiary, the states in relation to the nation present, then, as Woodrow Wilson once remarked, not so much a problem of sovereignty as 'a question of vitality.' "

Lack of vitality in state government is more glaring than ever before in the history of the nation. It is more glaring because the need for broad-visioned, courageous, and honest public administration on that level is greater than ever before.

There was a time when state government led in social, economic, and political advances. Under such Governors as Robert M. La Follette, Sr., in Wisconsin, James Stephen Hogg in Texas,* Hiram Johnson in California, Alfred E. Smith in New York, and others, state government was the spearhead of government "by the people and for the people" on all levels.

The ideals that were proclaimed and the advances gained reverberated far and wide. They uplifted the moral tone and stature of the whole national body politic. They gave to government a quality and dignity it has rarely had in American history. They set goals and inspired emulation in every level of public administration.

Where is that kind of exalting state government to be found in the nation today!

There are some enlightened, honest, and well-intentioned governors, legislators, and administrators. Their zeal, struggles, and bitter rebuffs are graphically portrayed in the pages of this book. But they are pathetically few in number and even more sadly thwarted and frustrated by the stifling inadequacies and imbecilities of state government.

The whole system of state government is moribund, corrosive, and deadening. It is riddled with senescence, incompetence, mediocrity, ineffectualness, corruption, and tawdri-

* Chapter X, Page 314, "Texas: *Owned by Oil and Interlocking Director-ates*"

ness. It pollutes instead of purifies; destroys and obstructs instead of building and improving.

Every chapter of this book records in dismal detail how state government has become the prime instrument of oppression, suppression, and obfuscation. From Massachusetts to California and Wisconsin to Louisiana, large states and small states, everywhere the sordid story is the same. Everywhere, state government in the grip of minority or vested interests; everywhere, flagrant reaction in the saddle; everywhere, dismaying retrogression; everywhere, gross lobby manipulation and even outright domination.

As James E. Lawrence,* William T. Evjue,† and Richard V. Hyer ‡ recount in their penetrating studies, even once notable reforms have been perverted to gross and disruptive ends.

The elder La Follette's great regulatory innovations are now complaisant handmaidens of the powerful Wisconsin corporations they are supposed to regulate. Senator George Norris's unique Unicameral Legislature defiantly wipes out rent control at the behest of Omaha realty interests. And Hiram Johnson's "cross-filing" device to smash bossism is the grubby plaything of grubby party hacks.

In diverse forms this sinister trend of retrogression and maladministration permeates the whole structure of state government.

In Albany, an all-powerful insurance lobby cracks the whip; in Austin, it is done by insensate oil barons; in Harrisburg, by the Pennsylvania Manufacturers' Association §; in Little Rock, by the utilities; in Columbus,‖ by the rural sections allied with assorted corporate interests; in Sacramento,

* Chapter IX, Page 278, "Nebraska: *Norris: In Victory and Defeat*"
† Chapter VII, Page 216, "Wisconsin: *A State That Glories in Its Past*"
‡ Chapter XII, Page 373, "California: *The First Hundred Years*"
§ Chapter II, Page 96, "Pennsylvania: *Bossed Cornucopia*"
‖ Chapter V, Page 166, "Ohio: *Oxcart Government!*"

by the liquor trade and race tracks. The underworld tentacles of gambling overlord Frankie Costello are to be found in state government from New York to Florida and from Louisiana * to California. Illinois, that hallows the name of Abraham Lincoln, rejects an FEPC, while Georgia, which enthrones the racist son of racist Gene Talmadge, enacts a law to deprive both whites and blacks of voting rights. For years, states in every section have lawlessly violated specific constitutional requirements for reapportionment, thus preserving minority rule.

The whole malodorous story of state government is summed up in a remark by Governor Earl Warren of California. He was asked about the control wielded by Gargantuan lobbyist czar Arthur Samish. This was Warren's doleful answer:

"On matters that affect his clients, Artie unquestionably has more power than the Governor."

That is the shocking depth to which state government has sunk in the United States.

A curious aspect of the grave problem of state government is the silence about it.

Infamies of municipal rule and the misdeeds and shortcomings of the national government are an old tale. They are constantly in the public eye, and innumerable volumes and articles have been written about them. But material on state government is relatively sparse. There is not one outstanding book on the subject, comparable, for example, to Steffens' celebrated *The Shame of the Cities*.

This strange blackout is not new.

Two eminent authorities noted the phenomenon in their classics on American government. Lord Bryce, in his famous *The American Commonwealth*, published in 1895, wrote,

* Chapter VIII, Page 245, "Louisiana: *Beak Too Big For Its Belly*"

"This is the part of the American political system which has received the least attention both from foreign and from native writers. They have practically ignored the state governments." Four decades later, in his memorable *The Autobiography of Lincoln Steffens,* the indomitable little exposer of local misrule, one of whose pungent phrases serves as the title of this Introduction, commented on the same fact.

Bryce attributed it to overabsorption by "American publicists" in municipal and national affairs. Steffens vouchsafed no opinion. But he was emphatic regarding one thing: that "the state is the unit for action for good or evil." In this, he was inferentially corroborated by his scholarly predecessor in this observation, "I call state government a field. Actually it is rather a primeval forest where the vegetation is rank and through which scarcely a trail has yet been cut."

That statement is as true today as when Bryce made it fifty-four years ago.

The noxious vegetation that befouls this primeval forest is of varied kinds. Some are inherent in the system of state government itself, such as pronounced geographic and population disparities within states, and boundaries which no longer make sense economically, socially, or politically.

A number of states are actually two states in one. Catholic South Louisiana is far different from Protestant North Louisiana, which is much more akin to Arkansas. Upstate New York is as distinctly different from the boroughs of New York City as Chicago is from downstate Illinois. Comparable disparities exist in California, Alabama, Texas, Florida, and other states.

Similarly, many state boundaries are disruptive anachronisms. Washington, D.C., for sound local administration, should include adjoining areas in Virginia and Maryland. One-fourth the Capital's 1,250,000 population resides in these sections. Silver Spring, second largest city in Maryland, is a

Washington suburb that owes its growth from a crossroads village solely to Washington's huge wartime expansion. Philadelphia, for every practical reason, should include a considerable portion of southern New Jersey. Camden, New Jersey, is as much a part of Philadelphia as Silver Spring is of Washington. On the same score, portions of Connecticut and New Jersey should be incorporated into New York City, just as suburbs in Indiana and Wisconsin should be a part of Chicago.

Most state boundaries are artificial in origin. Many were determined solely by political considerations long since invalid. Extensive revamping of state lines is as urgently necessary as reapportionment within many of the states. A number of them, as already pointed out, have violated their constitutions for decades in this latter regard.

There are authorities on government who go so far as to contend that the entire structure of state government is an oppressive anachronism that should be replaced with a system of regional commonwealths.

Other rank vegetation clogging the primeval forest of state government is of a different category. It arises from maladministration, corruption, monopoly, and sinister undemocratic forces. The Pandora boxes of ills caused by these evils are numerous and critical. They cover the whole gamut of public administration. Uppermost among them are:

Archaic constitutions.
State-local relations.
Low-grade and corrupt Legislatures.

The constitutions of the states are their greatest shame. Every chapter in this book bears detailed witness to this shocking fact.

The whole dismal story is summed up in Richard Maher's *

* Chapter V, Page 166, "Ohio: *Oxcart Government!*"

scathing commentary in his study on Ohio: "That heritage is a form of government less representative than when the State was created in 1803."

Some of the state constitutions were perpetrated in outright iniquity and have been preserved in it by equally nefarious methods.

With no exceptions, these basic foundations of state governments are a disgrace to a people who pride themselves on being among the most advanced and democratic in the world.

The simple fact is that the primary intent of a number of these documents is to abort honest and democratic government rather than to sustain and further it. Some are outrightly oligarchic. Georgia is a leading example of this. Its constitution directly disenfranchises Negroes and indirectly several hundred thousand white urban voters. This is the "new" constitution. When adopted in 1945, it was acclaimed as the brightest gem of the liberal regime of Governor Ellis Arnall. The "old" constitution was a frenetic shambles. Here is the way Tarleton Collier describes it in his vivid chapter.

"The old constitution was written in 1877, when Georgia was emerging from reconstruction and was bitter with memories of violence and carpet-bag prolifigacy. Accordingly the 'Constitution of Redemption' was a maze of prohibitions. It required an incessant process of amendment merely to keep up with the times. When Arnall was elected the constitution had been amended 300 times."

The same can be said of most state constitutions. Many are large tomes, running into the tens of thousands of words. They bear no more resemblance to a constitution than a garbage dump does to a park. They are massive refuse heaps of accumulated layers of fleeting trivia, much of it long since meaningless. Louisiana's constitution, adopted in 1921, already has been amended 257 times. It is the longest in the country.

Introduction

The chaotic magnitude of these junk-swollen documents is strikingly demonstrated by these contrasts with the 7,500-word Federal Constitution:

Louisiana	85,000 words
California	72,000 words
Alabama	40,000 words
Oklahoma	36,000 words
South Carolina	31,000 words
Missouri	30,000 words
Georgia	25,000 words
Colorado	24,000 words
Maryland	22,000 words
New York	20,000 words

Even such sparsely populated states as Wyoming, Utah,* Montana, North Dakota, South Dakota, Nevada, and New Mexico have constitutions of 15,000 to 20,000 words—an over-all average of approximately one constitutional word for every three registered voters.

It is of interest to note that the thirteen Founding States had short constitutions. Modeled after the federal document, they were concise and coherent. The trend to swell state constitutions with innumerable items of basic statutory import is relatively recent. New Hampshire's original constitution was only 600 words in length. Today it totals 10,900 words. Virginia's first constitution covered only four printed pages. Today it fills a fair-sized book of 23,101 words. Pennsylvania started statehood with a constitution unusually long for that period, 4,000 words. Today it totals 15,092 words.

What Hart Stilwell says in his penetrating Texas study applies to most state constitutions: "[Texas'] constitution . . . is a document that is difficult to revere. In addition to the Bill of Rights and provisions for a state government, it

* Chapter XI, Page 345, "Utah: *Contrary State*"

embodies a tremendous mass of material that rightfully belongs in the field of statutory law."

Another striking characteristic of state constitutions is their archaic features. Some are grotesque parodies on modern government.

Typical is Massachusetts' Governors' Council. A colonial relic of royalty, this eight-man body has served chiefly as a breeder of pardon scandals, administrative stultification, and partisan turmoil and knavery. The Council performs no useful or intelligible function. Its mediocre members are virtually unknown. Yet repeated efforts to eliminate this aberration have been unavailing. It persists as a costly and baneful constitutional bottleneck.

Such bottlenecks are dead hands in the path of progress, efficiency, and honesty. In most instances that was their original deliberate intent. Powerful interests rammed them into the constitutions for the express purpose of preserving profitable inequalities and to thwart majority rule.

Uppermost among these inequalities is taxation.

Numerous efforts at constitutional revision have foundered on this shoal. Great business, utility, and press interests have violently resisted clamor for modernization of state constitutions because of fear that this would open the door to recasting tax structures that benefit them at the expense of the many.

Chicago has writhed painfully in the crippling coils of Illinois' seventy-five-year-old constitution. Under this archaic encumbrance, the second largest city in the country has become a governmental morass of numerous overlapping independent agencies and staggering administrative costs. Yet every attempt to revitalize this antiquated constitution has been savagely balked by the business forces of Chicago, spearheaded by the *Chicago Tribune*. Chief reason for this opposition is hostility to a State income tax.

Comparable situations exist in virtually every state. In Nebraska, constitutional anachronisms bar vitally needed state improvements; in Alabama and Colorado, other anachronisms bar the shedding of old plunder-bund shackles that have made the two states the pawns of absentee corporate owners; in Michigan, Connecticut, and Missouri, they bar the modernization of cumbersome, inefficient, and wasteful administrative set-ups; in New York, Ohio, Louisiana, and Oregon, the wiping-out of deadening curbs imposed by narrow-minded rural sections manipulated by vested interests.

The annals of every state are cluttered with the wreckage of unsuccessful attempts to lift the pall of oppressive constitutions. Tremendous battles have been waged in this endeavor, only to come to naught.

Even after surviving the laborious processes of revision, final victory frequently has been smashed at the ballot box or through sabotaging judicial interpretations. Maher recounts a flagrant instance of this by Ohio's dead-hand Supreme Court.

In some states, the ponderous curbs on constitutional revision are staggering. In Illinois, only one constitutional amendment can be submitted at an election. Minnesota's constitution was adopted in 1857. It is so antiquated that it is practically moribund. Popular demand for remedial action finally became so insistent that more than forty proposals were introduced in the 1947 Legislature. Under this pressure, the Legislature took steps. They consisted of creating a twenty-one-member commission to make a study and report to the 1949 Legislature. Minnesota is still grappling with the tortuous problem of bringing its pre-Civil War constitution up to date.

Tennessee's 1870 constitution has never been amended, the only one in the country. The 1945 Legislature finally empowered the Governor to set up a seven-man Constitutional Revision Commission. After laboring two years, the body recommended nine major changes. Three bills were introduced in the 1947 Legislature to submit the proposals to the electorate. Whereupon the State Attorney General produced a legal opinion that the Legislature has no authority to initiate constitutional revision. The Governor disagreed. But nothing came of the three bills.

Kansas's constitution was adopted in 1861, Maryland's in 1867; eighty-eight and eighty-two years old respectively. Both have long urgently needed extensive rejuvenation. A determined effort was made in the 1947 Kansas Legislature to set such action in motion. A majority voted favorably, but the constitutional requirement was two-thirds. So the proposal got nowhere. Similarly, the 1945 Maryland Legislature empowered the Governor to appoint a committee to recommend constitutional changes. Nothing came of that. The Governor disregarded the Legislature and didn't name the committee.

It was significant that in 1945, when the war was drawing to a close and the states began planning for peace and the atomic era, only three of them made even a gesture toward modernizing their fundamental law. Nothing came of the gestures.

In Illinois's 1949 Legislature, Governor Adlai Stevenson earnestly pressed for constitutional revision. Forthright, liberal, and courageous, he understood clearly the crucial need for this. He made the issue one of his major campaign targets. In hundreds of speeches he had argued the case for a sweeping constitutional housecleaning. Presumably the voters agreed, for he was elected by the greatest majority in the history of Illinois. But when Stevenson offered a bill for a constitutional convention, he was stopped dead in his tracks in the State Senate.

The crowning irony of this defeat was an offer by a bloc

of Chicago legislators to abandon their obstructionism on this question of so much moment to the welfare of their city, to say nothing about the State as a whole, if Stevenson would support a measure to legalize gambling.

Three main obstacles bar the path to lifting this greatest shame of state government.

One is the hostility of officials and politicians, who fear loss of jobs, patronage, and numerous other benefits they enjoy under the existing anachronisms. Another is a combination of public ignorance and apathy regarding the supreme importance of vitalizing outmoded and oppressive constitutions. Parenthetically, despite all the evidence to the contrary, many people still seriously consider constitutions as divinely inspired and untouchable sacred instruments.

Third, and perhaps the greatest obstacle, is the unceasing resistance of great corporate and financial interests. In every struggle for constitutional revision, these powerful forces are the wellspring of the opposition. Chambers of Commerce, manufacturers' associations, railroads, utilities, oil, coal, timber and other natural-resource monopolies incessantly fight constitutional modernization every inch of the way. That is the unbroken record in every state.

Still, the need will not down, and the clamor for change will not silence. The Council of State Governments, the National Municipal League, civic organizations, labor, civic leaders, liberal groups, and champions talk about the matter year in and year out. But the situation is much like Mark Twain's famous remark about the weather—everybody talks about it but nobody does anything about it.

Long-strained state-local relations have become so inflamed that cities are openly talking rebellion.

Mayor George W. Welch of Grand Rapids, Michigan, gave voice to the defiant fury of the harried municipalities in his presidential report to the 1949 United States Conference of Mayors.

"American cities are under the control of unsympathetic state legislatures dominated by agricultural oligarchies," he declared. "City people have a sympathetic ear for the problems of rural residents. But the reverse is not true. There will never be any long-range program for home rule, for financial stability of our cities, or for full and complete local responsibility as long as the present dictatorial attitude of state government persists.

"We once had a little affair known as the Boston Tea Party. Perhaps a few Boston Tea Parties in some of our states might serve a useful purpose."

The outrages of state government against municipalities are many, grievous, and long-standing.

Uppermost among them are grossly inequitable representation in legislatures, lack of local autonomy, and tax mulcting and juggling.

Fifty-nine per cent of the nation's population lives in cities. Yet these 84,000,000 elect only 25 per cent of the state legislatures. The 66,000,000 rural residents choose the other 75 per cent. The following are a few characteristic examples of how the rural tail is wagging the city dog:

Los Angeles County, with 39 per cent of California's population, has only 2½ per cent representation in the State Senate; Baltimore, with 47 per cent of Maryland's population, has only 29 per cent membership in the Legislature; Wayne County (Detroit), with 40 per cent of Michigan's population, has only 27 per cent representation in the State Assembly; and eight urban counties in New Jersey with 80 per cent of the State's population have only 8 State senators as against 12 of 13 rural counties with only 20 per cent of the population.

Scores of similar illustrations could be cited. This system

of "rotten borough" misrepresentation is practically universal throughout the country.

It stems out of two old evils: one legal, the other lawless.

The first is constitutional anachronisms that discriminate against the cities. Some are the normal result of changed conditions, such as the shift of rural population to urban centers, the influx and development of new industries, and the rise of war plants. Others of these provisions are deliberate. They were put into the constitutions for the express purpose of maintaining rural dominance of legislatures and taxing powers.

But whether inadvertent or deliberate, these "rotten borough" anachronisms have been tenaciously maintained. Employing every advantage and stratagem their legal domination gives them, the minority rural sections have steadfastly refused to relinquish control. In this die-hard obstructionism, they have invariably found powerful allies in business quarters and the courts. The reason is obvious. Farmer-controlled legislatures are anti-labor, anti-spending, and anti-liberal.

It is significant that every state that enacted a "little" Taft-Hartley law is rural dominated.

The other root cause of gross legislative discrimination against cities is the deliberate violation of constitutional mandates requiring reapportionment every ten years. Some states have not reapportioned since the 1920 census. As in the case of the discriminatory constitutional provisions, attempts to force reapportionment have encountered unyielding resistance.

Today, as a result of the war, the long-crying need for reapportionment is more pressing than ever before. Tremendous intra- and inter-state shifts in population have taken place.

Chief of these was the great westward movement between 1940 and 1946. In these six years, the population of California, Oregon, and Washington increased more than 3,290,000, or 33.9 per cent. Of this influx, California got the bulk, 2,485,000. Since then, the State's growth has continued to an estimated total of over 10,000,000. Other states also were big gainers: Michigan, 797,000; Ohio, 594,000; Texas, 419,000; Florida, 358,000.

In all, sixteen states underwent large population expansions during the war. Of this group, five states and the District of Columbia added more than 20 per cent, five other states between 10 and 20 per cent, and the remaining six between 5 and 10 per cent.

In twenty-seven states the changes were relatively minor, and five others experienced losses, ranging up to 16.3 per cent in North Dakota.

These striking figures demonstrate clearly the magnitude and urgency of the need for reapportionment. The problem will be squarely before all the states in their 1951 legislatures, following the 1950 national census. But on the basis of past performance, it is safe to predict many states will do nothing. They will continue their "rotten borough" violations of their constitutions.

Directly related to this reapportionment question is another serious problem of state government. This is the huge multiplication of local governmental units.

Until recent years, little was known about this vast horde of splinter empires. They are still largely a virgin subject. Authorities even differ widely as to their exact number.

The last (1944) U.S. Bureau of Census report puts the total at over 155,000. For the country as a whole, this is at the rate of one unit of government for every 850 people, or one unit for every 19 square miles of land area.

Illinois leads in multiplicity of these devices with 15,854. Kansas is next with 11,115, followed by Missouri with

10,740; Minnesota, 10,398; Wisconsin, 8,508; and New York, 8,339.

States with the lowest numbers are Rhode Island with 54; Delaware, 70; Nevada, 163; and Maryland, 207. It is of interest to note that in contrast to Rhode Island, Champaign County in Illinois, with approximately the same area but with less than one-tenth the population, has 349 local governmental units.

The following are the last Census Bureau figures on the pyramidal structure of governmental units in the United States:

TYPE OF GOVERNMENTAL UNIT	NUMBER OF UNITS
U.S. government	1
States	48
Counties	3,050
Townships (or towns)	18,919
Municipalities	16,220
School districts	108,579
Special districts	8,299
TOTAL	155,116

Of this total, school districts constitute 70 per cent. If they are excluded, municipalities approximate 35 per cent, townships 41 per cent, and counties less than 7 per cent.

The "special districts," comprising more than 5 per cent, cover a wide array of agencies, all with taxing powers. Among their functions are road-building and maintenance, drainage, irrigation, sanitation, water purification, mosquito control, power, airport, harbor and inland waterway projects.

The countless functional deficiencies and the cost of these swarms of splinter empires are staggering. Not only do they impose tax burdens all out of proportion to services rendered, but they make impossible centralized budgeting, purchasing, and other measures of modern administration; they dissipate political responsibility and public control of local institutions and thwart community-wide action to meet community-wide problems.

Numerous remedies have been proposed for this grave problem. They have got nowhere. With legislatures under rural domination, every effort to prune, integrate, and reorganize has been defeated. The innumerable small but potent "courthouse gangs" and county machines determinedly see to it that any attempt at reform is scuttled in the rural-ruled legislatures, which lawlessly refuse to reapportion.

The claim of states to complete legal supremacy over municipalities was forcefully enunciated in a famous Iowa case more than eighty-five years ago. Judge J. F. Dillon, in *City of Clinton v. Cedar Rapids and Missouri Railroad Co.*, laid down this dictum:

"Municipal corporations owe their origin to, and derive their powers and rights wholly from, the legislature. It breathes into them the breath of life, without which they cannot exist. As it creates, so it may destroy. If it may destroy, it may abridge and control. Unless there is some constitutional limitation . . . the legislature might, by a single act, if we can suppose it capable of so great a folly and so great a wrong, sweep from existence all the municipal corporations of the state, and the corporations could not prevent it."

This doctrine of local subserviency was challenged by other jurists. One noted dissent was handed down by a Michigan judge only five years after Dillon's pronouncement. Judge Edward Cooley, in *People v. Hurlbut,* held that municipalities possess certain inherent rights of self-government. Cooley's contention was sustained by courts in other states, particularly Indiana, Kentucky, and Texas.

But the U.S. Supreme Court refused to recognize this claim of inherent right of local self-government.

In 1903, in *Atkin v. Kansas*, the tribunal upheld Judge Dillon's doctrine that municipalities are wholly the creatures of states. That edict is still in force. Under it, state governments are continuing to wield oppressive and disruptive whip-hands over metropolises that, individually and collectively, are superior to their masters.

In the last several decades, some grudging concessions have been made to home rule. In every instance legislatures have been forced to make these grants under the pressure of mounting urban rebellion, severe economic strains, such as the great Hoover depression, and through sheer physical inability to cope with the tremendous task of administering local affairs. But the principle and the structure of this system of state supremacy remain unimpaired.

Many incongruities exist as a result.

In some states, localities must still go to legislatures to obtain charters, by special acts. In many states, a large part of the legislature's time and effort are consumed with purely local matters—for instance, bills dealing with such momentous problems as authorizing Frederick County to reduce from $5 to $2 the annual license fee for unspayed female dogs, or to "empower the town of Hyattsville to purchase on a deferred payment plan one modern hook-and-ladder fire truck."

In one session of the Maryland Legislature, two-thirds (509) of the bills passed dealt with local affairs. Maryland has only one city, Baltimore, of over 100,000 population. The 1949 legislatures are estimated to have adopted more than 10,000 acts dealing with purely local details.

The immense amount of time required to handle this heavy load leads to many evils.

Many legislatures operate under specific time limitations. Inevitably, a burden of this magnitude prevents proper consideration being given either these measures or those of statewide import. The result is widespread log-rolling and legislative irresponsibility. That in turn plays into the hands of self-seeking and obstructive forces. These elements always have greatest sway when legislators are overtaxed, harassed, and harried.

Equally vicious are the effects on local government. Chief among them are confusion and instability, the injection of purely local affairs into the maelstrom of state politics, and, above all, the deprivation of control by local citizens of their own local households.

Some of the absurdities resulting from these evils are weird. It is not uncommon for a legislature to enact local laws that are contradictory, not only as among localities but in the same locality. One group of municipal officials will slip across an act, and another group a completely opposite measure.

Similarly, it is not unusual during legislative sessions for Mayors and other key city officials to have to spend a large part of their time seeking essential local legislation or trying to block hostile measures. It is practically axiomatic that the ability of a municipality to secure special legislation is in direct proportion to its pressure and manipulative facility.

These and other evils arising from this system constitute one of the greatest barriers to efficient, honest, and forward-looking municipal rule.

These evils are also one of the main reasons why municipalities have turned increasingly to the federal government rather than to the states for aid and support.

There is a curious anomaly in this significant development.

At the very time that the cry of "states' rights" has crescendoed to new heights of vehemence, the standing of state government as an effective governing agency has sunk steadily lower. The two opposite levels are practically in direct ratio. The higher the "states' rights" screams, the lower the stature of state government.

The reason for this is very simple.

Since 1930, state government has dismally failed to meet responsibilities and obligations in virtually every field. In every crisis, individuals, groups, municipalities, and the states themselves have had to turn to the federal government for support and succor. There is much clatter in state circles about "federal encroachment upon the domain of the states." That is pure balderdash. The federal government has not encroached on state government. State government has defaulted. It has either refused or been unable to meet the requirements of its people and subordinate governing units.

That is really what has happened. Through its inadequacies, defects, and failures, state government created a void that had to be filled by some responsible governing force. Otherwise there would have been chaos and violence. The only governing force capable and willing to step into the breach was the federal government. It came forward when state government proved incapable of meeting its obligations to protect the welfare of its people. That is why the people are increasingly turning to the federal government, why the localities are doing so, and why the states are, too.

This default of state government is particularly discreditable because it is due to deliberate unwillingness to act. This is flagrantly true in the field of taxation.

Although states have infinitely greater fiscal strength than localities, state government has not used these tremendous powers to meet its responsibilities. In fact, the exact opposite is the case. Local revenues are derived chiefly from property taxes. States have a wide range of taxable sources, if they will employ them. But the primary concern of state government in recent years has been "economy" and surpluses. In

1945, the debt burden of the states was less than one-sixth of that of the localities, while state surpluses were 75 per cent larger than those of localities. Since 1940, state debt retirement has been double the rate of localities. Yet, throughout this period, new administrative functions and greater financial burdens have been thrust on the localities.

States are superior to localities legally and financially. But localities are relatively more efficient administrative units. New demands for services are constantly being made upon them. This has been particularly true in the postwar era, with its pressing problems of housing, education, slum clearance, health, recreation, transportation, public works, and other developments. State government has done little to help solve these problems. In some instances, it has been deliberately crippling. Urgently needed revenue was either denied or siphoned off from the localities for the benefit of rural areas.

That the cities turned to the federal government was inevitable. It was simply a case of the people resorting to the governmental unit that, in some measure at least, met their vital social and economic needs That was why at their 1949 conference, the Mayors of the country went on record to ask Washington for aid and not their state governments.

Professor Carl M. Frasure, head of the Department of Political Science, West Virginia University, summed up the situation in a few lines. In *The Book of the States, 1948-1949*, published by the Council of State Governments, he warned:

"As time goes on we can take for granted that the people will demand increased services from one governmental unit or the other. . . . If their wants are not satisfied by the unit of government closest home, they are going to appeal to some higher authority for assistance. . . . In other words, if the states are slow to move in attempting to solve matters of concern to the people, we may expect that the people will turn to the federal government for legitimate assistance. State governments are

xxx

under obligation to take all necessary action to protect the welfare of the people, and if they fail in their responsibility, federal intervention is inevitable, and it will be welcomed."

The legislatures are the bawdy houses of state government.

Without exception, legislatures, as a whole, are a shambles of mediocrity, incompetence, hooliganism, and venality.

Lord Bryce voiced that opinion, and so did Lincoln Steffens. Said Bryce in his monumental study: "The money power, which is most formidable in the shape of large corporations, chiefly attacks the legislatures of the states." Steffens's *Autobiography* was even blunter: "The legislators came from the country, and they came to be bought. They had no vision, received low salaries, and they took orders absolutely."

These conditions are more true today than ever before.

State legislatures are the most sordid, obstructive, and anti-democratic law-making agencies in the country.

Their annals are filled with the blackest pages of corruption, frustration of popular will and public good, obscene irresponsibility, and the squandering and pilfering of fabulous natural resources and rights.

The record of the 1949 legislatures is an unrelieved waste of inaction, reaction, and retrogression. The malodorous details of this shocking record are unfolded in every chapter of this book. In the very few instances where enlightened measures were enacted, they were won only after ferocious battles and as sorry compromises.

Governor Chester Bowles of Connecticut, Governor G. Mennen Williams of Michigan, Governor Adlai Stevenson of Illinois proposed broad-visioned, integrated, and desperately needed programs of social, economic, and administrative reforms and projects. In every instance these programs were torn to pieces on the rack of crass partisanship, gross re-action, and defiant offishness. The few bits-and-pieces the three Governors did suceed in salvaging after titanic efforts were puny shadows of what they had sought.

Governor Williams publicly denounced the legislative session as a "lamentable fiasco."

In different forms, the same thing happened in virtually every other state. Political alignment had nothing to do with it. Democrat, Republican, non-partisan—it made no difference what their nominal political label was—legislators ganged up to obstruct, scuttle, and mutilate.

Nebraska's unique, one-chamber Unicameral Legislature is elected on a non-partisan basis. The late great Senator George Norris conceived it as a select body of law-makers. Yet this elite legislature perpetrated an outrage at the behest of the insensate real-estate lobby—an outrage which the lobby could not put over in Congress. Over the outcries of veteran organizations, civic groups, labor, and housewives, the Legislature wiped out rent control. When Governor Val Peterson indignantly vetoed the act, it was passed over his head in an orgy of hooliganism.

One legislator seriously offered as an argument the ingenious idea that Nebraska could score a costless, nationwide publicity coup by being the first state to kill rent control.

In Massachusetts, reform proposals by Democratic Governor Paul Dever were garrotted by Democratic legislators. In Wisconsin, the Republican legislature sabotaged an anti-trust agency created by a Republican Governor. In Georgia, a rural-controlled Democratic legislature wiped out electoral reforms wrought by a Democratic Governor. In California, Governor Earl Warren came within a hair's breadth of being turned down by the Republican legislature on his demand for continuance of a State Crime Commission he had established to cope with a sinister rising tide of gambling and vice.

In every legislature in the land, the story was the same.

Leading causes for the sordidness of legislatures are absurdly low pay and crippling limitations on the duration of sessions.

These vicious factors play squarely into the hands of reaction, monopoly, and corruption. That is why these forces always fight every attempt to raise legislative salaries and to modernize legislative processes. These interests want inferior, low-paid, and time-harried legislators. Law-makers of that stripe can be easily bought, pressured, and manipulated. They are eager and complaisant tools of lobbyists and corporate interests.

Legislative pay scales are among the worst anachronisms of state government.

They have no relation to current costs. They are an open invitation to bribery and corruption. More than thirty states pay legislators $10 a day or less. Nine states pay $5 a day. One of them pays $4 a day. Even mighty New York, with the highest scale, pays only $5,000 a year. The next highest are Illinois and New Jersey, with $3,000 a year; Michigan, $2,900; Massachusetts, $3,750; Ohio, $2,600; and Mississippi, $1,500.

The following are typical examples of legislator pay:

Connecticut, $300 a year; Idaho, $10 a day for 60 days; Kansas, $5 per day, up to $300 for a regular session and $150 for a special session; Maine, $850 per session; Missouri, $125 a month; North Carolina, $600 a session; North Dakota, $5 a day, with a $5 per diem maintenance allowance for 60 days; Oregon, $8 a day for 30 days; Rhode Island, $5 a day for 60 days; Tennessee, $4 a day for 75 days; Utah, $300 a year; Vermont, $750 for two years; West Virginia, $500 a year.

The widespread practice of limiting the duration of legislative sessions is equally vicious.

It is an open invitation to obstructionism and irresponsibility. Even if all other adverse factors were eliminated, it would still be physically impossible, in the brief periods in which the majority is allowed to function, to give conscientious consideration to the mass of complex measures that confront legislatures. Inevitably, last-hour "jams" result, which lobbyists and other forces utilize to ram through their measures or kill desirable ones. Frequently such chaotic melées are deliberately created by these elements.

Twenty-six states have restrictions upon the length of regular sessions, ranging from 40 to 90 days. Sixteen states also limit the duration of special sessions. In the 22 states, where there is no legal limit on the length of the session, sessions in recent years have averaged 118 days. This is striking proof of the vital need for unrestricted sessions.

All governors have power to call legislatures into special session and to specify the matters to be considered. However, in North Carolina the Governor can convene a special session only on the approval of the Council of State. In three states, New Hampshire, Massachusetts, and Connecticut, the legislators themselves can invoke special sessions. In four other states, Louisiana, Nebraska, Virginia, and West Virginia, the Governor is required to call a special session if two-thirds of the members of both legislative houses sign a petition. Georgia has a similar provision but with a three-fifths requirement for each chamber. In all these states, the Governor alone has the actual convening power.

Legislatures meet annually in only six states. They are Massachusetts, New York, New Jersey, Rhode Island, South Carolina, and California. All other states have only biennial regular sessions. In 1948, twelve legislatures were summoned into special session.

Introduction

Flagrant and scandalous lobbying is the bane of every legislature.

It is the symbol of their shabbiness and sordidness.

All legislatures are lobbyist-ridden. Some are openly ruled by lobbyists. In California, Georgia, and other states, they have virtually semi-official status as the "Third House."

Every chapter in this book records shocking lobbyist domination, manipulation, and corruption.

Earlier this Introduction pointed out specific corporate interests which control various legislatures. Here are more details. In Ohio, a former Republican State Chairman rules the lobbyist roost, serving potently a wide variety of interests ranging from oleomargarine to pension-seeking judges. As Richard Maher relates in his study, this lobbyist can "do tricks with either Republican or Democratic Assemblies." In Texas, the lobby of the giant oil combines controls the legislature with an iron hand. In Arkansas it is the power trust; and in California the fabulous Artie Samish cracks an all-powerful whip for the liquor industry, race tracks, and such other interests he deigns to represent.

In Utah, the legislature gave a banquet for a mining lobbyist who had decided to retire.

Lobbyist scandals are the common rule in legislatures. Occasionally, there is a flurry of investigation. But nothing ever comes of it. Thirty-five states have laws regulating lobbying in some form. Some of these laws date back more than fifty years.

There has never been a single prosecution under these laws.

History was made during the 1949 Wisconsin legislature when one official did attempt to enforce laws against lobbyist corruption.

It is significant that he was not a state official. He was a young, crusading County Attorney. He didn't get far. The legislature went through the motions of an investigation that concluded as anticipated. It was a whitewash.

The shame of the legislatures is nowhere demonstrated more strikingly than in their failure to suppress the widespread evils of lobbying.

Of the thirty-five states that have lobby-regulating laws, not one contains a clear and specific definition of lobbying. Most of the acts are obviously deliberately vague and meaningless. They are patent shams. Some are outright farces. The acts of Louisiana, Texas, Georgia, and Tennessee are examples of this. Those of the first two states define unlawful lobbying as "private or secret attempts to influence a legislator except by appealing to his reason." In Georgia and Tennessee lobbying is illegal in instances of "any personal solicitation of any member of the General Assembly . . . not addressed solely to his judgment."

Twenty-five states require paid lobbyists to register. In seventeen of these states lobbyists must also file statements of expenditures. In most instances, these laws are vague as to what expenditures must be reported. It is noteworthy that submitted accounts invariably record only modest outlays. Similarly, the penalties for violations are solicitously mild. In eleven of the states maximum penalties range from thirty days to one year.

Probably the most vicious form of lobbying is that done by legislators themselves.

A large percentage of legislators are lawyers. Many others are insurance agents, realtors, contractors. It is a simple matter to bribe them through fees, contracts, and other "legitimate" business transactions. This form of lobbying often has been denounced. During his incumbency, Governor Herbert Lehman of New York attacked this evil in the course of a bitter fight to enact his anti-crime program. In a scathing statement that focused public attention squarely on a group of recalcitrant legislators, he declared: "One perceives in them a still more sinister conspiracy than that of politics, the conspiracy of lawyer-legislators to perpetrate for their profession the obstructions to justice by which it prospers."

The operations of legislator-lobbyists finally became so scandalous in Michigan that public pressure forced action. But when the Legislature finished adopting a corrective law, it was a joke. The statute prohibited persons interested in legislation from employing legislators at higher pay than non-legislators would receive.

That is the extent to which legislatures have gone to police their own ranks.

No wonder Artie Samish observed sagely, "Give me an Assemblyman and you can have all the mayors in California."

What can, or will be, done about this Stygian stable of legislative anachronisms, evils, and inadequacies?

In 1946, the Committee on Legislative Processes and Procedures of the Council of State Governments published a penetrating report on this problem. Twelve far-reaching reforms were recommended:

1. Restrictions upon the length of legislative sessions should be removed.

2. Compensation of state legislators should be increased.

3. Legislative terms should be lengthened and staggered.

4. Skilled and essential full-time legislative employees should be appointed on basis of merit and competence.

5. Committees should be reduced in number and organized with regard to related subject matter, equalization of work, and co-operation between legislative houses.

6. Public hearings should be held on all major bills.

7. Legislative councils or interim committees with adequate clerical and research facilities should be established.

8. Reference, research, bill drafting, and statutory revision services should be provided.

9. Improved methods of drafting, printing, and introducing bills should be considered.

10. Legislative rules should be reviewed and revised.

11. An adequate legislative budget should be provided.

12. The amount of local and special legislation should be reduced by provision for judicial settlement of claims against states and by increasing home rule for political subdivisions of the states.

To date, only four states have done anything at all about these vital proposals. They are New York, Connecticut, Alabama, and Missouri. What they have done is very little: a slight modification here, a minor change there. Not one basic reorganization has been instituted.

None is likely in the foreseeable future.

Our Sovereign State ★

MASSACHUSETTS ★ ★ ★

Prisoner of the Past

WILLIAM V. SHANNON

"It is curious how much of the organized intellectual energy of New England goes into a past which almost nobody attacks and ignores a present which almost nobody defends."

—*Howard Mumford Jones*

THE cannon roared on the Common. High above, on Beacon Hill, dapper, dark-eyed Robert Fiske Bradford took this as his cue.

It was the initial round of a nineteen-gun salute to his successor. It signalized that Bradford was no longer His Excellency, the Governor of Massachusetts. Earlier he had surrendered the picturesque tokens of office, the gavel made from wood of the U.S.S. "Constitution" and the Ben Butler Bible. (With all the strait-laced Yankees who have ruled the "Bible Commonwealth," it is curious that the malodorous "Pirate Ben" should have left his copy of the sacred Book!) Now, in accordance with the morbidly dramatic ritual set decades ago, Bradford walked alone down the terraced steps of the Statehouse. With a wave and a fixed smile, he acknowledged the cheers of several hundred onlookers. At last he

★

WILLIAM V. SHANNON is a native of Massachusetts. He was graduated from Clark University and did graduate work at Harvard. He is now Research Associate in History at Massachusetts Institute of Technology, and is writing a history of Massachusetts.

reached the street and stepped into the waiting automobile. The car moved slowly off, carrying him back to the obscurity of private life.

His solitary walk down from the heights of power was over. The crowd melted away. Upon it all, two sculptured giants of the past, Horace Mann and Daniel Webster, looked on serenely. They had seen many Governors come and go for they were old and Massachusetts was old.

Inside the great gold-domed Statehouse another part of the ceremony was going its appointed way. Forty-five-year-old Paul Andrew Dever, son of an Irish father and a French mother, raised his right hand and solemnly swore to "bear true faith and allegiance to the Commonwealth of Massachusetts."

Looking on from a reserved gallery were thirty-five Dever relatives. Below him sat the first Democratic Legislature in Massachusetts history. The great television floodlights beating down from all sides gave the heavily ornate, mid-Victorian setting a garish tone. But these "atomic era" trappings could not destroy the inner harmony; the scene was from out the past. It symbolized a Commonwealth that is prisoner to its past.

Paul Dever has been an active politician all his adult life, is the son of a politician, and looks as if he were designed by God to be a politician. He is a short, fat, rolypoly, good-natured bachelor. Very much a *bon vivant,* he loves nothing so much as to be with a crowd, swapping stories, eating heartily, and puffing an endless chain of cigarettes.

But there are more than the conventional elements of the politician in Dever's make-up. The thin, wide mouth, the large, dark eyes, and the eyebrows customarily arched, as if half expecting the other person to say something very witty or very unbelievable, give hint of the quick, shrewd, skeptical

24

mind that lies behind them. Dever's speeches, cluttered with clichés and delivered in a ponderous, old-school manner, obscure his real acumen. He loves a funny story but his own wit is often flecked with sarcasm. In Dever, the sentimentality traditional to the Irish is deeply veined with Gallic cynicism.

He was elected a State Representative at twenty-five and Attorney General at thirty-one. In the latter job, he made a record by cracking down on the racketeers, small loan sharks, and "bucket-shop" operators. In 1940, at the age of thirty-seven, he lost the governorship by a hairbreadth.

After wartime Navy service, Dever made a comeback attempt in 1946. He teamed up with then Governor Maurice Tobin and ran for Lieutenant Governor. Both went down to defeat. By 1948, it was victory or oblivion for Paul Dever. This accounts for his sudden alliance with Jim Curley, with whom he had never been too friendly. Ironically, the move was unnecessary. Maurice Tobin, his friendly rival for the nomination, vaulted suddenly into the Washington big time; and the general Democratic tide swept Dever in with a record-smashing majority of 390,000 votes.

The triumph vindicated the patient optimism of his political backers. Dever, like every other leader in the amorphous political system peculiar to Massachusetts Democrats, has had to build a personal machine. His strength rests on the support of veteran politicos throughout the State who felt they knew a "comer" when they saw one. For more than a decade, they stuck with the Dever band wagon through victory and defeat. Nineteen forty-eight was the pay-off.

A professional politician, known and trusted by other professionals, Dever has never enjoyed that personal adulation which many voters have given to the more magnetic Curley and Tobin. Dever is well aware of this. He knows that his huge majority was the result of certain unusual

25

forces, such as the presence on the ballot of highly controversial labor and birth-control referenda. But on the other
hand Dever is an agile performer who makes few mistakes.
He will always roll with the punches. He is almost certain
to win re-election, though it will probably be by a much
closer margin than 390,000 votes.

A portrait of the late Senator David I. Walsh hangs in
Dever's office. (One of Sam Adams was removed to make
way for it.) It is significant that Walsh, a conservative and
a bitter-end isolationist, is Dever's political hero. Walsh and
Roosevelt, for political reasons, masked with friendliness an
intense mutual dislike. During the 1940 campaign, both
Walsh and Dever were certain Roosevelt was going to lose
Massachusetts, and they hastened to form Willkie-Dever
clubs. Roosevelt, well aware of this Democratic-Republican
entente, was something less than grief-stricken when he carried the State and Dever did not.

Yet Dever is not unacceptable to Massachusetts liberals,
though they know he is not one of them. His similarity to
Walsh resolves the paradox. Dever's basic point of view,
insofar as he has a coherent philosophy, stems from the economic thought of modern Catholicism which stresses social
justice for the underdog. The emphasis is not on class conflict but on equity. Dever, and Walsh before him, therefore,
oppose only the bad actions of individual businessmen, and
not the domination of society and government by the business community as a group. That explains why Dever is
friendly to many specific liberal objectives and yet is alien
to the spirit of the New Deal.

The governmental machinery Dever took over is still in large
part that which John Adams designed when he wrote the
State Constitution in 1780. Later generations tinkered with
it in 1853 and 1917, but they did not alter the basic plan.

Napoleon once said "a constitution should be short and

obscure." The Massachusetts Constitution is quite un-Napoleonic. It is a long, wordy document, cluttered with details.* Matters such as the allocation of gasoline taxes are minutely provided for. Because a housing shortage existed during the constitutional convention of 1917, the delegates gave the State specific authority to build houses for its citizens, but added the cautious proviso that the structures could not be sold for less than cost.

The Constitution permits a flat income tax but not one graduated according to ability to pay. Dever has recommended this be changed, but the cumbersome amendment process will require a minimum of four years.

Typical of the Constitution's many archaic features is the Governor's Council. This "relic of royalty," as Jim Curley accurately called it, has for its chief function the approval of all appointments, contracts, and pardons. To perform these important but unglamorous jobs, eight Councilors are elected from specially constituted districts which have little relation to the political or economic facts of life. This system would seem to have been cleverly devised to encumber the Governor with obscure political leeches. If so, it serves its purpose admirably. A quiz show would have a hard time disposing of its refrigerators in Massachusetts if the question was: "Who is your Executive Councilor?"

Occasionally a competent man gets elected to the Council by mistake, but no Councilor has ever been known to go anywhere in public life. While in office, however, hostile Councilors can easily undermine any attempts at strong executive leadership. Maurice Tobin, though he had a Democratic majority, was plagued by two personal enemies who consistently voted with the Republicans. Jim Curley solved

* As the authors of the chapters on Louisiana and Texas point out, those state constitutions also are encumbered with details that are properly the subject of legislation.—Ed.

a similar problem by kicking two Republicans upstairs into choice jobs and replacing them with Democrats. Republican editors wailed loudly about this "destruction of the people's barrier!"

The more sordid ramifications of this constitutional bottle-neck concern the Council's power to approve pardons. A few years ago, a legislative investigating commission declared: (1) "substantial sums of money have been paid out for the procurement of certain pardons"; (2) the Governor and Council "were influenced by considerations other than the merits of the case"; (3) "pardons, especially in the closing days of administrations, were rushed through with indecent haste and in utter disregard of the [proper] procedure."

This investigation climaxed a series of shocking pardons, including one to Raymond Patriarca, former Rhode Island Public Enemy No. 1, after he had served eighty-three days of a three- to five-year sentence. "Just an example of the Christmas spirit," pontificated one Councilor, but the legislative report showed clearly that some Santa Claus had received more than union wages.

Leverett Saltonstall, Governor during the war years, and his one-term successors, Tobin and Bradford, cleaned up this corner of the political barnyard somewhat. But Chairman Matthew Bullock of the Parole Board told a legislative committee in 1949, "You have no idea of the terrific pressure we are under."

The practice of conferring pardons on the clients of politically friendly lawyers is still common. Bradford, for example, during his last days in office, commuted the sentence of nightclub owner Joe Rubin, serving time for murder. Rubin's lawyer was Reuben Lurie, a particularly stanch Bradford supporter. There was apparently nothing irregular, yet Bradford felt constrained to issue a public statement in defense of his action.

28

Dever, blessed with a comfortable six-to-two Democratic majority on the Council, has thus far got along with it with a minimum of public controversy. But even he early surrendered to the relentless nepotism of the "little Senate." The brother of one Councilor and the son of another were appointed deputy tax assessors, though it would be charitable not to examine their qualifications for such specialized jobs.

The political system in Massachusetts breeds the curse of irresponsibility and divided authority. Although the Governor serves only two years, the major policy-making officials have appointive terms ranging from three to seven years. As a result, a Governor usually takes over an administration staffed at the top with people hostile or indifferent to his program, yet so entrenched they cannot immediately be removed. In critical cases, he has to resort to impeachment.

Under this system, he prefers charges against the officeholder, then presides as judge while his Executive Council hears the case. The public hearings are a public farce. Everyone knows that the commissioner will be sacked. Nevertheless, each side makes vigorous statements for the sake of the record, the Council weighs the evidence, and the commissioner is impeached. The minority party leaders assure the victim that they will make his ouster an issue in the next campaign; they will see that he is "vindicated."

With these critics out of the way, the Governor then appoints his own man and all goes on as before. No matter what heinous offenses an official has been charged with, no one is ever prosecuted later in the courts. The lawyers make a nice distinction between impeachment and "removal from office for cause." Like a South American revolution, everything proceeds according to a mutually understood routine.

The office of Commissioner of Public Works has most often been involved in these controversies. This post is, next to that of the Governor, the most important in the whole administration. The Commissioner awards contracts to politically friendly contractors, who reciprocate by making heavy campaign contributions and by hiring loyal party men. The principal duty of the Commissioner is to supervise road building, and for many a Governor, re-election has turned on the success or failure of his highway program. For these reasons, Saltonstall ousted Curley's man and Tobin threw out Saltonstall's. Dever in turn was about to get rid of Bradford's appointee, when the latter discreetly resigned. Dever completed the cycle by appointing colorful, energetic William F. Callahan, the man originally ousted by Saltonstall.

To synchronize the terms of the chief officeholders with that of the Governor is a reform too sweeping for this respectable Commonwealth. After all, wouldn't that imply that politics entered into the filling of these jobs?

Three decades ago, a constitutional convention sought to further economy and efficiency by consolidating one hundred and twenty-two boards and bureaus into twenty executive departments, each headed by a commissioner directly responsible to the Governor. The Legislature, however, recently passed an act taking the appointment of the Commissioner of Education away from the Governor and granting it to an unpaid, nine-man advisory board. This plan has been extended to cover the State Airport Director and the head of the Boston Port Authority. The terms of these advisory boards are long, and staggered to prevent rapid turnover. This cramps strong executive leadership and represents a retrogression in the struggle for responsible government.

Accompanying Dever into office were five other State officials, all Democrats and none distinguished. Charles F. "Jeff" Sullivan, a stocky, thick-jowled man, holds down the do-nothing job of Lieutenant Governor. A self-educated restaurant owner, he rose through the ranks of ward politics to become Mayor of Worcester, the State's second largest city.

He received Boston support in 1948 in a calculated effort to "balance" the ticket. Honest, plodding, uninspired, Jeff Sullivan has aspirations for the governorship which seem sure to be frustrated.

The new Attorney General is flamboyant and indefatigable Francis E. Kelly. "Frankie" has run for State office in each of the last nine elections and has come out ahead only twice. In the 1948 campaign, he was still bragging about his victory over Saltonstall for Lieutenant Governor a dozen years earlier. During that previous term in office, Kelly had the worst possible relations with his nominal chief, Governor Charles Hurley. The latter hated to leave the State in the hands of Acting Governor Kelly even for a week end. Hurley saw to it that during his first extended absence the executive offices would be occupied by painters and repairmen. Kelly, not to be denied, moved in anyway and "transacted the affairs of the Commonwealth" at a desk covered with painter's canvas and flanked by buckets and stepladders.

In 1938, Kelly ran for Governor on an antiutility platform. He promised every housewife a free electric light bulb. His solution for the tax problem is a State lottery.

On taking office in 1949, Kelly inherited an investigation of racketeers and bookies. The probe was centered in Revere, suburb of Boston where the underworld cesspool first overflowed. Although the trial initiated by his predecessor ended in failure, Kelly promised that the fight had just begun. Months have passed but nothing has been heard of the investigation. Instead, Kelly has been busy condemning comic books, setting up a book censor in his department, attempting to ban the novels of James M. Cain and Erskine Caldwell, and acting in similarly subtle ways to preserve unblemished the purity of the Commonwealth. Perhaps the Attorney General is too busy cleaning up *God's Little Acre* to worry about the Devil's patch in Revere.

The roots of Kelly's popular appeal are to be found in the harsh experiences of Boston's low-income immigrant community. Like a hundred other ward politicians, he reproduces the life pattern so familiar in Boston politics—the slum tenement, the widowed mother, the large family, the early hardships, the self-education, the years of night law school, the bruising ward battles, the eventual emergence as full-blown . . . leader or demagogue?

The other elective State posts, Treasurer, Secretary, and Auditor, are adequately filled. The new Secretary of State is a likable stub of a man whom nobody ever heard of before. But he had a good Irish name—Edward Cronin—and he came from the right neighborhood—Greater Boston. For 1948, these were sufficient.

To correct this geographic and racial imbalance, some Democratic Party managers favor a shift from the open primary to the party convention. Judge Frank W. Tomasello told a legislative committee, "My son shouldn't be barred from gaining high public office merely because the 'o' comes at the wrong end of his name." GOP leaders also favor this move as they seek to sprinkle the Bradfords and Woods with an occasional Olander or Maginnis.

Massachusetts was once a trail breaker on the frontiers of social welfare. It was in the Bay State that Horace Mann in 1835 successfully led the fight for a bill creating the country's first state board of education. Here Dorothea Dix first crusaded for better care for the insane. And here Lemuel Shattuck drafted his epochal report in 1851 which led to Massachusetts' setting up the first department of public health.

But all that was long ago.

Massachusetts is today the only state in the Union without minimum standards for teacher certification. The Mental Health Commissioner, with an undermanned staff, struggles to care for the insane in overcrowded, dilapidated buildings financed on a penny-ante budget. Public health authorities hold conferences to find ways and means of achieving the goals Shattuck charted a century ago.

Mental Health Commissioner Clifton Perkins, in his crisp annual report for 1948, summed up the problems in the care of the mentally ill with "Not Enough." Sixteen hospitals handling thirty thousand patients do not have enough physical facilities. Effective segregation is almost impossible when, as at Bridgewater, one ancient hospital houses chronic alcoholics, delinquent defectives, and criminally insane. Because of the lack of family-sized living quarters and low wages, there are not enough psychiatrists, nurses, and ward attendants to care for the mentally ill.

It is in the ward, according to Dr. Perkins, that personnel shortages "really hurt." For here an undermanned staff means "delays in cleaning excrement from floors . . . fights among patients . . . weeping patients with no one to comfort them . . . epileptic children suffering injury because one attendant cannot be two places at once . . . vermin multiplying without check."

To stimulate interest in these problems, Commissioner Perkins has formed a large committee of citizens. But what Massachusetts needs is a second Dorothea Dix to level the walls of smugness and put the penny pinchers to flight.

Massachusetts does not go forward because so much of her energies are spent in trying not to slip back.

Typical was the fight in early 1949 to save Dr. Miriam Van Waters as Superintendent of the Framingham Reformatory for Women. A former president of the National Conference of Social Work and author of many books and articles, Miriam Van Waters was widely recognized as pre-eminent in her field. She also possessed crusading faith in the possibilities of human rehabilitation. Her basic principles were that no

33

criminal was beyond redemption and no society could afford a "human scrap heap." At Framingham, inmates were called "students" and activities ranging from sewing classes to glee clubs were organized to give them chances to develop new habits.

Miriam Van Waters became the idol of her staff, but she was perhaps not the easiest colleague to work with. Prison bureaucrats and adherents of the "knock-their-teeth-in" school of penology called her idealism self-righteous and her advanced views the inevitable intellectual snobbery of a Ph.D. in anthropology. Her most relentless foe was Deputy Commissioner of Correction Frank Dwyer, a tough-minded cop who got his penological training as Governor Hurley's bodyguard. But not until Elliott McDowell became Commissioner in 1948 did Dwyer have a chief of similar outlook. McDowell, a civil engineer, had gained his experience as director of the Norfolk Prison workshop where he supervised the manufacture of furniture and highway curbstones.

McDowell later testified that on the day he was sworn in, Dr. Van Waters came to him and pledged her "loyalty and co-operation." He retorted, "Your loyalty is mandatory and your co-operation is required by law." Eventually, egged on by Dwyer and the Hearst press, McDowell fired her. His stated reasons ranged from the hiring of ex-inmates as reformatory officers to lurid charges of homosexuality in the reformatory. Spicy stories of a full-fledged "doll racket" at the reformatory, complete with "queen" and "studs," titillated newspaper readers from one end of the State to the other.

Following the ouster came two long public hearings, one presided over by McDowell and the second conducted by a three-man commission appointed by the Governor and headed by Dean Erwin Griswold of Harvard Law School. Dozens of civic organizations and hundreds of private citi-

zens led by Mrs. Eleanor Roosevelt formed the "Friends of
Framingham" to support the elderly, white-haired reformer.
Beneath the bright glare of public censure, McDowell and
Dwyer and their "charges" slowly shriveled.

The inquiry ended in a resounding vindication of Dr. Van
Waters. The three-man committee ordered her reinstatement
and rejected the accusations as "trivial and indeed captious."

The "Friends of Framingham" are now urging that for the
first time in a quarter century the laws regarding women
offenders be overhauled. But achievements in this line will
come slowly. For the present, the Van Waters case represents a hard-fought holding action, not an advance.

> "Experience, not logic, is the life of the law."
> —*Justice Holmes*

Years ago a lawyer in the Boston Probate Court was ad-
dressing the bench in extremely unctuous terms. Somewhat
bored, Judge John V. Mahoney cut in, "Sir, a judge is only
a lawyer who knew a Governor."

In the years that have passed, nothing has happened to the
Massachusetts judiciary to revise that classic definition. The
overwhelming majority of Massachusetts judges were money-
raising, speech-making, back-slapping politicians before their
appointments. For some, their elevation seems to have had
no significant effect on their activities.

The Massachusetts judicial system enshrines old men and
old ideas. The Governor appoints all judges for life. Only
Massachusetts and New Hampshire give life tenure to every
judge, including even special justices in the municipal court.
Nor is there provision for compulsory retirement. A judge
may be blind as a bat and deaf as a haddock, but he can
go tottering and quavering on indefinitely.

In the top echelons, the appointive system has worked
fairly well on the whole. Stanley Qua, Chief Justice of the

Supreme Judicial Court, is proof of this. A middle-of-the-roader appointed by a Democrat and elevated to the chief justiceship by a Republican, Qua is no Oliver Wendell Holmes. But he is respected by all, liberals and conservatives alike. Tall, erect, with shrewd, friendly eyes and a full, strong face, he rules the court with tact, dignity, and impartiality.

His six colleagues complete a respectable high bench, notable more for legal competence than social conscience, more for personal honesty than insight. None is a liberal. Two are men of inherited wealth; all had big-business connections in private practice.

Over the years, this high tribunal has constructed a severe and extreme conception of property rights unequaled in the nation. The ghost of a property-loving Puritan past still haunts the courtrooms of the Commonwealth. Many "backward" Southern states have more liberal case law than Massachusetts.

In the present housing-hungry society, this body of conservative precedent means that landlord-tenant law is sharply slanted for the landlord's benefit. For example: It is almost impossible to prove negligence against a property owner in an accident case. The tenant, therefore, pretends he had a verbal agreement with the owner to keep his sidewalk clear of old banana peels, or whatever. This automatically shifts the case from the area of law technically known as "torts" to that of contract law, where different precedents apply. In more important cases involving banks and insurance companies, the vested interests always start with this initial advantage.

Legal conservatism, by bolstering the "spendthrift trust," tightens the dead hand of the past on the economic pulse of the community. Most states permit rich men to tie up their wealth in trust funds whose principal cannot be touched. But only Massachusetts permits trust funds of which even the income can be spent only for stated purposes. Spend-thrift heirs may buy yachts on credit or run up bills at the Stork Club, but such creditors cannot attach Uncle Jed's money.

The constitutional revolution carried on by the United States Supreme Court in the last decade has done little to thaw out Massachusetts precedent. The local judges have taken the position that they will comply only "if they tell us specifically." When the Supreme Court did directly over-rule them in a decision which said leaflets could be distrib-uted even though it did mean "littering" the streets, a Mas-sachusetts court declared in *Commonwealth vs. Nichols* that it was obeying because it was "constrained to do so."

Nowhere is the dictum that "the law is what the judges say it is" more evident than in labor law. Union agreements are enforceable in the courts, but the Supreme bench has ruled that a strike to obtain such an agreement—whether it be closed shop, union shop, or maintenance of membership—is not legal. As a result, in such a strike, injunction-happy judges may ban picketing no matter how peaceful. The U.S. Supreme Court has ruled that peaceful picketing is a form of free speech, but the Massachusetts court has as recently as 1947 remained blandly indifferent to this edict.

In 1935 a "baby Norris–La Guardia Act" was passed which was designed to solve the injunction issue. The courts, by their interpretations, tortured the statute to death. In the Legislature, labor has failed to obtain the resurrection of this corpse.

The courts with which most citizens have contact are those at the local district level. The district judge handles all nonjury cases, both civil and criminal. As one wit remarked, the district courts are called, with more significance than in-tended, "inferior" courts.

The seventy-two District Courts, like Topsy, just "growed."

Poor country roads and winter weather were the chief architects. Thinly populated areas like the Berkshires have four courts where two would easily suffice, but it is as easy to remedy this as it would be to deprive Nevada of one of its Senators. Many abuses have crept into this haphazard judicial system. Of these, the policy of appointing part-time, special justices is one of the most flagrant. Often a court in a small town has not enough work for a full-time judge; but in the adjoining district there may be too much work for one judge but not enough for two. Instead of making the thorough streamlining and consolidation that is needed, politicians prefer to appoint special justices who continue their private practices on the side. Justice is something less than impartial when the morning's defendant in Judge Jones' court may have been yesterday's client in Attorney Jones' office.

Between the District and the Supreme Courts come the thirty-one justices of the Superior Court. All jury trials are heard before a Superior judge. At this level the political coloring of the Massachusetts judiciary shows up in its darkest tones. The thirty-one judges include four former Governor's Councilors, a former Lieutenant Governor, an ex-Attorney General, a Democratic State Chairman, a Governor's secretary, and three unsuccessful nominees for statewide office. The majority of the remaining judges were active in miscellaneous political activities. In theory, the appointive system removes the judiciary from politics. In practice, for a lawyer aspiring to a judgeship, taking out nomination papers for elective office is second in importance only to passing the bar exam.

Typical of the bench he rules is Superior Court Chief Justice John Patrick Higgins. Son of immigrant Irish parents, he entered politics after working his way through Harvard. Higgins fought the legendary Martin Lomasney for control of Boston's Ward Eight until the crafty old boss took him into his own organization. Lomasney, bald as a bullet and grimly taciturn, was for the first thirty years of this century the ruthless kingmaker of Boston politics. Under Lomasney's tutelage, Higgins went quickly up the ladder. In 1937, when Governor Hurley named him to the bench, he was a Congressman and an active aspirant for Mayor. Twelve years have passed and the suave, silver-haired Higgins has thus far resisted the temptation to return to the political arena.

Criminals convicted by a judge in District Court may appeal for a jury trial in the Superior Court. This two-trial process produces curious results in the cases of powerful bookies and gamblers. The judges of Boston Municipal Court conducted a few years ago a confidential survey of criminal cases appealed from them to the Superior Court. It revealed that more than half the defendants they had imprisoned or heavily fined were subsequently freed by juries.

There are many reasons for this phenomenon. Women, who might be more severe on panderers, were, until 1949, barred from jury service in Massachusetts. The mechanics of jury selection are something less than foolproof. The Boston City Council provides Suffolk County with jurors by selecting names at random from a roster drawn up by the city board of election commissioners. These three commissioners are required by law to eliminate from the list "known" criminals. One of the present election commissioners served more than a year in jail, while a second was once indicted, though not convicted, of conspiracy to violate the election laws. The Massachusetts Judicial Council has repeatedly recommended that professional jury commissioners be appointed to draw up these lists. Politicians merely laugh at such naïveté.

But behind the faulty mechanism lies a deeper meaning. The Boston community has a pervasive gang code. Ambitious immigrants have long found politics, sports, and crime the most available routes to power and prestige. The rewards, the spirit, the *espirit de corps* of the three activities are basically similar. The first political speech, the first prize-fight for a two-dollar watch, and the first game of craps may all take place in the same clubhouse on the corner.

Only the few succeed and become Mayors or boxing champions or big-time gamblers. But the many who do not succeed carry into adult life the code of ethics learned in grammar- and high-school days. They still "go with the gang," they still "cheer for our side," they still expect their leaders to take care of the weaklings and the failures. From the boyhood gangs of yesterday come the complaisant, softhearted juries of today.

The recent graft trials in Revere, Boston's "Little Cicero," proved this once again. Five city councilmen were charged with accepting thousand-dollar bribes in connection with a $1,250,000 housing project. This case of the alleged petty graft of stupid political "front men" was only an offshoot of a probe into the activities of certain big-time numbers-racketeers whom the newspapers quaintly identified as "prominent figures in the sporting world."

On the opening day of the trial, City Councilor Leonard Ginsburg stunned his codefendants by turning State's evidence. On the stand, the twenty-five-year-old war veteran was a pathetic figure as he testified in a panicky, tear-choked voice that he feared he would be "bumped off."

The jury was unconvinced. After a sensational three-week trial high-lighted by ugly charges of anti-Semitism bandied back and forth by both prosecution and defense, the jury brought in a verdict of not guilty. The three indictments against Ginsburg were nol-prossed and the investigation collapsed.

Ginsburg had broken the gang's dearest principle: loyalty to his own. In the eyes of the average Bostonian, Ginsburg was no hero—he had "ratted on his pals."

40

In addition to political judges and softhearted juries, Massachusetts suffers from a surplus of lawyers; nine thousand glut the legal market. Intense competition is in part responsible for the Boston "corridor-justice" scandals now under investigation by the Bar Association and the Supreme Court. A dozen or more lawyers with remarkable regularity obtain the business of criminal first offenders. They work through police, bondsmen, and jail attachés who act as "runners." Such shysters not only collect a fee but also squeeze the confused, heartsick defendant for sums as high as $1,500 to "buy off" the judge and "gag" the newspapers. If the victims were more sophisticated, they would know that judges usually put first offenders on probation and reporters never file stories on petty cases. This work forms a valuable side line for lawyers who derive their regular income handling the legal affairs of pimps, prostitutes, "treasury-pool" collectors, and the other expendable small fry of the underworld.

Probate Court is a special part of the judicial hierarchy. Probate cases are less technical than most civil suits and less sordid than many criminal cases. Here, therefore, is the happy hunting ground of the human-interest writer and the publicity-seeking judge who loves to see his name in print.

Probate Court handles contested wills ("Everybody knows the old man was crazy . . ."), divorces ("He ate crackers in bed, your honor . . ."), child custody ("I want my mummy . . ."), annulments ("Take my advice, my child, and forget you ever knew him . . ."). With all these opportunities, a judge with a talent for wisecracking and a ready fund of corner-drugstore philosophy can grab off a headline every edition.

A seat on the probate bench is also a choice political plum. This is the judge who chooses lawyers for lucrative jobs as guardians, administrators, and executors. Governors always try to select a "reliable" man, for in this way they pay off

41

not just one but many loyal party lawyers in the district.

Labor groups are currently urging a constitutional amendment to make judges elective. By this means they hope to get at least a few liberals and labor lawyers on the bench. Given the present conservative temper of the bar, however, Massachusetts is not likely to see this reform adopted for a long time to come.

It is impossible to take the politics out of politics, whether they be judicial politics or any other kind. The location of the Boston courthouse at Pemberton Square symbolizes this fact. Pemberton Square and Scollay Square are back to back. Together they form a shabby island in the business district where judges and bookies, cops and touts, lawyers and pleasure-seeking sailors rub elbows together. Here "characters" abound. When someone says "Hi ya, Judge," you never know whether he's greeting a demimonde moocher or one of the luminaries of the Superior bench.

Towering over all is the white, five-million-dollar courthouse built a decade ago by the PWA. Lawyers and reporters complain endlessly of its terrible ventilation. The air conditioning does not work except in reverse. Over innocent and guilty alike, it spreads a thin film of oil and soot.

Few judges can equal its fine judicial impartiality.

"Massachusetts politics sublimated its corruption in the tacit understanding of allied respectabilities. Raw money and raw whisky were not potent in the legislature." *

"The wonder of our society is not why feeble-minded people get into state prisons, but why feeble-minded people can get into state legislatures."
—*Miriam Van Waters*

The Legislature is in the limelight in Massachusetts. In November, 1948, the Democrats, carrying every doubtful dis-

* William Allen White, *A Puritan in Babylon*. (New York, Macmillan, 1938), p. 75.

42

trict in the State, squeezed into a 20–20 tie in the Senate
and a two-vote majority in the House. It is the first Democratic Legislature in the whole history of the Commonwealth.

The House of Representatives organized quickly along
straight party lines. The new speaker, Thomas "Tip" O'Neill
of Cambridge, is a local political ally, though not a personal
pal, of Dever's. O'Neill is tall, broad-shouldered, and sturdy,
with a sober, impressive appearance and a fine oratorical
manner. His career is rather undistinguished but he has the
great asset of looking like a statesman. One of O'Neill's
earliest moves was to appoint a Catholic priest to serve for
the first time as House Chaplain.

The Senate became tangled immediately in a struggle to
elect a President. The twenty Democrats steadfastly supported Boston's sharp-featured Chester Dolan, an honest,
hard-working, unmagnetic bachelor. Not long ago, Dolan
was a local star in semiprofessional baseball, but like Tobin
and Dever he entered politics early. Now, at forty, he is already a well-worn veteran of seven terms in the State House.
The Republicans, with equal determination, sought to re-
elect Harris Richardson of Winchester.

For four weeks the futile balloting dragged on. Bad puns
about the Senate's 20–20 eyesight went the rounds. The
Lieutenant Governor, having no connection with the Legislature, was powerless to break the deadlock. Dever took no
active leadership because the prospect of party regularity in
the Legislature did not appear good enough to make Democratic control a special benefit in the passage of his program.
Cannily, he saved his patronage for future crises when it
could be used to pick up the marginal votes, Democratic or
Republican, needed to pass his major bills.

Behind the scenes the lobbyists busily tried to manipulate
the struggle for their own ends. Senator Edward C. Peirce,

New Bedford Democrat who enjoys the rattle of skeletons, spoke out on the Senate floor. "Lobbyists are attempting to dictate our choice of a President. The situation is vicious and gains have been made by this group in stirring dissension in both parties."

Most active in this undercover fight were the representatives of the insurance companies and the horse and dog tracks, led by Clarence F. King of the Revere Racing Association. Their favorite candidate was Democratic Senator William Nolen, a shrewd legislative veteran from western Massachusetts who is much less a strict party man than Dolan. Nolen had also been an intimate of the late Robert Bottomley, a long-time political power, who at the time of his death in 1948 was general counsel for the Suffolk Downs race track. Running interference for the special interests on this play was Senator Charley Innes, Republican chief of Boston's Back Bay. But neither Dolan nor Richardson would release his supporters from their caucus pledge and ultimately the two-year presidency was divided between them. Dolan took the post for 1949, possibly as a springboard from which to seek the Boston mayoralty in the fall election.

Smart lobbyists, as in this case, usually work both sides of the street. Sometimes the policy is carried right to the top, as illustrated by the Pappas brothers. A couple of Greek boys who made good, John and Tom Pappas control the State's largest dog track, a big chunk of Suffolk Downs horse-racing track, and almost a sixth of the wholesale liquor business in Massachusetts. John Pappas is a Judge and a Democrat; Tom is a Republican and bank-rolled the abortive presidential boom of ex-Speaker Joe Martin in 1948.

Three hundred and forty lobbyists are registered at the Statehouse. On paper, the law makes a meaningless distinction between the two hundred and eight legislative "counsels" who only argue before committees, and the hundred and thirty-two "agents" who do the corridor buttonholing. Allowing for some duplication, there is still better than one lobbyist for each of the two hundred and eighty members of the Legislature.

The groups represented at the Statehouse range from the Massachusetts Bowling Association and the Lord's Day League of New England to the CIO and the New Bedford Cotton Manufacturers Association. The people they employ are just as diversified. Unemployed politicians and smooth young lawyers, self-conscious idealists and money-conscious careerists all mingle in the Senate and House lobbies.

The lobbyists were naturally interested in packing the key committees with friendly members. But in Massachusetts every one of the approximately three thousand bills introduced receives a joint committee hearing and must be reported to the floor and voted on. The hard-working lobbyist has to think up other methods to choke off nuisance bills. Here the Senate President is the strategic man.

He appoints the Committee on Third Readings which studies bills in the final stage of passage to eliminate technical and constitutional flaws. The Senate counsel ordinarily does this routine job and the Committee rarely meets. But some bills "obviously" require more study than others and a sympathetic Committee on Third Readings can sit on an objectionable bill for many weeks.

Comes a day, however, when the chief proponents of the measure all happen to be absent. The Chairman on Third Readings spots this; the Committee promptly concludes its judicious scrutiny and the bill is reported out for its third and final vote. An adverse vote kills the proposal unless someone immediately makes the saving motion for reconsideration. Or again, the Committee may hold back the measure until the final days of the session in the hope it will be trampled underfoot in the rush for adjournment.

Even though they failed to get this backstop in 1949, lobbyists have many other means at their disposal. The weapons used differ according to whether the interests involved are predatory or merely defensive. The racing interests illustrate a pressure group on the make. Horse- and dog-track owners spend freely and bribe readily to stave off the relentless attacks of moral and civic groups. The operators are anxious to hold down the tax on their lush profits as well as to get the Racing Commission to assign the full legal quota of racing dates. One of the hottest fights in the Legislature raged around Dever's proposal for a one per cent hike in the racing tax. The racing crowd wept loudly over its poverty-stricken condition. A sympathetic Taxation Committee brusquely rejected the proposed increase. Ultimately a compromise was worked out, with the substance of victory going to the tracks.

Every four years, the question of retaining race-track betting comes up on the ballot as a referendum. The lobbyists put across a provision that racing taxes be earmarked for old-age assistance. In each campaign, therefore, the horse and dog tracks fill the newspapers with heart-rending pictures of a wispy-haired, sad-eyed old couple. Underneath is the caption: "Make Their Last Years Secure and Happy. Vote for Pari-mutuel Racing!" It is always the same couple and they never look any happier or more secure, but the appeal hasn't failed yet.

The power, insurance, and railroad companies are interests that only want to hold what they have. Of some two hundred bills introduced in an average year dealing with electric light and power, not more than a half dozen are sponsored by the companies themselves. The more respectable interests, having operated at the Statehouse for decades, work with artistic finesse. They know that the overwhelming majority of the legislators are already in leading strings to the business community in a hundred different ways. These lobbyists spend as much time cultivating the important people in the Representative's home town as they devote to the Representative himself. There are far subtler ways than bribery to reach a legislator who in private life is a salesman of building materials or an insurance broker writing up industrial fire coverage or a plumber working on bank-owned real estate.

But even among lobbyists for the business interests there are changes in fashion. A relative newcomer on Beacon Hill is the Association of Real Estate Boards, whose high-paid spokesmen first appeared after the war. Leading them into battle was big, hulking, red-faced Clarence Roberts. He has the glib, velvety manner of a professional toastmaster, and with equal facility can furnish good stories, good whisky, and good reasons to vote against public housing. The 1949 Legislature was a flop from Roberts's point of view. He did weaken somewhat the bill to stay evictions for twelve months, but the measure eventually passed, as did a law strengthening the State housing program.

By contrast with Roberts, Jarvis Hunt's tactics have all the zip and freshness of a Hoover campaign button. A pudgy State Street lawyer, Hunt works for the Associated Industries of Massachusetts, the local equivalent of the NAM. In his spare time he also represents the Association of Master Plumbers. Hunt was Republican President of the Senate in 1943-44. In the latter year he was jostled from his place on the party escalator by Robert F. Bradford, who defeated him for the nomination for Lieutenant Governor and two years later went on to the governorship. Hunt retired to the lobby where he has functioned with dubious effectiveness ever since. A fellow townsman of ex-Speaker Joseph Martin, Hunt exhibits the same brand of unimaginative, grimly serious conservatism. He sees every tax increase, every upward revision in workmen's compensation, every proposed hike in the forty-cent minimum wage for sweated service employees as the last death blow to Massachusetts industry. He even predicted that an FEPC would drive industry from the State. "Jarvy" Hunt has been playing "Horatio at the bridge" for so long that even tried-and-true Republicans stifle a yawn when he steps forward to testify.

The insurance interests are a potent but little-noticed pressure group. Ordinarily, insurance lobbyists put a premium on silence. Some bills are desired by all companies and these are hurried through with as much speed as circumspection will permit. Helping considerably are the soothing ministrations of the Insurance Federation's Ben Priest, an astute Republican who once served in the Legislature as Chairman of the Insurance Committee.

Sometimes, of course, these bills are aimed at one set of companies by another set. Private concerns like Metropolitan and Liberty regularly wage a violent undercover feud with "real" mutual companies which return a larger share of their profits to policyholders. But these family quarrels are never unseemly. The measures in dispute deal with premiums, reserve fund requirements, and other technical problems about which the public is grossly ignorant. Many legislators, including some Insurance Committee members, confess privately they don't know what the score is. Even the most conscientious reporters never bother to dig for stories in such a deathly dull subject. The insurance lobbyists are therefore free to wage their internecine struggles in secluded hearing rooms and to pick the public's pockets with the long, thin fingers of finely printed clauses.

Representatives of the insurance companies have many devices to protect their freedom of action. One of the most effective is to have fire and accident cases—those handled by lawyers who are also legislators—settled out of court on generous terms. Half the Legislature is made up of smalltime lawyers.

But in 1949, new social pressures put the insurance companies on the defensive and their lobby, ordinarily a staid, soft-spoken lady, became a shrieking, bespangled Jezebel. First, Representative Daniel Rudsten of Boston offered a bill to create a workmen's compensation fund operated by the State. He pointed out that this form of insurance is compulsory for every firm and that over the years Massachusetts employers had paid $191,000,000 in premiums to private insurance companies, but their workers have collected only $101,000,000 in benefits. By contrast, Ohio's State-operated fund has paid out over ninety per cent of the premiums collected. The insurance lobby shrieked frenzied protests. In the crisis, Rudsten's Democratic colleagues lost their nerve and the bill died. Some twenty legislators, of both parties, who are insurance agents in private life, voted against this measure. This was in direct violation of a specific House rule forbidding members to vote on bills in which they have a private interest. But this victory did not end the lobby's troubles. Governor Dever opened an attack. He proposed a State-operated compulsory sickness-insurance plan. The insurance interests cast the last vestige of gentility to the winds. Their lobbyists tripled in number. Hundreds of insurance workers were furloughed and marshaled for service on Beacon Hill. In jammed committee rooms, they jeered and hooted supporters of the bill and applauded company spokesmen. These pressures again turned the trick and the Governor's bill was axed.

Many spokesmen for special interests, to line up legislator support, now make important use of the disposal of jobs in private industry. Old-time political bosses built their machines by dispensing pick-and-shovel jobs to unskilled immigrants. But in this day, when most of the sewers have been laid and the subways dug, public contract work has become less important for modern-style bosses than jobs in private industry.

On any morning, Statehouse corridors are thronged with jobless constituents waiting to see their Representatives. When business slumps, finding jobs becomes a legislator's full-time occupation. Here the lobbyist steps in and acts as broker. He invariably collects his price even though the sum is never mentioned and payment may be long deferred.

Businesses like construction companies and race tracks, which are clearly dependent on the good will of the Legislature, follow this practice religiously. Racing interests have a definite patronage schedule which prorates so many jobs to each Representative and Senator and the rest to the Governor's office. Other businesses, like the railroads and public utilities, have a less rigid system. Thus, if a jobless constituent wants to handle the two-dollar window at Suffolk Downs, paint telephone poles, or be a water tender on the Boston and Albany, his shortest route is by way of Beacon Hill.

The chief mediator between the Dever administration and the job mart is State Senator John E. Powers of South Boston. Powers was Dever's campaign manager and is much closer to the Governor's office than is Senate President Dolan. Powers is a short, squared-off man with a dark, florid face and a firm, aggressive manner. He is the prototype of the tireless, efficient machine politician.

Outside his Statehouse office are two long benches always crowded with job seekers. In the Senate Reading Room, adjoining his office, he interviews two hundred applicants a day. Three secretaries handle the crowd as well as answer the hundreds of letters he receives. Usually when Powers goes down to breakfast in the morning, there are five or six people waiting for him in his living room. When he goes home in the evening, there are sixty to seventy more waiting for him.

"The number has been steadily increasing," Powers says. "They're all able people looking for jobs. I try to get them employment in private industry. There's just no State work, and most of what there is comes under Civil Service. I served in office during the WPA days and that was always a source of employment. Now we have to try outside."

Pressure groups like the Consumers League, the Frances Sweeney Committee, which serves as a watchdog against discriminatory racial practices, and the Massachusetts Civic League have no axes to grind. But they can only nibble the edges. Reformers have not yet found a way for society to dispense with the Senator Powerses.

The only effective counterweights to the business interests are the spokesmen of organized labor. In place of the conventional weapons of the lobbyist, labor swings the club of its mass voting strength. The local labor unions, whose membership by the end of 1948 had climbed to 598,000, have produced broad-gauged, non-Communist leadership. There are no Ben Golds or Willie Bioffs in the Massachusetts labor movement.

Organized labor's chief spokesmen on Beacon Hill are authentic members of the labor movement, not outside "experts." Agent for the AFL is Kenneth Kelley who came up through the ranks of the butchers' union. "I was," he says jokingly, "the best left-handed butcher in all of New England." An able, hard-hitting Irishman, Kelley is of medium height and brick-red complexion, with the trim figure, quick movements, and taut, earnest expression of a welterweight boxer. Kelley and his close associate, the very alert and astute Robert Segal of the Radio Artists Union, are two of the "young guard" which is giving the AFL in Massachusetts an intellectual face lifting. But not without a struggle. The liberals fought a furious struggle in the 1949 convention to save Kelley's job as legislative agent from the clutches of a waning clique of old-timers who sought to transfer it to William V. Ward of the Municipal Employees union, a close pal of Jim Curley's.

Albert Clifton of the CIO is a ruggedly built, serious man in his late fifties who could easily pass as a prosperous business executive. But having started in the labor movement as a teenager in 1911, he knows what it is to work with his hands, to tramp hours in a straggly picket line, and to hold together a band of dispirited strikers in moments of despair and crisis.

In 1946, business interests began a drive to shackle labor. Their shining Galahad was Republican Attorney General Clarence Barnes, a bull-necked, Yale-educated, small-town lawyer with the crew haircut of a college boy and the social philosophy of a troglodyte.

Emblazoned on his shield was the motto "Intra-Union Democracy." The two bills he sponsored called for a ban on union political contributions and required unions to file public financial reports far more detailed than those required of corporations. The Legislature turned the measures down twice, but in 1946 the public voted for the second in a referendum after the courts had ruled the first off the ballot. Barnes had championed this referendum procedure, although in 1918 he opposed adding the initiative and referendum to the State Constitution. Senator Taft later told Barnes that his bills were a model for his own Taft-Hartley Act.

In 1947, the Bradford administration pushed through three more antilabor laws curbing the closed shop, jurisdictional strikes, and disputes broadly defined as "affecting the public health and safety." Also, under pressure from the Small Businessmen's Association, Bradford fired as Labor Commissioner a veteran AFL man who had served several governors.

Success intoxicated Barnes and his front group, the Massa-

52

chusetts Citizens Union. Three more referendums were placed on the ballot in 1948. Literally backed against the wall, organized labor awoke from a mood of postwar lethargy to wage a fierce counterattack. At the last moment, Barnes disavowed the parentage of his embarrassing offspring and even came out against one of the three proposals. It was too late. On November 2, a tidal wave of aroused labor submerged the three referendums by half a million votes and flushed Barnes into oblivion.

Labor's political star now hangs high over Beacon Hill. There was some grumbling that labor's services were not sufficiently reciprocated by the Democrats in the Legislature. But this is only a temporary phenomenon. Labor's political action committees provide the Democrats with their only doorbell ringers. Of the State's three hundred and fifty-one cities and towns, fewer than one-third have Democratic committees, and of these not more than ten actually function. The rest are the private preserves of dead beats and stuffed shirts who sniffle over Al Smith and long for the good old days when they had an "honest-to-God" issue like prohibition. With the Americans for Democratic Action serving as a catalytic agent, scores of tough, practical labor politicians are vitalizing these local Democratic organizations.

The morning after his election, Dever's first public act was a courtesy visit to the residence of Catholic Archbishop Richard J. Cushing. To many, this merely symbolized the deference which all men in public life pay to the most pervasive social force in Massachusetts. Other observers would also rank the Catholic Church as the most potent political influence in the State. The former judgment is perhaps true; the latter surely is not. It may be seriously doubted if the Church as such was ever a very effective power politically.

The late Cardinal O'Connell, a strong-willed man of great personal force and charm, ruled the Boston archdiocese for thirty-seven years, until his death in 1944 at the age of eighty-five. Most writers grossly overestimated his political influence. The Cardinal felt it unwise to participate directly in political controversies. This forced him into the awkward position of endorsing or criticizing certain men and measures obliquely and somewhat ambiguously. This, in part, is why he was often thwarted. He could not destroy political figures whom he disliked. An amendment to the State Constitution which he attacked was carried overwhelmingly in a popular referendum. On another occasion, his personal attorney was defeated for Mayor of Boston. The Cardinal was influential only when public policy impinged on private morality, but even here it should be remembered that book-banning and birth control are areas which the average politician considers unimportant. As a political force, the Catholic Church under Cardinal O'Connell had a terrific potential, but little kinetic energy.

His successor, Archbishop Richard J. Cushing, a big, friendly man with engaging, democratic manners, has tried to bring some of this vast power into play in solving social issues. He does not try to manipulate politics either on-stage or from the wings. He did, however, strongly champion Fair Employment Practices legislation. He invited the Catholic Industrial Welfare Conference to hold its convention for the first time in Boston. He constantly urges that nobody let "an evil thing like Communism be confused with liberalism or 'progressive democracy.'"

But essentially Archbishop Cushing realizes that political leadership is not the job of the hierarchy. The clergy can state broad principles, but only laymen can effectively carry out practical programs and political maneuvers. Unfortunately, Catholic lay organizations traditionally have not been encouraged to act independently of the priest. Yet if the dry matter of secular life is to be infused with the vigor of Catholic ideas, the laity must kick aside its clerical crutches and do the job that it alone can do.

In a significant but little-noticed address to the 1948 convention of the Union of Holy Name Societies, Archbishop Cushing admonished the priests to remember that these key parish groups were lay organizations and must have lay leaders. "If this organization ever fails," he declared, "I don't want it attributed to you, my brother priests, or to me. I have absolute confidence in our lay leadership. I never interfere with the plans of archdiocesan officers," he added meaningfully. The Archbishop went on to urge an active approach to community problems in which Catholic men "must not remain segregated."

But self-reliance and creative community action are not the products of an hour. The same convention responded by passing two resolutions; the first urged the freeing of Archbishop Stepinac, and the second condemned "brutal" comic books. The one issue was cosmic, the other trivial; neither was a problem the average Holy Name Society member could grapple with constructively as a Catholic citizen in the Commonwealth of Massachusetts.

"BABY BORN AT BRIDGE PARTY. WOMAN AT WEEKLY GAME BIDS TWO SPADES, THEN LAYS CARDS DOWN, BABY ARRIVES BEFORE DOCTORS."

This thrilling headline topped no two-inch titbit on page twelve; it introduced the lead story on page one of the February 24, 1949, *Boston Post*. The *Post* calls itself New England's "great breakfast table newspaper" and every morning, true to its word, it relieves the monotony of orange juice and cornflakes by serving up a healthy ration of the morbid and the maudlin. The *Post* is the State's only important Democratic journal. Three years ago, a shift in the paper's trustees caused a softening in its traditional anti-Curley stand. Generally, however, the *Post* sticks to safe, "homey" subjects.

On the Republican side, the most important spokesmen and the most unwavering champions of business interests are the *Herald-Traveler* papers in Boston and the *Telegram-Gazette* group in Worcester. These papers invariably wear an editorial suit of ready-to-wear comfortable conservatism. The tailoring is orthodox Republican and the material is sturdy, but intellectual blue serge can become monotonous. In western Massachusetts, the Springfield press is entirely owned by the famous Bowles family, but the present generation has forgotten Samuel and disowned Chester.

The *Boston Globe* is the tragedy of Massachusetts journalism. It is a mature, independent, family-owned newspaper which lacks the fighting spirit to attack the powerful and the privileged. "Uncle Dudley's" column, an unsigned composite production, is the editorial voice of the *Boston Globe*. Uncle Dudley spins out some penetrating analyses, but just when he should logically recommend a cure, the pattern ravels away, leaving to the reader only bits of verbal fuzz.

Last and least, there is the Hearst press. The *Record* and the *American* are currently crusading for public-power development. There are plenty of combustible materials available for their editorial pyrotechnics. The people of Boston pay the highest electric-light and power rates in the country, and of the next eight cities at the top of the list, seven are also in Massachusetts. Local stockbrokers give this situation a touch of grim humor by running huge ads entitled: "How You May Pay Your Electric Bills." Their solution: Buy common stock of the New England Electric System, the region's largest public-utility holding company. Its shares pay a dividend of more than nine per cent.

The Hearst papers sponsored a joint resolution calling on Congress to develop hydroelectric power in New England.

The public utilities were too smart to oppose such a resolution directly. Would the Hearst group accept an amendment? They would. The resolution as passed read, therefore, that any power developed "should be distributed over privately owned transmission lines." The legislators, most of them ignorant of the history of the public power issue, passively accepted this amendment. The utilities thus disemboweled the resolution; the Heart press got another "victory" to boast about; and the legislators were safely on record for power development as well as for the Flag, Good Friday, and the American Home. Everybody was so happy.

Antivivisection is the subject of another Hearst crusade. General Sherman Miles, representative for the Beacon Hill district, introduced a bill providing that stray animals be turned over to medical centers for research purposes. Experimentation on live animals has led to many brilliant discoveries including that of insulin, the savior of thousands of diabetics. But opposition formed quickly.

The Hearst press led the way with screaming headlines: "Youngsters Rally to Save Their Pets." Hundreds jammed the Statehouse for the public hearings, and they brought their cats, dogs, and lizards with them. The Bull Dog Society sent a representative. The Anti-Vivisection Society sent its president, George R. Farnum. Farnum, a bespectacled, thin-lipped lawyer who served as Assistant Attorney General under Coolidge, is a sincere humanitarian. "Remove this blot from the record of the Commonwealth," he cried. The Farnums have no children but several pets, including a huge, fourteen-year-old elkhound named Sonya. Another opponent saw in the plan a dark plot by Harvard to save its medical school the $9,000 spent each year to buy animals.

The 1949 Legislature, like its predecessor, lacked the courage to buck this tide of sentiment. It voted to postpone the measure indefinitely.

During the debate, supporters of the bill asked: "Does Massachusetts want live dogs or dead babies?" So far, the Legislature seems to be betting on the dogs.

The vivisection and public-power controversies reveal clearly that the local liberal movement lacks stature. Massachusetts politics still suffer from the divisive and intellectually crippling effects of yesterday's Irish-Yankee conflict. Time has bleached the purple past, but politics is still streaked with its dye.

Able, courageous progressives like Congressman John Kennedy and ex-Congressman Joseph Casey have emerged. Among Democrats in the Legislature, however, for every genuine liberal there are a score of easygoing mediocrities who owe election solely to personal popularity in their home districts. They run lawn parties at the church and "Irish Night" at the Elks. They sound off on comic books, Communism, and high electric-light rates, but in a crisis their liberalism wobbles badly. The social climate of the New Deal, the rise of the labor movement, and the infusion of ADA intellectuals are all working to provide the necessary social and political underpinnings.

The course of the Democratic majority in the 1949 session of the Legislature exhibited a flabby state of political liberalism.

Dolan in the Senate and O'Neill in the House, aided by their respective Floor Leaders John Powers of South Boston and Robert Murphy of Malden, did a competent enough job of party management. The middle bracket of leadership, however, creaked and groaned from intellectual hardening of the arteries. Under the seniority rule, key chairmanships went to a clique of time-servers. Having always been in the minority, they had no experience in putting through a comprehensive program. Whatever flame of zeal they may have once possessed had burned low. After losing a month over the Senate presidency fight, they squandered another month getting the legislative machinery rumbling into action. Then more weeks were lost wrangling over the Governor's $100,000,000 highway program and the precise nature of a superhighway into Boston along the Charles River. It was May and lilac time before any important action had been taken. The metropolitan Boston transportation tangle, labor's anti-injunction bill, and Dever's tax program clamored for attention.

At this point, a corporal's guard of some thirty or thirty-five liberals swung into action in the House. They first bared their teeth in a revolt against the emasculation of the bill wiping out segregation in the Massachusetts National Guard. The measure came out of committee amended so as to be merely permissive. In this form it was carried and the issue seemed settled. But when the bill came up for its second reading, Representative James L. O'Dea of Lowell, a dark-eyed, thin-lipped, granite-featured young man, moved to strike out the amendment. In support of his motion, he delivered his maiden speech, an eloquent appeal that the high purpose of the legislation not be made a "mockery." General Sherman Miles, Beacon Hill Republican and Army G-2 at the time of the Pearl Harbor debacle, militantly championed the amendment. Miles pontificated weightily, but with public opinion focused on the issue by the sharpness of the debate, the Republicans deserted the General, and the amendment was killed, 156-44; the antidiscrimination bill became law without qualifying teeth-pullers.

Two other freshmen, Edmund Diníz, Portuguese Democrat from New Bedford, and Harold L. Putnam, Needham Republican, gave O'Dea vital assistance. Putnam, a natty, self-assured young man with sandy hair and smooth, regular features, writes the Veterans' Column in the *Boston Globe* and is one of the most engaging members on the GOP side of the House.

After this resounding victory the liberals turned to the anti-injunction bill. Mario Umana, East Boston Democrat and nephew of former State CIO President Joseph Salerno, was in charge of this measure. Umana is a dark, deceptively slender (he won a boxing championship at Harvard College) fledgling lawyer with an intense manner and a ringing voice. With the doors locked to keep a quorum present, he and his supporters drove the bill through in a stormy session which roared from early afternoon to midnight.

Sparking the newcomers were two slightly older Boston Democrats, James A. Burke of Hyde Park and Daniel Rudsten of Dorchester. Burke is an able, aggressive, colorful leader who is never averse to standing up and snapping: "Let's get to a vote. We've had enough 'soft soap' for one day." Rudsten is a burly ex-stevedore who served in the war for four years as a Marine Corps sergeant. Fast-talking and personable, Rudsten is the Legislature's most articulate and tenacious liberal.

The Senate, voting on party lines, killed the anti-injunction bill, by a 20–20 vote. It was then revived by an emergency message from the Governor and in modified form again went through the House. For a time, it seemed likely to be salvaged due to the courageous mediation efforts of two liberal Republican Senators, Charles Olson of Ashland and Christopher Phillips of Beverly. But in the showdown, the GOP caucus cracked the whip of party regularity and both men bid labor good-by. The long fight had once more ended in defeat.

Phillips, wealthy son of Roosevelt's ambassador to Italy, is at twenty-seven the youngest and most ambitious man in the upper House. His money, brains, and blue-blood lineage make him a strong prospect for the top level of the Republican Party in Massachusetts. Banker Sinclair Weeks and his successor as State GOP boss, United State Senator Henry

Cabot Lodge, best exemplify this leadership of caste, class, and clique.

Weeks, son of Calvin Coolidge's Secretary of War, is a millionaire and the director of a dozen corporations. As National Committeeman and chief money raiser, he held Republican machinery in the hollow of his hand for nearly two decades. It is said of him that "he can raise more money in five minutes than anyone else can in five months." His critics attributed the 1948 disaster to too many "Week-lings" in high party positions. After that defeat, Weeks yielded active leadership to Senator Lodge, who installed his cousin Mason Sears as State Chairman.

State Street supplies the money, the brains, and the political generalship of the GOP, but Main Street furnishes the noncommissioned officers and voting rank and file. The mass of Republican legislators are rural and small-town men. They inherit their conservatism, and years of Grange-going or Rotary Club attendance reinforces it. They go to Congregational bean suppers and find it expedient to "wear the ring" (of the Masonic Order). Like Calvin Coolidge, their perfect archetype, they deeply respect the almighty dollar and the almighty men who possess it. Republican-controlled Legislatures are superficially more decorous and less of a threat to civil liberties simply because they are amenable to pressure from the powerful and responsible elements.

It is significant that the only strong man to emerge among the Republican legislators in their first year of adversity was not a native type. House Floor Leader Charles Gibbons is Kentucky born and was relatively unknown. But as a result of his deft, moderate leadership, he stamped himself as potential governorship material. With good handling, the tall, lanky, Lincolnesque legislator could be built into a potent candidate.

By contrast, Senate Republicans continued in the ruck under the staid management of Harris Richardson, a mediocre, small-town politico. Not since the early 1930's, when the late Gaspar Bacon presided, have the Senate Republicans produced a really able man. Richardson's three predecessors were Jarvis Hunt, now counsel of the Associated Industries; Arthur Coolidge, "stage Yankee" in everything but his garrulousness (as Lieutenant Governor under Bradford, Coolidge used to free the Lithuanians and redeem "ravished Poland" at a banquet table practically every night of the week); and Donald Nicholson, now in Congress and one of the blackest reactionaries Massachusetts or any other state ever produced.

Local problems and local politics are the consuming interests of Republican legislators. No opportunity is too small to be exploited. Old-age assistance is given in Massachusetts only to those who can prove they need it. A strategic town job, therefore, is a seat on the welfare board which makes up budgets for the needy aged. Naturally, the system reeks with political favoritism; many legislative bigwigs built their local machines by dispensing little favors from the welfare-board kitty. The Commonwealth is now in danger of losing federal aid because it is the only State which does not handle old-age assistance through qualified civil service employees.

When these rural and small-town politicians come to Boston, they have to grapple with far bigger problems than whether the town should pay Aunt Nettie's milk bill. Hostile to a "corrupt" Boston they know only by reputation, ignorant of urban and industrial problems, they come with minds sterile if not malevolent.

Efficient gerrrymandering of the Legislature keeps the State's urban majority in the inexorable grip of a rural minority. The present slender Democratic margin is a freak which the 1950 elections will probably reverse. Yet the Legislature has to pass on city problems sweeping in scope and fantastic in detail. No municipality can borrow outside its legal debt limit without specific permission from the Legislature. If a legislator is at odds with his home-town Mayor, he can easily frustrate his rival by blocking approval of an important bond issue. No municipality can change its form of government except by switching to another of the five basic plans drawn up by the State. The Legislature's power to alter these plans at any time makes home rule a farce. In the last municipal elections, several cities adopted Plan E, the main features of which are proportional representation and an appointive city manager. Yet the Legislature this year only narrowly defeated a proposal to deny these cities the right to elect their councilors by PR.

Boston* is the stepchild of this irresponsible system. The city operates under a special charter which means that representatives from Pittsfield and Cape Cod are called on to determine all sorts of odds and ends such as the salaries Boston city councilors should have. The police commissioner, the port authority, and the liquor license board are appointed not by the Mayor but by the Governor. The city has been stripped of control over its subways, parks, parkways, sewers, water system, and bathing beaches. State-appointed commissions manage all these functions. Only two of the last eight Governors have been Boston residents, and the average chief executive when he makes these Boston appointments is less interested in the city than in his own political fence mending.

Over fifty years ago, a special State commission pointed out that this system "constituted a wide and serious departure from the political principles upon which this state and

* The problem of municipal home rule in Ohio is treated at some length in the appropriate chapter.—Ed.

nation are founded. . . . A system of metropolitan control which permits the Legislature, representing the entire Commonwealth, to tax the people of a district not for state but for local purposes, and then, having deprived them of all but a fractional voice in the levying of the tax, decrees that the money shall be spent by those whom the payers of the tax have no voice in appointing and over whom they can exercise no control, is not a system which can be reconciled with American political methods."

Eight hundred thousand people live in the city itself, but they are not the only victims. Within fifteen miles of Boston's City Hall live half the State's 4,500,000 people. The problems of this vast metropolitan community have been consistently neglected and mishandled. The continuing rapid-transit fiasco exemplifies the three-ring circus of State, city and suburb in which nobody gets the brass ring.

One of Dever's chief campaign issues was opposition to a subway-fare increase to fifteen cents. A mounting deficit endangered the dime fare on the publicly owned network that services Boston and thirteen adjacent communities. Bradford lamely protested he would not approve a fare hike, but that didn't keep him from going down under the Democratic deluge.

Dever, saddled with the promise to maintain the fare at a dime, faced an almost insoluble dilemma. Like many another Massachusetts problem, its roots go deep into the past.

In many ways, it is the legacy of the fabulous Matt Brush, self-made Irishman from Minnesota, who was head of the Boston Elevated Company in 1918. Matt was a great storyteller, with all the wit and inventiveness an Irishman is supposed to have. And he told the public in 1918 a truly doleful tale of what would happen to poor old Boston if the State didn't hurry and bail out the stockholders and thus prevent a suspension of transit service. On the side, he showed many legislators how they could buy Elevated stock at $20 a share and make a killing when the State guaranteed dividends. As a result of these blandishments, the Legislature took over the bankrupt company, whose books carried as assets "rolling stock which had ceased to roll, equipment which had become obsolete, and lines which had been abandoned," and guaranteed holders of preferred stock eight per cent dividends, and holders of common stock six per cent. Also, just as Brush had predicted, the shares soared from $20 to $80. The "smart" legislators pocketed their profits; Matt blithely left for the green fields of Wall Street where he became one of the biggest plungers, and the State settled down to wrestle with a problem it has yet to solve after thirty-one years of trying.

Dever accurately declared, "It is doubtful whether, in the entire history of the State, there ever was legislated a measure which more shamefully conferred special benefits on a privileged few or which more shockingly disregarded the interests of the public."

If the Metropolitan Transit Authority should go into the red, the Legislature jauntily provided that the deficit be met by Boston and the other municipalities in the district. Thirteen times there has been a deficit. But the administrative and financial complexities do not end there. The Transit Authority does not own these properties outright. It rents the Boston subways from the city, the Cambridge subway from the State, and certain streetcar lines from a private firm. The Authority also pays taxes to all the cities it services, and this naturally increases the deficit which they in turn are taxed to meet.

Dever proposed to eliminate these anomalies, refinance the bonded debt, and transfer to the State the burden of subway maintenance. The funds for this would come from gasoline taxes, if the subways were defined as "public highways." But the Supreme Court, in an advisory opinion, promptly ruled out this convenient reinterpretation.

Dever's plan was the toughest issue confronting the Legislature. Upstate politicians raised the cry that their constituents never ride the Boston subway so why should they have to pay its costs? One columnist even suggested the rest of the State should secede and call itself "Berkshire," while the Boston metropolitan area could call itself "Messochusetts." Eventually the Legislature passed a bill refinancing the debt burden but withholding State funds to meet the remaining deficit, thus making a fare increase inevitable.

Thus Boston still limps along like a sick old lady, snubbed by her suburban daughters and forced to appeal to an indifferent, tightfisted State government every time she wants to have her glasses straightened or her shoes mended.

Massachusetts has lost faith in herself. Like a hypochondriac she peers anxiously in the mirror to see if, beneath the postwar bloom, the flesh is gray. Another textile mill moves to Dixie, the Waltham Watch Company flounders through another reorganization, the machine-tool business sags. These are but the fatal telltale signs. They awaken no sense of urgency. For the sake of the record, politicians bleat mournfully for tariff protection. "Swiss watches. English woolens. The competition of slave labor." Cant. Nothing but cant.

The hypochondriac at the mirror scarcely listens. This is what she always expected. It was bound to come sooner or later. She stands, she waits, she savors her melancholy satisfactions.

But there are those who would save Massachusetts in spite of herself. Dever urges the piping of natural gas from the Southwest. This may become a reality by 1951. More fundamental is the demand for large-scale development of hydroelectric power. For many, public power has beccme more

66

than an expedient; it is the new deliverance. Labor, business, and politicians all murmur pious "amens." But once again, no one takes decisive initiative. Politicians shadowbox. Business groups like the New England Council sponsor an expensive, lavishly documented survey which tends to minimize the importance of the whole subject. Labor unions, still shaky and defense-minded, expend their energies repealing the laws that cramp them. Soggy inertia blankets the issue.

Moreover, power alone is not the key to New England's future. The problems of the Connecticut River Valley are far different from those of the Tennessee or the Columbia. New England is an old, complex industrial area, thickly settled and highly developed. Her ailments are those of age, not stunted growth. To cure them, not only an integrated regional program of hydroelectric development, flood control, reforestation, and soil conservation is required, but also industrial diversification and plant modernization.

New England's economic history offers dreary parallels to that of old England. The United States is now engaged through the Marshall Plan in stoking the run-down British industrial machine. If New England continues its relative economic decline as it has for the last thirty years, the American South and West may one day find it necessary to provide Massachusetts and her neighbors with a Marshall Plan.

Essentially, the probem is one of human leadership. Massachusetts needs a civic renaissance, a liberation of creative energies, a cutting away of the tangled growth of prejudice and misunderstanding. For such a task, Massachusetts desperately needs a leader. She already has the people; among both Yankees and immigrants there is a hunger for purposeful action. She already has in her many universities a wealth of inteilect only waiting to be tapped as Smith and Roosevelt tapped the university faculties in New York. What Massachusetts lacks is a leader to inspire a broad forward movement, a man to strike from her giant resources the shackles of the past.

Some say that no man could make such a difference. But great men do make all the difference. Wisconsin still bears the imprint of La Follette, and New York City of La Guardia. No one can say from where this leadership may come. Perhaps one of the young men now emerging will be that leader. Perhaps he will be one who is still unknown.

The hour is late. Massachusetts anxiously scans the horizon.

NEW YORK ★ ★ ★

Backslider

ROBERT G. SPIVACK

It is Monday night in Albany. The lights in the Capitol are ablaze. The corridors are crowded. The Assembly and Senate chambers are jammed. Lobbyists for the banks, cemetery associations, chiropractors, railroads, teachers, labor, the air lines, utilities, and realtors are everywhere.

A former Senate leader pleads the cause of flophouse owners making a fortune on their firetraps. Western Union's Republican leader saunters about, with legislators showing proper deference. The all-powerful and ubiquitous insurance companies parade new schemes for high-rental apartments with juicy tax exemptions. This, their spokesmen proclaim, is real public housing. Of course, not all the public will benefit from it, and especially Negroes will fail to benefit. Property values must not be depressed. The Dewey administration agrees.

In the present State government of New York, that is prac-

★

ROBERT G. SPIVACK, thirty-four, is a political writer for the New York *Post Home News*. He has covered the New York Legislature for the last six years, was elected president of the Legislative Correspondents Association, and covered both of Governor Dewey's presidential campaigns. Spivack is a frequent contributor to magazines on New York politics, and wrote a chapter in the book version of Henry R. Luce's "The American Century."

tically the whole story. Protection of private property and special interests—for a price.

In the uneven battle between the forces of good and bad government in the Empire State, Albany is the arsenal of corruption. The moral standard of the bulk of the legislators and politicians is graphically illustrated in an incident involving the late Paul Lewin, factotum to Irwin Steingut, Democratic boss of the Assembly.

Eight reporters were seated around a poker table in the pressroom on the night of March 4, 1944. Periodically they would get up to check with Dewey's office on the case of Louis "Lepke" Buchalter. For over two decades the hoodlum had terrorized and murdered. That night, it was his turn. After exhausting every legal stratagem, his life was about to end.

Shortly after 11:16 P.M. the press phone rang. Ossining reported that the executioner had pulled the switch. The reporters phoned their offices and departed. In the corridor loitered diminutive "Paulie."

"Well, Lepke got it," a reporter said.

"De bum was no good," Paulie growled.

"Why do you say that?" asked one of the newsmen, with feigned amazement.

"I'll tell ya why," was the answer. "Every year I'd go to de bum and ast him ta kick in with de dough for de boss. He never gave us a penny, de louse. He got what was comin' ta him."

Paulie Lewin's viewpoint and standard of measurement are not exceptional in Albany. Only his outspokenness was.

Irwin Steingut, Paulie's boss, is a perfect case in point. Steingut has been an Assemblyman for more than twenty-five years, and Democratic leader of the chamber for nineteen years. He's what the boys in the back room call "a sweetheart." There is practically nothing he won't do for

70

anyone with the right connections—a very accommodating fellow, a sweetheart.

One of Steingut's chief claims to fame is that he does not have a prison record.

Several efforts have been made to incarcerate him. In one of the more recent, Special Prosecutor Hiram C. Todd uncovered, among other things, nearly $100,000 in a safe-deposit vault. Steingut blandly produced a remarkable explanation. It had been bequeathed him by his deceased stepfather. Others in the immediate family seemed unaware of this legacy. There had been an impression, rather widespread, that the stepfather died a poor man. Todd held that belief, and went to the courts. They evinced interest, but were seemingly powerless to make Steingut change his story.

In the end, a Republican Assembly committee found Steingut blameless, and the Republican Assembly itself gave him a clean bill of health. Some legislators remarked how wonderful it was that the Republicans rose above party differences and refused to condemn a Democrat. Others had a different idea. They thought the Republicans were merely making sure that Steingut spilled no beans. That he wouldn't start "singing."

Flabby Mr. Steingut loves to pass himself off as a New Dealer. Although a dull speaker, his speeches are replete with assurances of his devotion to the administrations of Al Smith, Franklin D. Roosevelt, and Herbert H. Lehman. As leader of the Assembly, particularly in 1935, when the Democrats for the first time in years controlled the Legislature, Steingut has been in a position to play a role in the enactment of some of the State's most advanced social legislation. Actually, he had virtually nothing to do with the inception of these measures, but he has boastfully lived in the reflected glory of the great Democratic Governors who championed them.

In the absence of latter-day Tweeds, Crokers, and Murphys, a host of lesser bosses, of whom Steingut is but one, have come to the fore in New York State.

Livingston Platt, as befits the boss of wealthy, Republican Westchester County, is polished and far more at home in a yacht club than in Hogan's Third Avenue Bar & Grill. Platt's law partner, William Bleakley, speaks often for the utilities —and is respectfully listened to.

Probably the most intelligent New York boss is urbane Edward J. Flynn. The Democratic chief of the Bronx can not only read, but he can write, as his cynical autobiography, *You're the Boss,* attests. Flynn is honest enough to admit that an enlightened electorate can overturn any political machine. He has been astute enough to keep his own machine relatively free of scandal, thus avoiding popular revolt.

Other bosses have remained true to the old traditions. An example is J. Russel Sprague, of Long Island's Nassau County, with its Gold Coast and spacious estates. While he leads the Republican blue bloods, Sprague is at the same time a business associate of Steingut, the Brooklyn Democrat. Sprague, right-hand lieutenant of Governor Dewey, lacks the subtle touch. Once he sent newspaper and radiomen in his area crisp new $20 bills as a "Christmas present."

All the bosses operate on the ancient concept that anything and anyone can be bought. On most matters before the Legislature, party lines vanish. The Spragues, Steinguts, and Platts work together hand in glove.

The Democrats aver—that's the right word—that they put human values before property values. At every legislative session the chambers ring with the high-school orations of Steingut and Elmer F. Quinn, his Senate counterpart. Both vehemently proclaim that they mean business. But it is just so much empty clatter. They know it, and their colleagues know it. The only ones apparently fooled are the voters.

Quinn is a portly, back-slapping, caricaturist-type politician. His district includes Al Smith's old Fulton Fish Market. He has become wealthy in the years he has "served the people," and his law clients range from great chain-store corporations to theater-ticket scalpers. His name appears on one of the State's most advanced measures of social legislation, the law barring discrimination in employment, though it is extremely questionable if Quinn had any great share in formulating it.

Until recently, the Senate Republican Leader was Benjamin F. Feinberg. He had a habit of springing to his feet and screaming imprecations at Quinn. Everyone, of course, knew it was all in fun. The same was true in the Assembly. Speaker Oswald D. Heck would often good-humoredly shut off debate with, "Are you all through, Mr. Steingut?"

Sometimes debate in the Legislature grows bitter and makes good newspaper copy. But, as in Congress, the oratory is for the "folks back home." It is in the quiet of the suites of Albany's comfortable DeWitt Clinton and Ten Eyck hotels that the freewheeling political entrepreneurs carry on their business. And on that level it matters not whether a man is a Republican or a Democrat. What counts is whether he can deliver what he promises—votes, money, or both.

Despite the shabbiness and tawdriness of its politicos, New York State's reputation as a bellwether in social legislation is well deserved. However, it is significant to note that important social changes take years to enact. The struggle for such legislation is as unending as the battle for decency and honesty in politics.

New York's great social reforms came about only through the untiring efforts of high-minded citizens. The political bosses and machines had no part in this leadership. They

73

were merely "free riders." When they couldn't thwart or sabotage or defeat, they went along. But only because they had to. Now, as then, they still sneer and mock the "do-gooders."

The Democratic Party has been the vehicle for these changes. This is not because the party is more enlightened and honest. It is due to the fact that the focal point of demand for social legislation is New York City, and it is Democratic. Charles Murphy, Tammany's ablest boss, summed up what still remains the attitude of the back-room boys. In 1911 the Triangle Shirtwaist Company went up in flames, burning to death scores of girl workers. Frances Perkins led the fight for corrective legislation. Murphy told her he had opposed such laws but had changed his position because "they will make a lot of votes for us."

New York boosters never tire of enumerating the glories of the State. It is true they are many—as are its inglories. Magnificent parks and highways and, also, foul Gowanus Canal; mighty Empire State Building, and fearsome slums; Niagara Falls, and polluted Harlem River; modern dairy farms, and marijuana dens; Wall Street, and the Bowery; *The New York Times* and the New York *Daily News,* and Roy Howard, Frank Gannett, and William Randolph Hearst. And but for railroad and utility obstructionism, the State might now be leading the nation in cheap electricity from the St. Lawrence and Niagara rivers.

New York does have a great deal. More television sets, longer subways, the biggest harbor, 60,000 industrial concerns, and 14,400,000 people. Their income has topped $23,000,000,000 a year. Economically, the State possesses 12.6 per cent of the nation's wealth. It also boasts of more art galleries, more overworked psychiatrists, more foreign-born, more political parties, dingier night clubs, more churches, temples, and cathedrals, thicker telephone books, the tallest

74

showgals, the largest newspapers, the tastiest salami, and more singing commercials than any of the other forty-seven states.

But it had only one Fiorello H. La Guardia.

To millions of New Yorkers, La Guardia, with his squeaky voice, fireman's hat, and five-star police car, was the symbol of clean government. Although they were not close friends, he and Herbert H. Lehman left an imprint on the governmental and social structure of New York comparable to that of Franklin D. Roosevelt on the nation.

Despite his many faults, mostly temperament, La Guardia was an honest man. He gathered able, intelligent, and for the most part honest men around him.

Under him, the begrimed, weather-beaten City Hall became a bastion of clean government. If an appointee went wrong, La Guardia would denounce him in the shrillest language heard outside a fish market. Sometimes he even got suspicious of the scrupulous men about him, and then would humbly apologize. Once he appointed a judge who turned out a bigot. In one of his few dispassionate observations, "Butch" remarked ruefully, "When I make a mistake, it's a beaut."

La Guardia took over a bankrupt and crime-ridden city. He led it through a depression and a war and brought it out solvent. He made many mistakes, some of them whoppers. One of the worst was yielding to intolerant churchmen and refusing to permit Bertrand Russell to lecture at City College. Another that was a real "beaut" was paying an exorbitant price for the city's broken-down private subway lines. It was a completely honest transaction, but a stupid one. But with all his human shortcomings, La Guardia gave the city the finest, ablest, and most invigorating government of its entire history.

He was not only the conscience of the big city, but of the

entire State. The impact of his personality was felt up north among the dairy farmers, in the steel mills of Buffalo, among the clothing workers at Rochester. It was even felt in the legislative halls in Albany, normally insulated against the forces he represented.

The change since his death has been gradual, but fundamental. For a decade New York advanced. Since La Guardia's death, retrogression has set in.

New York is two states.

Fifty-five per cent of the population lives in the Babel-like, giant, Democratic metropolis. The entire upstate is largely Republican. Actually, the two richest and most Republican counties, Nassau and Westchester, are next door to the metropolis. In reality they are its suburbs. Large numbers from the big city are constantly overflowing into the two counties, and it is only a matter of time when they will cease to be GOP strongholds. Buffalo, Syracuse, and Rochester veer back and forth as the voters seek political relief. The State is so gerrymandered that the Republicans, except for 1935, have consistently controlled the Legislature despite repeated Democratic sweeps. Moreover, this situation is aggravated by an onerous provision in the State Constitution which prohibits New York City from having more than half the State's Senators.

The two key officials in New York are the Governor and the Mayor of New York City. The retrogression which the State has suffered is due largely to Republican Governor Thomas E. Dewey and Democratic Mayor William O'Dwyer. For different reasons they failed to maintain the high governmental standards of their predecessors, Lehman and La Guardia.

While lacking in popular appeal, Thomas E. Dewey is intelligent, has administrative ability, and lives on his salary

—three qualities rare in a New York politician. Insatiable ambition has destroyed Dewey.

Members of Dewey's staff have almost all been bright, capable, and cautious men. His running mates, Nathaniel L. Goldstein, the Attorney General, and Frank Moore, State Controller, are able, honest, nonspectacular public servants.

One of Dewey's first rules on taking office was that no one could get a State job who had ever been convicted of crime. This policy has kept his administration free of obvious thievery. But Dewey closed his eyes to the type of Republicans elected to the Legislature. Except for a handful, they are owned by business interests.

Once he stepped out of the District Attorney's Office, Dewey laid down his shining armor. As he refused to face up to issues in his 1948 campaign, so throughout his seven years in Albany "Tongue-tied Tommy," as he has come to be known, has tolerated bad government in local communities and in the Legislature. The rare occasions on which he has lifted a lance have been to tilt with decomposed Democratic machines.

What Dewey has given New York is cautious, unimaginative government. Within the limitations he has set for himself, it has been competent and personally honest. But he has not evinced any burning interest in social progress. The most important advance of his administration was the enactment of a State FEPC. With New York's huge minority groups, the legislation had obvious political value. How the law will be administered in a period of social stress is yet to be seen.

Dewey boasts he has given the State a businesslike administration. In part this is true, although his budget has been nearly triple that of Lehman's. In temporary veterans' housing, Dewey ran wild in expenditures—building firetraps at much higher cost than decent permanent housing.

During the years in which Dewey was seeking to impress

big Republican contributors as an economizer, he pinched pennies on education. But the schoolmarms, after lengthy submission and being kicked around, finally acquired a sense of their own strength. At Buffalo a teachers' union shut down the schools in an effective strike. In the course of the bitter fighting over aid to the schools, Dewey developed a phobia about what he called the "teachers' lobby," although none of the other lobbies seemed to bother him at all. But after his second defeat for the presidency, he offered an olive branch, and it was accepted.

Dewey has had a good New York press in Albany. His attitude toward the newspapers is calculated, and he uses news conferences for all they are worth.

What no newsman could write about in day-to-day coverage is the real tragedy of Dewey's career. This was not his second defeat for the presidency. Dewey's great tragedy is that he started out an ardent foe of corruption and has ended up tolerating it.

Probably no man in the State was as well informed about the interests corrupting officials. What Dewey did not know himself, he learned from his highly competent legal counsel, Charles D. Breitel.

With Lazarus around, Dewey has had no excuse for his unwillingness to clash with corruption. When he laid aside his racket-busting role, it was a deliberate decision. He was convinced by his brain trust that the public would not look with favor on the idea of a prosecutor as President. What they failed to tell him, and what he could not comprehend, was that the public likes a fighter in any role.

Mayor William O'Dwyer is a different story.

A reporter once credited O'Dwyer with the observation, "To be a successful politician you have to be on intimate terms with sin." A product of one of the worst machines in the State, O'Dwyer has seen a lot of the ways and deeds of

78

political racketeering. Yet most of his original appointments were mediocre or outright bad, and many of his second choices were not much better.

O'Dwyer has talked New Dealish and acted Old Dealish. In almost every department, usually after newspaper exposés or in fear of them, O'Dwyer has been forced to remove many of those whom he named and whose taking ways he should have known about even if he didn't.

But a number of them with underworld connections were kept in office. O'Dwyer himself was on friendly terms with Frank Costello,* prime minister of the underworld. Before O'Dwyer became Mayor he was often a guest in Costello's swank Central Park West apartment. The boys would feast on caviar, thick steaks, and vintage wines. O'Dwyer and Costello also lunched at a luxurious West Twenty-third Street restaurant.

Underworld influence has always been strong in New York politics. In recent years, Costello has been the most influential racketeer. He has potent friends in the Legislature, in the New York City Council, among businessmen, and on the bench. His wide circle of acquaintances also takes in Joe "Adonis" (real name, Doto), who has a lot to say in Brooklyn politics; Willie Moretti, alias Moore, the gambling king of New Jersey; and water-front racketeer Albert Anastasia. During the O'Dwyer administration Costello has often seemed to be the *Oberburgermeister* of the metropolis.

Costello is shrewd and personable. Also, he has the distinction of being intelligent enough to want to keep the racket boys from needlessly using strong-arm tactics. His repute and connections extend far beyond New York borders and he has often acted as impartial arbiter for mobs in other states unable to settle their differences amicably.

*This gentleman is not unknown in Louisiana and California, as the reader will learn.—Ed.

One place where it is extremely difficult to keep peace is on the city water front, and an incident of a few years back is the key to understanding the O'Dwyer city administration's peculiar relations with the Dewey State administration.

Before O'Dwyer became Mayor, Dewey appointed a prosecutor to look into the operations of the Brooklyn District Attorney's office where O'Dwyer had established a reputation as the nemesis of Murder, Inc. Within a very short time a special grand jury, guided by Prosecutor George J. Beldock, charged O'Dwyer's office with "gross laxity, inefficiency, and maladministration" on such a scale as "to imperil the very foundation of our system of government in the enforcement of its penal laws."

For reasons never fully explained, Dewey turned down a request by the grand jury to continue its probe after Beldock had been defeated in 1945. But the jury did go into the activities of Anastasia.

The jury came up with an extraordinary presentment on December 20, 1945. This presentment was expunged from the records after O'Dwyer became Mayor.

Among other things, the presentment said:

"The undisputed proof is that William O'Dwyer and Edward A. Heffernan (his chief of staff) were in possession of competent legal evidence that Anastasia was guilty of first-degree murder and other vicious crimes. This proof, admittedly, was sufficient to warrant Anastasia's indictment and conviction, but Anastasia was neither prosecuted, indicted, nor convicted."

It then quoted portions of O'Dwyer's testimony under oath:

Q. Anastasia was not only one of the biggest of the big-shots, but you found that he played a hand in every murder committed in Brooklyn, and you finally got him in the . . . case, didn't you?

A. [By O'Dwyer] Yes.

Q. And you could have gotten an indictment against him, couldn't you?

A. Yes.

Q. And sent him to the electric chair?

A. Yes.

O'Dwyer had described the evidence in his hands as constituting a "perfect murder case" against the powerful gangster. But the grand jury noted that every case against Anastasia was "abandoned, neglected, or pigeonholed."

O'Dwyer for his part did not deny the facts, but blamed his subordinates for not carrying through. They, in turn, shifted the blame from one to another, each one absolving himself. The grand jury declared that the failure to proceed against Anastasia was "neither denied, justified, nor satisfactorily explained."

O'Dwyer testified that his chief concern was to convict Anastasia, but said he was not aware that his chief aide had presented an almost complete case against him before a grand jury and then had suddenly abandoned the presentation. O'Dwyer was called before the special grand jury eight separate times and spent approximately fourteen hours answering questions. At one point he said:

"I haven't the slightest doubt where the responsibility lies, Mr. Beldock. I have no fault to find with this grand jury for making the complaint that they have made because that complaint is justly founded. That thing should have been followed through, but to blame me for that, that is not right."

The presentment was given some attention by the press. But O'Dwyer had just been elected and the prevailing sentiment was to "give him a chance." Almost his first act after election was to drive to Albany to see Dewey. What occurred in their talk has never been told, but in his subsequent relations with the Governor, O'Dwyer has been exceedingly respectful.

O'Dwyer mastered the New Deal vocabulary, but his four years as Mayor have been costly and illiberal.

During his administration there reappeared open gambling, prostitution, pay-offs, cops carrying night sticks on strike duty, protection for racketeers, payroll padding, and other characteristics of a lazy, phony government that usually ends up with underworld rule.

La Guardia set a pattern of honest and efficient government. It meshed well with Lehman's pattern of State social welfare.

The disastrous results of O'Dwyer's administration are not merely that the patronage-hungry Tammany Tiger was fed and fed well—27,000 non-civil service jobs, approximately $100,000,000 in patronage for the machines. The greater disaster is that through a series of deft maneuvers, O'Dwyer has dissipated the energies of New York's normally alert and vigilant liberal leaders, and divided and confused them.

This craftily induced paralysis of New York's forces for good government has not ended at the city line.

Under the State Constitution, the City is a creature of the State. Most of its major problems cannot be settled in City Hall. The City has to go to Albany. During the La Guardia era, the liberals were active and vocal in the Legislature and they worked closely with him. O'Dwyer's formula has been to tell the liberals to leave everything to "Billo."

Now, Billo O'Dwyer is, indeed, a charmer. At the City's expense, he has wined and dined civic leaders at Gracie Mansion, the Mayor's home, simulated an interest in their viewpoint, impressed them with his knowledge of Yeats and other Irish poets, and displayed grief and despondency at the shenanigans of the boys in the rear rooms. His listeners have departed feeling he was in their corner and sorry for the woes that beset such a sentimental and beautiful soul.

But when the chips were down, O'Dwyer never fought for the City's interests at Albany nor against the financial overlords who own the City's bonds. Not once in his entire administration has O'Dwyer stood up and slugged it out toe-to-toe with these interests. Thus it inevitably followed that with O'Dwyer and the Democrats, who profess to be the liberal champions, doing nothing, Dewey and his upstate Republicans, who make no such pretensions, have had no reason to agitate themselves.

That has been Billo O'Dwyer's greatest offense to his City and his State.

There is scarcely a basic issue on which O'Dwyer has moved forthrightly and steadfastly against corporate greed. And every time he capitulated, the way was made that much easier for the Republicans on the State level to move several steps farther in the same direction. They always had a convenient Democratic precedent.

What happened on the subway-fare issue is a case in point. The five-cent fare was long sacred in City politics. Even the GOP didn't dare tamper with it, despite the clamor of real-estate and banking interests. At the start of his administration, O'Dwyer solemnly promised that the fare would not be increased. Then banker–real-estate pressure began to operate, and, where others had feared to tread, O'Dwyer plunged in.

He repudiated his announced policy and only went through the motions of examining alternatives to meet the transit deficit. After staging a public hearing, at which he resoundingly whacked real-estate operators for demanding increased fares, he then proceeded to climb aboard that grab wagon himself. His demand created a furor in Albany. But since it was the Democrats who asked for it, the Republicans were quick to grant everything O'Dwyer and the bankers and

83

realtors asked for. Dewey sat back and with a Cheshire-cat grin watched the floundering O'Dwyer break a final pledge: that the voters would be given an opportunity to pass on a fare boost. O'Dwyer carefully ducked a referendum on the issue.

The fare was doubled. The increase amounted to a tax of $50 annually on every New York family. But a year later, the subways were still dirty, unventilated, and overcrowded.

Once O'Dwyer showed the way, the Public Service Commission, now headed by the former Republican Senate Leader Feinberg, went hog-wild in granting increases to private bus lines and other utilities throughout the State.

The ease with which O'Dwyer flimflammed liberals and clean-government groups is no credit to them. The normally vigilant Citizens Union was virtually lulled to sleep by his magic. Others, including some of New York's most distinguished citizens, were busy arguing at cocktail parties whether a man who appeared to know so much about literature could be talking out of both sides of his mouth at once. The debate is still going on.

Perhaps O'Dywer's most flagrant surrender of a traditional Democratic position was in the controversy over State aid to municipalities. Reduced to its simplest terms, this was an argument over what portion of revenues collected in the cities by the State should be returned to those cities.

Dewey had fixed ideas on the matter. He felt the larger communities should quit seeking State "handouts" and should impose new local taxes.

O'Dwyer posed as the champion of the cities against the "miserly" State. He declared he was sick of coming to Albany each year "hat in hand" begging for a pittance. Those were strong words. But Dewey said "No," and the Democratic Mayor edged farther and farther away from his original stand. By 1949 he did not even refer to it.

84

O'Dwyer's abandonment of this stand cut the ground from under the other municipalities in their fight for State aid.

Without such funds, the cities had to turn to other sources for the revenue they urgently needed. Among these were raising the constitutional limit on real-estate taxes or the bonded indebtedness. Here again O'Dwyer started to lead, but did not go far. Real-estate boards and banks quickly flashed the stop signal. O'Dwyer stopped.

The average good intelligence of the New York voter has put a heavy strain on the two major parties to keep alive the myth that they think and act differently on basic issues.

The *real* difference is between the Democratic voter and the Republican voter.

Each election they go to the polls and vote their convictions, and each time they get more and more of the same thing. On the State level the Democratic "outs" have surrendered their function as watchdogs over the Republican "ins." And the Republicans, led by Dewey, have done nothing to uncover the malodorous practices of the O'Dwyer regime in New York. A "gentleman's agreement" has seemed to be in force to keep out of each other's territory.

There are Democrats and Republicans who blush at the arrangement. In this very small group are Democratic State Chairman Paul E. Fitzpatrick, an enlightened Buffalo businessman, and W. Kingsland Macy, Suffolk County Republican leader. But they have been able to do very little.

The bipartisan connivance extends to the bench, although politicians will say with a straight face that the reason for two-party endorsement of judicial candidates is "to keep politics out of the courts." Actually, only the Court of Appeals, highest tribunal in the State, is free of politics. Attempts have been made to inject it there, but they have been thwarted.

85

The lower courts, however, are literally of a low order.

There are a few distinguished jurists on these benches, but they are the exception. A horrible example is the New York Supreme Court. A court of almost limitless jurisdiction, its judges receive higher compensation than the Governor and have more power in issuing decrees. Yet many of the judges have to rely on their clerks to write opinions. There have been reported instances of judges paying as much as $125,000 for their places. District leaders have often been named secretaries to the judges, and handle the lucrative patronage that passes through their hands.

With the present make-up of the New York bench, the expression "sober as a judge" has become obsolete, and more than one smart lawyer has warned a client against trying to have "his day in court."

Still, in comparison with the Legislature, the courts appear of a high order. The center of most of the clamor for judicial reform is in New York City, although the caliber of upstate Supreme Court judges is higher. Some of the judges in the metropolis definitely owe their "elevation" to racketeers and other politically unsavory elements. Few, though, have been as candid about this as Supreme Court Justice Thomas A. Aurelio. He telephoned Costello and thanked him for his backing and further underscored his gratitude with a pledge of "undying loyalty" to the slot-machine czar.

But New York has produced celebrated jurists. Benjamin N. Cardozo graduated from the New York bench to the United States Supreme Court, and other nationally known judges are Samuel Seabury, Irving Lehman, brother of the former Governor, and Thomas D. Thacher, vigorous foe of corruption. The present Court of Appeals is headed by Chief Judge John T. Loughran, who has a more conservative social outlook than some of his predecessors. But among the judges is a young man in his forties, Stanley H. Fuld of New York

City, who shows promise of becoming one of the nation's great jurists. He was appointed by Dewey and has established himself as an outstanding authority on constitutional law. Fuld's appointment was one of Dewey's best and least publicized. All the young lawyer had to offer was exceptional intelligence and integrity; he had no political connections that could have helped Dewey in any way.

One of the first things a freshman legislator learns when he comes to Albany, even before he knows the location of his office, is that the Legislature is a big fraternity in which all the brothers stand together against the outer world, come what may.

Once, one of the brethren, a Manhattan Democrat, questioned another brother's "investigation" of milk interests. Was it not true, he inquired, that the "investigator's" law firm represented an important segment of the milk trust? Although the object of the attack was a Republican, the look of horror that came over the faces of the Democratic brethren was a ghastly sight to see. As soon as they could recover from the shock and shame, they leaped on their erring colleague. The Democrats forced him to retract his heinous outburst. "He shouldn't had ought to of done it," was whispered throughout the lobbies. To this day the incident is recalled with shudders by both Republicans and Democrats.

The bipartisan collaboration begins at the top and trickles down. Aside from the *entente cordiale* between Dewey and O'Dwyer, based on the latter's apparent determined desire for peace at any price, these are the high lights of the Albany story:

O'Dwyer was saved from an investigation of his administration by Republican Senate Leader Arthur Wicks, one of O'Dwyer's closest friends. Wicks has probably the most extensive business connections in the Legislature. Once a Democrat, he switched parties when he moved upstate. He owns two bus lines, a large hotel, a huge laundry, and has other interests.

Republican Chairman D. Mallory Stephens, of the Assembly Ways and Means Committee, in addition to selling coal, insurance, and bonds, is the spokesman for banking interests. He is also a board member of the City Title Insurance Company of New York, in which Democratic Assembly Leader Steingut is a dominant figure. Stephens is an intelligent conservative. He is aware that the world is changing in a sense that most of his party colleagues are not. But beyond that he doesn't do much about it.

Senate Democratic Leader Quinn's most likely successor is Francis J. Mahoney of Manhattan. Mahoney is a law associate of Manhattan Republican Chairman Thomas J. Curran.

In politics you meet the most interesting business allies. Or is it the other way around?

Five men control the fate of every piece of legislation in Albany. They are the Speaker of the Assembly, the Assembly Majority Leader, the Chairman of the Ways and Means Committee, the Senate Majority Leader, and the Chairman of the Finance Committee. If any one of them turns thumbs down on a bill, its chances of passage are virtually nil. Similarly, when the group backs a measure, nothing except a veto can stop them. Every one of the Big Five is conservative, wealthy, and has numerous business interests.

Every Monday night during the legislative session, the pleaders for special interests flock to the gaudy old Capitol. With its million-dollar staircase, first cousin to the Tweed courthouse in New York City, the building is a costly monument to the boodle boys of an earlier era.

But while the lobbyists still appear in droves, their practices have changed. In the days of fierce competition between the expanding railroads and retreating canal-boat operators, the legislators would hang their coats in the cloak-room, and "bag men" would silently deposit envelopes in the pockets of the deserving. Even as late as the Seabury probe in the 1930's, open bribery was common. But in this stream-lined day, such crude methods are old hat.

Now the business interests have legislators lobby for them. There is nothing illegal about it. It's all very proper. The lawmaker's firm is retained, or it gets a big order or insurance policy. Very simple, safe, and productive.

Al Smith is credited with a keen observation made while walking through a law library. Noticing a student diligently poring over his books, Smith remarked, "That boy is learning to take a bribe and call it a fee." *

Next most effective lobbyists are ex-legislators. One who has done handsomely at this is former Senate Republican Leader George R. Fearon. Among his well-paying clients are flophouse owners, utilities, banks, and industries.

What can a lobbyist-lawmaker do? Former Senator Warren T. Thayer, once Chairman of the Committee on Public Service, is a graphic illustration.

Thayer was quietly hired by Associated Gas & Electric Company. He served the utility well and loyally for years. Unfortunately for himself and his employer, Thayer had a weakness for writing letters. In one, to a utility executive, he reported, "The Legislature adjourned last Friday. . . . I hope my work was satisfactory to your company, not so much for the new legislation enacted, but from the fact that many detrimental bills which were introduced we were able to kill in Committee."

Thayer was not alone, and what he did years ago is still being done in Albany today.

* As the chapters on Pennsylvania and California make clear, Al Smith's remark is certainly applicable to those states—and possibly to many others.—Ed.

The stakes are great. A recent fierce battle over millions was fought between rival race-track interests: pari-mutuel machine companies versus bookmakers. Each vied hectically for legislators' favor. Another epic struggle was over a so-called "merit rating" plan under which big industries receive large rebates from the unemployment-insurance reserve fund. Since the enactment of this grab, corporations have collected more than $350,000,000. The size of the prize indicates the degree of fervor that went into putting the scheme over. Financial experts of giant General Electric Company masterminded the bill through the Legislature against labor opposition.

It is customary at Albany to postpone important and controversial legislation for the hectic closing hours. Then the measures are high-pressured through without debate. Example: Several bills were passed in this manner in the 1949 session at the request of the O'Dwyer administration. One authorized a special tax on certain personal commodities, and another, the sale of condemned slum areas at bargain prices to private builders. Under this craftily drawn bill, the City Board of Estimate could condemn property and resell or lease it to favorites of the Board.

Such far-reaching and suspicious legislation warranted closest scrutiny. It would have escaped unnoticed but for Charles Abrams, public-spirited attorney. He exposed the bipartisan scheme. That the business-minded Republicans should approve such measures was no surprise. But that the O'Dwyer administration was deeply involved in them was a jolt, particularly as the bills contained no prohibition against racial discrimination in the new housing projects. In fact, they did not even provide that evicted tenants from condemned slums should be cared for in the new developments —or somewhere. To Dewey's credit, he vetoed them.

Cynics used to say that the chief difference between a

Democratic and Republican politician was that the Democrat was a petty grafter. That distinction no longer exists.

One of the more flagrant examples of bipartisan connivance was the attempted suppression of a report on the investigation into the operations of the New York City Rent Commission, loaded with ward heelers and hacks.

Set up to enforce rent control and prevent evictions, the Board aroused a storm of outcries by its antitenant rulings. The situation burst into a scandal when Charles Abrams revealed that a member of the Commission was voting rent increases for clients of a firm in which he had an interest. The Legislature ordered an inquiry and the job was given to Louis E. Yavner, Investigations Commissioner for La Guardia.

Yavner produced a devastating report. He found that the Rent Commission had allowed residential hotels increases totaling $10,000,000. These were granted at the very time O'Dwyer was in Washington "fighting" for stronger rent controls. Yavner also uncovered extensive collaboration between some members of the Commission and property owners to devise rent-kiting formulae.

The report was submitted to a subcommittee. Assemblyman Samuel Rabin, able young Republican from Queens, demanded immediate adoption of the report. But Democratic Senator Francis Mahoney strenuously objected. In this stand he was vigorously supported by the third member of the committee, Republican Senator Charles V. Scanlan. Scanlan is from the Bronx, where for years the GOP has been merely an adjunct to the Democratic machine. Scanlan "discovered," despite Yavner's evidence, that the Rent Commission had done a "fine job." For a time the report was suppressed. Only the threat to make public additional evidence gathered by the investigations, with the possible implication of high New York City officials, reluctantly led the whole committee to agree to adopt it—without any public announcement of this decision.

The irony of this sordid affair was that the Yavner report was an exception in its fearlessness. The usual technique is for a joint committee with a large appropriation to "study" a situation leisurely for several years. Juicy patronage plums are a much prized feature of such inquiries. Also other things. One group, studying juvenile delinquency, presented mink coats to showgirls, silk shirts to its members, and ran up large bills in swanky hotels and resorts throughout the State.

Once the railroads and the public utilities ruled the Legislature. Now the great insurance companies, led by Metropolitan, hold politicians and legislators in an iron grasp. The legislators who head the insurance committees have almost always been pro-company, and it is a rare occasion when the insurance moguls cannot block a bill or put through one they favor. The insurance laws are administered by a State Insurance Department headed by an able, but conservative, young lawyer, Robert E. Dineen of Syracuse. Much of his experience, before being appointed by Dewey, was as the attorney for insurance firms.

In New York politics the insurance octopus has many friends. Numerous legislators and politicians are insurance brokers. Downstate, many of the insurance company housing schemes were born in the fertile brain of Robert "Bob the Builder" Moses, and those which he did not father personally, he supported. In the Legislature, the insurance companies look to Stephens, one of the Big Five, for protection of their interests.

Volumes are yet to be written on the history of insurance company grabs. Their most flagrant violation of democratic rights was Metropolitan's lily-white "Stuyvesant Town" within the boundaries of the world's most cosmopolitan metropolis.

New York politicians scoff at Dixiecrats and editorial writers wax heated about "white only" signs of "benighted" Southerners. But the Legislature which approved a State antidiscrimination act also refused to interfere with Stuyvesant Town's ban on Negroes. Most of the New York press has been editorially unconcerned about the matter. Negroes pay taxes in New York, like everyone else. But Stuyvesant Town, the Caucasian village, got tax exemption for twenty-five years, to the tune of $53,000,000. Even the city's streets were given to Metropolitan "for free" and have now become private driveways.

Despite the general sodden level of the New York Legislature, there are a few men of high caliber on its rolls.

One is Philip Schupler, a high-school teacher. He not only earned a Ph.D. while serving in Albany, but repeatedly beat the Coney Island Democratic machine against vicious opposition. Another is Manhattan Assemblyman Samuel Roman. He was a small coal dealer minding his own business when he became so outraged by the corruption he saw around him that he got into politics and twice beat Tammany candidates. A third is Senator Thomas Desmond. A trustee of Massachusetts Institute of Technology, he represents the section once dominated by reactionary, isolationist Congressman Hamilton Fish. A wealthy man, Desmond has fathered more reform legislation than probably any other member of the State Senate. There are a handful of others.

New Yorkers are an angry people who have marched in many causes.

In this State was born the Fight for Freedom Committee that effectively smashed the isolationist shibboleth of the America Firsters. Much of the New Deal developed in New York from the little-known League for Industrial Democracy. In the last few years there have been Americans for Democratic Action, Freedom House, the American Association for the United Nations. New ideas find a ready outlet in the State. No voice is entirely a voice unheard there, even if a man has to go to Union Square to be heard.

On the whole, the New York press has not done an outstanding job in exposing the waste, incompetence, and corruption in State offices. A few exceptional newsmen have distinguished themselves.

The struggle to make the government of New York State more responsive to the needs of all its people is a never-ending one. Neither political party has a monopoly on virtue or evil. In the Legislature there is a Republican who does little else but guard the interests of the New York Central Railroad, and another who has done the same for Niagara Hudson Power Corporation. There are Democratic members from tenement districts who spend more time protecting racketeers than fighting for slum clearance, while pari-mutuel operators have their zealous defenders and liquor dealers their champions.

Is the outlook hopeless? Emphatically not!

William Jay Gaynor, while on the bench, once ruled on the constitutionality of a statute permitting five citizens to petition the State Supreme Court to demand an accounting from public officials, even if the charges were based only on hearsay.

"This statute," he declared, "was passed to help the rent-payers and taxpayers to keep watch on the conduct of their officials, and in the hope of enabling them by publicity to prevent official betrayals of trust which had come to be so persistent and common, and were so low, base, vulgar, and heartless as to make many believe that we had reached an era when the permanent decay of our civilization had set in. . . . If it be said that it [the statute] enables the citizen to

94

be meddlesome, the answer is that purity and integrity in government can be obtained and preserved only by the wholesome vigilance and meddlesomeness of the citizen."

New Yorkers will stand for a lot, but they do have a limit. And when they finally break loose, they mow 'em down.

PENNSYLVANIA ★ ★ ★

Bossed Cornucopia

HERMAN A. LOWE

IF PENNSYLVANIANS were as extroverted as Californians, or had the bombast of Texans, or the brass of New Yorkers, they could brag about their State with adjectives that would shame a circus press agent.

But, unfortunately, Pennsylvanians lack the bluster and braggadocio.

When a Pennsylvanian remarks that his State has the most churches and colleges, the largest number of cities and towns, the most miles of paved highways, the biggest coal production, and the greatest iron and steel output, that its mills turn out one-fourth of the nation's knit and woven goods, that it is second in industrial output, and the value of its agricultural crops exceeds that of most of the so-called farm states, the Pennsylvanian is merely reciting a few items in the book.

Similarly, when he soberly mentions that his State possesses a string of "firsts" unparalleled in the land—first oil well, first exclusive natural-gas well, first paper mill, first

★

HERMAN A. LOWE is a Washington correspondent who operates his own news bureau. Previously, he was a member of the Washington staff of the Philadelphia *Inquirer,* and prior to that, city editor of the paper. In 1946 he won a Sigma Delta Chi special citation for outstanding Washington correspondence.

elevated railway, first university, first medical school, first law school, first abolition law, first labor union, first labor strike, first daily newspaper, first great American painters, and that even the famed Kentucky long rifle and the West's great pioneering covered wagon originated in Pennsylvania— well, it's just matter-of-fact, unembellished truth. And when a Pennsylvanian recalls that in his State was the first capital of the nation, that within its boundaries are Independence Hall, Liberty Bell, and Valley Forge, that the Declaration of Independence and the Constitution were drafted and signed there, and that even earlier, William Penn laid the groundwork for the first experiment in democratic government in the Western world with equal rights to all, and that there were no witch burnings nor exile for religious dissenters, the Pennsylvanian is again simply asserting unvarnished history.

Of course, there are other things Pennsylvania has: a Legislature with a built-in lobby that manipulates the little statesmen like puppets on a string, a deeply ingrained tradition of political bossism, a lavender-and-old-lace Constitution in an atom age, some lulus in graft and corruption, and a web of political machines which have begun to creak from age and ineptness.

Yes, sir! With a straight face and no sarcasm intended, it can be truthfully said that Pennsylvania has everything. The only trouble is, Pennsylvanians don't know their own strength. If, unlike Texas and California and New York, Pennsylvania doesn't brag—it doesn't have to.

There is a euphemism afloat in the corridors of the Capitol in Harrisburg. It is "legislative engineers." That is a soft and delicate way of saying "lobbyists."

As state governments go, Pennsylvania's is probably as good as any. But there are the "legislative engineers."

The unvarnished fact is that the Legislature is lobby-run, lobby-ridden, and lobby-captive. In Harrisburg, the legislative statesmen live intimately, cosily, and cheek-by-jowl with the pressure boys.

A session of the Pennsylvania House or Senate—particularly when important bills are up—is a spectacle to witness. Along the side wall of each chamber "inside the rail" are special seats reserved for the families and personal guests of the legislators. It is in these seats that lobbyists are to be found, packed tightly as raisins in a fruitcake, and up in front where they can readily confer with the official law-makers.

It is all as subtle as a punch in the nose at the corner of Broad and Main. Any newsman or legislator will point them out for you: the lobbyist for the railroads, for the Mine Workers, for the truckers, the teachers, the soft-drinks interests, the utilities, coal operators, and many others. Does one of the lobbyists want a little privacy? He thinks nothing of appropriating one of the lounges, as if he owned it.

Best estimate is that more than one hundred lobbyists, some resident full time in Harrisburg, others only for specific bills, swarmed over the 1949 Legislature. That was a record number, but the State had also done itself proud at previous sessions.

But this is only part of the picture.

There is nothing in Pennsylvania's laws to prevent a member of the Legislature from accepting a retainer from one or more special interests. In some recent sessions, as many as forty of the fifty Senators were reportedly on the payrolls —legally—of organizations having a direct dollars-and-cents interest in bills under consideration. To a lesser extent the same situation prevails in the House. Smartest trick is to engage a committee chairman as a "legal consultant." That ensures that an undesired bill will not see the light of day.

The only thing that saves the Commonwealth from complete subjugation by the minions of organized industry and organized labor is that the lobbyists don't gang up. They are usually sharply at odds, frequently cancel one another out. Otherwise, God save the Commonwealth!

Aside from "retaining" legislators, which is legal, there is little, if any, passage of money. Obviously, there need not be. Also, where the need for additional stimulus arises, there are other safe ways to operate. One is campaign contributions, a very popular formula. Another is poker and other forms of entertainment. All legitimate and all productive.

What the lobby spends during a session is wholly a guess. It has been estimated at anywhere from $100,000 up. Old-timers around the Capitol laughingly stress the "up."

Monday and Tuesday are the big entertainment nights in Harrisburg. On these nights the "legislative engineers" dine the legislators. Most-courted are the majority members of the Senate (currently Republican). The Senate is a legislative bottleneck. It is the most effective place to block a bill.

Above all, there is one thing about which there is no doubt. That is, the most powerful lobby of them all.

Practically everyone, lobbyists, legislators, State officials, the public, give the laurel to the Pennsylvania Manufacturers Association. There is controversy over the runners-up, but PMA leads everybody's list. It is the undisputed tops.

PMA is interested mainly in tax and industrial matters, but that does not keep it from bestriding the entire field of legislation. In doing so, it functions discreetly. During the 1949 session, while other lobbyists sat openly in the House and Senate, PMA operated off-stage. It established headquarters in a spacious suite in the nearby Penn-Harris Hotel, and its representatives kept away from the Capitol throughout the session.

Labor is one of the foremost PMA runners-up in lobbyist

99

influence, now ranking third or fourth in that regard. It is generally predicted that in the event of a Democratic administration in Harrisburg, labor would take first place. Its political influence is exerted practically entirely on behalf of the Democrats.

Despite disagreements on the national level, the CIO and AFL operated in close harmony at Harrisburg from 1938 to 1947. After this amicable decade, the AFL split away. The CIO carries great weight in industrial areas, and boastfully claims it was responsible for defeating eleven Republican Congressmen in 1948. The AFL has some Republican ties, but not many.

Harrisburg is the only State capital in which John L. Lewis' United Mine Workers maintain a full-time lobbyist and office. They are financed by the seven UMW districts in the State. Miners' influence is restricted to matters of their own special interest. To a lesser extent they are involved in local politics. UMW is the only large labor organization in Pennsylvania that has influence in the Republican Party. This is largely concentrated in the anthracite region in the northeastern portion of the State.

Miner chiefs have a lot of respect for the lobby of the coal operators. The miners say the coal bosses are the real power in the State government. On occasion the two lobbies team up. This happened in the 1949 session on an amendment to Governor James Duff's "tax everything" law. The measure authorized local governmental units to tax everything not being taxed by the State.

Miners and operators got coal exempted.

Railroad influence is also a dominant power in the Pennsylvania Legislature, probably second only to PMA. One of the big fights of the 1949 session was over a bill to allow trucks to carry heavier loads on the State's highways.

The truckers' lobby, no slouch itself, succeeded in wheel-

100

ing the measure through the House. Then it was stopped
by the railroads, working closely with township and borough
officials (another strong lobby). They claimed they did not
want their streets ruined by heavier loads. At the crucial
moment, the railroads and their allies received potent aid
from PMA, which quietly passed around the right word.

Pennsylvania legislators make no bones about these things.
In informal conversation they said frankly it was a case of
the truckers versus the railroads and the latter won. Next
time, perhaps, it will be different. No question of good government or public interest. Strictly business.

Pennsylvania's school teachers, who muster a lot of votes,
are a highly regarded lobbying force. Also, in other specialized fields, there are the lobbies of the liquor interests, real-
estate associations, soft-drink manufacturers, Joseph N. Pew,
Jr., speaking for oil, etc., etc., etc.

Yes, no state can boast of a finer crop of "legislative
engineers."

The Pennsylvania Legislature may have saddle sores
from the hard riding of the lobbyists, but it never permits
itself to be tethered too tightly to yesterday. It is always on
the lookout for new ideas to keep out of the rut. It is willing
to learn from anybody, and keeps one inquiring eye on
Congress in Washington.

For example: After the war, Congress voted itself a $2,500-
a-year tax-free expense account. Pennsylvania's wide-awake
Legislature snapped to instant interest. In practically no
time at all it followed suit, voting itself a tax-exempt $1,200
expense account.

In Pennsylvania, folks seem to be born with built-in insula-
tion against local and State scandals. The characterization,
"corrupt and contented," pinned on Philadelphia many years
ago by Lincoln Steffens, not only still applies there but to a

considerable extent to the State as a whole. Pennsylvanians take small and medium-sized scandals in stride, the way certain South American countries take military revolts.

In the spring of 1949, the "hot" story involved the Pennhurst State School, an institution for mentally deficient children. An investigation by the State Auditor General and the State police disclosed shortages in accounts, farming out of inmates as virtual slave labor, widespread petty thievery, and other sordid scandals.

It was discovered that five hundred and fifty-two tons of coal had vanished from the powerhouse, and hundreds of gallons of paint and turpentine had been diverted to a contractor who was the brother of a Pennhurst employee. Also, that employees were bringing in "guests" for free meals on a scale large enough to send the institution's food bill soaring by thousands of dollars.

A short time before this shocker was uncovered, Philadelphia underwent one of its periodic, though futile, soul searchings. Builders and property owners revealed that they had been compelled to cross the palms of fire department officials with silver to obtain permits and safety clearances. Another scandal came to light with the discovery that employees in the Tax Collector's office had filched hundreds of thousands of dollars from the municipal wage tax.

Still, these exposés were by no means so colorful as the 1929 Grand Jury probe of police graft. That brought out such tasty titbits as the Philadelphia policemen who, despite $35-a-week salaries, managed to accumulate bank accounts of $40,000 to $50,000 in a few years. They attributed the feat to profits from raising canaries and goldfish in their kitchens!

Still earlier, a real shocker was uncovered in Eastern State Penitentiary, a maximum-security prison near the heart of Philadelphia. The penitentiary had come under the dom-

102

ination of a band of criminal inmates called "the Four Horsemen." They virtually ran the institution, mauling those who would not obey their edicts. The "Horsemen" imported liquor, dope, and even prostitutes. The prison authorities took their cut and let things ride.

But of all the scandals Pennsylvania has known and taken in stride, the real heller was the malodorous stink attached to furnishing and equipping the State Capitol.

The Capitol was destroyed by fire in 1897. A year later work was begun on the present structure which was dedicated, with appropriate fanfare, by President "Teddy" Roosevelt on October 4, 1906. The building was—and is—magnificent. Together with furnishings and equipment, the tab to taxpayers came to more than $13,154,000. And that was back in the days when eggs were fifteen cents a dozen, and a dollar had one hundred cents of real purchasing value. But in May, 1906, even before T.R. had given the structure his toothy blessing, William H. Berry, a Democrat, was sworn in as State Treasurer. Digging into the Republican administration, he struck pay dirt. Berry uncovered a sewer of graft and theft in the equipping of the new building.

He promptly notified the press and turmoil broke loose.

Under public pressure, the Republican Legislature finally authorized a full-scale investigation. It wrote an amazing Alice-in-Wonderland story. Furniture and other items had been paid for by the linear foot, the square foot, the cubic foot, and by the pound. It all seemed to depend upon how John H. Sanderson, the principal supplier, wanted to sell the equipment.

For example: He sold $5.50 clothes trees at $18.40 "per foot." One batch of one hundred forty-five cost taxpayers $4,057. Some sofas were sold for $21.79 per linear foot, others by the square and cubic foot. An eleven-foot-long leather sofa for the Senate chamber was listed as containing 151¼ feet and was billed at $1,951.12. At the trial, the manufacturer who sold it to Sanderson said the regular retail price was $280.

Similarly, the chair used by the Speaker of the House was purchased on the basis of the number of cubic feet it would occupy if crated for shipping. The rostrums for the House and Senate were built by a carpenter who charged Sanderson $2,060 for the job. But, on a cubic foot basis which included the empty space beneath the rostrums, Sanderson billed Pennsylvania for $90,748. An ornate $182.50 bootblack stand for a locker room cost $1,619.20; Senate desks, which should have cost $90 each, were palmed off at $265; and filing cabinets were billed by the cubic foot—most of this being the empty space inside the files. Similarly, chairs, umbrella stands, mirrors, all were sold by the foot, as were marble trim, bronzes, and upholstery.

Chandeliers, purporting to be solid bronze, were sold by the pound. When some were sawed open, it was discovered the bronze was merely a shell. Lead and iron rods had been wedged into the hollow parts to make them weigh more. Entire iron wheels were built into some of the large circular chandeliers. Fancy hand-carved wood wainscoting turned out to be putty and plaster.

More than $5,400,000 was paid Sanderson. The law required the bills be approved by the Board of Public Grounds. He actually received more than $3,000,000 before the Board ever saw a bill. In many instances, he was paid his padded prices months before the items were delivered in Harrisburg.

Out of this affair came a suicide, a flock of jail sentences, and $1,500,000 restitution to the State. However, it was estimated that, even after restitution, Pennsylvania taxpayers lost well over $2,000,000.

For most people, Pennsylvania is synonymous with two things—industry and politics. While industry feeds the largest segment of Pennsylvanians, politics is the name of the game they all play.

Politics, Pennsylvania style, is tricky, intricate, and largely of the boss-ruled variety. The major lubrication is money, enormous sums of money.

Despite the Hatch Act, no one knows how much is really spent in a Pennsylvania election. Democrats insist the Republicans are by far the largest spenders. That was certainly true in the past. Now, unions raise and spend huge sums, and as labor is virtually all on the Democratic side, that party is probably spending at least as much as the GOP.

One thing is certain. Neither party lacks for funds, no matter what kind of tearful, raggedy-Ann story may be unloaded on the public.

The 1946 Republican primary was not regarded as particularly close. That was the one in which James H. Duff was nominated for Governor and Edward Martin for Senator. Insiders estimate that nearly $500,000 was used to put the ticket over.

During the 1938 gubernatorial primary between Arthur H. James and Gifford Pinchot—a Kilkenny cats scrap from the opening gong—more than $1,000,000 was expended by the two camps. In hot gubernatorial years, combining primary and general elections costs, outlays in Philadelphia alone have run over $1,300,000.

The state-wide expenditure for the 1948 presidential election is estimated to have been well above $2,000,000—although no indication of that was to be found in the official reports.

However, the fact that big money is spent in Pennsylvania electioneering does not mean big corruption per se.

It costs a good-sized fortune to reach Pennsylvania's five

million potential voters with "literature," posters, radio time, stump-speech traveling, etc. Then, on election day, it costs another fortune for paid watchers, those who haul voters to and from polling places in automobiles, and for other legitimate purposes.

While there is some bought-and-paid-for support, political corruption has tapered off considerably in the last twenty years. The onetime ugly pressures on labor, threats of firing if they did not vote right, have virtually disappeared. There was a time when Pennsylvania factories posted blunt signs before an election: "This mill will shut down if the town does not go Republican next Tuesday." Allegheny County, in which Pittsburgh is located, and formerly tightly controlled Republican territory, was notorious for the way election returns were held up while ballot boxes were stuffed to deliver the votes needed.

They still talk about the Republican gubernatorial primary of 1926 in which John Fisher beat out Edward Beidleman by the hairline margin of 18,000 votes out of 1,400,000. The Vare machine in Philadelphia went down the line for Beidleman. It delivered the works, from homeless drifters in the flophouses to tombstones in the graveyards. It looked sure for Beidleman on election night. But Pittsburgh, which was in Fisher's camp, was a mite slow in making returns. In fact, it was not until Thursday, almost two days later, that Allegheny County succeeded in getting its ballot boxes all neatly stuffed, weighed, and sorted. Then it came up with just enough margin to nominate Fisher.

Those were the days, too, when in the tough anthracite sections, bully boys waylaid known opposition voters with the challenge, "Turn back, or fight your way through to the polls."

Philadelphia politicians relate this typical incident of the "bad old days." In one of the swankiest Germantown sections,

106

a wealthy citizen drove to his polling place. As he stepped from his limousine, he was greeted respectfully by a party worker with, "Mr. ——, you've already voted."

The prominent citizen paused a moment, blinked, then said quietly, "Er, oh yes, thank you." Then he climbed back into his car and drove off.

But things like that have simmered down. As one leader summed it up, "Luzerne and Lackawanna County [in the hard-coal region] politics are crooked. Delaware County is rotten, but on a high scale. The State, as a whole, is much cleaner than it used to be."

The long Republican monopoly came to an end when Pennsylvania became a two-party State with the advent of the New Deal.

Except for public consumption, no informed Pennsylvania Democrat will contend that all current sins in the State's politics are Republican and that his own party is pure and undefiled.

The southwestern quarter of the State now votes Democratic as solidly as Mississippi, with Pittsburgh the Democratic core. The Democratic rulers in the area get their funds in the time-honored fashion, from the protection of vice, gambling, and rackets. And, Hatch Act or no Hatch Act, they mulct their national payrollers for funds in a fashion that even the most practical Republican would not be ashamed of.

In the State's Republican organization, they don't speak of Governor Thomas E. Dewey with the same old affection. For if he had won the presidency, the organization's troubles would be much smaller and fewer, and the 1950 re-election prospects of Democratic Senator Francis J. Myers would be considerably less than they are. Likewise, there

107

would be no likelihood of a strong primary revolt by Governor Duff.

That likelihood started in a smoke-filled room early in 1946. Then-Governor Ed Martin, Attorney General Duff, G. Mason Owlett, president of the Pennsylvania Manufacturers Association, and several others were trying to agree on who should succeed Martin. Finally, the Governor pointed to his close friend, Duff, and said, "We're not getting anywhere. What about Jim, here?"

That did it. The Republican ticket became Martin for Senator and Duff for Governor. It won handily.

The new administration started off in fine style. But, by the end of 1947, the organization became acutely aware that Duff had gone into business for himself. Over the vehement objection of old-timers, he re-established the General State Authority which incurs debt and floats bonds for improvements.

Duff said it was the only way to get things done. The organization retorted it was a trick to avoid submitting spending proposals to the people. Under the State's archaic Constitution, its bonded debt is limited to $1,000,000 except for proposals approved by popular ballot.

A second major source of cleavage was presidential politics. Martin was the favorite-son candidate. All factions were agreed on that. Martin's friends figured that in the event of a deadlock, he would have a real chance for a place on the national ticket. The organization began making contacts, while Martin hit the sawdust trail, making speeches across the nation so the folks could get to know him.

Then things began to happen in Harrisburg. Duff's friends decided he was pretty good presidential timber, too. So he began to sound off with headline-making speeches. On one occasion a press agent arrived surreptitiously in Washington with advance copies of a speech Duff was to make in

108

Philadelphia. These were distributed to a select list of columnists, together with an interpretation of what the speech really meant—a break between Martin and Duff.

The already existing coolness between Duff and Martin turned frigid. But, after the fashion of women and politicians, the two men made it a point to embrace publicly on all occasions and proclaim their disavowal of any enmity. Duff vehemently denounced Dewey and said his personal choice for President was Senator Arthur H. Vandenberg, after Martin, of course, as the favorite son.

Pennsylvania had seventy-three delegates to the 1948 convention, second only to New York. Backed by the full power of State patronage, Duff started out to round up delegates.

The organization had kept very quiet on the subject. But for months it had been secretly planting men not dependent upon State jobs in the delegation. The showdown was at the convention. Two days before it opened, Martin dropped a bombshell by announcing he would not offer his name. Instead, he would put Dewey in nomination and urged united support for the New Yorker. The surprise maneuver broke up the ball game.

On the first convention ballot, the organization gave Dewey forty-one of the seventy-three delegates, despite advance claims by Duff leaders that they had a substantial majority. Thus, had Dewey won in November, Martin would have controlled all federal patronage in the State, enough to counterbalance Duff's hold on State jobs. But Dewey didn't win and Martin has had no taste of federal pap. Duff, however, has had full control of State jobs, and the organization is very unhappy and very annoyed.

A knockdown Republican primary fight would considerably enhance the chances of Democratic Senator Myers for a second term.

109

The complexity of Pennsylvania interests makes for equal complexity in its political control. The State is still as basically Republican as it has been since the Civil War. In the 1948 Democratic landslide, the Democrats swept the big Pittsburgh industrial area, narrowly carried Philadelphia, and unseated eleven Republican Congressmen. Yet the State as a whole went for Dewey by 150,000 votes, his largest plurality by far in any state.

In Pennsylvania, despite the fact that Philadelphia and Pittsburgh are two of the nation's ten largest cities, the majority of votes are in the rural and small town sections. It is this support that maintains Republican supremacy. One Democratic spokesman sums up the situation:

"The Democratic Party is the party of labor. We are also the party of the newer immigrants. Our basic strength lies in a coalition of minority groups, the Slavs, Italians, Jews, Negroes, Catholics. The Republican Party is the party of industry. It has the money and the prestige. Its basic strength lies in the old stock, the farmers, the small-town businessmen, the little white-collar workers, and the Protestants."

The Democrats have still another source of strength, although they have been losing some of it. Formerly, the bulk of the sturdy, conservative Pennsylvania Dutch farmers were strongly Democratic. Now, however, as industrial workers in the Pennsylvania Dutch counties line up more and more with the Democrats, the farmers tend toward the Republican side.

Prime factor in the control of Pennsylvania Republicanism is the Grundy-Martin-Owlett leadership. This combine is generally known as the basic State organization. It is a combination of the Pennsylvania Manufacturers Association, dominated by Joseph R. Grundy and G. Mason Owlett; the followers of Senator Edward Martin; and the various allies

110

of these leaders. The combination has worked together for years. Formerly Grundy was the unchallenged boss. Now basic decisions are made at conferences.

Another dominant factor, thanks to Dewey's fiasco, is Governor Jim Duff, a gruff, blunt, husky redhead who can charm a bird off a tree. One of his ardent friends describes him as "an old-fashioned Scotch-Irish Presbyterian, outspoken, stubborn, and with all the vices and virtues of the Scotch-Irish Presbyterian."

Oddly enough, his former close friend, Senator Martin, comes from exactly the same stock. However, instead of bluntness, Martin is distinguished by an infinite patience, courtly courtesy, and the ability to conceal what is on his mind.

The real struggle in the Republican arena is between these two men.

Duff's chief strength is his control of the huge State patronage until the end of his term in January, 1951. In his camp is Republican State Chairman M. Harvey Taylor, who, when the chips were down in 1947 and 1948, quit the organization where all of his political life had been spent. Taylor has long experience and wide contacts. To some extent this tends to counteract Duff's main weakness, his lack of a state-wide organization and the fact that, once he leaves the governorship (Governors may not succeed themselves under Pennsylvania's Constitution), he loses the patronage.

On the Democratic side there is, first, Pittsburgh. Control of its vote has made Mayor David Lawrence the Democratic boss of Pennsylvania. No Democrat has a chance in a state-wide contest without Lawrence's support. Second is labor, a steadily growing force. The bulk of labor is registered in the Democratic Party. This applies even to most of the one

111

hundred and eighty thousand coal miners who still vote the ticket of FDR, no matter what John L. Lewis bellows.

It is difficult to understand what makes Pennsylvania tick without knowing about the Pennsylvania Manufacturers Association, otherwise known as PMA, the Grundy machine, and a number of less fancy names applied by labor.

For a generation PMA and its allies have been the underlying Republican organization of the State. PMA moved in to fill a vacuum created by the death of Senator Boies Penrose, the old boss. It took over because there was no one else to do the job. That PMA assumed this role is further proof of the prime importance of industry in Pennsylvania.

PMA is largely the story of one of the unique figures in State politics. He is Joseph R. Grundy, eighty-six-year-old bachelor, woolen mill owner, and the high priest of high tariffs as the key to American prosperity. He is a Quaker who has never turned the other cheek in a political or tariff fight. And he is the only living survivor of the "little smoke-filled room" where Warren G. Harding was selected at the 1920 Republican convention.

These days Grundy is a little hard of hearing. Otherwise, he has surprising vigor and good health, a full head of snow-white hair, sparkling eyes, and the amiable, disarming manner of a retired clergyman. He professes to be in semiretirement, but PMA makes no important political decision without his OK. He has become almost a legendary figure and even Democrats speak of "Mr. Grundy" with a certain affection. But there was a time when the name Grundy was a fighting challenge to liberals in Pennsylvania and elsewhere.

The Grundy saga started in 1890 when his father, then operating the family woolen mill in Bristol, outside Philadelphia, went to Washington. The senior Grundy helped write the complicated wool schedules in a high-tariff bill

112

being prepared by William McKinley, then Chairman of the House Ways and Means Committee. In 1897, after his father's death and after McKinley had become President, Joe Grundy started his own treks to Washington to work on wool schedules. During these trips, he would drop in on Senators Matthew S. Quay and Boies Penrose, the State's political bosses, to seek their support on matters before the Legislature. It is a curious fact that most of the Commonwealth's bosses have operated from Washington rather than from Harrisburg.

During one of these calls in 1908, Penrose told Grundy: "You go to Harrisburg and see John Scott. Tell him I sent you." State Senator Scott was Penrose's first lieutenant in the Legislature. Grundy saw Scott and explained his problem.

"You know," Scott advised, "this thing is pretty big. You ought to have somebody in Harrisburg all the time to look after matters."

From that little acorn grew PMA.

Grundy returned home and invited some of his manufacturer friends to a meeting. They agreed to finance a lobbyist in Harrisburg. Later, discovering that their agent was becoming the spokesman for an increasingly large share of Pennsylvania industry, they decided that manufacturers all over the State should help foot the bill. So, in January, 1910, the Pennsylvania Manufacturers Association was born in Philadelphia. Grundy became its first president, and held the office until he voluntarily relinquished it in 1943.

The Association grew rapidly. It established regional and county groups, entered politics via the customary route for businessmen—campaign contributions—allied itself with Penrose, became his money-raising arm, and fought on his team until his death in 1921.

Grundy, himself, became probably the best-known politi-

113

cal fund raiser in the country. In those days there was no federal income tax, no Hatch Act, no limitation on campaign expenditures, and no reports required on income and outgo. When Grundy set out to get money, he got it—big money. Industrialists paid well for low taxes in Pennsylvania and high tariffs in Washington.

In late years, PMA has mellowed. It has greatly broadened its base of contributions, and it encourages county leaders to get a larger share of the money. Its tactics are marked by more finesse and a greater understanding of the workingman's viewpoint.

Example: The Association was a prime mover in enacting the Workmen's Compensation Act.

PMA's more than eight thousand members make it the largest organization of its kind in the country. Toward its own workers, PMA is a model employer. It operates a cost-of-living pay system, geared to federal statistics. At Christmas it passes out ten per cent bonuses to all its people from the president down.

As a political force this can be said about PMA: Since the death of Penrose, no man has received the Republican gubernatorial nomination unless he has had the approval of Grundy. And only one of those nominees was beaten in the general election.

To PMA, control of the State administration is No. 1 priority. It is less interested in the United States Senate and has been less successful there. For almost a year, from December 11, 1929, to December 1, 1930, Grundy served in the Senate by appointment, filling the vacancy caused by the Senate's ouster of William S. Vare.

Vare's expulsion was a significant factor, because it broke the back of a drive by the Vare machine of Philadelphia to wrest State control from Grundy. Vare went to the Senate in 1926, following a primary that was a barroom brawl and a general election that was a riot. The then-Governor was reformer Gifford Pinchot, elected with the support of Grundy. Instead of the customary certificate of election issued to Senators-elect, Pinchot gave Vare a "certificate of doubt" which stated that "William S. Vare appears to have been chosen by the qualified electors."

And, just to make sure that nobody mistook his meaning, Pinchot wrote a letter to the Senate in which he asserted: "The form of words customarily used for such certificates by Governors of this Commonwealth and the form recommended by the Senate of the United States both include certification that the candidate in question has been 'duly chosen by the qualified electors.' I cannot so certify because I do not believe that Mr. Vare has been duly chosen. On the contrary, I am convinced, and have repeatedly declared, that his nomination was partly bought and partly stolen, and that frauds committed in his interest have tainted both the primary and general election. The stealing of votes for Mr. Vare and the amount and the sources of the money spent on his behalf make it clear to me that the election returns do not in fact represent the will of the sovereign voters of Pennsylvania."

The Senate delayed action on Vare until late in 1929 when it finally denied him his seat. He suffered a stroke after this bitter blow, and that wrote finis to the effort of the Philadelphia Vares to rise from city to State rule.

In the 1930 special election, for Vare's seat, Grundy was soundly beaten by James J. (Puddler Jim) Davis. And that was when Grundy was at the height of his powers!

The upset was sensational. It showed that PMA had an Achilles' heel and could be chopped down to size, as Franklin D. Roosevelt later proved repeatedly. In 1936, 1940, and 1944, he took the measure of the organization, plus the Philadelphia machine, three times running.

PMA is an organization of large and small factory owners. But, oddly, its strength has always been in the rural and suburban areas. This support it inherited from Penrose, and to this day the farm vote goes down the line for PMA.

Before the Pittsburgh area was transformed into a Democratic stronghold by New Deal alchemy, PMA could normally count on important alliances there. But it has never had a real foothold in Philadelphia. The Vare brothers, who fought Penrose, also were hostile to Grundy. The present diluted Philadelphia Republican organization carries on this old tradition, although without the old bitterness.

PMA has lasted because it stands for something. It wages never-ending war to keep industry from leaving Pennsylvania and to attract new industry. It does this principally by pushing pro-industry bills through the Legislature and fighting measures it considers inimical to industry. What PMA is, what it believes in, and what it stands for, are best summarized in testimony which Grundy gave before a Senate Lobby Investigating Committee on October 24, 1929. Grundy was summoned because he had spent months in Washington working on the Smoot-Hawley Tariff Act. The Committee was made up of Senators from the deep South and from the wide-open spaces of the cattle and wheat West. They expected to chew up this high priest of high tariff. He strode blandly into the Committee room and read a prepared statement which presented the proud, arrogant, and unabashed position of Pennsylvania industry. He said in part:

"Perusal of the figures here submitted justifies the statement that if volume of voice in the United States Senate were proportioned to population, productive power, or the total sum contributed toward the national upkeep, some of those states which are now most vocal would need amplifiers to make their whispers heard. The truth of the matter

116

is that such states as Arizona, South Dakota, Idaho, Mississippi, etc., do not pay enough toward the upkeep of the government to cover the costs of collection, and states like Pennsylvania, hamstrung as they are by adverse legislation, support these backward Commonwealths and provide them with their good roads, their post offices, their river improvements and other federal aid, figuratively on a golden platter."

At another point Grundy observed regarding the great Senator William E. Borah:

"The Senator from Idaho, who speaks so eloquently for agriculture, represents a state which has only one-fifth the number of farms that are in Pennsylvania, only two-fifths of the farm value of Pennsylvania, less than one-fiftieth of the industry of Pennsylvania, and which contributes to the national treasury the magnificent sum of five one-hundredths of one per cent of the total income tax."

The "backward Commonwealths" speech was a national sensation. It drew headlines everywhere, and a flood of furious retaliatory oratory in and out of Congress. Many Western and Southern candidates were elected the following year on platforms denouncing Grundyism and the haughty and rapacious Easterners.

Twenty years later, Pennsylvania still feels the same way, although no one has said it as bluntly since.

That is why the Pennsylvania Manufacturers Association is in politics and that is what it stands for—high tariffs and low taxes for industry, and keeping the burden of the "backward Commonwealths" as light as possible on Pennsylvania's pocketbook.

A few weeks after his spectacular foray before the Lobby Investigating Committee, Grundy was a member of the Senate. His appointment followed a tradition which antedates the Civil War, of having the State's political bosses sit in the

117

Senate. Ed Martin, one of the group currently running the organization, is in the Senate.

Pennsylvania's bosses have never lacked color and varied backgrounds.

First of them was durable Simon Cameron who was one hundred years old when he died in 1899. Before the Civil War, he was successively a newspaper printer and publisher, canal builder, railroad builder, banker, politician, State Adjutant General, and United States Senator. He went to the Senate on five different occasions, the first in 1845, the last in 1877. Cameron succeeded Edwin Stanton as Abraham Lincoln's Secretary of War and later served as Minister to Russia. At the age of seventy-eight, shortly after his last election to the Senate, he resigned and jockeyed the State Legislature into electing his son, Donald, to succeed him.

Donald Cameron's leadership didn't last long. After a few years the reins were taken over by Matthew Stanley Quay, the only political boss in American history to win the Congressional Medal of Honor. Quay got the decoration as a Civil War officer. He started his political climb in the Legislature. By 1887, he was a United States Senator and, the following year, he became Chairman of the Republican National Committee.

In those days the Legislatures named Senators. Quay was re-elected in 1893 but ran into trouble in 1899. The Assembly deadlocked. Quay simply had Governor William A. Stone declare a vacancy and appoint him to fill it. But trouble developed in Washington. The Senate refused to seat Quay. So he had a special election called and this time the Quay machine worked without a hitch. He won and remained in the Senate until his death in 1904.

Most spectacular of all Pennsylvania's bosses was lusty Boies Penrose, the huge-framed, earthy son of Philadelphia aristocrats, tremendous eater, tremendous drinker, and un-

118

blushing frequenter of bawdyhouses. Born in Philadelphia in 1860 and graduated from Harvard in 1881, Penrose launched into politics almost immediately. He was elected to the Assembly in 1884, two years later became a State Senator and, in 1889, was made President Pro Tempore of the Chamber. Here his pell-mell progress slowed down. It was not until 1897 that he was able to negotiate the leap to the United States Senate.

Once in Washington, he never let go. He was re-elected four times. He died on the last day of 1921. His friends say it was overeating, rather than overdrinking, that did him in.

Pennsylvania remembers Penrose for his frankly extroverted personality and because a large, bronze, full-length statue of him stands on the Capitol grounds in Harrisburg.

From Penrose such men as Grundy and Martin learned the business of politics. He was a master at the adroit and effective use of flag waving and Bible quoting. It was not until fifteen years after his death that Pennsylvania began to get rid of its eighteenth-century Sunday Blue Laws, a slow process which still continues. Penrose made himself the public defender of the Blue Laws, thus nailing down the hinterland vote. Once when a clergyman publicly congratulated him for his stand, Penrose snapped:

"Hell, I'm not for the preachers. But it isn't good for the people to run wild on Sundays."

It was the Legislature which elected Penrose to his first three terms in the United States Senate. Then in 1913, the Sixteenth Amendment to the Constitution, providing for the popular election of Senators, was ratified. Penrose went into the 1914 primary campaign with the crepe-hangers predicting it was all up with the Old Master. They argued that he had always been a behind-the-scenes string-puller, and could never win votes on the stump. He won with more votes than all his opponents combined.

It was at this time that young Ed Martin, veteran of the Spanish-American War and a rising young politician in southwest Pennsylvania, first encountered Penrose. Martin took him to a country fair. As the farmers began to cluster about Penrose to shake his hand and talk politics, the big city aristocrat asked to see the livestock. The party adjourned to the barns. Penrose inspected the sheep and cattle and discussed their fine points expertly. He spoke of the need for adequate tariffs to protect wool, hides, and meat production. The farmers listened in fascination. He had not said a word about his campaign.

Finally he turned to his host.

"I don't know," said Penrose in a loud voice, "when I've enjoyed an afternoon so much. But I have a hard campaign. They're making a tough fight on me."

Martin describes Penrose's handling of the incident as a connoisseur's handling of a priceless porcelain. He relates: "That's all the politicking Penrose did at the fair. But it was enough. The story went around among the farmers that 'they' were making it tough for this man who knew cattle and sheep and the farmers' problems."

In Penrose's younger days, Quay and other leaders felt he should marry. Penrose, who went through life a bachelor, laughed and retorted, "If the organization will select the woman, I'll marry her."

Although his main base was Washington, Penrose frequently held week-end office hours in Philadelphia. There he was visited by hundreds, carefully making note of the information they brought and the favors they asked. Ostentatiously he would put the notes on an iron spike on his desk. At the end of the day, after the last visitor had gone, Penrose would empty the spike into his wastebasket.

He never forced candidates down the gullet of his people. He would counsel and confer with local leaders, sometimes

120

for weeks. Finally, he would announce, "It looks as though sentiment has crystallized in favor of ——." But, even then, there would always be a final session with a half-dozen top leaders before the decision was clinched. He also pursued the theory that Pennsylvania's Senators should come from the big cities at the opposite ends of the State and its Governors from the rural region. This has been the formula in Pennsylvania for half a century.

"I learned from Penrose," says Martin, "that the great secret of politics is to have enemies, but to pick them very carefully."

Perhaps the first real Democratic boss in the State was Joseph F. Guffey. Although active in the Wilson administration, he achieved his stature after the election of Franklin D. Roosevelt opened the treasure trove of federal patronage. In 1934 Guffey went to the United States Senate.

He was the last of the old-school Democratic politicians. He ruled with the assistance of State Chairman David Lawrence. But long before the end of his last Senate term, Guffey had been replaced as boss by Lawrence, who operates a true big-city machine in Pittsburgh, where he is Mayor.

There is still one other political boss in Pennsylvania. He is in a class by himself.

The patsy of Pennsylvania politics is multimillionaire Joseph N. Pew, chairman of the board of the Sun Oil Company. He revels in an undeserved reputation as a national political boss.

From Maine to California, political commentators and writers have propounded the myth of the "Pew-Grundy machine," and of Pew as a real powerhouse of national GOP politics who names Pennsylvania State tickets and controls droves of delegates at Republican conventions. Pew loves these reports and tales. He collects politics the way some collect stamps. He has shown himself willing to pay generously

121

in contributions and "loans" for the privilege of being known as a big shot on the political campus. Whatever he has achieved in that field has been solely and only through his bank roll.

Among smart politicians the belief is general that Pew is a soft touch, that he has paid inflation prices, and has been "took" for plenty. Actually, Pew lacks political savvy and understanding of people. He sincerely believes that he wants nothing but good government.

This is the story of this boogie man of Pennsylvania Republicanism.

In 1934, in the first tremendous surge of New Dealism, GOP fund raising in Pennsylvania, as elsewhere, was tough. Grundy cast about for new contributors to finance that year's gubernatorial and senatorial races. He invited Pew to try his hand as a money raiser.

The oil magnate proved highly successful. Best of all, there was no rubber band about his own rich roll. But he was a natural target for the opposition. He was not only a millionaire, but an oil millionaire. It was duck soup for Democratic orators and such rabid party organs as the late Philadelphia *Record*.

He became "Oily Joe" Pew, the symbol of entrenched wealth seeking to bar the people from the more abundant life. His own Bourbon outlook and blunt opinions of the New Deal at a time when FDR was riding the crest of the first great wave of his popularity, made it all the easier for the opposition to flay Pew. Also, it was a natural to label the Grundy organization the Pew-Grundy organization. That year the label helped to elect the first Democratic Governor, George H. Earle, in more than a generation, and the first Democratic Senator, Guffey, since 1875.

That was the springboard from which the Pew myth launched.

122

To keep it alive, he gave with an even more generous hand, his contributions frequently showing up in congressional contests as far west as the Pacific Coast. Pew reached his pinnacle in 1938. He was one of the leading backers of Judge Arthur H. James, who won the governorship. From Texas, Pew imported Carl Estes, an anti-New Deal Democratic newspaper publisher and associate in the oil business. Traveling under an assumed name, Estes campaigned with James as a public-relations adviser. After James took office, Estes disclosed his real identity and announced he was going to take the Governor right up to the steps of the White House.

This idea intoxicated not only Estes and James but, most of all, Pew. He, the Governor maker, was going to become a President maker.

At the 1940 Republican convention, Pennsylvania's delegation was a resounding exemplification of "too little and too late."

Pew was the mastermind of the delegation. He determinedly announced he would put James over, despite the fact that the rest of the Pew family was enamored of a flashy, hard-hitting crowd-pleaser named Wendell Willkie. Pennsylvania professionals, who were shoved into the background and not allowed to say or do much, did not learn until too late that Pew had hypnotized himself into believing he had the votes. He figured Estes could deliver a large part of the Texas delegation and that Oklahoma and other oil states would rally behind the Sun Oil banner. But all that Pew had actually done was to throw James' hat into the ring and wait for the lightning to strike.

It didn't, by a million miles.

While Pew was insisting there would be a deadlock and refusing to release the Pennsylvanians, Willkie stampeded

123

the convention. He had the nomination in the bag while the Quakers were still wrangling among themselves.

That killed the Pew myth among the professionals, although he has remained a hardy perennial in other quarters.

Pew has had no better luck in a much smaller arena. For years he has sought futilely to wrest control of Delaware County—where the Pew oil refineries and shipyards are located—from its hard-boiled leader, former State Senator John J. McClure. McClure is as strongly entrenched today as ever.

Probably the one place where Pew had real influence for a while was in Philadelphia. This sway was bought and paid for through a series of loans. These loans, used for campaign purposes, were made in exchange for personal notes from the city machine leaders—David W. Harris, Edwin R. Cox, and Frederic D. Garman. The money was not used personally by these men; it went to the Republican City Committee.

At one time the notes aggregated between $300,000 and $400,000. It was common talk that the Philadelphia organization was in hock to Pew. The loans have been gradually reduced. The last payment made on them was $25,000 in 1946. Notes now outstanding total around $80,000.

However, if he hasn't done so already, Pew might just as well write that off as a bad debt and claim a tax deduction. When William F. Meade took over as Republican City Chairman, he quietly gave the old books of the Committee the heave-ho, thus unilaterally wiping out the Pew debt. A new set of books was instituted. They do not list the Pew debt.

Finally, there was the 1948 Republican convention at which the Grundy-Owlett-Martin organization engaged in a knockdown battle with Governor Duff for control of the delegation.

Pew, a delegate, joined the "Stop Dewey" movement

124

early. He announced he was backing Duff for Senator Robert A. Taft. To the uninformed it appeared Grundy's partner had deserted him and that the organization was due for a licking. But the organization held fast to a majority of the delegation. Grundy and Duff leaders did agree on one thing. That was that Pew's strength consisted of one vote, his own. Thus another political immortal passed into the twilight.

However, as long as Pew's money holds out, there is no doubt he will continue to be courted by politicians in Pennsylvania and elsewhere.

Regardless of what the future holds, Pennsylvania is riding high now.

Second only to New York in industrial output and one of the leaders in mineral wealth, it also crowds the top in wholesale, retail, and service establishments. Pennsylvania ranks first or very close to first in all of these industrial categories: coal, steel, woolens, silk and cotton goods, knitwear, lace, hats, carpets, rugs, oilcloth, blankets, linoleum, cork products, leather and rubber goods, sugar refining, confectionery, foodstuffs, malt and alcoholic beverages, tobacco, limestone, slate, cement, chemicals, paper, printing, glass, clay, stone products, electrical equipment, radios, lumber, building materials, railroad- and street-cars, electric power production, locomotives, merchant ships, tankers, aluminum and aluminum products, men-of-war, auto trucks, cannon, soap, clothing, shoes, petroleum and petroleum refining, and many others.

During 1947 and 1948 alone, more than twelve hundred new industrial plants located in Pennsylvania. This growth represented a capital investment of more than $2,000,000,000.

But there was a time, during the 1920's and the 1930's, when the State was deeply alarmed over the loss of industry to the South and Southwest where the baits of tax exemp-

125

tions and low-wage and unorganized labor were held out. The exodus cost the State scores of plants, particularly in the cotton-textile field. Small, one-industry communities faced the threat of ruin and ghost-town status.

Three things changed the picture.

The first was the federal minimum wage law which upped hourly wages in the low-cost areas. Pennsylvania strongly favors further increase in the minimum wage, as it would tend to obliterate most of the remaining advantages held by the South.

A second factor was the great rearmament program of 1940 and 1941, and then the war. Employment soared and everything Pennsylvania could offer was hungrily clamored for.

Third has been the growing unionization of the South. As Southern advantages have been overcome, Pennsylvania has noticed that some of its strayed mills have headed home where, even though the labor is not cheap, it is highly efficient.

But taxes have risen in the State. Duff claims the increase has been less than in other states, and that, because of the pay-as-you-go policy which has prevailed for many years, entangling debt has been avoided. Also, he points out there is no State income tax or general sales tax.

Spokesmen for industry, however, do not view the situation through the same rosy spectacles. They say that unless the brakes are put on spending and taxation, and the tax base is broadened, factory owners will again pack up and move when times get tough. Their contention is that, despite the progress made, Pennsylvania's position industrially has been slipping and that its tax system "places an unduly heavy burden on business and industry."

After having kept things well in hand for years, manufacturers were severely jolted in 1935 when the New Deal

126

administration of Governor George H. Earle boosted business taxes. (Ironically, in 1949, Earle quit the Democratic Party in protest at Truman's spending policies.)

There was little change during the four years of Arthur H. James. When Martin became Governor, he laid about him with a pruning knife. He helped pave his way to the Senate by eliminating the four-mill personal property tax, the municipal loans tax, mercantile tax, emergency corporate loan tax, the emergency bank and trust company shares tax. Martin also cut automobile registration and driver's license fees, the gross receipts tax, and, by instituting an experience-rating law, reduced employer assessments for unemployment compensation.

With a flourish of trumpets, Martin claimed $322,000,000 in tax savings during his four years in Harrisburg.

Today, it is claimed, the Commonwealth still collects a relatively greater share of its revenues from business and industry than do competitive industrial states. Industry clamors for a sales or income tax—or both. Particularly annoying to business is the capital stock franchise tax, based on capital rather than on earnings. This must be paid whether a corporation makes or loses money.

In these business taxes is one bone of contention between Duff and the organization. The organization points out that taxes were slashed under Martin. Duff people argue he has run into inflation and soaring costs.

The antiquated State Constitution prevents imposition of a graduated income tax. Yet the very people who favor such a tax would rather do without it than to take a chance on a new Constitution.

Pennsylvania is still mighty in natural resources, but has passed its peak. The problem is to conserve these resources and at the same time make the most of them. For Pennsyl-

127

vania's greatness feeds largely upon this raw material. When it is gone, much of the State's industry will leave for greener pastures.

Up to 1900, Pennsylvania produced half the mineral wealth of the United States, pouring it out with lavish and careless hand. Rich men got richer, but subsoil Pennsylvania got poorer. However, the State continued to lead in mineral output until 1935. In that year, oil-rich Texas flashed to the front, waving its ten-gallon hat a little contemptuously. But while Pennsylvania may have appeared a mite swaybacked to the new champ, the State has still not done too badly for an old gaffer. It is holding its own in second place and is still tops as a processor of minerals, thanks to the steel mills, oil refineries, and coke ovens.

Of all the resources, the most romance attaches to oil.

As early as 1820, petroleum from surface seepage was being collected and bottled as "Seneca Oil" in western Pennsylvania. It was sold by medical quacks as a cure-all. By the early fifties, it had become known as "coal oil," and was being refined as kerosene to light lamps. Then in 1859 the oil era had its beginning when Colonel Edwin L. Drake sank the first well at Titusville. Within a few years, the slopes of northwestern Pennsylvania sprouted hundreds of derricks.

Pennsylvania oil reached its peak by 1891 with an output of 31,424,000 barrels of crude. From then on it declined. Of the 200,000 Pennsylvania wells drilled since 1859, some 75,000 still operate, tired little holes in the ground with a daily average output less than half a barrel per well. Coaxing the stuff out is like burping a baby. Total current production is now around 13,000,000 barrels annually.

World famous for its industry, coal, and other minerals, Pennsylvania has its bucolic side. Of its 45,000 square miles, forty-six per cent is in timber, although part of this is scrub second growth and reforestation is only now getting under way. Also, more than 170,000 farms provide a rich agriculture. Ten per cent of the State's people make their living on the soil, and Lancaster County, in the heart of the colorful Pennsylvania Dutch country, is the second richest agricultural county in the United States.

This factory giant, mining colossus, and farm and forest Titan is also a mother of cities.

Pennsylvania is the only state that has within its boundaries two of the ten largest U.S. cities—Philadelphia and Pittsburgh. It also has more cities and towns than any other state.

Pennsylvania's great civic rivalry has been between Philadelphia, the blasé old metropolis of the east, and Pittsburgh, bulging with iron and steel muscles in the west.

Philadelphia is in the lead and is certain to remain there a long time.

Philadelphians worry only about New York City. Massive Gotham, with its sneers about "sleepy" Philadelphia, its overwhelming edge in population, and its great port, is a bare ninety miles away. Its long shadow reaches down across Philadelphia and gives it an inferiority complex. Some businessmen reside in Philadelphia and commute to offices in New York.

If Philadelphia were to consult a psychiatrist, it would probably learn that one reason for its constant jibes at Pittsburgh is its own deep-rooted New York-inflicted inferiority.

While Philadelphia shows marked evidence of hardening of the arteries, Pittsburgh of late has been coming on like a race horse. Its pace is fast and strong. Pittsburgh has about one-third as many people as Philadelphia, but it is the core of a tightly knit web of heavy-industry suburbs. They are booming, and so is the metropolitan area of two million of which they are a part.

Pittsburgh is characterized by the spirit of the old college

129

try. Philadelphia is largely stuck in the doldrums of its glory-spangled past. Philadelphians are ancestor worshipers; Pittsburghers, go-getters.

Typical of the difference between the two giants is the story of the Hoover depression, when the New Deal was getting up a head of steam. Philadelphia disdainfully turned thumbs down on a proferred $60,000,000 in PWA projects. The Republican organization did not want to be beholden to the Democrats. Pittsburgh took every penny of federal money it could get and asked for more.

It is of interest to note that the Republicans still rule Philadelphia, while Pittsburgh has gone over to the Democrats lock, stock, and barrel. From that point of view, the Philadelphia GOP was canny, even though the city lost heavily.

While the large cities and many of the smaller ones eye each other competitively, what really makes them nervous is the encroachment of the State government. Year after year the State has been reaching down to the towns and counties, taking over more and more of what were originally purely local functions.

Health, welfare, education, and roads once were handled within county boundaries. They are now practically entirely ruled by Harrisburg. It is like the old tale of the camel that stuck his head in the Arab's tent. In exchange for cash benefits, the State has taken over control from local authorities.

Not so long ago, Pennsylvania's counties used to pay, on a per patient basis, for inmates they sent to State mental hospitals. Today the State foots the entire bill. When this change took place, some counties, seeking to reduce expenses, cruelly swept their poorhouses of the aged, labeling them mental cases and unloading them on State hospitals.

Pennsylvania boasts of its vast "State plan" highway system. For twenty years this boa constrictor has been swallow-

130

ing local road systems. Today, in nearly all of the sixty-seven counties, the roads formerly maintained by county officials have been turned over to the State. The township roads are fast slipping into the same vortex. Even city streets are being absorbed into the State plan.

Many of the big arteries of Philadelphia have been surrendered to the State Highway Department. Pennsylvania used to contribute to the city for upkeep of these "mainstems." Then the State decided it did not like the idea of the Philadelphia GOP organization having all that money to spend. So the State took over the main highways.

The matter of patronage in all this is, of course, of more than passing importance.

Pennsylvania has a permanent State payroll of over $90,-000,000 with 35,000 full-time employees and usually another 18,000 to 20,000 on a per diem basis. The large bulk of these job holders are under the spoils system, with the biggest single chunk in the Highway Department. Most of the per diems, for example, maintain roads and streets. It is obvious, therefore, why State officials are so eager to get hold of the highways and byways—and their accompanying pap.

The tide is running strong from little to big to bigger government. Local governments seek desperately for an alchemy that will recoup their revenues and their powers. They grumble over what they have lost, though the muttering is yet in a minor key.

But one day it may be louder. And when it is, there will be hell to pay at the crossroads. Pennsylvania doesn't flaunt its biceps like New York, California, or Texas. But it has them. And when Armageddon comes between the State and local governments, buy your tickets early. The brass knuckles will be sharp.

And they will proudly bear that label of quality, "Made in Pennsylvania."

GEORGIA ★ ★ ★

Paradise of Oligarchy

TARLETON COLLIER

GEORGIA is rich in lore and curious natural phenomena. Of these, Georgians are given to talk expansively and with pride, as if they were tokens of a special grace. Take, for example, Stone Mountain. It is one of the State's vaunted Ten Wonders—"the world's largest monolith," a stupendous block of naked granite in full sight from windows in Atlanta, twelve miles distant. Stone Mountain is two miles long, seven miles around, and rears eight hundred feet above a broad plateau; verily, an authentic phenomenon.

Georgia is also a State of unique social and political institutions, which bring forth comment of an entirely different nature. Thus, Stone Mountain is identified with revels of the Ku Klux Klan, the crest of the monolith being the historic stage for monstrous cross-burnings.

The spectacular sheer side of the mountain is deeply scarred as a result of another debacle. Thirty years ago a

★

A native of Alabama, TARLETON COLLIER lived for twenty-five years in Georgia, where he was reporter, city editor, and, for five years, writer of a daily column on State affairs for the Atlanta *Georgian*. He is author of a novel with a rural Georgia background, and two studies of the Georgia penal system, which had a part in the prison reforms of the Arnall administration. He is now an editorial writer on the staff of the Louisville *Courier-Journal*.

project was launched to carve a vast relief showing leaders of the Confederacy in attitudes of eternal spirited movement. The equestrian figures were to be a hundred and fifty feet high. Scandal, waste, and fierce rivalries beset the enterprise. The original grand outlines were blasted away by new hands. Two sculptors have died, one in exiled bitterness, the other in futility. At the mountain's base the rubble is heaped high, a mute judgment on this worship of the past.

Georgia's Ten Wonders do exist. But each is somehow stamped by a particular convention that seems to make it different and of a kind that could not exist anywhere else. It is in this spirit of jealous pride, sensitiveness, and turbulence that Georgia rationalizes a political system which was bluntly described by the late Judge Orville A. Park of Macon, in a study for the Citizens' Fact Finding Movement, as follows: "Georgia's politics have become a mere squabble for office. We have voted for men and not for measures. We are divided into factions and not into parties. We are controlled by passion and prejudice and not by principles. We have produced demagogues and not statesmen. We have quarreled among ourselves over small issues and petty offices, while the State has lost her position as the Empire State of the South and in many respects is trailing behind all the states of the Union."

This political structure which Judge Park inveighed against not only incites conflict and chaos, but perpetuates it. For under this system Democratic candidates for State offices are nominated by county units and not by popular vote. The vicious system permeates not only the political but also the social and economic life of the State, determining attitudes, customs, fortunes, and the quality of freedom.

Today, as a result of this "rotten borough" system, a condition approaching bankruptcy envelops Georgia's schools and colleges, and many agencies of the State government are crippled for lack of funds.

In the peculiar anatomy of Georgia politics and controls, this system is the heart. And being Georgia's own, it is justified by that simple fact, as well as by the consciousness of class and race (city *vs.* country, white man *vs.* Negro) in which it is planted and which the Talmadge element, the natural product of the system, unwearyingly keeps fertilized. It is imbedded so deeply in tradition, and no less in shrewd purpose, that no one aspiring to State office, however liberal in intent, dares condemn the system without surrendering his chance of election at the very start. It would be sheer political suicide to point out the plain truth that the county unit system makes Georgia's government less a democracy than an aggregation of one hundred and fifty-nine oligarchies. That is the number of counties or, rather, of political sovereignties.

The essential fact of the county unit system is inequality of representation.

It is based on an arbitrary dictate, bedrocked in the State Constitution, giving three members in the lower house of the Legislature to each of the eight most populous counties, two each to the next 30, and one each to the next 121. Thus, under the primary election system, each county has a unit vote of twice the number of its Representatives in the Legislature. The first eight counties have six unit votes each, the next 30, four votes, the other 121, two votes each.

The eight largest counties vary in population, from around 500,000 for Fulton (Atlanta) to 45,000 for Troup. Yet both have the same number of votes in the convention which technically nominates the candidates after the primary. Of the smaller counties, seven have fewer than 5,000 inhabitants each, 48 fewer than 10,000. These 55, with a total population less than that of Fulton County, still have 110 unit votes to the latter's six.

The State's total unit vote is 410; a majority, 206.

It is possible, and indeed it has happened more than once, for a candidate to carry 103 of the small, two-vote counties, with only one-third the State's population, and win nomination. His election, in this one-party State, follows automatically. In 1946, for example, the late Eugene Talmadge received 297,245 votes for Governor. Against him, James V. Carmichael scored 313,000 votes, 16,000 more than Talmadge. Yet "Ol' Gene" was nominated by 242 unit votes to 146 for Carmichael.

In keeping with this "rotten borough" system, the smart politicos have evolved a special method of operation. They concentrate their campaign efforts entirely on the small counties and blandly ignore the others. This procedure calls for deftness and an anatomist's deep knowledge of the counties, their nerve centers, and the men, interests, and mores that control them. Above all, it calls for a knack of ingratiation that will convince a rural boss in a dusty, tobacco-stained courthouse that he is important beyond any measure of the few hundred votes he can swing. His importance is further magnified by the fact that similar campaigns are in progress in a hundred fifty-nine other sovereign and, in a sense, unrelated jurisdictions.

A specialist agilely equal to this kind of manipulation is Roy Harris, the shrewd, knowing, tough, tireless politico from Augusta (Richmond County, six unit votes). Harris and his career, particularly the part he played in the 1946 campaign, are a graphic exemplification of the Georgia system. He is a product of Augusta's old Cracker Party, which for two generations tightly controlled the city and county. Recently, a citizens' revolt overthrew his machine, effectively aided by removal of the poll tax, lowering of

135

the voting age to eighteen years, and a U. S. Supreme Court decision admitting Negroes to primary elections.

In the past two decades, Harris has been in and out of every faction. He was high in command in three of E. D. Rivers's campaigns for Governor, two of them successful. Harris also was prominent in Ellis Arnall's 1942 winning fight against Eugene Talmadge. Four years later, Harris helped elect Talmadge. And Harris is generally regarded as the engineer of the 1947 *coup d'état* by which the governorship was seized and held for Herman Talmadge for sixty-three days after the death of his father. The following year it was again Harris who masterminded Herman's successful campaign against M. E. Thompson, who as Lieutenant Governor had become Acting Governor after the State Supreme Court refused to approve Herman's brazen grab of the office.

Roy Harris's wide and frequent fluctuations do not mean he is a mere political soldier of fortune. They are due to the fact that he is a man of large capacity and driving ambition to be Governor himself. He has exercised great influence for years as a member of the Legislature, as Speaker of the House and lobbyist, usually with close ties in the administration. His shifts are attributed to bitterness at what he regards the flouting of his ambition by men he helped to power and who he felt should repay him in kind. That may well explain why, when Eugene Talmadge set out to run in 1946 to recapture the governorship from Arnall, Harris, having meanwhile broken with Arnall, applied his specialist's skill to mapping Talmadge's strategy.

Harris's survey is reported to have shown seventy-five rural counties practically certain for Talmadge. Harris counseled concentrating efforts on thirty other counties, mostly in the two-unit group. The rest could come along or not. The strategy proved sure-fire. Talmadge won the nomina-

136

tion with less than forty-three per cent of the popular vote.

There is a definite economy in such a process. Whether to organize or to buy outright, it costs less to campaign in a dozen small counties (total unit vote, 24) than in a single sprawling urban center (six votes). However, that does not mean electioneering in Georgia is cut-rate.

The large number of counties and the exactions of Georgia's peculiar system make state-wide campaigning expensive. Campaigns have cost up to $300,000. Blunt charges of corruption are frequent. An example is the following in the Eastman *Times-Journal* (Dodge County, two unit votes), October 21, 1947, under the signature of Editor Edwin T. Methvin:

"In a large degree, Dodge County was placed on the auction block last Wednesday and sold to the highest bidder. Votes were sold to opposing candidates for appalling figures. One man's family of five received $100, another family of four received $80. Individuals were given from $2.50 to $50 each for theirs.

"For years it has been known in Dodge County that votes can be bought. They can be bought elsewhere, too—in Telfair, in Pulaski, in Bleckley, and in many other counties over the State."

On the whole, however, the use of such crude methods is not necessary. To nail down a rural county and its precious two unit votes, all that is often required is to get the backing of only a few persons. They may be the boys in the courthouse, or the members of a certain family; old landed gentry, the banker, the mill owner, or the supply man.

These counties are tiny. They average 369 square miles; twenty have less than 300 miles, the smallest only 114 square miles. They are so small, indeed, that it is a wonder they can marshal taxable resources to sustain basic services.

Several years ago, the annual budget of one mountain county included the munificent sum of $2.75 for public health. Until the State guaranteed a minimum seven-month school term, the annual school period in some of the counties was only ninety days, and salaries for teachers were as low as $30 a month. Even today, local resources to supplement the State grants are often infinitesimal. The average salary of teachers is $1,539, third lowest in the country.

Occasionally, the question is raised whether the counties are doing enough for themselves and are not leaning too heavily on the State. Many of them can do little more than that. But some, definitely indulging business and other privileged elements in local taxation, refuse to carry their proper load.

A typical example is Jones County (two unit votes). This rural county's schools cost $134,355 last year, and were far below standard. Of this amount, the State provided $112,-600 and local utility taxes $8,991. The residents of the county put up only $12,764 of their own for their 1,653 pupils. But they spent $118,759 for the courthouse, jail, and rural roads, the select domains of the local politicos.

In addition to the county unit system's restrictive political controls, it also operates as a stifling blanket on the social and intellectual life of the State. The controls exert powerful influence on thought and habits. The "leading citizen" maintains a sharp watch for pulpit rebels, to guard against a "social gospel" that questions the status quo. There are many examples of this.

One was the young Baptist minister in Talmadge's own county, Telfair (two unit votes), who was dismissed for protesting a piece of local political immorality. More often than not, the county tycoon sits in or close to the economic controls of the small sovereignty. The importance of jobs, of credit, of leases, of tax assessments—of tolerance, in short

138

—is obvious; and if conformity is the price, who is to blame a fellow for paying?

Through this "rotten borough" system, liberals, city dwellers, labor, and Negroes are isolated and overwhelmed. By law they are made permanent minorities, and prevented from liberating themselves and Georgia from political, economic, and social thralldom.

Every effort to get rid of the system has failed. After Talmadge's abnormal 1946 victory, with fifty-nine per cent of the unit vote and only forty-three per cent of the popular vote, a little band of liberals took the unit system into court. They passed the hat, employed the late Charles S. Reid, former Chief Justice of the State Supreme Court, and fought the issue up to the U. S. Supreme Court. Their only consolation was a restatement of the familiar principle that though the system was reprehensible, it could be remedied only by legislative action. At last report, the group still owed some of the money they had borrowed to make the costly fight.

A generation earlier, the great Hoke Smith, running for re-election as Governor, persuaded the Democratic State Committee to shift to the popular-vote system in the primary. Thomas E. Watson, the pre-Talmadge agrarian idol who had supported Smith two years previously in return for his aid in disfranchising the Negro, turned fiercely against him and Smith was beaten.

Watson was impelled by bitter personal experience. In his vigorous younger days, as a Populist leader, he had been twice defeated for Congress by outrageous frauds in Augusta, the one large city of his district. This was before the perfection of the county unit system. To Watson, the system was an instrument of virtue; and, indeed, city-machine corruption supported this view in the beginning.

It is an old story in American politics that a practice that starts out as an instrument of reform is debauched by misuse into a weapon of evil and misrule. Georgia's county unit system is a perfect example of this. It has been a long time since city bossism held sway in the State, but the myth of its existence is still kept alive by arrant demagoguery. In the same manner, Watson held Negro voting an insuperable evil, not because Negroes were black, but because in that era of exploitation they were corruptible, and had been used to his undoing. It was characteristic of the Southerner's classic approach to morality in this sphere, that the obligations of white leadership, example, and conscience were ignored and the onus placed upon the Negro as an inferior and unworthy creature.

After the defeat of Hoke Smith, pressure intensified to seal the victory for the county unit system. There was a spurt to create more counties. In the next decade, a large number of new counties were carved out, each with its two unit votes. The creation of counties became a kind of lobbyists' racket. A genial old professional, Clayt Robson, set up as a specialist in this field; and between 1910 and 1924, when Peach County, the last, was formed, it was common knowledge that a group, faction, or community could get a county of its own for as little as $25,000 properly laid out in the Legislature.

This would, indeed, be a bleak ending to the story, but for one thing. Faced with the reality that they have to live with this system, liberal elements have set out to do something about it within its own pattern. Their strategy is to infiltrate into the machinery of local controls, winning places on school boards, in parent-teacher associations, luncheon clubs, and other important groups that offer forums of action and appeal.

In the important textile center of Dalton (Whitfield County, four unit votes), this strategy has already done much to change old social mores. Ostracism and segregation of millworkers' children in schools and community activities have been broken down. In the Seventh Congressional District, the only one as yet in which the CIO vote is a cohesive influence, Henderson Lanham, a stanch liberal, ousted old-fashioned Malcolm S. Tarver. With Negroes beginning to vote in primary elections, the poll tax gone, eighteen-year-olds becoming electors, immensely heartening political upheavals have also taken place in Savannah, Brunswick, and Augusta.

To some, these instances appear hardly noticeable against the overwhelming pattern. For every oligarchy that is broken or threatened, a dozen remain secure and untouched. But the professional politicos are uneasy, nevertheless. They see danger to their cherished "rotten borough" structure. That explains their recent frantic efforts at patching, both with laws, and with ceaseless reminders that bloc voting (new euphemism for "nigger") and "Communism" (another word for CIO) are undermining Georgia traditions —and, naturally, all American society at the same time. Both lines of attack flowered lushly in the 1949 General Assembly, which young Herman Talmadge dominated.

The system is a solidification of seventy-five years of struggle for control, in which the high points of popular resistance were the agrarian revolt of the late eighties, the first Hoke Smith administration in 1907, the high tide of the New Deal in 1936, and Ellis Arnall's administration. Each was marked by a partial loosening of the grip of the interests which control Georgia. Each of these hard-won victories was followed by a dismaying period of reaction. But, still, not all the gains were lost. Each time some of the advances were preserved.

After the War Between the States, the first struggle was

between the Unreconstructed Confederates and the New
Departure Democrats, who accepted defeat and were willing to come to terms with Northern industrialism. These
realists prevailed through the Bourbon triumvirate that held
sway for years, handing around the governorship and other
key posts among themselves. The popular saying of those
days was that War Governor Joseph E. Brown had the
money, General John B. Gordon had the medals, and Alfred H. Colquitt had the religion. Northern capital came
in, the railroads were given tax exemption, and the foundations laid for absentee economic overlordship. There seemed
to be no obloquy involved when Collis P. Huntington, of
California, the colorful freebooter of the Southern Pacific
Railroad, referred to Gordon as "our man in the Senate."

This period saw the start of the sharecropper system, devised by large landholders to solve the problem of operating
plantations without slave labor. A condition of mass dispossession and debt was created which still existed fifty years
later, when Eugene Talmadge arose to exploit rural discontent. It was already chronic when hard times and distress
fired the Populist and Alliance movements around 1890,
and Tom Watson emerged as the bitter, strident, and often
intemperate voice of protest of the inarticulate "Wool Hats."

The Populists never quite elected a State administration;
the Democrats were too experienced in herding Negroes to
the polls, plying them with whisky and silver dollars, and
marking their ballots. Georgia did not have a mandatory
secret ballot until 1949. But the State did get a taste of
social legislation in 1891, with benefits for workers and
farmers. Black-listing of labor was forbidden, and the work
day of locomotive engineers and trainmen was reduced to
thirteen hours.

But with the return of better times, Populism waned and
the Bourbons returned. Hoke Smith was the next great

threat. Nominated Governor in Georgia's first primary election, he abolished the convict lease system, under which for thirty years the privileged Bourbons had grown rich on cheap labor. Convicts had manned Brown's mines and mills, and had worked on the railroads, plantations, and in the lumber camps and turpentine mills of Gordon's friends. Many present-day Georgia fortunes were started under this system. Hoke Smith also smashed the grip of the railroads on the State, imposing rigid regulations and dismissing "Little Joe" Brown, son of the Bourbon tycoon, from the Railroad Commission.

But, again, reaction set in swiftly. All the powers that Smith had affronted united to undo him. Brown, whom he had ousted, opposed him and won. Liberal zeal was confounded. Though Smith came back two years later to defeat Brown in his turn, Smith did not hold the governorship long. A vacancy in the Senate gave him the chance to go to Washington, and he departed.

A succession of unspectacular administrations followed. A few Governors of good intentions found themselves frustrated by a settled order of privilege and indifference. Aging, broken by emotional excesses, Tom Watson came back into politics on the wave of isolationism after World War I. He defeated his old enemy Hoke Smith, but two years later, a thin, muted shadow of his old self, Watson died in the Senate. The "Wool Hats" had no spokesman until Eugene Talmadge appeared a decade later, with an instinct for perfecting the county unit system that the hate-ridden Watson would have admired.

In the long period of restricted suffrage and factional rivalries, the growth of influence of the vested interests was steady and consuming. The scope and power of this control is shown by the swarm of lobbyists who dominate the State Legislature. Georgia, of course, is no exception in this.

143

But in few other states is the lobby so pervasive and all-powerful. So openly recognized is this situation that the lobby is amiably referred to as the "Third House." *

In recent years, a latter-day carpetbagger has emerged in the exploiting and corrupt lumber, wood pulp, and paper industry. Georgia has twenty-two million acres of forest land. Now that the versatile pine has been turned to paper-making, large plants have grown up, and millions of acres of piny woods have been bought or leased for pulpwood. The pressure for low taxes and resistance to regulation for proper forest management have been powerfully felt both in the State Capitol and the county seats. A pulp mill is a tempting prize for a poor community, and a new element in the competition for political and economic control is a natural consequence.

Another new force is the Georgia Farm Bureau Federation, headed by H. L. Wingate, a "strong man" in ability as well as in physique. The organization has burgeoned swiftly in the last ten years and is moving toward a goal of a hundred thousand "family" memberships, with associates among merchants, bankers, and professional men, and general classifications in cities and towns. As there has never been a lack of farmers' advocates in this predominantly rural State, an obvious question arises as to the aims, alliances, and sponsorship of the organization. Could it be that it is a protective coloration for interests other than agricultural?

For example: Wingate throws the Farm Bureau into the forum as an official champion of extreme antilabor laws. And the farmer-dominated Legislature enacts Farm Bureau bills bearing strong evidence that the measures were drafted by representatives of the Cotton Manufacturers Association.

The core and symbol of Georgia substance and influence

* Use of the term "Third House" is by no means confined to Georgia. See the chapter on California.—Ed.

144

is fabulous Coca-Cola. This Olympian of American business and model of modern enterprise, organization, and merchandising is a kind of fraternity of the fortunate and the propertied. The increment of its stock has made millionaires of those who had the good luck to get in on the ground floor of its reorganization in 1919.

Of late, a new lobby has appeared on the scene and is playing the game of influence for all it is worth. The education groups entered the lists under the pressure of a desperate worsening of the lot of teachers and schools. To show they meant business, they hired as their counsel none other than the Warwick of the Talmadge administration, Roy Harris himself. It was a good arrangement for Harris: a righteous cause, a highly respectable clientele, quite different from his usual run of customers, and a numerical power that could be very helpful to a man of his ambitions. On their part, the teachers got an expert. But however they may have helped themselves in the Statehouse, it turned out in a subsequent referendum that they had lost face with the people. The proposals of the teachers were overwhelmingly defeated.

The dominant role of business interests in the State government of Georgia is graphically shown in an article in the Atlanta *Constitution,* May 21, 1948. At the top of page one a 60-point, three-column headline read:

BIG BUSINESS CHOICE FOR
GOVERNOR LOOMS IN "THIRD
HOUSE" SESSION

Below this was a one-column bank, "Hideaway Meet Set Tonight," and under the by-line of M. L. St. John, the eminent newspaper's Capitol reporter, was the information that " 'Third House' members would decide whom they will support for Governor and what bills the corporations will

145

spur or fight in the 1949 Legislature." It was to be, Mr. St. John reported, "a confidential talk in a cabin near Lakemont," on the shores of the magnificent lake created as a power development in the foothills ninety miles north of Atlanta. The matter-of-fact tone of the article indicated the incident was considered merely routine.

The Legislature, upon which these forces converge, is keenly aware of the realities in the political situation. Otherwise it would be hard to explain the variation of mood and action from one session to another. Basically, the legislators remain the same, men out of the same background and overwhelmingly rural, even for the South, because of the small-county system. Yet, while the 1935 General Assembly approved Eugene Talmadge's executive orders of his previous term (including three-dollar auto tags rejected by the 1933 session, and ouster of the Public Service Commission and Highway Board), two years later, with Talmadge out and Rivers in, the Legislature whooped through the "Little New Deal," abjuring "thrift and economy." Again, in 1940, with Talmadge back in the saddle, the shift was to the right, only to see another complete about-face in 1942 when Ellis Arnall's spectacular reforms were enacted.

In the 1947 Legislature, fifty-eight members were lawyers and a large proportion were retainers of utilities, railroads, and banks. Speaker Fred Hand, one of the wealthiest men ever to sit in the General Assembly, is an ardent Talmadgeite. Re-elected in 1949, Hand is vice-president and general manager of the extraordinary Hand Trading Company of Pelham, a mercantile establishment that completely dominates the town. He is also a director of banks, mills, warehouses, and numerous other enterprises all over Georgia, and has close family ties in the textile empire.

It is of more than passing note that the small city of Pel-

146

ham is also the home town of H. L. Wingate, the virulently antilabor boss of the Georgia Farm Bureau.

If the county unit system is a prime factor in conditioning life in Georgia, the Talmadge influence is a natural outcome of that conditioning. It has become in itself almost a natural phenomenon, like Stone Mountain or mysterious Okefenokee Swamp. As long as Ol' Gene was alive, it was easy to regard him as a unique personality—a colorful, willful, designing politician who loved power and used it shockingly. Or, he might be viewed as an able, if miserly, administrator, who endeared himself to the economic powers by his dogged refrain of "thrift and economy" and his immovable resistance to the New Deal, while at the same time swaying the rural masses by his carnival antics, his invectives, prejudices, and promises.

"Keep a man poor," Gene would say, "and you'll keep him honest. And that means government, too."

Generally, the complacent belief held that after a while he would disappear and with him his demagogic tricks and manners. But his son's lightning succession, the swift, powerfully organized, forcible establishment of young Herman in his father's place, indicates clearly that for many Georgians, Talmadgeism holds more than mere fascination of a name or personality. That Herman, ejected by the State Supreme Court, was able a year later to win nomination easily (76 per cent of county unit votes, 51.77 per cent of popular vote), demonstrates the depths of Georgia's peculiar social conditioning. Neither the unsuccessful nor the subsequently successful drives to seat Herman were altogether sentimental, though carefully stressed sentiment for "Gene's boy" helped, of course, in vote-catching.

The Talmadge "condition" began in a time of great rural distress—the boll weevil, cheap cotton, cheap hogs. It is note-

147

worthy that Talmadge fortunes rise and their appeal sharpens in times of need, fear, and emotion. When Richard B. Russell, Jr., the "boy wonder" Governor, decided to run for the U. S. Senate rather than to seek a second term, Talmadge, then Commissioner of Agriculture, entered the race with a dozen other candidates. He courted the label, "The Wild Man from Sugar Creek." He ranted that he didn't expect and didn't want the vote of any county that had streetcars. He introduced red suspenders, the drinking gourd, and rural vernacular to campaigning. He promised things that the depression made highly appealing to farmers—three-dollar auto tags, cheap power rates, lower taxes, more roads. He got 22,000 votes less than a popular majority, but his county unit majority was 59.

It was a cinch. The more candidates the better—a fact which Talmadge never forgot. His defeats came when he ran against a single opponent—for the Senate, against Russell; for Governor, against Arnall.

Talmadge instituted rule by executive order. He dismissed members of the Public Service Commission, though they had been elected by the people, and did the same to the Highway Board. He filled both agencies with henchmen eager to do his bidding. When the Legislature refused to cut the auto fee, based on weight, he waited until the session was over and by executive fiat substituted a flat three-dollar charge. The farmers whooped with glee, while overlooking the fact that though they saved a few dollars, the big truckers pocketed thousands.

Another executive order reduced the State property tax from five to two mills, but it was not until later that opponents arose to point out that while Ol' Gene's "little fellow," with but a few acres and belongings, had been spared in many instances less than a dollar, large landowners, utilities, and corporations had profited heavily. Similarly, Talmadge endeared himself to large employers by calling out troops and

148

ordering concentration camps for pickets and demonstrators in the 1934 textile strike. He also used troops to kick out the State Treasurer and the State Auditor, both constitutional officers elected by the people, because they would not honor his warrants in a dispute over the legality of an appropriation bill.

Talmadge was powerless, however, to hold back the New Deal at the height of its popularity. In 1936 he ran against Senator Russell. The result was Talmadge's first and most ignominious defeat. He carried only sixteen counties. Talmadge lost another try for the Senate in 1938, this time against Senator Walter F. George. In 1942 Talmadge was balked in his fourth try for the governorship when an incendiary race issue which he had dredged up with apparent deliberate calculation was turned against him. He professed to have found evidence that teachers in the University of Georgia were planning to admit Negroes. The charge was baseless, but he juggled the Board of Regents, held noisy hearings, and fired several key men.

Talmadge soon found he had taken on more than he had anticipated. Alumni of the University rose in arms. Ellis Arnall, the young Attorney General, announced against Talmadge as the embattled champion of youth. Organized students, alarmed for their credits, beat the bushes for votes. "Little Boy Blue," as Talmadge dubbed his opponent, won by a close margin.

Four years later Talmadge tried again, this time with a stronger appeal to his "fellow countrymen." The U. S. Supreme Court had handed down several decisions upholding the rights of Negroes as voters, as travelers, and as entitled to an education on the same level as whites. Talmadge incited the race issue for all it was worth. Confederate flags were whipped out. The Klan marched. The result was inevitable. Talmadge

149

won with 242 unit votes, though on the minority end in the popular count.

But Ol' Gene was deadly ill. Shortly after the primary he collapsed, with a series of stomach hemorrhages. Among his coterie, worry rested like a pall. Examining the new Constitution to see what it said about succession, they discovered an unfamiliar item to the effect that if the General Assembly found that no candidate had received a majority, "then from the two persons having the highest number of votes, *who shall be in life* . . . [it shall] elect a Governor *viva voce.*"

Talmadge had no announced opposition in the general election save an obscure aspirant, who was asking people to write his name on the ballot. That name was D. Talmadge Bowers, the Talmadge being purely coincidental. In secret haste word went out to local leaders to make certain that there were write-ins of the name of Herman Talmadge—just in case.

In the election, Talmadge received 147,279 votes against fewer than 2,000 write-ins for Bowers, Herman, and James V. Carmichael, whom Gene had beaten in the primary. No one seemed to notice this trivial detail, and Georgia made ready to accept Gene as Governor for the fourth time. But on December 21, twenty-four days before he was to be inaugurated, he died.

The situation was without precedent. The new Constitution was only a year old, and not a line had been interpreted. Under its provisions, Georgia for the first time had elected a Lieutenant Governor, who ordinarily would succeed if a Governor died. But the point was raised that there was no Governor for him to succeed, for Talmadge had not taken office. Then and there the wheels began to churn to install Herman.

Most of the patronage of the forthcoming administration already had been allocated. An organization, if not a dynasty,

150

had to be preserved. Roy Harris, the expert manipulator, took charge of the strategy.

He faced a number of difficulties. When the General Assembly met, it was found that the official returns placed Herman third in write-in votes. The totals were Carmichael 669, Bowers 637, Herman 617. The ensuing events were vividly described in an editorial in the Columbus *Enquirer-Ledger*: "At the absolutely strategic moment, the Telfair canvass was challenged [Telfair County is the home of the Talmadges]. There was a fussing around with papers and envelopes and—lo and behold!—up came these fifty-eight missing votes, every last one of them for Herman. And quick as a flash the vote result was changed. Herman took the lead instead of the tail-end, just an even half-dozen votes more than Jimmy Carmichael and a scant thirty-eight more than Bowers. It was a close squeak—but they made it."

The Atlanta *Journal*, scenting fraud, sent a crack reporter, George Goodwin, down to Telfair. He soon uncovered gross irregularities. The boys had concocted the "missing" votes, by dint of "voting the graveyard," stay-at-homes, and absentees.

But in the meantime, the subservient Legislature had elected Herman Governor, and he, backed by State troopers, seized the executive office and mansion. He remained in possession for sixty-three days, until the State Supreme Court, in a five-to-two decision, ruled that the General Assembly had no right to elect him.

The tribunal held that Lieutenant Governor M. E. Thompson was the legal successor to Ol' Gene. It was a foregone conclusion that Thompson and Herman would be the candidates the next time.

Thompson evoked no enthusiasm, particularly after it became evident that the real power behind him was former Governor Rivers. The people got the forlorn feeling that the contest was not between Talmadgeism and liberalism, but

151

between two shabby machines. The campaign fell into the familiar pattern of rival political squabbling. Nearly half a million registered voters stayed away from the polls. It was significant that Negroes, of whom 125,000 had qualified in their new emancipation, were uninterested. Herman won easily, with 130 counties (most of them small ones) to 29 for Thompson.

Herman started his lawful term like a true chip off the old block.

His first assault was on the State penal system which had been reconstructed by Ellis Arnall. Two henchmen were appointed to the State Board of Corrections, and the able Director of Corrections was replaced by the Sheriff of Wayne County (two unit votes). Next, the Board of Education was gutted. One of the first victims of this deal was the Superintendent of the Academy for the Blind, the best man ever to hold the post.

Ripper legislation came early to reduce the powers of State Treasurer George Hamilton, who had been re-elected ever since Eugene Talmadge had had him carried out bodily by troops in 1936. The Governor, not the Treasurer, now has power to designate State depositories, an obvious political advantage. Before the Legislature adjourned, it had erected an elaborate structure of dynastic political controls. To prevent another Supreme Court from spoiling the fun, the Legislature gave uncontestable power to the State Democratic Committee to say whether Herman may run again in 1950 (the Constitution has a one-term limit), and also to settle all other questions of eligibility.

Another act wiped out the voters' registration lists, to require reregistration (with tests) in two years. Also, newspaper libel laws were tightened, an obvious attempt to stifle criticism. Some of these measures may not be constitutional, but their enactment is indicative of Herman's viewpoint and brass-galled tactics.

Strangely, the Legislature also approved the largest budget in the State's history, totaling $108,574,026 in positive commitments and $46,000,000 in contingent appropriations, subject to referendum vote.

The last sum included $23,000,000 for schools. Herman nominally approved the proposed expenditure, but carefully dodged any commitment on how the money would be raised. Georgia's tax system is a hodgepodge that embraces every source of revenue from real estate to rolling stores. There are twenty-seven items of taxation and thirty sets of fees—everything save the unpopular sales tax, and Herman was not going to be stuck with that if he could help it. He insisted he was for progress and was not averse to spending when necessary to get it. But it was up to the people to impose more taxes.

To no one's surprise, the people voted three to one against taxing themselves further. Nothing had been said about the nature of the new taxes, and the voters balked at giving Herman a blank check.

The episode is significant in its bearing on the future of the Talmadge dynasty. It demonstrated that despite Herman's outward slickness and glibness, he is not the man his father was. Cold-eyed realists like Roy Harris, doubtless, never were deluded on that point. Ol' Gene would grimly insist on bulling through, to occasional disaster. Herman is the leader only in flashes, and then with a kind of shrewd plausibility. For example, three months after his dubious performance on the tax referendum, he called the Legislature in special session and in four days ran through bills for new revenue. Characteristically, he asked for less than half the amount the voters had refused to approve—not enough to do the job, as Roy Harris complained, but enough for a substantial sop to the pressures—schools, hospitals, old folks. At the same time this lesser amount showed that Herman was not deaf to the people's voice as it had spoken three months earlier.

Despite the current wave of reaction, Georgia is still stamped by the progress of the Arnall administration. In Georgia lights, that period was a phenomenon.

The voting age was lowered to eighteen years. Talmadge was strikingly outdone in financial management. The atrocious chain gang was abolished and other spectacular reforms introduced in the penal system, including wiping out pardon scandals. In the Rivers administration, 7,800 prisoners had been released by pardon, commutation, or parole, 2,700 of them by executive order and 800 in the final four months. The Talmadge record was somewhat less, but the total still reached 6,000 in one term. A small coterie of lawyers with political connections had handled most of the cases before the Prison Commission.

Arnall put through legislation divesting the Governor of indiscriminate pardon power and setting up a Board of Pardons and Paroles. To head this agency, he named an out-of-State expert.

That the State has a new Constitution is another part of the brilliant Arnall record. The old Constitution was written in 1877, when Georgia was emerging from Reconstruction and was bitter with memories of violence and carpetbag profligacy. Accordingly the "Constitution of Redemption" was a mass of prohibitions. It required an incessant process of amendment to keep up with the times, and when Arnall was elected, the Constitution had been amended three hundred times. Every effort to get a constitutional convention failed because of rural suspicion. Under Arnall, the Legislature set up a Revision Commission, which worked two years. The resulting new Constitution, in the form of amendments, was submitted to the people and adopted in August, 1945.

154

While far from perfect, the new Constitution is a great improvement. It confirmed most of the Arnall reforms, and ended the old tyrannical system, still in force in some states, of allocating certain revenue to definite projects. All revenue now goes into a common fund.

But the new Constitution, like the old, is a mass of legislation that has no place in a basic document. It includes such items as the salaries of the Governor, $12,000; Lieutenant Governor, $2,000; Supreme Court Justices, $8,000; members of the Legislature, $10 a day plus $5 maintenance.

The new Constitution did make a gesture toward freeing communities from the crippling grip of the rural Legislature. For the first time machinery was provided to establish home rule. But getting the necessary enabling acts is a virtual impossibility. Two sessions have come and gone since the 1945 Constitution was ratified, but home rule is still a wistful dream. Sixty per cent of the bills introduced are concerned with purely local affairs. County and municipal government in Georgia find themselves at times powerless to function under the blighting authority of the Legislature.

The nature of this oppression may be judged from a few of the hundreds of local bills passed at the 1949 session: "To permit the microfilming of certain documents by the Fulton Superior Court Clerk"; "To permit the City of Atlanta to sell a portion of the waterworks property"; "To permit Dekalb County to use voting machines and to set voting hours between 7 A.M. and 7 P.M"; "To permit East Point to construct a veterans' home."

One of the most priceless examples was a bill making it unlawful "for owners of goats to allow their goats to run at large in Candler County, to require all owners of goats to keep them in fenced enclosures, sufficiently built to prevent goats from getting out and running at large and trespassing on lands of other parties."

Perhaps the most widely acclaimed Arnall reform was repeal of the poll tax. Next to Alabama's poll tax, Georgia's was
the most repressive, permitting accumulation of the debt for
seven years, at $1.50 a year, with interest and process fees.
Arnall moved warily in striking at the tax, as it had become
a symbol of resistance to Yankee incitements. It had been
maintained with jealous watchfulness, like a grail. When at
last Arnall announced his intention to act, his proposal was
acclaimed, to everyone's surprise, by Eugene Talmadge. That
did it.

Actually, Talmadge had long had doubts about the poll
tax. On apparent impulse, he made an interesting admission
about this to a newspaperman in the intimacy of a Pullman
stateroom, back in 1936.

"You know what I've been thinking?" he said. "I'd like to
suspend the poll tax. I could do it by executive order, pending the next session of the Legislature. My fellows (referring
to the little farmers, tenants, and croppers) didn't make a
crop last year. They're suffering. They can't pay the tax and
they can't vote for me." He hesitated a moment. "But I reckon
I won't do it. If I do, all those damn boondoggling easy-
workers will be able to vote against me."

Whether he was aware of it or not, Talmadge summed up
the unanswerable argument against the poll tax. It was a financial limitation on the ballot. His fellows couldn't pay, so they
would be disfranchised. Similarly, it was a device knowingly
used to restrict suffrage. The opposition would be controlled
and hostile votes eliminated.

In view of Ellis Arnall's remarkable record of accomplishments, it may seem strange that his political fortunes have
been in eclipse. The answer is to be found in the mercurial
nature of Georgia politics, its inhibitions, and endless preoccupation with factionalism. Some Georgians have called their
State an adolescent, given to tantrums. Roosevelt, to whom

it was "second home," called it an unfinished State. Arnall did a number of things that were simply bad politics in the purview of tradition.

For one, when the Supreme Court ruled that Negroes could vote in primaries and ride unsegregated in interstate transportation, Arnall refused to heed clamor for a special session of the Legislature to purge the statutes of all reference to primaries. It turned out later that this would not have been any more effective, but the white-supremacy politicians made vital use of the issue at the time. They also exploited fully Arnall's suspected acquiescence in an effort by the Legislature, self-convened in special session, to change the Constitution and qualify him for a second term. It was at this point that kingmaker Roy Harris, with burning ambitions of his own, turned against Arnall.

Also, Arnall lectured widely. His enemies spread the accusation that he was "talking against the South." The Wool Hatters were not impressed by Arnall's star performances on "Information Please," where he seemed to know all the answers on literature, music, and the arts. Arnall wrote two books. In rural Georgia they were regarded as hifalutin. He worked for the nomination of Henry Wallace as Vice-President in 1944. And Arnall talked and wrote against monopolists and the Georgia Power Company. Finally, in 1948, when Herman was running against Acting Governor Thompson, Arnall and Ed Rivers, formerly old enemies, formed an ostentatious alliance behind Thompson. Folks were easily persuaded that Arnall was a designing politician, throwing away principles for factional advantage.

Above all, Arnall ignored the anatomy of Georgia politics and the peculiar requirements of the county unit system, the deference to local bosses and courthouse rings. They complained they couldn't talk to him, that he had a swelled head, that he wouldn't play ball. It is a fact that when he beat Tal-

157

madge in 1942, much of his practical political support came from old-line politicians. But with all this, the Arnall stock and the Arnall ambitions are looking up again, because there is no other opposition to the Talmadge dynasty in prospect—opposition that has a meaning in the sense of contrasting philosophy, program, and experience.

The current situation in Georgia is explosive, particularly as regards Herman, the nominal heir of the old tradition.

Money troubles are acute in spite of help from able Commissioner of Revenue Charles Redwine, a banker whom Eugene Talmadge once ran for Governor, and from State Auditor B. E. Thrasher, Jr. The cities, saddled with the mounting burdens while deprived of the vote, are restive. Herman is indecisive. At a Gridiron party after the 1948 session, Capitol reporters trotted out two Governors. One was "Wool Hat Hummon," with all the tricks and intonations of his father. The other was "Civic Club Herman," perfect in apparel and erudite speech about bigger and better industry and agriculture. Everyone laughed, but the point struck home.

A big question has arisen throughout political Georgia as to how far Roy Harris will further support Herman, now that his weaknesses, his inclination to the convivial rather than the leader's life, have been revealed. If the Arnall recrudescence shows any signs of real vitality, nobody would be greatly surprised to see the "kingmaker" once more in the Arnall camp. It would be consistent with his special and purposeful brand of inconsistency.

In his middle thirties, Herman has had experiences his father lacked. He has a good war record, and in the first flush of his accession there was an idea that he aimed to go far, that his sights already were set on that Senate seat his father could never win. But that concept has undergone a big change.

158

Herman's political future is very uncertain, particularly as far as the Senate is concerned.

Another sign of Herman's somewhat vague intent to establish a name for respectability are his gestures of warning to the Ku Klux Klan, which openly supported him and his father before him. The gestures are not, to be sure, anything to worry the Klan—as when he says that "unlawful" acts will be punished. The Klan hastens to approve; that is, its more articulate segment, headed until his death last August by Dr. Samuel Green, Atlanta obstetrician and baby specialist, approves.

A fanatical little man with a Hitler mustache, Grand Dragon of the Georgia Association of Klans, Green insisted that Klansmen always uphold the law and do not tolerate lawlessness. Incessant acts of lawlessness by robed and hooded men occur, but the Grand Dragon's pretentious "investigations" always found these to have been perpetrated by others than genuine Klansmen. When Robert Mallard, a Negro, was killed from ambush in Toombs County in November, 1948, apparently for the offense of sporting a snappy automobile, investigations by the sheriff and the Georgia Bureau of Investigation first were directed toward proving the Klan was not guilty, rather than to finding the assassins.

As an organization, the Ku Klux Klan is not what it used to be. As a state of mind, it is. Twenty-five years ago, it was a sinister, powerful, and all-pervading force, a combination of calculated racket and indulgence for festering ignorance and prejudice. Then, and frequently afterward, there were signs of strange alliances. Labor organizers in textile centers might see from their rooming houses a patroling cluster of robed men, or a cross would suddenly flame. Or they might be seized at night to be flogged or dumped over the county line with a warning. One organizer related that as he sat in a mill manager's office, in a small town thirty miles from Atlanta, he saw through an accidentally opened closet door a pile of KKK robes. There is more than a suspicion that the Klan has long offered a purchasable service of terror.

However, what with public revulsion, scandals of income tax and other frauds, fading novelty, and a growing volume of condemnation, the official Klan dwindled. Juries occasionally convicted floggers identified as Klansmen. When Arnall revoked the Klan's charter in 1946, it was done by a court decree to which Hiram Evans's successor as Imperial Wizard, one Colescott, wearily consented. What remains today is an aggregation of groups, a sort of balkanization knit only by a common mentality.

There is an occasional disposition to argue that the Klan, having lost official status, is an empty force, and that Dragon Green was simply a strutting comic. However, when a bill to make mask-wearing a crime was offered in the 1949 Legislature, there was an instant and furious sortie to beat it down. Analyzing the vote that killed the measure, the Atlanta *Journal* showed that generally the legislators who opposed the bill had voted to seat Herman Talmadge illegally in 1947.

Atlanta, it should be noted, has done better, with a local ordinance outlawing hoods and masks. And, just before his death, Green issued an imperial edict to ban the mask—which is ignored by Klansmen who disputed his leadership and who turned to others as the racket proliferates.

Sensitive Georgians are sorely distressed that their State seems to be a breeding ground for Klan pattern movements. One reason is the license and protection such movements have received. Dan Duke, the vigorous young liberal who as Assistant State Attorney General courageously prosecuted the Columbians, one of these imitative groups, called them "the juvenile delinquents of the Klan." Duke, when still in his twenties, was one of the first to prove that Klansmen could be convicted.

The shibboleth of all Klan-type organizations is white

160

supremacy. This has been so since the Civil War. Now that the Negro is steadily winning the right to vote in primaries and becoming a force in politics, the feeling behind the classic prejudice is intensifying.

The last census reported 1,084,927 Negroes in Georgia. This was 34 per cent of the total population. Whites numbered 2,049,915, of whom 99.42 per cent were American-born. Negroes began registering heavily after the Supreme Court decision, and although there were widespread purges of the lists, 125,000 remained qualified in 1948. The potential is half a million, so it is small wonder the old-line politicians are seizing upon every device to thwart Negro balloting.

The Negroes have able and determined leadership. In civil-rights tests, the leaders prefer to work through the Georgia Defense Committee, rather than through the N.A.A.C.P., with its vulnerability to charges of Yankee meddling. A. T. Walden, an outstanding Atlanta attorney, heads an organization of Negro voters, the Georgia Association of Democratic Clubs, with 20,000 members, and branches in sixty counties. However, it is in the cities that the bulk of Negro balloting takes place. In rural areas it is still dangerous for a Negro to do so.* Maceo Snipes, the only Negro who voted in Taylor County (two unit votes) in the 1946 primary, was murdered the next day. The two white men who called him from his home and shot him were acquitted—on a plea of self-defense.

Few white persons have any concept of the infinite patience, caution, and courage with which members of the Negro com-

---

* It takes courage for Negroes to vote in Louisiana, too, as the chapter on that state makes clear. The authors of the chapters on the three Southern states (Georgia, Louisiana, and Texas) included in this volume agree that one hope of the South is the new Negro vote. Ralph S. O'Leary, who has written the chapter on Louisiana, expresses it as follows: "There is genuine hope in the Negro, both for himself and the whites. Once Negroes can make themselves felt at the polls, they may help all the underprivileged to better their lot."—Ed.

munity must wage their struggle against discrimination. The struggle is grimly perilous. But advances have been won. Atlanta has the only Negro daily newspaper in the country—*The Daily World.* The Atlanta University, endowed by private philanthropy, is an outstanding center of Negro education and culture. And though long barred from Democratic primaries, Negroes have voted in general and special elections on bond issues and other referendums. In urban centers, particularly Atlanta, they have often wielded decisive weight.

The average Georgian is inclined to be resentful of discussions that dwell on the political and social idiosyncrasies of his State. He is loath to concede that in Georgia the repressive political system has profound impact on social attitudes and economic authority. He asks querulously why the beauties and resources of Georgia are ignored—the Ten Wonders, the material progress. He is enraptured by apostrophes such as Stephen Vincent Benet's in *John Brown's Body:*

> "For wherever the winds of Georgia run,
>   It smells of peaches long in the sun . . ."

The Georgian has a case. His State, largest in area east of the Mississippi, has attributes of climate and variety that make it a lovely place to live in. There are times when it may appear an excess of captiousness to call attention to flaws, as when a doting native speaks of the lovely coastal islands—the Golden Isles of legend. Yet it is a fact that only a few places along that shoreline with its magnificent beaches are open to the public. This public area totaled barely one per cent until the brief administration of M. E. Thompson performed a lasting service by purchasing Jekyll Island as a park. For the most part the shoreline is privately owned, made up of posted and guarded baronies, hunting preserves, and rarely visited estates of absentee owners. The Cumberland Island fastness of the Car-

162

negies, with twenty-three miles of matchless beach, is deserted and forbidden, a graphic example of social waste.

Georgians are also much given to reciting the mineral wealth of their State—kaolin deposits sufficient to supply the world for a thousand years, barite, manganese, ocher, Fuller's earth, shales, feldspar. "But nowhere in the South," reported a study in the *Harvard Business Review* (January, 1948), "will one find an important manufacturer of glass, tile, enamel, or scouring powder." Georgia's inexhaustible clays go to potteries in the North and East.

In agriculture, Georgia is a bursting cornucopia. Cotton acreage is dwindling and the State is fast turning to diversified farming. More than fifty per cent of Georgia's 250,000 farms participate in the soil-conservation program, though only a few years ago Eugene Talmadge was heatedly opposing conservation districts as regimentation and meddling. Georgia is now the second state in the South in this, and ahead of the national average.

But reaction tugs constantly at farm progress, particularly in the one place it might least be expected—the State Department of Agriculture. Commissioner Tom Linder, an original Talmadgeite, has made of the official *Market Bulletin* one of the most virulent anti-Semitic and isolationist mediums. In its columns he has carried Talmadge hatred and calumny of the Roosevelts to an extreme. A publication supported by tax money and designed for information to farmers, it has been used by Linder to vent venomous attacks on reciprocal trade agreements, foreign aid, and to air dissertations on Linder's "discovery" that the Roosevelts were originally German Jews named Rosenfelt and that FDR's racial grudge against Hitler was really why this country entered World War II. Linder is secure and self-confident in his job. The county unit system and its rural tyranny have many triumphs like him.

However, more and more of late such things are being chal-

163

lenged. This is particularly true in the Georgia press. The newspapers are displaying a vigor and alertness that, with rare exceptions, was not evident a decade ago.

Today, the Atlanta *Constitution*, edited by Ralph McGill, and the *Journal*, owned by James M. Cox, former Ohio Governor, are militant and outspoken on public delinquencies and violations of civil liberties. The Augusta *Herald* played a leading role in smashing Roy Harris's Cracker Party. Similarly, smaller dailies like the Albany *Herald* and the Griffin *News* are doing yeoman service in the cause of clean and enlightened government.

The outstanding intransigent Tory is the Savannah *News*. Railroad-corporation-bank-owned, it has long advocated die-hard Republicanism nationally and the views of Georgia's economic masters locally.

Another heartening development is the fact that iniquities clearly linked with the political system appear to bring greater public shock. An instance occurred in the 1949 session of the Legislature.

Disclosure of the appalling conditions in the old mental hospital at Milledgeville flamed into outraged scandal, though these conditions had existed for years. Few State mental hospitals are adequate, but Georgians found that theirs was one of the worst. This condition was due not only to horrible overcrowding (some ninety-five hundred patients in a single enclosure, more than four thousand in seventy-five-year-old firetraps) and lack of staff and services (one qualified doctor to twelve hundred patients). It was also due to gross political chicanery. The Milledgeville Representative in the Legislature was found to have served as broker in the sale of equipment to the hospital. At the same time he was chairman of the Hospital Committee of the House. He was cleared, apparently, on the ground that this practice was honored by long custom. Hadn't the beatified Eugene Talmadge sold cattle to the hospital when he was Governor? But the affair created vigorous public outcry. There was a stirring of public conscience that surely bodes well for the future.

There are other encouraging signs of a new generation in Georgia. Herman Talmadge's voters' purge cannot wholly undo the grant of suffrage to eighteen-year-olds. How many voters are under twenty-one and how they are voting is difficult as yet to say. Many areas and usages are still uncharted by study. But the new voters, white and colored, are definitely a leaven for change. The League of Women Voters is alert and determined. The veterans are coming up. Increasingly, opposition is mounting against the Old Guard.

Above all, there is evident youthful skepticism of the county unit system. This was strikingly manifested at the 1948 Georgia Youth Assembly, which the Y.M.C.A. sponsors as a summer camp project.

The youngsters learn the processes of government by conducting a mock State government, with Legislature, courts, and executive branches. Herman Talmadge, smooth, pleasant, and close to the boys in years, pontificated about the surpassing virtues of Georgia government. He dwelt particularly on the blessings of the county unit system and how it keeps a great rural people from domination by the Sodoms and Gomorrahs of the populous centers. When he finished orating, sixteen-year-old Paul Simms rose. Paul was from Lumpkin County, one of the tiniest in Georgia, but with two unit votes. To this make-believe but deadly earnest House of Representatives Paul Simms offered a bill to repeal the county vote system. It was passed by overwhelming vote.

There was no report of Herman's comments or thoughts.

OHIO ★ ★ ★

Oxcart Government!

RICHARD L. MAHER

OHIO, fourth state in population and third in industrial wealth, boasts an oxcart-model government in an atomic age.

This obsolete governmental machinery stands as a perpetual monument to the machinations of Marcus Alonzo Hanna, who made William McKinley President so that he (Hanna) could sit in the United States Senate.

Hanna's heritage to his State is control of its affairs by a rural bloc in the disproportionately constituted Legislature. This "Cornstalk Brigade," as it is known, has stifled progress in Ohio for generations.

The dead hand of Hanna rules the State almost as effectively as he did when alive. Much of the lawmaking is the handiwork of special interests. They put through their schemes by seeing to it that the Cornstalk boys are well taken care of.

Once, in a revolt, the people of Ohio wrote into the Con-

★

RICHARD L. MAHER gets his by-lines in the Cleveland *Press* as Politics Editor and legislative correspondent. He has been in newspaper work in Ohio since 1921, when he gave up his law studies to take a job with the Cleveland *News*. In 1940 he won the Cleveland Newspaper Guild award for news reporting. Maher also was author of the chapter on Cleveland, "Study In Political Paradoxes," in *Our Fair City*, published in 1947.

166

stitution provisions that Mark Hanna in his day called "social-istic." The people thought they were giving their cities the right of home rule. But despite this constitutional guarantee, a conservative Supreme Court and an obstructive Legislature are still forcing the cities to come, hat in hand, to the State Capitol to beg for money to run their households. The home rule amendment has been so emasculated by decisions of the Supreme Court that it is practically meaningless.

Mark Hanna was a born politician. He was a genius at organizing and a personality-plus man in an age when big business openly ruled politics and government.

He came from a family of antislavery Whigs. He joined the Republican party in 1860 and cast his first vote for Abe Lincoln. Hanna served in the Union Army and soon after returning home got into politics. Some folks said it was because he was interested in street-railway franchises. Hanna had discovered there was a direct relation between franchises and politics.

He organized businessmen in politics, and was so effective in this that he soon emerged as the boss of the West Side of Cleveland. It could hardly have been a coincidence that his chief street-railway interests were in this section.

Hanna dreamed for years of making a President. He failed with John Sherman, but succeeded with William McKinley. Then he proceeded to deal himself a senatorship. That was in the days when Legislatures picked Senators, and Hanna had to control the Assembly in order to keep himself in the Senate. For although he was the undisputed boss of the Republican party, he could not win elections in his home bailiwick. At the very time McKinley was being inaugurated for his second term and Hanna was basking in the Washington spotlight, Tom Johnson, Cleveland's greatest Mayor, was soundly trouncing Hanna in his home town.

Johnson was battling for a three-cent streetcar fare. Hanna

was determined to block him. The hectic struggle that followed was described by Johnson in his autobiography as "government by injunction." Johnson could win at the polls, but Hanna frustrated him at every turn in the subservient courts and Legislature.

After McKinley's death, Hanna's power began to wane. To remain in the Senate, he had to keep control of the Legislature. Thus he gave Ohio its evil heritage.

That is a form of government less flexible, efficient, and representative than what the State had when it was created in 1803. By an innocuous-appearing constitutional amendment, Hanna placed in the hands of a rural minority control of the lawmaking machinery and the power to tax and spend.

The name of Charles Rannells does not appear in any of the State's history books. An obscure legislator, he has been forgotten. But Rannells sponsored Hanna's measure that gave the rural areas permanent domination of the Legislature.

Rannells represented a district that included Vinton and Hocking counties, the former the smallest in the State. The constitutional amendment he offered in 1902 gave every county—eighty-eight in all—at least one representative in the House. Vinton County then had fifteen thousand residents. Today it has ten thousand. In 1902 Vinton was joined to another county to get one Representative in the Assembly. Today, Vinton has its own Representative—one legislator for ten thousand persons. Cuyahoga County, with a million and a half residents, has one representative for each seventy thousand.

The amendment sounded innocent in 1902. Hanna's machine worked hard for it. His term expired in 1904, and he wanted to be sure he had the Assembly votes to win another.

Hanna traded the birthright of the cities for a Senate seat that, ironically, he held only fleetingly. He died one month after his re-election.

In the half century since then, Ohio has changed from an

168

agricultural to an industrial State. Population has increased enormously in urban areas and declined in rural ones. Today seventy of the eighty-eight counties have seventy Representatives in the House, two more than are necessary to control. But those seventy counties represent only one-third of the population of the State.

The two-thirds of the population living in the other eighteen counties have only sixty-five Representatives.

Realization of the true nature of Hanna's heritage began to dawn in the lush twenties, when demands arose for State aid for schools and highways. A gasoline tax was enacted, whereupon the Cornstalk Brigade grabbed it to finance rural feeder-roads and other agricultural benefits.

Author of the tax was one Dallas Sullivan, a rip-snorting spellbinder from Union County, a rich farming area. He had one rule in lawmaking, and boasted about it.

"Soak the cities while we can," Sullivan would say. "It won't last forever."

Today, the gas levy is a major source of the State's income, but farmers are carefully given special treatment. The Cornstalk Brigade saw to that. Gasoline used in farm equipment is exempt from the tax.

The cities got another tax rooking in a cigarette tax. A levy of two cents a pack was voted. The tax produced nearly $10,000,000 and today raises $15,000,000. When adopted, the tax was earmarked for needy school districts. But not one urban district was able to qualify, even though some were on the verge of closing their schools.

The bulk of the tax has always come from big population centers.

In the thirties the cities got it in the neck again. Struggling up from the havoc and despair of the Hoover depression, the State enacted a three per cent sales tax. In 1935, the tax produced $50,000,000; in 1948, $140,000,000. It was set up to give sixty per cent to schools, forty per cent to local governments.

Again, the Cornstalk Brigade voted itself special dispensations. Food sales at farmer roadside stands were exempted, plus fertilizer and seeds. The city dweller paid the tax on everything he bought.

It was this sales tax that built up Ohio's much-vaunted hundred-million-dollar treasury "surplus." But while this huge sum lies idle in the State's coffers, the municipalities, from whose citizens the bulk of this money was obtained, are frantically grappling with desperate budget problems. To meet their soaring costs, they have been compelled to resort to payroll taxes and other harsh expedients.

When "Honest John" Bricker became Governor in 1939, he announced there would be a change in the allocation of sales-tax funds. Bricker succeeded Martin L. Davey, whose four years in office were marked by stormy tilts with political windmills, "legal graft" investigations, acrid feuds with newspapers and the Roosevelt administration, "hot mix" road-topping scandals, and "truckless trucking" contracts by the Liquor Department.

To "correct the evils" of the Davey regime, Bricker put through a series of "ripper" bills. One funneled revenue from the sales tax into the State's general fund. From this fund, appropriations were made to the schools and cities. In 1939 and 1940, local governments got $12,000,000 from this source —about forty per cent of the total—and it looked like a square deal.

But with the war, and greater employment and free spending, sales-tax collections soared. This increased revenue was promptly impounded by governors and the Cornstalk Brigade. Had the old 60-40 formula prevailed, the cities would have benefited handsomely. In 1948, they would have re-

170

ceived $56,000,000, instead of the $27,000,000 they got. But once again they were on the short end of the stick.

What has Ohio done to break the hold of Hanna's heritage? Very little.

Two decades ago, State Senator George H. Bender, later Congressman-at-large and Republican Chairman in Cleveland, launched a drive to reapportion * the Assembly through a constitutional amendment. He circulated petitions, got thousands of signatures, but, mysteriously, never filed them.

The widely reported reason was that the powerful Ohio Chamber of Commerce dissuaded Bender. Big business was—and is—satisfied with the status quo. It can generally get what it wants from the rural-dominated Legislature, and is strongly opposed to any change.

Later, Albert Ruddy, head of the Cleveland carpenters' union and powerful in State labor circles, started a new effort. Again, petitions for a reapportionment were circulated. The movement was gaining momentum when, suddenly, Ruddy was indicted for bribery in a building project. He went to the penitentiary, and his campaign dropped out of sight.

In Cincinnati today, Mayor Albert D. Cash, a rising young liberal Democrat, is endeavoring to initiate still another reapportionment program. He wants to go all the way. Cash proposes to put before the people a "Nebraska plan" Legislature. He would institute a one-chamber body of one hundred or so members elected on a proportional basis regardless of county lines.

His plan has been lauded in the press, but has received very little political support.

It is a curious fact that no Ohio Governor has dared tackle the reapportionment problem. Many have recognized the in-

* Reapportionment is a knotty problem in Illinois and Texas, too, where clear and mandatory provisions in the state constitution have been ignored, as the reader will learn in those chapters.—Ed.

equalities of representation, but none has spoken out against it.

Ohio has the habit of electing Democratic Governors and Republican Legislatures. The late Vic Donahey, who served three terms in the twenties, got along amiably with his Republican Legislatures because he was as rural minded as they. His administrations were as conservative as any Republican's could be.

Vic won the governorship as a result of a spectacular feat. As State Auditor he sternly refused to approve a charge for a baked potato in a judge's expense account. The deed won Donahey immense acclaim.

"Where I come from," he remarked with characteristic homespun candor, "you can buy a bushel of potatoes for the price of one of those fancy baked ones."

He was followed by Myers Cooper, a Republican accident; George White and Martin Davey, Democrats; John Bricker, the first Republican in forty years to break the "no second term for a Republican" tradition; Frank Lausche, Democrat; Thomas J. Herbert; and now, Lausche again.

But not one of them would stand up and make a fight for just representation in the Legislature. Also, not one of them gave the State the outstanding leadership it enjoyed under its last truly great Governor, James M. Cox, of Dayton. Thrice Governor and once Democratic presidential standard-bearer, Cox wrote into law more progressive legislation in his first administration than has been enacted in all the years since.

He became Governor in 1913 after a constitutional convention. His task was to put on the statute books the reforms the people had voted into their Constitution. Under Cox were instituted the direct primary, workmen's compensation (a radical departure in those days), civil service, home rule for cities, and a nonpartisan judiciary.

The question is frequently raised in Ohio, "Who runs the Legislature?" Certainly, it is not the people.

172

One of the leading arguments made against Mayor Cash's reapportionment plan is that it would "create a playground for lobbyists." The 1949 Legislature couldn't have been a more lush playground for lobbyists.

Speaker John Cantwell, from Mahoning Valley, has an ever-attendant ear cocked for suggestions from the steel operators of Youngstown. Cantwell publicly acknowledged that he owed one lobbyist a debt of gratitude for being elected. The lobbyist is Joe Thomas, spokesman for the potent Township Trustees Association, spearhead of the Cornstalk Brigade.

Most potent lobbyist in Ohio today is Ed D. Schorr, one-time Republican State Chairman. Schorr came to Columbus twenty years ago as Commerce Director in the cabinet of Governor Myers Y. Cooper. Schorr remained to head a large law firm and to become the big power in legislative matters.

He can do tricks with either Republican or Democratic Assemblies.

Currently, his chief interest is securing authorization for the sale of colored oleomargarine. For years oleo manufacturers have tried to get the restriction against yellow oleo removed. They got nowhere until 1947, when they astutely hired Ed Schorr as their lobbyist. It has been reported he is paid a $50,000-a-year retainer, and will get a $100,000 bonus when the discriminatory provisions are repealed.

Schorr always has a few irons in the fire. In 1945, he lobbied for pensions for judges. His connection with the bill prompted Frank Lausche, then Governor and himself a former judge, to condemn the proposal and to announce he would veto it if passed. That ended the matter.

In 1947, Schorr helped write the soldiers' bonus act. He did this job without fee, as a former serviceman. That year, also, he practically rewrote the election code. A year later the Democrats painfully discovered just what he had written into

173

the election laws. That little job by Schorr cost Harry Truman 100,000 votes in Ohio in 1948.

The Schorr code provided that only X marks were valid on ballots; any other mark invalidated them. In centers like Cleveland, Akron, Canton, and Youngstown, voters often mark their ballots with a check or cross, or even write yes or no. Previously, the law permitted such ballots to be counted if the intent of the voter was clear. When the Democrats discovered the X mark restriction, they bellowed in rage. But it was too late, and thousands of Truman ballots were tossed out because of illegal markings.

A major conservation problem in Ohio is strip mining, whereby coal veins near the surface are worked by "skinning off" the covering soil. The process leaves deep erosive scars. For a decade efforts have been made to do something about this destructive practice. But one man always blocked action.

That man was Robert Ellsworth Scott, lobbyist for coal operators.

"Scotty" was every inch a lobbyist for the privileged. In his hotel suite the drinks were plentiful and free and the company jolly and easygoing. His special legislator friends could charge such items as meals and taxis to Scotty's account. A swaggering, booming type, he loved to display his ownership of legislators. He frequently stalked through hotel lobbies with a pack of legislators trotting at his heels.

When Governors urged strip-mining legislation, Scotty went into action, always with success. Remarkably, he didn't function quietly, as do most lobbyists. He frequently got into brawls, such as the night he thought he could trap a critical newspaper reporter. Scotty attempted to photograph the reporter and a girl friend in the bar of a hotel.

On another occasion Scotty's activities attracted so much notoriety that the other lobbyists became alarmed. They held a meeting and told him to tone down.

174

It was thought Scotty's reign had come to an end in 1949. When the Legislature convened, he appeared in Columbus as usual. But within a few weeks he reportedly was dropped by his employers.

It was just a play, it seems. Scotty went into seclusion, but he emerged in the closing days of the session—which had dared to create a strip-mining commission, at Lausche's request—to scuttle two of Governor Lausche's appointees to that commission: one a crusading editor for strip-mining control, and the other an operator who advocated regulation.

A number of lobbyists swing more weight than legislators themselves.

A case in point is Isidore Topper. "Top" was one of the ablest men ever to serve in the Attorney General's office. That's why the liquor interests hired him as their Columbus lobbyist.

With municipalities clamoring for more funds, Governor Lausche asked the 1949 Legislature to boost liquor licenses fifty per cent to provide $3,500,000 additional revenue. He was elected on a "no new taxes" pledge, but stretched his conscience to propose this relief for the hard-pressed cities.

The liquor dealers screamed: "Why tax us? Put it on someone else."

Normally Lausche should have been able to put the tax over, as the Democratic Party controlled both branches of the Legislature. But Topper got busy. As a result, when the Democratic leaders called up the measure in the Senate, they didn't know where they stood. The Republicans were solidly against the bill for partisan reasons. Four Democrats bolted to them and that ended the bill. To prevent a direct rebuff to Lausche, Democratic leaders hastily withdrew the measure and sent it back to committee—where it died.

Scores of municipal officials had demanded the legislation, but one man, Liquor Lobbyist Topper, blocked them.

He showed himself more powerful than the Governor of the State of Ohio.

Then there is George Sheridan. For years he has represented retail merchants around the Legislature. Sheridan wields great influence among not only the lawmakers, but also with the other lobbyists. Sheridan doesn't strut, boast, or display his power. But the Legislature seldom does anything the retail merchants disapprove of.

The sales tax is Sheridan's specialty.

The tax is collected by the merchants. Ohio is the only State that employs the coupon system. The consumer paying a sales tax gets a coupon in return. When the merchant obtains these coupons, he actually is paying the tax in advance. For this the State gives him a three per cent discount on the face value of the coupons. Thus, a merchant doing a million dollars' worth of business collects $30,000 in sales taxes. For doing this he receives $900 in discount from the State.

With sales-tax returns soaring and the State surplus piling up, insistent demand has arisen for a reduction in the levy. Governors oppose this because of the deep cut it would mean in State income. The retail merchants also oppose it because they figure that if the State's income diminishes, a gross sales tax might be imposed on them. Sheridan's influence has kept the sales tax and the collection system securely in status quo.

Ohio's sales tax was the brain-child of a utility lobbyist. The late Harry Wilson, lobbyist for the Cleveland Electric Illuminating Co., is credited with planting the idea with Governor George White. Wilson had seen the tax operate in the West and had observed how easily it raised huge sums painlessly. Also, with the State casting about anxiously for new sources of revenue during the depression period, Wilson wanted to save his utility employers from further taxation.

He was an intimate of Martin Davey in the early days of

his administration. But they split, and Wilson showed the Governor just how much power he had over the Legislature.

Davey was a consummate egotist. He had taken a tree surgery idea his father hatched, and by pure salesmanship turned it into a three-million-dollar-a-year business. He made Joyce Kilmer's poem "Trees" the theme song of his radio program, and the official State song while he was in office.

After Davey and Wilson split, the lobbyist organized a group of Democratic Senators into what he called the "Hatchet Men," and they proceeded to ax the Governor and his program at every turn.

This precipitated a bitter feud, and out of that grew an investigation into a trucking contract to haul State liquor. The contract went to friends of the Governor, although they owned no trucks. Also aired were alleged kickbacks on a road-paving substance called "hot mix." The fierce internecine strife wrecked Davey and the Democratic Party for years.

That paved the way for "Honest John" Bricker. Had it not been for the bitter feuding of the Democrats, Bricker would never have been Governor, had the chance to make a bid for the presidential nomination, received the nomination for the vice-presidency, nor be in the United States Senate today.

Ohio has given seven Presidents to the nation, all Republicans.

Every four years the State gets "that way." Already, in preparation for 1952, Ohio has a budding Democratic aspirant in Governor Frank John Lausche.

Lausche is a strange combination of actor and politician, of conservatism and liberalism.

One of the greatest personalities ever to tread Ohio's political boards, he has the happy faculty of arousing antagonisms among politicos while retaining a powerful hold on the voters. He detests political bosses and loves to rail at them in public. Yet at the same time, he assiduously courts the

177

rural politicians who are far more powerful in their baili-
wicks than the city bosses.

Lausche is emotional. Many of his acts are dictated by
emotion. He has been known to worry for weeks after an
outburst of emotionalism; yet most of the time his instincts
are right and he lands with his feet on the ground.

An example was President Truman's 1948 campaign in
Ohio.

As a Democrat, Lausche likes to be known as an "independent" without strong party ties. When the President
toured Ohio, Lausche, as the State's Democratic standard-
bearer, was with him. From Cincinnati to Dayton and on to
Akron they traveled together, with the President enthusiastically boosting Lausche. But Lausche maintained a deep
silence so far as the President was concerned.

But at Akron, before a packed audience, Lausche was carried away. He burst out with a fulsome endorsement of the
President. It would not have been newsworthy except for
the fact that Lausche had said practically nothing about
Truman up to then and, it was recalled, had also said very
little for Franklin Roosevelt in 1944.

The endorsement unloosed a storm. Republican newspapers denounced Lausche and proclaimed he had pulled a
prime blunder. The GOP machine worked overtime flooding
the State with copies of Lausche's words. A number of political writers told Lausche privately he had stubbed his toe.
The few who told him his endorsement would help, rather
than hurt, were derisively pooh-poohed.

Lausche himself was uneasy. He avoided the Truman train
the next time the President came into the State. Lausche did
appear with Truman at Cleveland for the final rally, but
didn't let himself go as he had at Akron.

But the day after election, Lausche conceded that his

178

emotional instinct had been right. He had carried the State by more than 100,000.

Personally, Lausche is ingratiating and charming. But, somehow, he seems unable to get along with legislative bodies and organized groups, particularly unions. As Mayor of Cleveland he was constantly at odds with the City Council which the Democrats controlled. He also was in constant conflict with labor leaders. They have opposed him in all his gubernatorial contests, but he has won twice nevertheless.

During his first term, he had a Republican Legislature. He wooed the GOP leaders, consulting them more frequently than he did the Democrats. He developed a technique, however, of permitting his opinions on pending legislation to become known through statements to the newspapers rather than by messages to the Assembly. This infuriated the Republicans.

When he returned to the Governor's office, after a two-year lapse, Lausche was as surprised as the Democrats to discover that the party controlled the Legislature.

Though he disclaims being a politician, Lausche is one of the best in the business. When he won the gubernatorial nomination in 1948, over the opposition of practically every Democratic leader, he took over the party without firing a shot. He didn't say so publicly, but he let it be known he wanted Eugene H. Hanhart, New Philadelphia insurance man known familiarly as "Cheese," to be State Chairman. Hanhart got it, and Lausche backers took every stronghold in the State Democratic Committee, although Lausche would not admit he had anything to do with this seizure.

When the Democratic Legislature convened, Lausche professed a "hands off" policy on organization. But on the eve of the caucuses, it was apparent that Hanhart was in the thick of it and that he was acting for the Governor.

In the House, the contest for Speaker was between John

Cantwell, a stodgy, sincere, but mediocre man who had served as Leader of the insignificant Democratic minority in the previous Assembly, and James M. Carney, young Cleveland attorney and war veteran with a brilliant record. It was recognized that the man with Lausche's support would win.

Hours before the balloting, Carney called on Hanhart and was told he didn't fit into their program. Carney had supported Ray T. Miller, former Cleveland Mayor and long-time foe of Lausche, in the primary. So he was punished by being sidetracked for Speaker. However, before the 1949 session, longest in the State's history, ended in late July, Lausche was consulting Carney as much as anyone else in the Assembly, and it was Carney who carried the ball for much of the Governor's taxation program.

In the Senate, the fight for Democratic Leader was between Howard M. Metzenbaum, young Clevelander with several terms in the Assembly behind him; William M. Boyd, another Clevelander; and Clingan Jackson, Youngstown political writer.

The day before the caucus, word went out from Hanhart that he was supporting Metzenbaum. Then, mysteriously, a few hours before the meeting, Metzenbaum was dropped. Hanhart's support was shifted to an entirely new candidate, Miss Margaret A. Mahoney, Cleveland attorney. Miss Mahoney became the first woman Senate Leader in Ohio history.

It was openly stated that Metzenbaum was ditched on orders from Lausche, after business interests protested that Metzenbaum was "too liberal." But, although he didn't get the job, he was the real Senate Leader. Miss Mahoney leaned heavily on him.

Having picked the legislative leaders, Lausche then let them just drift along, floundering, pulling boners, mainly through inexperience, and making slow headway.

180

Lausche's presidential yearning is unmistakable, although he would be the last to admit it. Whether he can make the grade is doubtful. He has a curious political philosophy. It can be summed up as follows: Reward your enemies and forget your friends.

Lausche rarely has appointed a friend to office. On the whole, the men who went into his cabinet when he was Mayor of Cleveland had not been associated with him previously. The same has been generally true of those he has named to State posts.

Lausche's hostile attitude toward politicians is strange in view of his own career. He came into poltitics as a professional, first running as an organization candidate for the Legislature. Later, he became a Democratic ward leader in his home neighborhood, the most heavily Democratic section in the city. In his first mayoralty campaign, he had the united support of the Democratic organization and of organized labor.

But of the men who stumped nightly with him, not one got an office.

Fortune smiled on Lausche then, as it generally has. He picked as his law director a young lawyer whose campaign role, if any, had been minor, but who soon proved to be the mainstay of Lausche's administration. This young attorney was Thomas A. Burke, the present able and liberal Mayor of Cleveland.

When Lausche first became Governor in 1945, he named two of his primary opponents to cabinet posts. They were Frazier Reams, soft-spoken, Tennessee-born Toledo lawyer, who as Prosecutor had put nearly every crook in Lucas County in jail, and James W. Huffman, son-in-law of Vic Donahey, who later succeeded to Vic's seat in the Senate.

None of Lausche's cabinet had been close to him, either politically or personally.

Similarly, practically the same thing occurred when he returned to Columbus in 1949. Several members of his old cabinet were back, but all the others were new. Significantly, Reams did not return. Sharp feeling had developed between him and the Governor, and Reams was dropped.

Lausche frequently acts on impulse. As Mayor of Cleveland, he appointed a welfare director whom he had met only forty-eight hours before. Within a month, Lausche knew he had made a mistake. In much the same way he named a highway chief while Governor.

Shortly before Lausche's inauguration, he received a call from Theodore J. Kauer, one-time Ohio highway departmental engineer. Kauer applied for the job as director. Lausche invited him to Cleveland, was impressed, and named him.

When Lausche returned to Columbus in 1949, he foresaw an era of declining revenues. He shouted "wolf" so much about this that legislators accused him of putting on an act But the scoffing ended abruptly when an official survey disclosed the State running nearly a million dollars a month in the red.

Lausche had pledged no new taxes, and he had difficulty keeping the Democratic Legislature in line on this.

His jousts with labor have been due chiefly to his dislike of "pressure." That sort of thing always riles him from any source. It goes against his deep sense of personal independence. The Building Trades openly fought him in 1948. The CIO refused to back either Lausche or his opponent. But all the labor factions were united on Truman.

Yet, despite the stand of the labor leaders, Lausche carried the great industrial centers, Cleveland, Youngstown, Akron, Canton, and Toledo, and came within a few hundred votes of winning Cincinnati.

As titular Democratic leader of Ohio, Lausche has been sound in his choice of a State chairman. Eugene H. Hanhart

182

is personable, smart, young, and experienced. He has functioned quietly and efficiently. Wisely, he has not tried to toss out the professionals. Hanhart is one himself. He didn't try to dislodge National Committeeman Albert A. Horstman, easygoing, wealthy Dayton printer who financed the party during its lean years.

(Horstman paid the bill for an Ohio float in the Truman inaugural parade after everyone else backed out when it came to putting up cold cash.)

Hanhart runs the party the way Lausche wants it run. That means no levies on State workers, no kickbacks, no favorite contractors, no shakedowns. There have been times when Hanhart has had to scrape for postage money.

Lausche looks like a man with a date with destiny. But whether that destiny is the White House . . .

Ohio's gravest problem is home rule for municipalities.

It is a problem as old as the State. Ohio became a State largely because the people resented the crusty, dictatorial rule of Territorial Governor Arthur St. Clair. Sent out in 1787 to govern the vast Northwest Territory, he bitterly resisted efforts to achieve Statehood because it would mean the end of his job.

The first major battle for municipal home rule took place in 1889 under Democratic Governor James E. Campbell. He and another Democrat, James M. Cox, rank as Ohio's greatest chief executives.

Although a Democrat, Campbell actually owed his election to Mark Hanna. Hanna had decided that Republican Governor Joseph B. Foraker, seeking a third term, had been guilty of "treachery" and had to go.

The Democrats campaigned for home rule for cities and, with the Republicans split, carried the State. Campbell believed in keeping campaign pledges. He sent the Legislature a broad municipal program. But like Lausche, Campbell had trouble with his Democratic Legislature.

Home rule came to the fore again in 1902 when Hanna and Cleveland's great Mayor Tom Johnson locked horns in a gigantic struggle.

Johnson was licking Hanna politically in the city and making the master politican look silly on his own home grounds. Also, Johnson's ideas about three-cent carfare and three-cent electric light were "socialistic" in Hanna's eyes. As he couldn't beat Johnson at the polls, Hanna attacked him in the servile Legislature.

A special session was convened in 1902. In sweltering mid-summer heat, a new municipal code was made law. It wiped out the few puny reforms Campbell had been able to put through. The new Hanna code made mayors mere figure-heads, and set up city governments by boards. Aimed directly at Johnson, the code even barred mayors from taking part in discussions before city councils. Numerous other restrictions were placed on local rule.

But for all his power, Hanna met his match in Johnson.

Re-elected overwhelmingly in 1903, Johnson was able, with the aid of a friendly Council, largely to circumvent the code. Then he decided to run for Governor. He captured the Democratic nomination, and wrote a platform calling for municipal home rule, just taxation, initiative and referendum, city operation of public utilities, and public balloting on franchises.

Hanna was so enraged, and scared, that he took the stump bellowing, "Tom Johnson is a carpetbagger followed by a train of all the howling vagrants of Ohio with a crazy-quilt ticket and pretending to stand upon a Populistic, Socialistic, and Anarchistic platform."

Johnson lost for Governor. Hanna died the next year.

Although Johnson didn't live to see it, his ringing crusade

184

had not been in vain. In 1912 a constitutional convention met and drafted forty-two amendments to the State Constitution. Of these, the voters approved thirty-four.

Chief among them was a home-rule amendment, which progressives thought would end the pall of the Hanna heritage. This was a vain hope. Today, four decades later, the intent of the amendment has been largely wrecked by a conservative Supreme Court.

Commenting on this in the Cleveland *Press* in January, 1948, Julian Griffin wrote, "For fifteen years following the adoption of the amendment, the State courts rendered opinions generally favorable to home rule. Then the judicial tide changed."

After the adoption of the amendment, the cities hurried to write home rule charters to set up the kind of governing machinery they wanted. Cleveland adopted the mayor-ward-council form; Dayton, the city manager-city commission.

Home rule opponents attacked the Cleveland charter first. They took the city into court. But Hanna's device of "government by injunction" no longer operated. The courts upheld Cleveland.

"The clear intent of the amendment," read a court decision, "was to confer on municipalities all the powers of local self-government which were not included in the limitations specified."

But by 1927, the Supreme Court had begun to whittle away at home rule. The great boom era was in full tide, everywhere Republicans were enthroned, and the stand-pat philosophy of Cal Coolidge held full sway. In that year, the Ohio Supreme Court took its first big whack at home rule. The blow came in a decision on an Akron ordinance fixing the rate of speed in a hospital zone lower than the State law specified. The Court pronounced the ordinance invalid. The issue involved was minor, but it was the opening wedge.

Soon home rule took another licking, a worse one. The Court declared that State budget laws prevailed over those of municipalities.

During the Hoover depression, Ohio adopted a constitutional amendment to permit counties to modernize their governments. The amendment passed so easily that its backers were startled—until they discovered the reason. There was no altruism in the support that put it over. The amendment abolished the constitutional limitations on the terms of county officials, sheriffs, treasurers, etc. These gentry and their courthouse rings turned out strongly for the amendment.

When Cuyahoga County, which includes Cleveland, sought to modernize its government, it got a crushing jolt. A commission had worked for months to draw up a plan. But the Old Guard Supreme Court again thundered no. In a highly legalistic decree, the tribunal not only scuttled the charter but, in effect, placed veto power over reorganization of county governments in the hands of the small, and hostile, communities.

Other similar reactionary decisions have still further bound the hands of the cities in running their own affairs. The Court has prohibited them from setting up educational requirements for police and firemen, from regulating local pension systems, from prescribing civil service rules.

The climax came in a decision that the City Manager of Cincinnati could not preside at a hearing on charges against a policeman, even though the city charter provided this.

Carl D. Friebolin, who as a legislator had been in the thick of the home rule struggle in the Cox era, sums up the situation as follows, "The way things stand now, the State says to the city, 'You are your own boss, subject to my control. Do anything you like, so long as you do exactly as I tell you to.'"

186

Ohio's Supreme Court is among the most antediluvian in the country.

It is headed by Carl V. Weygandt, an imposing Cleve-lander, who until a few years ago got his recreation by ref-ereeing football games. At sixty-one, he has been Chief Justice longer than any of his predecessors. Weygandt came up from the Common Pleas bench to which he was named by Governor Donahey. Weygandt had to wait six months before taking his first judicial job because he had not practiced law long enough to meet the statutory requirements. A Democrat, he sounds out public opinion, particularly rural, through appearances before church groups, luncheon clubs, and similar organizations. The torch of liberalism on the tribunal has been upheld shiningly for a decade by Justice Charles B. Zimmerman. A former Dayton lawyer, he looks like a Prussian general. He and Weygandt are the only Democrats on the tribunal.

Ultraconservatism is represented by two aged and often ailing justices. They are Edward S. Matthias, who always reminds the voters of his Spanish-American War record, and William S. Hart, who came to the Court late in life after years of scrambling to get there. In between is Justice Edward S. Turner, who thirty-five years ago, as a crusading prosecutor in Franklin County, put half a dozen legislators in jail for bribery.

The hope for a more liberal and vigorous Court, strangely, rests with two new and solid Republican justices.

James Garfield Stewart, as Mayor of Cincinnati, was one of the greatest vote-getters in the city's history. He defeated Tom Herbert for the Republican nomination for Governor in 1944 and in turn was licked by Lausche. Later (in 1947), Herbert, as Governor, appointed Stewart to the Supreme Court to keep him out of the 1948 race. Stewart is an able lawyer who made a fortune in private practice. He is highly

187

cultured, and is one of the best after-dinner speakers in the State.

In his two years on the bench, he has been generally on the liberal side.

The other bright hope on the Court is its newest and youngest member—a Taft. Kingsley Arter Taft, still under fifty, a veteran of World War II, won his toga in 1948, defeating Lausche's only appointee, stodgy, cautious, wealthy Robert Sohngen. Sohngen had been appointed to an interim vacancy created by the death of a member of the Court. Under Ohio law he had to stand for election to his post at the next balloting. Justice Taft is neither related to his namesake in the U. S. Senate, nor in accord with most of the latter's views.

Ohio needs urgently militant and broad-visioned leadership. It needs another Campbell, a Johnson, a Cox.

It needs men with courage, imagination, and faith in the people. The crippling heritage of Mark Hanna can be destroyed by a leader who will arouse the people to the evils of that heritage. It cannot be done by little men interested only in gaining office.

But the prospects for a leader who will overhaul Ohio's oxcart government are not bright.

ILLINOIS ★ ★ ★

The "New Look"

DON E. CHAMBERLAIN

SOMETHING is happening in Illinois.

Just what it is or what it will accomplish remains to be seen. But the old-line political leaders are viewing it with uneasy concern, while the voters are watching it with considerably more interest than they usually evince in State affairs.

The optimistic are predicting the end of boss rule, a festering sore that has plagued Illinois for years. The cynics say the change is just another passing fancy—in a few years everything will revert to the old order, with the bright gleam of the new, shining armor tarnished and battered in the free-for-all battle of spoils politics.

Meanwhile, at long last, there is a "new look" to government in Illinois. It came about as a result of two great election upheavals. The first, in 1947, installed Martin Kennelly, wealthy businessman and Red Cross fund-raiser, as Democratic Mayor of Chicago. The second, a year later, sent Adlai

★

DON E. CHAMBERLAIN is a veteran newsman. He was an ace war correspondent of the United Press in World War I, and has served in UP bureaus in Washington, New York, and Chicago. He headed the State bureau in Springfield for sixteen years and was on the editorial staff of the Chicago *Tribune* for seven years. He toured the U.S. in 1919 with the late King Albert of Belgium, who decorated him as chevalier of the Order of Leopold.

E. Stevenson, lawyer, United Nations delegate, and former assistant to the Secretary of the Navy and the Secretary of State, to Springfield as Governor, and Paul H. Douglas, professor of economics, Marine hero, and Chicago alderman, to Washington as United States Senator.

The ballot-box triumphs of these men have brought about a condition where Chicago has a Mayor and Illinois a Governor who are far more concerned about giving honest, efficient, and enlightened government than they are about political pap and boodle. It is a long time since the State has seen anything like that.

In 1932, Judge Henry Horner was elected Governor in a long-overdue revolt against the Republican machine headed by Governor Len Small. But with Horner's death in his second term, the Democrats rushed off in all directions. In 1940 Dwight H. Green, a prosecutor of Al Capone and the new fair-haired boy of the GOP, was swept into office on the slogan "Beat the machine—Go with Green." The machine was the Kelly-Nash alliance, headed by Mayor Edward J. Kelly of Chicago and the late Patrick A. Nash, Cook County Democratic Chairman and National Committeeman.

Eight years later, Green's machine, reeking with sordid scandals, mine disaster, padded payrolls, and pay-offs, was booted out by Stevenson with the largest plurality ever scored by a gubernatorial candidate.

The old-line politicos of Cook County still don't know what to make of Kennelly. His impregnable honesty and immovable decency baffle them. They can't buy him, scare him, or get rid of him. Similarly, they speak of Stevenson as a "queer bird" because of his bland insistence on carrying out campaign pledges.

Depending on where you are, Illinois is known by various names. On the Atlantic seaboard it is called "the flatlands."

190

Britons call it "the American midlands." On the Pacific Coast, the State is "in the East."

In his book, *State Names, Flags, Seals, Songs, Birds, Flowers, and Other Symbols,* George Earlie Shankle designates Illinois as "The Prairie State because so much of its area is composed of prairie lands." But he adds that "Sucker State" is also widely used.

One version of the origin of this nickname centers around the Galena lead mines in 1822. An old miner is credited with saying about his peripatetic fellow workers, "They put me in mind of suckers. They go up the river in the spring, spawn, and all turn down ag'in in the fall."

Malcolm Townsend has another version. He attributes the nickname to the fact that "in many places in the early days the western prairies were filled with crawfish holes out of which the early travelers by means of long reeds would suck up the pure water from beneath. When a traveler would find one of the crawfish holes, he would call out 'A sucker! A sucker!' meaning thereby a reed; and in this way the name probably originated."

The name "Prairie State" came into vogue later. Illinoisans prefer it because of its association with Abraham Lincoln, who came to the Illinois prairie lands in 1830.

Since the rise of university football, still another nickname has come into vogue, particularly on sports pages. This is "Illini," used to denote the University of Illinois. The term derives from a tribe of Indians. They called themselves "Illini" to distinguish themselves from the Iroquois, whom they considered savages.

But whatever differences may exist on its nickname, Illinois is officially on record about its language. That is not "English." By a statutory edict, the official language of the State is "American." A law passed by the 1923 Legislature

191

formally proclaimed that thereafter "American," and not "English," was the language of Illinois.

The schools disregard this technical distinction. Textbooks continue to use the term "English." Few people are even aware the law exists. But both educators and politicians regard changing it as unwise, on the sound theory that it is best to let sleeping dogs lie.

The statute is a product of the fantastic era when the late William Hale Thompson was the "Cowboy" Mayor of Chicago. His passionate ambition was to "bust King George on the snoot." The feeling found sufficient backing in the Legislature to put through the law.

Illinois is actually two states in one.

In the north is giant Chicago, surrounded by the sprawling region the Chicago *Tribune* calls "Chicago-land." Illinois has one hundred and two counties, but more than one-half the State's population is in Cook County (Chicago). Those one hundred and one other counties, "downstate," constitute an entirely different domain. Its big centers are Peoria, famed for its whisky distilleries, Rockford, East St. Louis, and Springfield, the State capital.

These two states in one have divergent, and often bitterly hostile, economic, social, and political views and interests. In the Legislature, the ever-present and overshadowing struggle is between Chicago and downstate, which always has control of the lawmaking body.

Cook County has only fifty-seven seats in the House of Representatives as compared to ninety-six by downstate. Similarly, in the Senate, Cook County has nineteen Senators as against thirty-two downstate. Repeated efforts to reapportion the Legislature have always ended in either outright defeat or in a commission to investigate.

Big-business fears of reapportionment and a State income

192

tax have blocked modernization of Illinois' Constitution for decades.

While the Legislature usually grants Chicago and Cook County requests, they are still a long way from home rule. Although the city and county have a combined population greater than that of downstate, they have to come hat-in-hand to the rural-controlled Legislature for permission to conduct their household affairs.

They must not only obtain approval on the taxes they levy, but also on such minor matters as pensions for policemen and firemen.

State government in Illinois is completely dominated by the minority downstate. Chicago's only opportunity to make itself felt is in general elections. Since 1933, the Governor has been a Chicagoan (an exception was for a period of one hundred days in the latter part of 1940 when Lieutenant Governor John H. Stelle of McLeansboro, in southern Illinois, succeeded to the governorship on the death of Governor Horner); the other State officers are divided between the city and downstate.

But while able to elect Governors, Chicago is blocked by law from equitable representation in the Legislature. So intense is this Chicago-versus-downstate struggle that it led to a bill several years ago to divide Illinois into two states. Nothing came of the measure.

Cook County and Chicago are the biggest contributors to the State treasury. Their returns greatly exceed the combined total of downstate's hundred and one counties. More than half the gasoline tax comes from Chicago. Yet, under the division of this revenue, the metropolitan area receives considerably less than half for highway purposes. The same disproportionate situation exists on other State taxes, notably the sales tax.

A glaring instance of downstate domination in still another key sphere is the State Supreme Court. Six of the seven justices are downstaters, yet more than half of the cases before the tribunal come from Chicago and Cook County. Again, Chicago is now conducting an experiment in municipal ownership. It has its own transportation system. But even here, the State has a finger in the pie.

The Legislature passed a law in 1945 creating the Chicago Metropolitan Transit Authority, with power to issue bonds to take over the city's bankrupt and antiquated transportation lines. But in doing this, the Legislature also specified that only three of the five members of the Authority could be named by the Mayor of Chicago. The other two are appointed by the Governor.

Illinois is regarded as a normally Republican State, because of the usual heavy conservative vote of rural downstate. But Illinois has been so doubtful in recent years as to make it a pivotal State, particularly in national elections. In the last five presidential elections, the Democrats have carried the State every time.

Greatest vote ever given a candidate in Illinois was Roosevelt's in 1936—2,282,999.

Early in 1948 it seemed as if the State was finally headed back into the GOP column. Truman's chances appeared so hopeless that some Illinois Democratic leaders started looking for another candidate. Chief among them was Jacob M. (Jack) Arvey, head of the Chicago organization. He hit on General Eisenhower to save the State and local tickets. Paul Douglas, running for United States Senator, also went out on a limb against Truman.

Many of the leaders were as pessimistic about the local slate as they were about the national standard-bearer. The Republicans, headed by Governor Green, seeking a third term, and Senator C. Wayland Brooks, seemed unbeatable. The party had unlimited funds and patronage. Also, the

194

GOP held every State office but one—Secretary of State Edward J. Barrett—and the State payroll was at an all-time high, more than 35,000.

It looked like a Republican cinch and some of the Democrats mentioned as possible candidates acted that way. A strong move developed to draft Barrett, but he wasn't having any. He was content to stick to his own certain office. The bosses didn't like the outspoken liberalism of Paul Douglas, so Stevenson, an unknown, was finally picked for Governor. Douglas, who really wanted that nomination, bowed and consented to run for the Senate.

The slate was unopposed in the primary except for the attorney generalship. As though to show the weakness or lack of enthusiasm of the Democratic organization, Ivan Elliott, downstate country lawyer, the official choice, barely nosed out Joseph Burke, Chicago attorney. The electorate was so listless that Elliott, who campaigned, beat Burke, who didn't make a speech, by only 14,965 votes.

But many surprises were to occur between April and November. Stevenson, the socialite Princeton graduate and "striped pants diplomat," as Green, to his regret, called him, and Douglas, the University of Chicago economics professor, author of learned tomes and Marine combat hero, proved to be the most dynamic campaigners Illinois has ever seen.

Green's derisive reference to Stevenson, in an early campaign speech, backfired fast. The Chicago *Daily News* was unable to find a picture of Stevenson in striped pants, but it did uncover one of Green wearing them. Stevenson promptly announced he would be glad to wear striped pants if Green would lend him a pair.

Stevenson toured the State from stem to stern, often making as many as twelve speeches a day. Aided by three crack newsmen—James W. Mulroy, former managing editor of Marshall Field's Chicago *Sun,* who as a star reporter won a Pulitzer prize for breaking the famous Leopold-Loeb murder case, William I. Flanagan, formerly of the United Press and former city editor of the *Sun,* and Frank Millhouse, publicity director of the Democratic State Committee—Stevenson turned a searing beam on Green's administration. The results were devastating.

Douglas started campaigning before the primary and continued right down to election day. He made hundreds of speeches, many from the top of the jeep that jolted him thousands of miles through every county.

Illinois was astounded the morning after election to find the impossible had happened. The entire Democratic ticket had won. Truman, widely predicted as certain to lose Illinois by hundreds of thousands, slipped through. Stevenson scored the most impressive victory in the State's history, winning by 572,067. Douglas was not far behind. He retired the ineffable "Curly" Brooks by 407,728.

How did this miracle come about? What happened between April and November that turned an apparent Republican landslide into a rout?

A number of factors were responsible. High on the list is the immensely attractive personality of Adlai E. Stevenson. After eight battered years in office, the Green administration was highly vulnerable. But vulnerability does not necessarily mean defeat. To bring that about requires a candidate with the ability to dramatize the opposition's vulnerability, to catch the imagination of the independent voter, and to capitalize on the dissatisfaction and disgruntlement within the incumbent administration. The Democrats, in nominating Stevenson, had, to their own surprise, chosen just that kind of personality.

Also playing a decisive role in the GOP debacle were a long succession of scandals, the Centralia mine disaster, gambling, chiseling, and election-petition forgeries.

196

No study of Illinois State government would be complete without reference to the Centralia tragedy, where one hundred and eleven miners lost their lives after appealing vainly to Green to do something about the dangerous mine in which they were working.

The disaster occurred during the Chicago mayoralty campaign. The Green machine, seeking to take over control of the metropolis, had arrogantly served notice on the voters that if they wanted State aid to bolster weakened finances, they would have to elect GOP candidate Russell Root—"or else." Also, Green's machine was charged with "putting the bite" on coal-mine operators for heavy campaign contributions. Obviously, the pay-off for these donations would be indifferent enforcement of the mine safety laws. The contributions were collected by mine inspectors and other State employees.

The shocking Centralia disaster knocked Green's attempt to make himself master of Chicago into the ash can.

Robert Medill, former coal operator who headed the Department of Mines, was indicted on charges of failing to enforce the mine safety code. The charge was only a misdemeanor, and an indignant court threw it out in disgust. Said the court, "If these men are guilty in connection with this terrible disaster the charge should be involuntary manslaughter, at least."

A legislative commission then investigated and severely condemned Green's administration. The report declared the mine had been allowed to operate "under such hazardous conditions that even a common layman could see that a catastrophe could happen." The commission strongly recommended tightening of the civil service laws so that mine inspectors would be free of political interference.

Another monkey wrench that hit Green's machine was the slaying of Bernie Shelton, one of the notorious Shelton brothers. Gang murders are no novelty in Illinois, but the shooting of Bernie in a gambling war in Peoria, where gambling had been a source of city revenue for years, aroused a storm of outcries.

This indignation intensified when other gambling killings followed in Springfield and elsewhere. The crusading St. Louis *Post-Dispatch* began digging into the foul mess. The paper's ace investigator, ex-Marine Ted Link, pried open the lid in Peoria and found plenty of scandal and corruption.

The frightened and crude local officials retaliated by indicting Link on the charge of "intimidating" a punchboard peddler. The peddler had disclosed that Shelton was killed because he had made a recording of a bribe offer by an intimate of the State's Attorney.

The *Post-Dispatch* was undeterred. It pressed its cleanup drive with added vigor. In full-page advertisements in Illinois newspapers, the *P-D* charged Link's indictment was "an irresponsible act inspired by desperate men." Also, that the grand jury that did the indicting was controlled by aides of Republican Attorney General George F. Barrett, "whose pay roll has included collectors of graft." The *P-D* further asserted that it had uncovered evidence that gamblers in six downstate counties had been "shaken down" for $100,000 for Green's campaign in 1944, and that collectors were again making the rounds for Green's third-term bid. In return for contributions, the gamblers were being promised protection from interference by both local and State law-enforcement officers.

The barrage of scandals and exposures had profound effect on the November balloting. Illustrative was Peoria County. Usually strongly Republican, the County went overwhelmingly for the Democratic candidate for attorney general, and gave substantial pluralities to Stevenson and Secretary of State Barrett.

Three months later, the phony case against Link was dismissed, on the motion of the new Democratic State's Attorney. The *Illinois State Register* of Springfield termed the dismissal "a vindication of common decency." Another aftermath was the surprise defeat in 1949 of Peoria's Republican Mayor Carl O. Triebel by a political unknown, Democrat Joe Malone, a printer.

The whir of the slot machine is still heard in Illinois, but it is not so noisy as it used to be. Even the mild nickel bingo game has been suppressed in some areas, and Springfield, long known as an "open" town, has been shut down tighter than a drum.

Another factor that contributed importantly to the collapse of Green's machine was a report by a committee of the 1947 Legislature on State welfare institutions, hospitals, and insane asylums. As the Legislature was Republican-controlled, the committee was GOP-ruled.

But the conditions it uncovered were so appalling that even a Republican committee could not justify or excuse them. Overcrowding and lack of personnel were to be expected, but not cheating and graft in the purchase of food and other supplies, at the expense of the aged and sick.

These and numerous other outrages, such as the Chicago *Daily News'* exposure of wholesale forgeries in the nominating petitions of the Republican candidate for Treasurer, were pounded home by Stevenson. The GOP repeated its 1946 tactics. The party rarely mentioned Illinois affairs, but noisily assailed President Truman, the late FDR, the no-longer-existent OPA, and other distant subjects. Its only answer to Stevenson's blasts and the newspaper exposés was to cry, "Smear!" Coming from these bedraggled sources, the cry had an obvious hollow ring.

Particularly, as the Republicans were rent with internal dissension and were smearing one another with gusto, Green, who had denounced FDR for seeking a third term, came in for strong blasts for seeking a third term himself. Similarly, there was much resentment at increased local taxes and Green's bumbling attempts to land the 1948 vice-presidential nomination. Also, a number of party leaders were furious at the peculiar evaporation of Green's opposition. Two candidates filed against him. They were Lieutenant Governor Hugh W. Cross, and former Republican State Treasurer Warren Wright (not to be confused with the Warren Wright of baking powder and horse-racing fame). But both withdrew. Cross quit on the patently lame ground that promised support had failed to materialize. Immediately thereafter Wright dropped out on a specious excuse: that Green had promised to support a veterans' program, in the interest of which Wright had entered the race.

Stevenson, as Governor, has been fairly nonpartisan in his appointments. On occasion he has named Republicans to key positions, in the face of strenuous protests from hard-boiled leaders of his party. Labeled a "reformer," he readily admits it, if by "reform" is meant "a restoration of honesty and integrity in Illinois."

In grappling with his job, Stevenson's droll sense of humor has stood him in good stead. An instance was his veto of a "cat" bill. As a result of a supercharged campaign, a lot of heat had been generated for the measure. It required that cats be leashed when outside the premises of their owners. Stevenson vetoed the legislation with these remarks:

"As is often the case, this bill which was fraught with so much human interest, attracted far more attention than an important measure like constitutional reform. People wrote to me all the way from Maine to Texas [but] I felt obliged to veto it because it is in the nature of cats to do a certain amount of unescorted roaming. . . ."

200

Similarly, he ribbed himself during a discussion of the State budget. Referring to himself as a frugal man, Stevenson added, "That may account for the letters I have been getting from friends who have seen me pinch pennies and can't understand why, after criticizing the past administration for extravagance and waste, I propose to spend more in the next two years."

Many stories are told of Stevenson's frugality. One is that he would take a streetcar to campaign meetings rather than hire a taxi; another, that he will walk three blocks to take a bus to a railroad station rather than call a cab.

Stevenson took office committed to a definite program. This included long-overdue modernization of the Constitution, a fair employment practices law, strengthening of civil service and mine safety regulations, cleanup of the State police, increased aid to schools, consolidation of welfare activities, and improved conditions in State institutions. But in pressing execution of this program, Stevenson was faced with a divided Legislature. The Democrats controlled the House, 81 to 72, but the Senate remained Republican, 32 to 18, with one seat vacant because of death of a Republican Senator. Despite this situation, he launched a determined drive to enact his pledges.

Stevenson had surrounded himself **with** a group of able lieutenants. Some of these "brain-trusters" were little known as far as the public is concerned. Others, like Mulroy, Flanagan, and Richard J. Daley, former Democratic leader in the State Senate, were more to the fore. Other important members of this inner group were Frank Annunzio, CIO leader, State Welfare Director Fred K. Hoehler, State Finance Director George W. Mitchell, and administrative assistants Lawrence Irvin, Walter V. Schaefer, James Edward Day, and Louis Kohn.

Mulroy is Stevenson's closest adviser. Graduate of the

University of Chicago and a veteran of the onetime famed
New York *World*, Mulroy is tall, genial, and good looking.
He is very popular with newsmen and politicians because of
his forthrightness and fair dealing. When he talks it is for
the record, or he doesn't talk at all. As the legislators came
to know him, they liked him for the friendly but firm way
he stood up to them and talked back to them.

Flanagan is in charge of the Governor's press relations.
An experienced Springfield and Chicago reporter, he knows
his way around in politics. One of Flanagan's first acts was
to houseclean an army of Green press agents he found when
he took over. He retained several career men and after re-
vitalizing the staff organized it along the lines of the city
room of a newspaper. Every man reports each morning to
Flanagan, who as "city editor" keeps close to Stevenson and
makes a good team with Mulroy. Mulroy and Flanagan usually are to be found wherever Stevenson is.

When Daley was leading the Democratic minority in the
State Senate, he was known as a "good" legislator. That
means he was considered an "honest" man despite his prominence in the Chicago Democratic organization. In 1946 he
ran for sheriff of Cook County but lost in the Republican
landslide. He was brought into Stevenson's cabinet because
of his great legislative knowledge and his integrity.

Annunzio and the CIO backed Stevenson while the Illinois State Federation of Labor, through its executive board,
endorsed Green. This stand was directly counter to that of
the national AFL League for Political Action, which vigorously opposed Green. Later it was disclosed that many of
the State leaders were on Green's State payroll. Despite this
and their opposition to Stevenson, the AFL opposed his appointment of Annunzio. Subsequently, Stevenson brought
another laborite to his staff, Fern Rauch, a top AFL leader
who accepted the appointment over the squawks of other AFL

chiefs. Annunzio is a shrewd, liberal labor politician and is the Governor's closest adviser in this field.

Hoehler gave up the $25,000-a-year job as head of the Chicago Community Fund to take the $8,000 post as State Welfare Director. He did this at Stevenson's appeal for aid to clean up the odious conditions in the State mental hospitals and other institutions. During the war Hoehler was a Major General in charge of relief and rehabilitation work under Eisenhower.

Mitchell was an official of the Federal Reserve Bank of Chicago when Stevenson drafted him as State Finance Director. Former president of the National Tax Association, author of numerous articles on public expenditures and taxation, Mitchell is somewhat academic and serious. At first the legislators and politicians were amused by this, but they got over it quickly as he gained their respect by his detailed knowledge of State finances.

Irvin, Schaefer, Day, and Kohn were the four "passion-for-anonymity" brain-trusters. By preference they keep in the background. Because of their intellectual backgrounds and reputations they have ruffled the feelings of the legislators more than have the other brain-trusters. They were regarded as inexperienced upstarts and their ideas amateurish. But Stevenson stuck firmly by them. They were his friends and he knew better than anyone else that they had not come with him merely to get a job, prestige, or money. They had worked tirelessly to elect him and had offered their help in Springfield when he won. Kohn has already returned to his law practice and the others will go back to their private affairs unless Stevenson is able to persuade them to remain.

Kohn is an ex-GI who became a Stevenson zealot long before the latter was even suspected as being gubernatorial timber. Now that Stevenson is Governor, Kohn probably will not rest until Stevenson is in the White House. There are

203

many others in Illinois who feel the same way. Schaefer is on leave from Northwestern University, where he is a law professor. He is a former Assistant Corporation Counsel in Chicago and commands high fees when he occasionally acts as consultant in a case. Day, thirty-four, teams up with Schaefer as Stevenson's legal aces, particularly on legislative enactments.

Stevenson quickly ran into trouble from old-line legislators, who long have been accustomed to making deals for personal rewards in return for their votes. With them it is a strictly business proposition. "You scratch my back and I'll scratch yours."

But this time the boys did not hit pay dirt. Stevenson is not a stiff-necked prude. He simply refuses to play that kind of politics.

As a result, major features of his program were defeated. They included an FEPC and a constitutional convention to free the State and cities of reactionary and obstructive shackles.

It is significant that Stevenson suffered his first setback on the Constitution issue in the Democratic House. His proposal for submitting a constitutional convention to the people received ninety-seven votes, five short of the necessary two-thirds. The GOP, aided by a coterie of Tory Democrats, did the knifing.

The issue was still technically alive in the House when the Senate Republicans administered the final blow. They did this by the device of submitting a so-called "gateway" amendment to the voters. This diversionary substitute proposes liberalizing the cumbersome process for amending the Constitution.

Even if adopted, the scheme leaves the Constitution still untouched. But for the politicos, the stratagem had the advantage of giving scared legislators an "out" to excuse their rejection of Stevenson's demand for an outright overhaul of the Constitution.

Illinois functions under a Constitution that dates back to 1870. The voters approved a constitutional convention in 1918, but nothing came of it. The revised Constitution, submitted to popular ballot in 1922, was defeated overwhelmingly.

Only once since then has the question of another constitutional convention been before the electorate. In 1934 a proposal received 691,021 votes to 585,879 against. But this was equivalent to rejection, as on such issues a majority of the total vote cast, not on the measure itself but in the election, is required. "Gateway" amendments have been defeated five times, the first in 1892, the last in 1946.

Not only have all efforts to rewrite the obsolete Constitution been frustrated, but its provisions have been ignored. Under the Constitution, the Legislature is required to reapportion the State every ten years. The last time this was done was in 1901. An attempt was made in 1922 to reapportion the Senate. It was defeated five to one.

Spearhead of the opposition to revision of the Constitution is the Chicago *Tribune*. In season and out, it carries on a virulent attack. At the bottom of this unceasing vendetta is fear of a State income tax and, in the past few years, civil rights laws.

The *Tribune* and its autocratic owner, Colonel Robert McCormick, are mighty powers in Illinois Republican politics. McCormick's views and injunctions are just about law in the GOP. At the slightest alarm of an income tax, McCormick roars into assault. Stevenson repeatedly declared he was not seeking such a levy, but the *Tribune* was taking no chances. It screamed its opposition and the Republicans, as always, heeded the voice of their master. But McCormick isn't their only master.

Another is the powerful Illinois Manufacturers Association. It too is violently opposed to an income tax, as well as a long list of other enlightened measures, and fights any attempts to overhaul the eighty-year-old Constitution. Astoundingly, in this stand the Association has had the backing of the Illinois State Federation of Labor. Its contention is fear of tampering with wage, hour, and other labor laws.

Stevenson turned down a "deal" that might have put through his constitutional convention proposal. A group of Chicago legislators offered their support in exchange for his abandoning a series of antivice bills. The Chicago Crime Commission had proposed the legislation to strengthen enforcement powers against gangsters and other criminals. The Chicago members wanted to block the measures and offered to back a constitutional convention if Stevenson scuttled the crime bills. He indignantly rejected the scheme and the Chicago group voted against him to a man.

Another major Stevenson defeat was on a State FEPC. Again, the GOP-controlled Senate did the axing. It was the fourth attempt to pass such a law, but Stevenson was the first Illinois Governor to back it. The measure was approved by the House, 69 Democrats and 12 Republicans voting for it. But it lost in the Senate, 25 to 23. Sixteen Democrats and 7 Republicans voted for it; 24 Republicans and 1 Democrat against.

One of Stevenson's first steps, after taking office, was drastically to revise the mine laws and thoroughly reorganize the mine inspectors. Their selection was removed completely from political meddling.

Similarly, Stevenson forced the State Commerce Commission out of politics. He created a well-paid, five-man bipartisan agency and named an able Republican, Walter Fisher, as chairman. He transformed this key agency from a political football into a career body. Instead of being made up

206

of five one-party commissioners, Stevenson made it into a bi-partisan commission. In addition, Stevenson named an outstanding Republican as chairman.

While putting through this long-needed reform, Stevenson was unable to get legislative approval for another. This was to merge the Public Aid Commission, which handles distribution of hundreds of millions of dollars of State funds, with the State Welfare Department. With their eyes on patronage and other gravy-train grabs, the legislators balked at this reform. But Stevenson has not given up the fight and will renew his proposal at the next regular session. Strong public support is behind his merger plan. Meanwhile, considerable good has been accomplished in eliminating waste, and worse, in State aid and State institutions. Welfare Director Hoehler has done away with a number of patronage jobs and weeded out many incompetents, misfits, and time-servers.

Illinois also now has a new system of State buying which is expected to save millions of dollars. In its first three months of operation, the benefit to taxpayers came to $500,-000. Also, much "waste and water" has been squeezed out of highway contracts. In his first six months Stevenson saved more than $600,000 on this item alone.

As already pointed out, Stevenson failed in his determined effort to get legislative approval for an FEPC. But he did put through measures which may pave the way for voting on three constitutional amendments at one time instead of only one. He also obtained a big increase in State aid for common schools, boosting this to $100,000,000, an increase of more than fifty per cent.

Stevenson's chief legislative lieutenants in these and other bitter fights were Speaker Paul Powell and Floor Leader James J. Ryan in the House, and William J. Connors in the Senate. Powell and Ryan had the easier job in the Democratic House. Connors was up against rough going in the overwhelmingly Republican Senate. Spearheading the attack against Stevenson's liberal program were Republican Leader Reed Cutler, John W. Lewis, Jr., and Clinton Searle in the House, and President Pro Tem Wallace Thompson and Charles Carpentier in the Senate.

Powell hails from Southern Illinois. Aggressive, well-informed, and an able speaker, he worked well with Stevenson, although no "yes" man. He gave the Governor frank pictures of what could and could not be done. Ryan is mild mannered and quiet spoken normally, but he can be very forceful when the chips are down. He was the choice of Chicago Mayor Kennelly for Speaker until it was decided to give the place to Powell. The two men made an able and harmonious team.

Cutler, 350-pounder from Lewistown in the strip coal-mining area, was a constant thorn in the Democratic side. A whip-smart parliamentarian, he effectively filled the role of "needler" as House Republican Leader. On occasion he voted as an individual for parts of the administration program. Ably aiding Cutler in causing Stevenson trouble were Lewis, auctioneer and farmer with a foghorn voice, and Searle, Rock Island attorney. Through dilatory and obstructionist tactics, they filibustered and scuttled a number of Stevenson's projects.

In the Senate, Thompson and Carpentier conducted a running fight to slash the administration's budget. They ripped out considerable chunks, but were forced to accept some House restorations. Thompson led the attack at the start, but as the Democrats began to make inroads, Carpentier, a Moline movie-theater owner, took over most of the GOP pot-shotting.

As Democratic Senate Leader, Connors was very effective in coping with the heavy Republican majority. Tall and

208

husky, he is a power in Chicago politics, as committeeman of the 42nd ward which takes in the Gold Coast, the Chicago *Tribune,* and much of the North Side. Two aides are Senator A. L. Marovitz, protégé of Boss Jack Arvey who induced him to switch from the Republican to the Democratic Party, and Senator R. V. Libonati, Chicago attorney who has defended two hundred accused murderers without losing one to the electric chair.

Lobbying may not be as profitable in Springfield as it is reported to be in other capitals, but it is no less pervasive. Lobbyists of the Illinois Manufacturers Association, utilities, railroads, banks, and other special-interest groups wield powerful influence on the Legislature. They have practically a free hand.

In Illinois, lobbyists do not have to register. In fact, the statutes are so vague they don't even define a lobbyist. Virtually the only restraint is a rule barring lobbyists from the legislative corridors. But while numerous and pernicious, the lobbyists keep adroitly out of the public eye.

A spectacular exception to this rule is George Ziller, former labor leader who, legend avers, weighs more than five hundred pounds. He is so huge he is unable to get through the door of a railroad car and has to travel in a specially built automobile. He once was questioned about lobbying activities but the affair blew over. One accusation was that he shouted instructions to legislators from the galleries.

The Illinois press is predominantly Republican. The Chicago *Sun-Times* was the only paper in the city to back the entire Democratic ticket in 1948. Of the ninety downstate dailies, less than ten supported Truman and only a few more, Stevenson. The same proportion existed among the eight hundred weeklies.

An aftermath of the election was a joint exposé by the St.

Louis *Post-Dispatch* and the Chicago *Daily News* that more than fifty newspaper publishers and editors had been on the State payroll during the Green administration—some of them secretly—and had received hundreds of thousands of dollars. The exposé rocked the State press and brought a storm of nationwide censure.

But the newsmen weren't the only offenders. More probing uncovered a number of AFL business agents on Green's payroll. This probably explains, as already pointed out, why the Illinois AFL backed him when the national AFL Political League was clamoring for his defeat.

One result of this sordid affair is that a CIO leader heads the State's new Department of Labor. The CIO, as already pointed out, went down the line for Stevenson and the rest of the Democratic ticket.

Illinois courts are fairly free of scandal, except the municipal benches in Chicago. But the State's judicial system as a whole is still of "horse and buggy" vintage. The bar associations go through the motions of recommending candidates for the bench, but the politicians do the picking. Both Democratic and Republican candidates for the supreme and circuit courts are selected at party conventions, with the result that in Chicago the hand-picked slate of the dominant party carries the field. Downstate, voters have a somewhat bigger voice in this regard. Sharp contests for circuit judgeships are common. But the panoply of party politics blankets practically every court in the State.

Chicago and Cook County have not elected a Republican to the circuit or superior bench for more than twenty years. Some Republicans did win, but they had to run as Democrats. The Democrats allow the GOP to submit a few names for places on a so-called "coalition" judicial slate which appears on the ballot under the Democratic label. Thus the hand-picked Republicans have to run as Democrats.

Downstate there is less of this in the selection of circuit judges. All are nominated at party conventions by delegates made up mostly of attorneys and politicians. But in a number of sections the Chicago practice prevails, with the dominant party controlling the judicial slate. Republicans hold more than forty of the fifty-one downstate judgeships.

Despite the leading role politics plays in the selection of judges, a number of them, surprisingly, are able and reputable. Outstanding are Harold G. Ward, former Democratic Floor Leader of the State Senate, and Elmer J. Schnackenberg, former Republican Speaker of the Illinois House, who had to run as a Democrat to get his judgeship. Both have made distinguished records on the bench. So have Circuit Judges Julius H. Miner and Cornelius J. Harrington, and Superior Judge Edwin A. Robson. The trio sponsored long-needed laws correcting glaring divorce evils.

Two outstanding members of the Supreme Court are seventy-year-old Walter Gunn and Francis S. Wilson. Both have been on the tribunal many years and are noted for the independence and vigor of their judgments.

The "horse and buggy" aspect of Illinois' court system applies more to the Supreme Court than to the other benches. More than fifty per cent of the State's population is in Cook County and sixty-five per cent of the appeals originate there, yet it has only one seat on the tribunal as against six from downstate. Also, prior to 1934, Illinois courts operated under the common law in its purest form. More than any other state Illinois emulated the courts of England. But after the enactment of the Civil Practices Act, by the late Governor Horner who had many years of experience as a judge, the distinction between equity and common-law suits was abolished and Illinois for the first time was brought more in line with the progressive policies of other states which had developed code pleading as their practice. This elim-

211

inated delay, expense, and long-drawn-out useless litigation.

Illinois criminal trial procedure was the target of a stinging rebuke by the United States Supreme Court several years ago. The case involved an appeal by Tony Marrino on the ground that he had been tried and convicted without having counsel. He was tried in Rockford in 1925 and sentenced to life for an alleged holdup murder. The U.S. Supreme Court ordered the case retried on the grounds that Marrino had been forcibly extradited from another state, held incommunicado for months, denied an attorney and rushed through an "assembly line" trial, and that his plea of guilty had been obtained through an interpreter and that he was not aware of what was occurring.

The U.S. Supreme Court was scathing in its condemnation. It denounced Illinois justice as "absurdly blind" and sharply advised the State Supreme Court to modernize its archaic and rigid rules of review. Marrino was an eighteen-year-old immigrant when imprisoned; he is now a man in his forties. In 1946 the U.S. Supreme Court listed five hundred and twenty-eight petitions from prisoners who claimed they had not had fair trials in Illinois.

Cook County courts attract numerous railroad-accident suits because of a reputation for generous verdicts and also because of a provision in the federal law which allows a plaintiff to file suit in any court where the railroad operates. Chicago, being a great rail center, is headquarters for many carriers.

Chicago's municipal court system was established in 1906 as a "poor man's court." The forty-eight judges are all Democrats. They handle four hundred thousand cases a year, more than all the other Illinois courts combined. Under a new law the city now has Sunday and night courts to expedite action.

Recently there has been much outcry against these municipal courts. Charges have been made of bribery, corruption, and inefficiency. One prominent attorney asserted that many of the judges did little work and ignored assignments. Also, that political favoritism played a big role in decisions, and that the taking of bribes, or "tips," was common among court attachés.

Nominally, the Democratic political machinery in Illinois is headed by Edward J. Kelly, former Mayor of Chicago. He is serving his second term as National Committeeman, and still has a devoted following. He meets regularly with party leaders and stands high with the White House due to his adherence to Truman when Arvey and others tried to draft Eisenhower. But although "Big Ed" bears the title of National Committeeman, the real leader of the organization is Arvey. As chairman of the Cook County organization, he is the one the boys look to for instructions and favors. Arvey is the "Boss" insofar as Illinois Democrats have a boss these days.

Mayor Kennelly, Governor Stevenson, and Senator Paul Douglas have one major factor in common. They are so-called amateurs in politics—amateurs who basically do not believe in bosses and machines. They do not reject the role of party organization, but primarily they place their faith in the people. In Illinois this kind of thinking and leadership is resulting in better government and better politics on the part of the Democratic leaders.

There are no indications that the GOP has any intention of abandoning the "old look" as far as the State organization is concerned. A new chairman, Carlos W. Campbell of Springfield, was named, but he is a Green-Brooks follower and an undistinguished representative of the old order. One of Campbell's first moves was to cancel the traditional Republican Day at the 1949 Illinois State Fair, presumably because the administration is Democratic. Campbell has freshened up the GOP press staff by hiring a new press agent for a reported $10,000 a year. He is Charles Allison, former United Press man in Springfield. Allison served a hitch as secretary to former Senator Brooks.

Brooks and Green appear to be washed up politically, although nothing is certain in Illinois politics, particularly Republican. But the two lame ducks are in bad odor, and there are a number of more promising aspirants crowding for the top places on the party's slate. Chief among them is Senate Leader Thompson. His maneuvers on old-age pensions, FEPC, and various budget cuts were interpreted as aimed at the governorship. A Republican press agent was quick to get the text of Thompson's remarks on economy into the hands of the press.

He can be counted on to play close to Colonel McCormick and the Chicago *Tribune* in bidding for the governorship. Thompson is credited with conferring regularly with the Colonel in the *"Tribune* Tower." There is a possibility he might try for United States Senator in 1950 in order to build himself up for Governor.

The question as to how far Stevenson will go is still too early to answer. But there can be no doubt that his "new look" is making a big impact on Illinois. Things already look a lot different—and better. It used to be that every State publication invariably contained a slick likeness of the Republican Governor, with his name repeated over and over. Similarly, the name was to be found in glaring letters on all State buildings, photographs of him were in the offices of all his satellites, and billboards blazoned his face and name in nonelection as well as in election years. It was that way under Green.

But that crass and blatant exhibitionism is no longer to be seen. The big signs advertising the State Fair merely read "State of Illinois." There was no reference to Stevenson. One of the first things Stevenson did was to order pictures of himself taken down and to have his name removed from displays of all kinds. On taking office he made a tour of State agencies and noted the elaborate display of his name and pictures. The next day they were down by his order.

Public reaction to Stevenson is mixed. A survey of newspaper editors showed they felt he is making an honest effort to give Illinois clean, efficient, and enlightened government. But whether for him or against him, all respected him as a man and as a public official—which is more than could be said for Illinois Governors in the recent past.

WISCONSIN ★ ★ ★

A State That Glories in Its Past

WILLIAM T. EVJUE

ROLLING meadows interspersed with rustling woods; cows pasturing peaceably in the fields; well-worked, clean farms; towns exhibiting a uniform pattern of a central main business street surrounded by lanes bordering modest houses and well-kept lawns; and an air of middle-class contentment hovering over the farm and city population—all this strikes the out-of-state visitor when he drives through Wisconsin.

Wisconsin was discovered in the course of the search for a northwest passage to China by the Frenchman Jean Nicolet, who came to Green Bay on the western shore of Lake Michigan in 1634.* Twenty years later two French fur traders entered Wisconsin by way of Green Bay and explored the country inland to the west and north of Lake Superior. Wisconsin was opened to the Europeans and for the next two hundred

★

WILLIAM T. EVJUE, founder, editor, and publisher of the *Capital Times*, was an associate of the late Robert M. La Follette, Sr. Evjue is still militantly carrying on the liberal spirit of an earlier day in his crusading newspaper. For thirty-two years the *Capital Times* has stood as a sentinel for good government under the shadow of the Capitol dome in Madison.

★

* The facts concerning the discovery and settlement of Wisconsin are based on material contained in *Wisconsin; A Guide to the Badger State;* American Guide Series. Compiled by Workers of the Writers' Program of the Work Projects Administration in the State of Wisconsin. New York, Duell, Sloan and Pearce, 1941.

216

years the exploitation of Wisconsin's wealth in furs was the determining factor in its development by the French, the British, and the Americans.

The struggle for the fur trade between the French and the British was part of a war of continental proportions which was raging in Europe in the middle of the eighteenth century. In America this conflict led to the defeat of the French and monopolization of the fur trade by the British. The British remained in possession of the Northwest until 1816, though the Americans came into nominal control at the close of the Revolution in 1783. The forts surrendered to the Americans in 1796 and actual American control began in 1816. Wisconsin, part of the northwest region, became a Territory in 1838 and was admitted to Statehood in 1848.

The earliest wave of settlement into Wisconsin occurred between 1820 and 1850, bringing Southerners into the lead-mining area of the southwestern counties of the State. Another wave of settlement took place after the great Indian Black Hawk War. The defeat of Black Hawk in 1832 was followed by a migration of Yankee farmers into the south-eastern counties of Wisconsin. Cornish miners began to arrive in the lead region of southwestern Wisconsin in 1830. Then came the Scots, the Welsh, and the Irish.

An important factor to be considered in connection with Wisconsin's history is German immigration. In 1850 there were fewer German-born than British-born inhabitants of Wisconsin. But between 1850 and 1860 there was such an increase in immigration from Germany that since then the Germans have been the predominant element of foreign stock in the State. They early ranked among the State's best farmers, built tanneries and sawmills, and started the brewing industry in Milwaukee.

Between 1840 and 1860 a large number of Norwegians also came into the State. They were followed by Danes and

Swedes, Dutchmen, Belgians, and Czechoslovaks. Poles began to come after 1863. The largest Polish immigration occurred between 1910 and 1920, when thousands settled in Wisconsin's industrial centers, especially Milwaukee.

The economy of Wisconsin went through several stages. Starting with the trapping of fur animals, it went into the exploitation of the rich forests from which many fortunes were made. The earliest form of agriculture, large wheat growing, gave way during the latter part of the nineteenth century to dairying, which is now the major agricultural industry of the State.

Eighty years ago, Wisconsin was listed among the highest wheat-producing states of the Union. Even in 1872, after wheat growing began to decline, Wisconsin produced twenty-six million bushels. Principal reason for the decline of wheat growing was soil exhaustion resulting from the one-crop system. Productivity was also ruined by the annually increasing invasions of chinch bugs.

The only way to rehabilitate the State's agriculture appeared to be crop diversification through dairying. The soil-regenerating value of dairying was so obvious that beginning with 1890 dairy farming spread rapidly, and Wisconsin became the principal dairy state in the Union. It attained a dominant position in the production of fluid milk, cheese, and condensed milk, and stands third in butter production.

The industry is one of rather small producing units. While Wisconsin farms have tended to increase in size in recent years, the typical Wisconsin farm is still a family-sized farm worked by the owner, and in a relatively small proportion by tenants, with the help of one or two hired men. Wisconsin's farm population constitutes twenty-eight per cent of the total population. The State is also an important producer of tobacco, fruits, potatoes, and vegetables.

As a result of the pre-eminent position which dairying

218

occupies, Wisconsin is thought of both at home and in the nation as an agricultural state. However, statistics indicate it is more industrial than agricultural.

Before 1890 the industrial population of the State represented only two to four per cent of the total population. National expansion of industries at the turn of the century had its effect on Wisconsin. The development of industry in the State greatly increased the number of wage earners and today they constitute thirty-five per cent of the population.

Although only fifteenth in population, and twenty-fourth in area, Wisconsin occupies tenth place among the states in the value of its products.

Except for the greater use of machinery on the farms, the numerous gasoline stations and heavy motor traffic on the highways, the State looks pretty much the same as it did forty or fifty years ago. But under this placid appearance great social and economic changes have taken place, which not only have had profound influence on Wisconsin but also powerful repercussions on the nation.

Wisconsin was the outstanding exponent of the American tradition, the essence of which is the concept of social changes as both evolutionary and fundamental.

The story of an American state presents a subject of momentous significance. The development of large-scale industry and the ever-growing economic and social interdependence of all elements of the population brought the states of the Union to a historical crossroads. Preoccupation with national affairs was supplanting local and regional interests. One of the determining factors in past American history, sectionalism, was giving way to economic and social nationalism. In Wisconsin this evolution was reflected in the changing fortunes of La Follette's Progressive Party which, starting as a purely State movement, was driven by social and economic forces to dissolution and absorption within the two

219

old parties. A study of these forces is important to the understanding of the historical role of Wisconsin as it is affected by national developments.

Whether it is the leader who determines historical events, or whether the leader is merely an agent of sociohistorical forces is a problem which still awaits solution. But the history of Wisconsin presents an interesting example of the interweaving of leader-activities and the action of social forces. At the turn of the century the time was ripe for social changes. A leader was needed to give expression to the latent forces which were developing as a result of the passing of the frontier. This leader appeared in the person of Robert M. La Follette, Sr. He was able to detect the evolution of social forces, and crystallize them in a popular and dramatic fashion. Through the impact of his personality he exercised such a powerful influence on translating trends into concrete achievements that the history of Wisconsin for the past fifty years is identified with his life and work.

The personality of La Follette runs like a gleaming thread through every aspect of Wisconsin life. His work is so strongly entrenched that even the anti-La Follette administrations of the past decade dared not attack the progressive fortress he built. The most they attempted was to undermine progressivism through reactionary execution of progressive laws or an unwillingness to enforce them.

La Follette's work had its immediate roots in the philosophy of the Granger movement. This farmers' movement originated in the seventies and was the first attempt to bring about a marketing system that would be free from speculation and the uneconomical activities of the middlemen who stood between the farmer and the consumer. In the long run, however, notably in the nineties, the movement developed into a revolt against the monopolistic hold of the railroads on transportation facilities.

Referring to this phase of the Granger movement La Follette said:

"Those hard-headed old pioneers from New England and from northern Europe who thought as they plowed, went far toward roughing out the doctrine in regard to railroad control which the country has since adopted. At that time there was no settled policy, no established laws, but their reasoning was as direct and simple as their lives. It was plain to them that the railroad was another form of highway. They knew that for the purpose of a highway, the public could enter upon and take a part of their farms. If, then, the right of passage through the country came from the people, the people should afterward have the right to control the use of the highway. It was this simple reasoning which was subsequently adopted by legislatures and courts." *

The revolt against railroad monopoly is of particular significance because of the dominating position the railroads had when America was entering the period of large-scale industry. The struggle waged by the Grange and Robert M. La Follette against railroad corporations led to the incorporation in federal and state legislation of laws regulating their operations. In the ensuing years it began to be recognized that regulation in itself was not sufficient and that only public ownership would accomplish the objects of public control. But the importance of the early successful struggle to regulate the railroads lies in the fact that it constituted the first substantial breach in the stronghold of rugged individualism.

The philosophy of rugged individualism held that the services which the pioneer railroad builders rendered in developing the continent entitled them to fix any rates they chose, to adopt any practices they considered profitable, and to use the government to guarantee them these privileges. The op-

* Robert M. La Follette, *Autobiography.* Madison, Wis., Robert M. La Follette Co., 1913.

posite philosophy, the outstanding representative of which was La Follette, held that the continued existence of these enterprises was conditioned by the toil and enterprise of the people and that therefore the people should not be exploited by the corporations, and that such exploitation is obstructive and hinders the development of the country.

Sporadic farm and labor movements existed before the advent of the Grange. But it fell to the lot of this rural organization and to the Farmers' Alliance, popularly known as the "Populist Party," to become the source of strength and vitality which developed into a movement embracing many phases of the country's life. This new movement, under La Follette, led to the enactment first in Wisconsin and later in the nation of numerous laws based on a philosophy opposed to that of the rugged individualism of the nineteenth century. It was founded on the concept of social purpose in human relations. It held that the interest of the individual must harmonize with the welfare of the social body. Unlike Marxism, which insists that this can be accomplished only through complete collectivization, American progressive thought as expressed by La Follette seeks to attain this objective within the framework of a free economy contained within our traditional political freedom.

The significance of the Grange and the Populist Party lies in the fact that they came at a time when changing conditions made it imperative, for the welfare of the people, to substitute the concept of social-purpose legislation for the theory of rugged individualism. Monopolistic inroads became so bold and widespread that the whole country was alarmed. "This was the heyday of the Standard Oil trust, the tobacco monopoly, steel rail pools, and railroad rate discriminations. There was real cause for fear that a few giant corporations would soon control all the major industries of the United States with the consuming public considered only

222

to the extent of what the traffic would bear by way of price exactions." *

The Grange and the Populist movement were the springs from which the activities of Robert M. La Follette originated. The real meaning of his work as a leader of the people is that he crystallized and translated into educational and legislative action the social and economic philosophy which changing conditions called forth. In the simple reasoning of the Grange farmer he saw a reaction against the unrestricted use of property regardless of the rights of the people and the welfare of the nation. The power of the railroads, which rested on property, to fix traffic rates arbitrarily, La Follette considered an obstacle to the growth of the national economy. And he applied the same reasoning to a similar use of the power of property in all those branches of economic activity which were being monopolized by great corporations.

Perhaps the finest expression of La Follette's views on the role of property is to be found in an opinion rendered by Justice A. J. Vinje of the Wisconsin Supreme Court in January, 1921. In this opinion Justice Vinje, after quoting Chief Justice Marshall to the effect that "The power of creating a corporation is never used for its own sake, but for the purpose of effecting something else," says:

"What is this something else? Obviously it is the transaction of lawful business. And it is equally obvious that the corporation is thus created for the primary benefit of the state and not for that of the corporation itself. The state creates this corporate entity because the business needs of the public and the state are hereby promoted. The moment a corporation becomes an injury to the public it has no valid reason for existence, because the object for which it was

* George F. Comer, "Price Leadership"; from a Symposium, "The Sherman Antitrust Act and Its Enforcement." Reprint of the Winter, 1940, issue of *Law and Contemporary Problems,* Duke University School of Law, page 61.

created has not only been thwarted but the creature has become an instrument of evil." *

When a corporation "becomes an injury to the public" it uses property in an antisocial way. By attacking the antisocial use of property in every branch of economic activity La Follette sought to harmonize public and private interest as the basis of our economic system. The numerous measures which he and his followers advocated, whether income taxation, railroad regulation, the Seaman's Act, general labor legislation, co-operative marketing, antimonopoly activities, to mention only a few, have one thing in common—they were all aimed against antisocial use of property.

Political measures such as the primary election law, of which he was the author, were intended to establish a medium for the fullest expression of popular preferences for political candidates. La Follette firmly believed that when the people are fully informed and are unhampered by predatory combinations, they will always support legislation favorable to the nation as a whole.

He understood that the passing of the frontier and the tightening of economic conditions made people feel keenly the effects of the antisocial use of property. He also perceived that the middle-class psychology inherent in all groups of the American population, including industrial workers, militated against the progress of socialism with its concept of the nationalization of the means of production and distribution.

The La Follette progressive movement relied on various heterogeneous elements—farmers, workers, and small businessmen. Under the leadership of the elder La Follette these various components were welded, in a somewhat unstable

* Nekoosa-Edwards Paper Company vs. News Publishing Company, 174 Wis. 107. *Cases Determined in Supreme Court of Wisconsin,* April 5–September 23, 1921, page 115.

manner, into a working organization. Whatever differences existed among these groups, notably between farmers and industrial workers, a common ground was found in their antagonism toward economic oppression. Because of its Granger and Populist origins, the Progressive movement was generally considered as primarily an agrarian movement, a successor of the so-called farmers' "revolts" of the latter part of the past century. The fact is, however, that the Milwaukee socialists and labor in general contributed just as much to the success of the movement as the farm elements.

In agriculture the traditions of the early Grange, and particularly those of the Populist movement, were carried on by the Society of Equity. This organization championed progressive farm measures, but concentrated largely on the development of co-operative marketing and purchasing associations. After the first World War it co-operated closely with the newly organized Nonpartisan League, a radical politico-economic farm organization which originated in North Dakota and which was largely confined to that state, Minnesota, and northern Wisconsin. The League advocated a certain degree of socialization in activities related to farming, such as government ownership of warehouses.

In later years the Equity co-operated closely with a national farm organization, the Farmers' Union, which represents the progressive trend in farm economics. This co-operation led to a merger into one single organization known as the Farmers' Educational and Cooperative Equity Union of America, membership of which is concentrated in the northern counties, the last to emerge from the pioneer stage. The other great farm organization, the Farm Bureau, is largely centered in the southern and central counties among the old settlers. This organization came into being after the first World War and was designed to counteract the militant radical activities of the Nonpartisan League. The national

Farm Bureau is distinguished by its strong conservative policies. In Wisconsin, however, many of its county units are strongly liberal, in keeping with the old Wisconsin progressive tradition.

The history of labor in Wisconsin is of peculiar interest because of its relation to the brand of socialism known as "Milwaukee socialism" which was mainly responsible for putting Wisconsin labor into politics. A Socialist Party was active in Milwaukee as early as 1870. With the rise of Victor Berger to leadership of the Party, its original Marxian aspect was considerably modified. Although professing the ideal of "production for use rather than for profit," the Party became reformist. It concentrated upon labor legislation and the improvement of civic government in Milwaukee. It succeeded in making the city one of the best-governed in the United States. Because of its reformist character and mild radicalism, the Party was able to work with the trade unions in furthering a general labor program. There was an overlapping of memberships in the Socialist Party and the trade unions. The latter represented the economic, and the Party the political aspect of the labor movement.

Most of the legislative successes of the Socialist Party as the representative of labor were won through alliances with the progressives. Since the Socialists were the political spokesmen of the trade unions, labor was able to avail itself of political action more fully than in many states. "To some extent legislative successes removed the necessity for economic action, and until recently Wisconsin ranked low in the proportion of workers organized in unions; but . . . Wisconsin is now one of the most completely unionized States." *

The usual antagonism between farm and labor interests

---

* *Wisconsin: A Guide to the Badger State;* American Guide Series. Compiled by Workers of the Writers' Program of the Work Projects Administration in the State of Wisconsin. New York, Duell, Sloan and Pearce, 1941, p. 77.

was mollified in Wisconsin through the influence of liberal ideas emanating from progressive leadership. The conciliatory methods of labor, its support of measures favorable to farmers, such as co-operative marketing, tended to develop a tolerant attitude on the part of the farmers toward labor's demands. But ". . . it is significant that both Progressive Party strength and the success of labor legislation have been greatest when the rural-radical ferment among farmers was most active: during 1905-15, when the Society of Equity was rising; in the middle 1920's, under the influence of the Nonpartisan League; and in the 1930's, as the Farmers' Union expanded after the milk strikes." *

Robert M. La Follette died in June, 1925, but the progressive heritage which he left was so strong that his younger son, Philip F. La Follette, was elected Governor in 1930, defeating the conservative Republican Governor Walter J. Kohler. After a two-year term, however, Philip was defeated in the Republican primary by Kohler, who, in turn, lost in the general election to Democratic candidate Albert G. Schmedeman. This upset was directly due to the landslide presidential victory of Franklin D. Roosevelt. It was the first time in forty years that a Democratic administration came to power in Wisconsin.

In the spring of 1934 the Wisconsin progressives took a fateful step. They broke away from the Republican Party and organized a party of their own under the leadership of the two La Follette brothers, Philip and Robert, Jr. The latter had been elected to the United States Senate following his father's death. As the Progressive candidate, Philip was again elected Governor in 1934 and at the same time his brother was re-elected to the Senate. Philip served two terms until he was defeated by Julius P. Heil in 1938. Robert remained in

* *Ibid.,* page 81.

the Senate until 1946, when he was defeated by Joseph R. McCarthy, a conservative Republican. Since Philip's defeat the State administration of Wisconsin has been continuously in reactionary hands with one exception. This was Governor Walter S. Goodland who, although elected as a conservative Republican, showed stanch independence and rebuffed onslaughts on the State's progressive legislation.

The peculiar circumstances under which the elimination of the La Follette brothers occurred present an interesting phenomenon. They can be understood properly only in the light of the development of progressive thought in this country since the early days of the Republic. Their analysis is also important inasmuch as it furnishes a clue to the sociopolitical trends which were revealed by the unexpected and dramatic re-election of President Truman in 1948.

A leader does not operate in a vacuum. The elder La Follette's great accomplishments were rooted in the soil of Wisconsin. Through a peculiar power of perception which set him apart as a great leader, he was able to crystallize and generalize into a practical theory the innermost thoughts of the farmers who rose against the domination of the railroads. Many historians hold that the Granger and the Populist movements were merely "farmers' revolts." But what distinguished La Follette as a man of vision and historical perspective was that he grasped the underlying significance of the great struggle against the encroachments of private interests upon public welfare. It was his genius for weaving this thought into the problems confronting the people, and for presenting his views in a popular and dramatic manner, that explain his great influence with the mass of voters.

But what contributed particularly to the wide scope of La Follette's practical and intellectual leadership was the fact that he was the personification of an idealistic trend that goes back to Thomas Jefferson.

228

The essence of Jefferson's philosophy is his concept of popular rights. Jefferson exerted decisive influence in giving the United States a definite turn to popular rather than aristocratic democracy. What gives a true insight into Jefferson's humanistic concept of social relationships is the preamble to the great historical document he wrote, the Declaration of Independence. This preamble refers to the inalienable rights with which all men "are endowed, by their Creator," as the right to "life, liberty and the pursuit of happiness." In his biography of Thomas Jefferson, Saul K. Padover points out that the words "pursuit of happiness" are original with Jefferson. "Ordinarily," says Mr. Padover, "the triplex of political values included 'life, liberty and property.'" * The substitution of the idea of "pursuit of happiness" for that of "property" reveals in Thomas Jefferson a uniquely idealistic concept of human relationships.

Jefferson's idealism has expressed itself throughout our history with varying degrees of intensity. In the nineteenth century, the energies of the nation were absorbed in developing a vast continent of unexcelled natural resources. There was room for everybody. European immigrants poured in by the hundreds of thousands every year. The moving frontier spared the country the hardships which followed in the wake of the Industrial Revolution in Europe.

The disappearance of the frontier and the tightening of conditions brought about a resurgence of Jefferson's idealism in the Granger and Populist movements. Rugged individualism, with its emphasis on self-interest, the sanctity of property, and unbridled competition, was revealed as a condition and injustice which hampered the evolution of a healthy and normal economic life. An environment was being created in which the humanitarian principles of Jefferson

* Saul K. Padover, *Jefferson.* New York, Harcourt, Brace and Company, 1942, pp. 55-56.

were bound to manifest themselves with intensity as a reaction against the ever-increasing encroachments of private power upon the national economy.

With the development of industrialization, the rise of great monopolistic combinations, and the consequent ever-spreading antisocial use of property, Jeffersonian idealism was translated into concrete terms dealing with the various phases of our economic life. Jefferson's idealistic concept of human rights found expression in numerous laws, state and federal, which regulate economic relationships in the light of social justice and consideration for popular rights. These laws were manifestations of streams of progressive thought which were flowing throughout the country. To mention only a few, there were the apostolic crusade of William Jennings Bryan, the antitrust activities of Woodrow Wilson as Governor of New Jersey, and, above all, the work of La Follette in Wisconsin.

But there came a time when the forces of history merged these streams into one mighty torrent. The unprecedented economic crisis of the thirties revealed even more vividly than the depressions which had preceded it, certain fundamental defects in our economy. The utter failure of the Hoover administration to realize the nature of the crisis and to take appropriate measures to deal with it brought into power the Democratic Party. It is in the light of the analysis of that progressive victory and the subsequent history of the Roosevelt administration and President Truman's re-election in 1948 that the second phase of the history of Wisconsin, that connected with the activities of the sons of "Old Bob" La Follette, must be studied.

At the time of Philip's election as Governor, the Hoover depression was in its second year and was still thought of in terms of a temporary decline. The belief was widely propagated that recovery was around the corner. The ever-deepening crisis was pictured as merely another "dip in the business cycle" that would follow the usual course of previous depressions. Throughout was preached the philosophy of rugged individualism, with emphasis on the futility and harmfulness of government meddling in business.

Phil La Follette tackled the problem of the depression from the point of view that it was fundamentally different from all others. He held the country was confronted with the need to rearrange economic relationships and that the government must take a leading part in effecting that. To that end he laid before the Wisconsin Legislature a program of immediate as well as long-time action based on this fundamental concept of the depression.

His plan was bold and pioneering in nature. It was particularly significant as it was undertaken at a time when the national government was still waiting for the depression to liquidate itself.

Relief of unemployment and State financing were the immediate problems with which La Follette grappled during his first administration. In addition, he coped with a number of problems of long-term significance, notably labor, agriculture, and public utilities. He put through a complete reorganization of the old Railroad Commission that transformed it into the Public Service Commission, with wide powers to regulate utilities. His ideas on social and economic relationships, particularly as they related to maldistribution of income, were the controlling precepts of his policies. His over-all guiding principle was his father's philosophy that the basic cause of the nation's economic ills was to be found in the "encroachment of the few upon the rights of the many."

But in Phil's subsequent administrations a pronounced change manifested itself, notably in his last term, 1936-37. He became preoccupied with the State government. This has long been the perennial hobby of conservative Republican Governors. As former businessmen, these Governors think of government chiefly in terms of bookkeeping efficiency. To them this is far more important than the needs and interests of the people.

La Follette brought about a certain amount of reorganization, that soon thereafter was re-reorganized by his successor, Julius P. Heil. The present conservative Republican Governor Oscar Rennebohm is having an efficiency study made, preparatory to embarking on still another reorganization.

Reorganizing activities consumed most of La Follette's efforts during his last term. What time he had left over was devoted to launching a new national political party. This came into being at a prepared rally in the Stock Pavilion of the University's College of Agriculture at Madison. In proclaiming the formation of the National Progressives of America, La Follette developed the thesis that the two old parties had exhausted their usefulness and the time had come to establish a new political medium for the expression of the true interests of the nation. The speech was sentimental and nebulous. It was in sharp contrast to his address to the Wisconsin Legislature less than six years before—an address that was a model of logic, forthrightness, and broad-gauged thinking. The undertone of his "new party" evinced such a departure from his previous progressive viewpoint that it was received with plaudits by conservative publications all over the country, and even evoked interest among business magnates. Wisconsin Progressives were either hostile or at best indifferent. Six months after launching this National Progressives of America Party, La Follette was swept out of office by an avalanche of votes. He has never sought election since.

The basic motivation behind La Follette's scheme was the belief that President Roosevelt and the Democratic Party had lost the confidence of the people and were faced with political bankruptcy. Relying upon the luster of his name, La Follette thought that he could rally around him the liberal forces of the country. But at the same time he made certain covert, but unmistakable, gestures toward reactionary forces. Neither the liberals nor the people were fooled. They grasped, simply and clearly, what was afoot and sent Phil packing.

While his political end was doleful, that of his brother, Senator Robert M. La Follette, Jr., was truly tragic. He had never wavered in his progressivism. To the end he fought stanchly for the liberal cause. But Bob failed to gauge trends of the times, and this brought to a close his career as a statesman.

In the spring of 1946, Progressive leaders of Wisconsin met to decide whether to dissolve their party. It was evident it was rapidly losing strength. In the 1944 election, the Progressive candidate for Governor had received only 76,000 out of 1,320,000 votes.

From the start it was obvious the decision rested largely with Robert La Follette. In his address to the convention, he strongly urged merging with the Republican Party. His justification was that "the unmistakable signs of dissolution and disintegration [of the Democratic Party] are evident" and that "the Democratic Party is now stalled on dead-center." * The convention followed Bob's counsel. The devastating shortsightedness of his view was fully exposed by the sweeping Democratic victory in the presidential election two years later.

In advocating the merger with the Republican Party, La Follette declared ". . . I am convinced that the Republican Party of Wisconsin offers us the best opportunity for the

* From "Complete Text of Senator La Follette's Address at Portage" published by the *Capital Times* (Madison, Wisconsin), March 18, 1946.

advancement of Progressive principles. I do not mean for a moment that the Republican Party as presently bossed and controlled is a liberal vehicle. Far from it. But I am convinced we have a better chance to put our Progressive ideals on the law books if we go into the Republican Party." *
In taking this position, he failed completely to appraise properly the record of the Republican legislatures. Also, he wholly overlooked the fact that the Wisconsin Republican Party is an integral part of the national Republican Party, and is thoroughly dominated by it.

The extent to which La Follette misjudged the Wisconsin situation was strikingly revealed during the 1949 session of the Legislature. Of the one hundred members of the Assembly, twenty-six are Democrats, a number are former Progressives elected on the Republican ticket, and the rest, a majority, conservative Republicans. A similar situation obtains in the Senate.

Toward the end of the session the Joint Finance Committee submitted the biennial State budget bill. Two of its major provisions were of a distinctly reactionary nature. One denied the Tax Commission much-needed funds to ferret out income-tax evasions, and the other slashed the appropriations for enforcement of the State Antitrust Act.

Wisconsin has had an antitrust law since 1893, but it was never seriously enforced. In the 1947 Legislature a bill was introduced creating an Antitrust Division in the office of the Attorney General and appropriating $50,000 yearly for enforcement. The bill had rough sledding. The conservatives tried to stifle it in committee. When that failed, they attempted to kill the measure by other means. But aroused public opinion proved too strong and the bill was finally passed.

* *Ibid.*

While chagrined by this setback, the foes of the measure were not too concerned. They confidently anticipated only lukewarm enforcement of the new law. But to their dismay that did not happen—thanks to the forthrightness of two high-minded officials.

Attorney General John E. Martin, now Justice of the Wisconsin Supreme Court, and Deputy Attorney General Stewart G. Honeck named Leonard Bessman head of the new Antitrust Division. A war veteran with a distinguished combat record, Bessman is a man of exceptional ability and high sense of duty. Also, he had experience in the Antitrust Division of the United States Department of Justice. He lost no time in swinging into action.

Bessman launched a series of attacks against price fixing in gasoline, milk, undertaking, and other fields. He followed up this opening barrage with a number of important cases involving unfair trade practices.

His drive proved highly successful. The attack on gasoline price fixing was sustained by Circuit Judge Charles L. Aarons of Milwaukee. On the basis of Bessman's argument, Judge Aarons handed down an opinion that dealt a severe blow to certain vicious forms of monopolistic practices which, because of their subtlety, are difficult to cope with.

This aggressiveness alarmed the Old Guard and the big business interests they represent. The Republican Joint Finance Committee set about to ax Bessman. In effect, his office was abolished as a separate agency and his budget was slashed from $50,000 to $25,000.

When this measure came before the Legislature a fierce battle ensued. The Democrats sought to restore the full appropriation and the Antitrust Division, but the Republicans beat them, with the assistance of former La Follette Progressives who had joined the GOP to "liberalize" it.

Instead of liberalizing the Republican Party, as Bob La

Follette had proclaimed, these men were now playing hand in glove with the reactionary elements which had consistently supported monopoly and fought the Progressive cause.

What both Bob and Phil failed to recognize was the fact that although some Democratic leaders have not always represented the interests of the people, and the party is not always free from the charges of catering to special interests, it is the party in which the Jeffersonian philosophy has always been present. With the emergence of Franklin D. Roosevelt and the resurgence of social consciousness resulting from the hardships of the Hoover depression, Jeffersonian idealism came aggressively to the fore in the Democratic Party. The philosophy of Jefferson is the substance of the American tradition of a free economy operating in an environment of political freedom. American progressivism is the twentieth century expression of the Jeffersonian humanistic concept of relations between men. Only a lack of historical perspective and failure to understand social forces and movements can account for the actions of the La Follette brothers.

Like Phil, Bob paid for his grievous mistake. Running for re-election in the Republican primary, he was defeated by a conservative opponent. On the other hand, the Democratic Party has continued to grow in Wisconsin. In 1946 it garnered 406,499 votes for Governor out of a total of 1,040,281. In 1948 President Truman carried the state by 56,000 over Dewey.

It is clearly evident that a large majority of the Wisconsin Progressives have discarded the counsel of their one-time leader and have gone into the Democratic Party.

The attack of reaction on the economic front, through the scuttling of the antimonopoly law, was duplicated by similar sabotage of the basic requirement of genuine democracy: representative government. The Republican Legislature has specifically and deliberately flouted the requirements of the State Constitution for a reapportionment of legislative districts after each federal census.

Section 3, Article IV of the Wisconsin Constitution reads as follows:

"At the first session after each enumeration made by the authority of the United States, the Legislature shall apportion and district anew the members of the senate and assembly, according to the number of inhabitants."

Despite the explicitness of this provision, the Legislature has disregarded it for four successive sessions. As was pointed out by the Madison *Capital Times*, "It [the Legislature] has arrogantly and brazenly refused to comply with the one guarantee the people have that representative government will be continued in the state."

Wisconsin is undergoing a far-reaching trend toward urbanization. But the existing structure of the Legislature is still based on conditions that prevailed decades ago; the desire to retain rural dominance of the Legislature is one of the underlying reasons for the persistent refusal to accede to the demands from urban centers for compliance with the constitutional provision for reapportionment.

The indifference of the Legislature toward this constitutional mandate is matched by the equal indifference of the Wisconsin State Supreme Court. In 1946, two war veterans, running for the Legislature, petitioned the Court to enjoin the Secretary of State from proceeding with the elections. They argued these elections were clearly illegal since they were based on a violation of the Constitution. The Attorney General supported this contention. He advised the Governor to call a special session of the Legislature to comply with the law. But the Supreme Court ruled against this view.

The recourse proposed by the tribunal bore all the earmarks of hypocrisy. The Court held the remedy was in the "political forum." In advocating this phony solution the Court chose to ignore a vital consideration. Commenting upon this, the *Capital Times* said: "How can a majority of the people find a remedy when they are forced by the existence of an unconstitutional amendment to elect only a minority of the Legislature?"

Similar indifference to the law was displayed by the Court in other instances, notably in the case of United States Senator Joseph R. McCarthy. When running for this office he continued to hold his seat as a circuit judge. This was challenged in the Supreme Court on the ground that McCarthy's action was in direct violation of Section 10, Article VII of the Wisconsin Constitution. This section provides, "Each of the judges of the supreme and circuit courts shall . . . hold no office of public trust, except a judicial office, during the term for which they are respectively elected and all votes for either of them for any office except a judicial office, given by the legislature or the people shall be void. . . ." The Supreme Court disregarded this specific requirement and upheld McCarthy.

On the court's decision the Milwaukee *Journal* commented:

"The court found that McCarthy practiced law 'for many years' and 'had not been derelict in the discharge of his duties and obligations as a lawyer.' Then it plunged into a turbid legalistic discussion of 'moral turpitude.' And the conclusion is this: That McCarthy is guilty of an infraction of the moral code, that he did not keep his solemn promises to support the constitution. But that all of this does not disclose 'such a degree of moral turpitude that he is unfit to discharge the duties of an attorney at law.' So there can be no suspension, no disbarment, no disciplinary action of any nature."

The record of the 1949 Legislature and that of the present State administration present a picture of subservience to special interests tempered in a limited number of instances by

238

a refusal to enact outright reactionary measures for fear of antagonizing the voters of a State which is still to a large extent progressive in temperament.

The Legislature represented in its majority the reactionary forces of the State. The Republicans predominated both in the Assembly and in the Senate. The progressive elements were represented by twenty-six Democrats in the lower house and six Senators. The former La Follette progressives who joined the Republican Party fell in step, for fear of losing the latter's support at the next election.

The Republican legislators found themselves to a certain extent in a quandary. On one hand, they were dependent on, and sympathized with, special business interests; on the other hand, they were uncertain, despite the Republican victory, as to the trend of political sentiment. The size of the vote obtained by President Truman, who won by 56,000 votes; the comparatively large increase of Democratic representation in the Legislature; and the election of the Democratic candidate to the important office of Attorney General made them apprehensive. This, combined with the feeling that the core of economic thinking in Wisconsin is generally progressive, made the Republican Legislature hesitant to undertake an outright assault on the progressive legislation inherited from the days of "Old Bob" La Follette.

A conspicuous instance of this was the refusal of the Legislature to consider a reactionary income-tax measure sponsored by the Governor which placed the burden of a proposed special tax on those least able to pay.

The usual tactics of the Legislature with reference to the more controversial problems was to leave the progressive laws intact but to reduce opportunities for their enforcement. The Legislature was afraid to tamper with a tax law that would arouse indignant opposition in the State, but it refused funds asked by the Commissioner of Taxation to enable him

239

to ferret out the law violators and evaders. In other instances, the tactics in favoring special interests were not to interfere with favoritism shown by State agencies in the enforcement of the laws. Two years ago when the Rural Electric Association, a co-operative organization, asked the Wisconsin Public Service Commission for permission to build a dam on the Flambeau River, the application was held up for twenty-six months. The reason for this protracted delay was that the private utilities were able to stall action while millions of dollars were added to the construction costs through rapidly inflating prices. In contrast to its failure to act for twenty-six months in allowing the Rural Electric co-operative to build a dam, the Public Service Commission disregarded the fact that a private utility started the construction of another dam before its application had been approved. This company began construction on the Pentwell dam project in August, 1947, but it was not until January, 1948, that the commission issued a permit for the dam. This and another instance of high-handed tactics by this utility condoned by the Public Service Commission were investigated by a legislative committee composed almost entirely of Republicans. But even this committee was outraged, and its report charged that the Public Service Commission had acted "contrary to the public interest" and that "the Public Service Commission is given the appearance of being nothing but a rubber stamp."

Yet, with this report before it and with the declaration of the Attorney General that the Commission went beyond its jurisdiction in the Pentwell dam case, the Legislature refused to act on proposals to reorganize the agency.

Similarly, it voted down a resolution introduced by two Democratic Assemblymen to investigate the Department of Agriculture and the College of Agriculture. Officials of the Department admitted that wholesale violations of pure-food laws were not enforced, and a professor of dairying, who occupies a strategic position in the College of Agriculture, was revealed as receiving $4,000 a year from large food processors.

The record of subservience to private interests on the part of the 1949 Legislature is revealed with particular vividness in two important fields—lobbying and State rent controls.

Lobbying is as nefarious in Wisconsin as it is in other states and in Washington, D.C. What is particularly interesting in the case of Wisconsin is the attempt made by a leading State Senator to provide lobbying with a show of decency by devising a clumsy "theory" in its support.

A month before the opening of the 1949 session, a party was staged in a Milwaukee hotel by the Wisconsin Conference of Association Executives. This is the name of the lobbyists' organization representing thirty-nine business associations in the State. Invitations were sent to Assemblymen and Senators. Eight Senators and twenty-three Assemblymen showed up. The invitation stated that "as in the past, this reception is merely a good old-fashioned get-together so that we, as well as yourselves, can become better acquainted."

The party was a gay affair opening with a generous supply of Manhattans and Martinis and closing with speeches stressing the good fellowship among legislators and lobbyists. The two Wisconsin newspapers which are known for their attacks on lobbyists, the Madison *Capital Times* and the Milwaukee *Journal,* were scored for their "pernicious propaganda" against lobbying.

The task of rationalizing lobbyists as "representatives" of business was undertaken by Senator Everett La Fond. He praised the lobbyists as "good fellows" with the exception of "one or two bad ones," and summarized his philosophy in the following memorable words: "It is good to meet over a glass of Coca-Cola, a beer, or a highball and discuss the State's business."

With the convening of the session, lobbying activities went

241

into full swing in the time-honored tradition. "Good fellow-ship" was cemented at entertainments in Madison night clubs, in northern resorts, and in less conspicuous places. But unlike the previous sessions, a fly fell into the legislative ointment in the shape of the Democratic District Attorney, Robert W. Arthur of Dane County (in which Madison is located). He started proceedings against lobbyists, with the result that the license of one was revoked, and others were threatened with the loss of their licenses. Arthur is the first District Attorney who has taken antilobbying out of the talking stage.

The legislative session also furnished another example of a high-minded official who thwarted an onslaught on progressive statutes. The Legislature not only reduced by half the appropriation of the State's Antitrust Division but abolished it as a separate entity and merged it with the office of the Attorney General. The expectation was that antitrust prosecutions would be crippled. Attorney General Thomas E. Fairchild, however, refused to permit this. He not only found means to continue antitrust activities but strengthened them through the addition of an Assistant Attorney General to the antitrust staff.

The apotheosis of pressures of private interests on legislation was reached in the passage of the bill that abolished rent control and enabled landlords to increase rents up to thirty per cent. It was in connection with this bill that Governor Rennebohm was torn between his big-business psychology and his apprehension of the consequences of approval of an antisocial measure.

He kept this bill on his desk until the very last moment before the deadline, and then signed it. He accompanied this by a statement indicating he had spent considerable time worrying about its merits, undecided until the last whether to sign or veto it.

Rennebohm's action and timid explanation were in keeping with the character and tactics of his administration. An honest man, but the wealthy owner of a drugstore chain, he has lofty political ambitions. He came to the governorship with business experience but without any philosophy of government, and devoid of an understanding of present-day social and economic problems. His record is bare of any leadership in legislation. A conservative at heart, he wants to appear a liberal but the "big business" psychology always gets the better of him. His political ambitions in a State with the great progressive tradition of Wisconsin make him timid and wavering. The consequent colorlessness of his administration is matched by that of the Legislature, which presented a striking contrast to the stirring sessions of the glorious epoch of the elder La Follette.

The University of Wisconsin, once famous for its contributions to social problems, has lost its luster and is adapting its thinking to the views of the big-business Board of Regents. The faculty of the Department of Economics has abandoned the tradition of the late John R. Commons's intellectual leadership in sponsoring progressive legislation. As an example, a large number of the economics faculty signed a resolution endorsing the reactionary taxation measure supported by the Governor—a measure which even the Legislature refused to consider. Among them was a prominent professor of taxation who was Tax Commissioner in the first administration of Governor Philip F. La Follette.

As to the future, there is significant food for thought in the fact that the Democrats, who have taken over the La Follette tradition, polled a tremendous vote in the most recent presidential election and increased their representation in the Legislature. At the 1949 legislative session it was the Democratic legislators who fought consistently for progressive ideals.

The course of politics in Wisconsin has long been closely attuned to national politics. For two reasons, it is safe to assume that the progressive trend, as represented by the State Democrats, will be strengthened. One is the generally reactionary record of the Republicans, the pronounced reactionary activities of the national Republican Party, and the traditional tie-up of the Republicans with big business. The second reason is the basic liberal tendencies of the Democratic Party—this, despite substantial deviations in Congress from party pledges and despite certain of President Truman's peculiarities in the selection of individuals for high posts in the government.

Wisconsin definitely looks forward to a resurgence of vigorous liberal leadership that will control its State government. But this time it will be under the banner of the Democratic Party.

LOUISIANA ★ ★ ★

Beak Too Big For Its Belly

RALPH S. O'LEARY

ALONG the southern coastline where the mighty Mississippi muddies the Gulf of Mexico with the topsoil of half a continent, there abounds a big bird with a bassoon of a beak and a junior-miss waistline. This winged creature is the pelican.

Also along the fringing shores live men who hold this queer bird in reverent esteem. Its awkward figure is on the great seal of their realm, and innumerable commercial establishments use its name in their corporate titles. A bassoon-beaked silhouette appears on their motor license plates.

This fetish extends even into the political life of these singular people. Often in the past they have gulped down assurance of a better life, greater liberty, and a freer pursuit of happiness, only to become uncomfortably aware that they had swallowed something larger and more gamey than they expected.

The strange folk in this unfortunate beak-too-big-for-their-belly predicament are the citizens of Louisiana. Appropriately, Louisiana's popular nickname is the Pelican State.

★

A native of New Orleans, RALPH S. O'LEARY was on the staff of the New Orleans *Item* from 1928 to 1942. Since then he has been with the St. Louis *Star-Times,* except for two years in the Army. In 1943, he won the Sigma Delta Chi award for distinguished service in general reporting and honorable mention for courageous reporting. He was also given an award by the National Headliners Club for outstanding public service in journalism.

Louisiana is bounded on the west by Texas, a vast territory of go-getters and big boasters, and on the east by Mississippi, still living in the horse-and-buggy age socially, politically, and economically. In between are almost 2,600,000 Louisianians. They feel the westward tug of the brash Texans, yet are bound by older and stronger ties to their conservative Mississippi neighbors.

Nature has fought hard to retain its grasp on Louisiana ever since the first colonists arrived shortly after 1700. Fever-bearing mosquitoes brought wave after wave of epidemics and misery. Even today, cattle are sometimes stung to death in the marshlands. Majestic tropical hurricanes frequently sweep inland from the Gulf, their hundred-mile-an-hour winds piling up tides ten to fifteen feet deep along the coastal lowlands. Until present-century advances in weather forecasting, these exposed sections were death traps for the few wary inhabitants bold enough to live there.

Also, like most of the Mississippi Valley, the State's interior is periodically ravaged by savage tornadoes, their knifelike winds cutting hundred-yard-wide swaths through towns and leaving nothing but kindling wood behind. And the treacherous Mississippi and its tributaries regularly threaten the State's heavily populated areas, no matter how high above bank level retaining levees are built.

The colonies on the Atlantic Coast reached political maturity much earlier than luckless Louisiana, which spent its first hundred years in vassalage to two of the most backward and feudal monarchies of Europe—France and Spain. The State's advancement was so slow that when the first American Territorial Governor, William C. C. Claiborne, arrived after the Louisiana Purchase in 1803, Historian C. E. A. Gayarré reports Claiborne notified President Thomas Jefferson that the Louisiana "Creoles" (generally persons of mixed French and Spanish blood) are "ignorant but kindly disposed beings . . .

246

unable to appreciate the value of American institutions and
. . . not susceptible of self-government."

Quite a few reminders of the rule of France and Spain sur-
vive. One is the use of the word "parish" instead of "county."
This came about through the Spaniards, who used the nineteen religious parishes of the Roman Catholic Church as their
chief political subdivisions in South Louisiana. When the
Americans sought to recarve these into twelve Anglo-Saxon
counties, the citizenry balked. They feared that the land obtained through French and Spanish grants might be lost in
boundary shuffles. As a result, Louisiana is the only State in
the Union which terms its political subdivisions parishes. It
has sixty-four.

The State also has a unique code of civil law. It is based upon
the Code Napoleon of France. Property owners demurred
about accepting the English common law because it was
largely unwritten. The American authorities gave in on the
civil law but did succeed in imposing the common law, with
its vital assumption of innocence for defendants, on the State's
criminal jurisprudence.

South Louisiana still observes the annual fete of Mardi Gras
(fat Tuesday) on the last day before the period of Lenten
penance begins. In New Orleans, the celebration has become
world-famous and attracts tourists from everywhere. A grace-
ful relic of Spanish rule is the picturesque architecture of the
French Quarter of New Orleans. The French gave nothing but
their name to this site of the original city. Most of the buildings were constructed during the Spanish reign after two great
fires in the decades before the Americans took over.

Modern Louisiana has also inherited a Hatfield-McCoy
feud between Protestant North Louisiana and the Catholic
South. Strait-laced pioneers of Anglo-Saxon origin poured into
the northern part after the Louisiana Purchase. They still distrust the easygoing Latin mixtures in the south and the feeling

247

has always been mutual. It is a political axiom that no Catholic can become Governor of Louisiana, nor a Protestant, Mayor of New Orleans.

The State also has odd nooks and crannies where time seems to have stood still since the feudal colonial days. Some are the homes of descendants of Pierre Lafitte's pirates, who gave up scuttling ships after helping General Andrew Jackson beat the English in the Battle of New Orleans, and became fishermen and muskrat trappers on islands and lowlands in the central Louisiana coastal areas. Others are the villages of the "Cajuns," whose ancestors were the Acadians who came to Louisiana after being exiled from Nova Scotia by the British.

Although the gold and silver deposits which the first French sought never panned out, modern Louisiana is a land of a million times greater natural wealth than John Law ever dreamed during his Mississippi Bubble Scheme days in France.

The State has never depended solely upon cotton as the base of its agriculture. It is the nation's leading continental producer of cane sugar and is second only to Texas in growing rice. It is near the top in lumber production and its teeming muskrat population makes it the nation's leading producer of furs in quantity although not in quality. It also has scores of specialty crops such as sweet potatoes, strawberries, oranges, lily bulbs, and practically all the world's perique, a vital tobacco for pipe mixtures, is produced on a few hundred acres near New Orleans.

And underneath its rich, alluvial soil, man has found a treasure trove of mineral resources far more valuable and useful than gold and silver.

Louisiana ranks third in petroleum production, outstripped only by such giants as Texas and California. It is second in the production of sulphur, and a leader in salt mining and natural gas utilization. The last census listed Louisiana twenty-

248

first in population but it was sixth in the value of its mineral production.

But despite these bountiful gifts, wretched poverty is the lot of most Louisianians. U. S. Department of Commerce figures show that in 1939 per-capita income was $354, compared to a national average of $539. When World War II was over, Louisiana's per-capita income had risen to $784, but the nation's average had climbed to $1,200. Only five other states, none of them anywhere near Louisiana's high rank in natural resources, had lower per-capita income.

The census also showed Louisiana at the very bottom in the literacy of its adult population, although it was doing a little better by its youngsters than some of the other tail-enders. Nearly thirteen per cent of those over twenty-five years of age had not completed even the first grade of school. For the nation as a whole, this figure was slightly below four per cent.

One of the chief causes for this widespread poverty and ignorance in the midst of such plenty is that too few Louisianians have been able to compete with the economic titans of the East and North. The overwhelming power of monopolies is largely to blame. Louisiana today is just as much a colony financially as it once was politically.

Since it is a satrapy, the cream of the profits goes out of the State. And when an absentee-owned property ceases to pay off, it is curtly closed down or abandoned. There is little concern for the workers. The Louisianians who manage and operate these absentee interests have always been among the State's most influential leaders. But they are all too prone to be unconcerned about the welfare of their less fortunate fellow citizens. Profits come first.

The plight of Louisiana natives eking out a bare existence on the big plantations never draws more than a shrug. So it was very startling to Louisiana when a furore arose over the plight of the displaced persons brought over from Europe to

249

work on the sugar plantations at the prevailing wage of $2.90 a day. In the State that was considered a high record for the industry.

Probably the greatest single obstacle to advancement in Louisiana is the ugly and undemocratic fetish of white supremacy. It serves as an anesthetic to dull the misery of the lower-class whites, while at the same time retarding the welfare of both whites and Negroes.

In education, for example, whites insist upon separate school systems. Yet, even though the system for Negroes is appallingly inferior, it still takes away enough funds to make white schools, in turn, also inferior.

Economically, Louisianians delude themselves into believing the reservoir of cheap Negro labor reduces their cost of living. Actually it does nothing of the kind. What it really does is to depress the living standard of the whole State.

The small independent farmer cannot compete with the large plantations, which always have masses of cheap manpower available. Even at the height of the World War II boom period, 49.1 per cent of Louisiana's farmers were tenants or sharecroppers. During the Hoover depression, 59.4 per cent were croppers. The full significance of these figures is understood only when it is realized that more than half of Louisiana's population is rural.

This fact has had profound effect on the composition of Louisiana. There are virtually only two classes in the State —a small, wealthy, owning group and practically all the remainder, in effect, peasants. There is no important middle class.

If Karl Marx were alive, he would, no doubt, lick his chops and sit back to await the uprising of the proletariat. Louisiana's economic rulers are fully aware of the danger. They are constantly on guard against what they call "Communist-type agitators." So relentless has their extermination campaign been that not even honest liberalism has had a chance to take root.

Yet, while truculently alert against Communism, Louisiana proved easy prey to a spasm of cowardly and buffoonish Fascism. When the right man appeared, the State submitted quickly to the most Nazi-like dictatorship in U.S. history. It took an assassination to end the terroristic reign. But the virus of that sordid period still remain. , and the madness may flare up again.

To understand Louisiana, it is best to begin at the top. And the top means the Boston Club, the New Orleans equivalent of the Union League in Philadelphia. The Club occupies a subdued, immaculately white, three-story building on famed Canal Street and exudes good breeding from every brick.

Untold numbers of Mardi Gras visitors have stood in front of the Club and watched Rex, the businessman chosen as king for the day, ride up on his elaborately decorated float. By tradition he toasts his debutante queen in champagne, then dashes the goblet to the pavement. It is a colorful and stirring spectacle.

But the Boston Club is the personification of the managers and factors of the absentee owners who really rule Louisiana. The Club itself does not rule. It merely executes the orders and dictates of its absentee rulers, the great commercial, banking, oil, shipping, rail, and utility corporations that own Louisiana.

The Boston Club was founded in 1841. When New Orleans was captured during the Civil War, federal troops looted it. During Reconstruction its members were leaders of the Knights of the White Camelia (Louisiana version of the original Ku Klux Klan) and the White League which restored white supremacy in the State. After Reconstruction, it was again Boston Club members who took over the reins.

This rule continued practically undisturbed until the turn of the century, when the white masses began to stir restlessly under their blue-blood masters. The ringing words of William Jennings Bryan and the embattled outcries of the Populists had deep effect. Finally, in 1904, there was a revolt at the polls in New Orleans and a crafty, potbellied, one-time drummer named Martin Behrman was elected Mayor.

Behrman was a man of the people at the start. He improved the efficiency of the city government. He made it possible for the poor man who voted right to get paroled from jail through the offices of a friendly Behrman henchman as easily as a rich man could get out by making bond.

New Orleans embraced him fervently. But after a while it discovered it had a bear by the tail. The city found that it had exchanged rule by the Boston Club for rule by the club of a political machine.

Behrman quickly built one of the most efficient machines in American history. It functioned long after his death and began to wane only in recent years. He served as Mayor for sixteen years.

After securely entrenching himself in New Orleans, "Boss" Behrman surveyed the rest of the State and saw inviting vistas. In each of the sixty-three other parishes he found cliques of small-bore courthouse politicians, feuding and bickering over office and boodle. Skillfully playing one off against the other, the Boss eventually gained political control of the entire State. Inasmuch as he was a Catholic, he made no attempt to run for Governor himself. But from 1912 to 1920, he literally ran Louisiana's Statehouse in Baton Rouge from his office in the City Hall in New Orleans.

252

The Boston Club had no difficulty getting along pleasantly with Behrman. In fact, he curbed New Orleans restlessness better than ever in return for the campaign contributions that kept his machine in power.

But despite his all-powerful organization, curiously enough Behrman was unseated largely as a result of an accident. Four of his policemen made the mistake of being caught red-handed in a graft shakedown in the far-famed bawdyhouse section. The *Times-Picayune* exposed the scandal.

Public outrage ensued. The Boston Club hurriedly shook its skirts clean and joined in the anvil chorus of denunciation of the "Ring." The Club sonorously announced it would support a "reform" candidate. Amazingly, this candidate turned out to be one of the Club's members, John M. Parker, Sr. A wealthy cotton broker, he became Governor, and a year later Boss Behrman was kicked out of City Hall.

Behrman was out but he had blazed a trail for an even greater evil. He demonstrated what a streamlined machine could really do. His ward bosses developed vote thievery into a science in which only the exact number of ballots needed to win, and no more, were produced at any election. It was so bald and so brazen that, ever since, the rest of the State has harbored a fierce distrust of the "city slickers" in New Orleans.

Since Behrman's success in Baton Rouge stemmed chiefly from manipulating blocs in the Legislature, there has grown up a practice which amounts to partial abandonment of the lawmaking power. Administrations have been afraid to trust pet proposals to mere bills, which could be repealed by a majority of the hundred and one Representatives and thirty-nine Senators. They have sought the more enduring security of the State Constitution. The present Constitution was adopted in 1921 while Parker was

253

Governor. In the twenty-eight years since then, this Constitution has been amended two hundred and fifty-seven times. It is the longest in the nation, containing eighty-five thousand words.

Socialite Parker's four-year term saw not only adoption of this Constitution but also the first effort to solve another big problem—the State's tax policy on its fabulous mineral wealth. The exploiters and the big oil companies had no reason to complain at Parker's solution.

The problem arose because the State had just had a painful lesson in exploitation.

More than fifty years before, a great dome of sulphur had been discovered near the southwestern coast in Calcasieu Parish. Louisianians had been unable to develop it because of the prohibitive cost in removing a covering layer of quicksand. The heavy outlay for this would have made it impossible to compete with the Sicilian sulphur monopoly, which employed 250,000 miners at fifty cents a day.

But in 1899, the quicksand problem was overcome by Herman Frasch, a Standard Oil engineer. He invented a process of melting sulphur underground with steam and pumping it to the surface from a well instead of hoisting it from a mine. When oil wells in nearby Texas assured a cheap fuel for the steam, the last advantage of the Sicilian monopoly was wiped out.

With backing from a brother of John D. Rockefeller, Frasch formed the Union Sulphur Co., a New Jersey corporation. In the next twenty-five years the concern steamed out an immense quantity of cheap sulphur from the Calcasieu deposit.

By the time Parker became Governor, the great sulphur dome had collapsed, threatening the area and Lake Charles, Louisiana's second deep-water port, with economic ruin. Also, strong sentiment had developed that greater State

254

revenues should have been derived from the ten million tons of sulphur taken out than the comparatively nominal ad valorem property tax.

It was then too late to do anything about sulphur. But Parker entered into negotiations for a new tax law with the oil industry, led by Standard Oil of New Jersey. The corporation had built one of the world's largest refineries just north of Baton Rouge. The result of these parleys was a so-called compromise. Under it, Louisiana imposed a "severance" tax of two cents a barrel on all oil "severed" from its soil. In return, the oil corporations got a provision inserted in the new Constitution prohibiting any other State levies on them. This provision barred tax assessors from boosting the valuation of oil lands.

While the tax deal was rammed through by Parker, it did not escape bitter denunciation. In fact, the deal gave Huey Long his start in politics as a crusader against big business.

He was then not quite thirty years old and hailed from Winn Parish, a one-time Populist stronghold in the heart of Protestant North Louisiana. Previously a supporter of Parker, Long now broke with him and distributed a circular charging that Parker had sold out to Wall Street. As a result, Huey was sued, convicted, and fined for criminal libel. In 1924, he retaliated by running as an independent candidate for Governor. Huey got nowhere in that race, but he left an indelible imprint. He split the rural vote so deeply that Parker's hand-picked choice lost, and Boss Behrman was able to make a resounding comeback and elect his gubernatorial candidate.

The Boss shortly thereafter completed the political cycle by returning as Mayor of New Orleans. But it was his last victory. Both Behrman and his Governor died early in their terms. With his death ended the long supremacy of New Orleans in State affairs.

By 1928, Huey was set to see to it that another split in the rural vote did not occur. He too, like Behrman, had been a traveling salesman. But Huey's territory had been rural, and he knew intimately the wants and mores of the farmer. Huey's speeches were studded with honeyed allusions to the plight of the "little man." His campaign program concentrated more on immediate benefits than on long-range reforms, although he did not overlook them, either.

But most important of all, Huey shrewdly organized the courthouse rings as they had never been before. He ended feuds and lined up the former feudists solidly behind his candidacy for Governor.

Huey won handily.

In office, he made good many of the benefits he promised. Free hospital care was expanded and improved; institutions for the insane and aged received larger appropriations; surfaced highways replaced dirt and gravel roads; free bridges replaced toll ferries; and free schoolbooks became the order. Also, he dinned incessantly his clatter about "sharing the wealth," while launching a huge construction program of new State buildings. A thirty-three-story skyscraper Capitol replaced the ancient "gingerbread fortress," as it was called by a river pilot named Samuel Clemens. And Louisiana's down-at-the-heel State University was expanded into one of the largest in the nation, with a brand new campus and numerous modern buildings.

While making good these campaign promises, Huey also took very good care of his own political interests. All jobs were distributed on a strictly "spoils" basis, with the courthouse rings heavily on the receiving end. Administrators for the new hospitals, institutions, and the great building programs were appointed because of their loyalty to Huey and not for fitness to do their particular jobs.

256

Inevitably, vast sums of State revenue were squandered and pilfered.

The oil boom reached its first peak shortly after Huey took office. He quickly boosted Parker's two-cents-a-barrel tax to six cents and the gas tax from one to three cents. The resulting increase in State income was very helpful to Huey. It enabled him to do a lot of free-handed spending without increasing general taxes.

Huey was also lucky in another lush windfall. Some of the largest oil pools were found under the thirty-five hundred miles of inland lakes, bayous, and other waterways that are State property. Awarding leases on these holdings not only poured millions into the State Treasury, but also opened the way for Huey to assure himself juicy campaign contributions from lease-hungry oil operators.

Huey's first use of the National Guard was to impress the courthouse rings that he was master.

Early in his term two parishes evinced signs of independence. They were Jefferson and St. Bernard, both adjoining New Orleans. Chief among the thriving industries of the two parishes were elaborate gambling houses. By a curious arrangement, the parish sheriffs appointed numerous special deputies, who served as doorkeepers, guards, and so on in these establishments. Their salaries were paid by the owners.

"Kingfish" Huey struck swiftly. National Guardsmen pounced on the gambling places. Expensive equipment was smashed, all money in sight was seized, and harassed patrons were searched thoroughly before being allowed to leave.

Overnight, the recalcitrant courthouse rings "got right" with Huey. On his part, he never again molested the gambling joints.

Shortly after these raids, the political boss of Plaquemines

Parish, occupying both banks of the Mississippi below New Orleans, assumed supervisory power over St. Bernard. The boss was Leander H. Perez, 38-year-old graduate of the State University's law school. He had served as judge of a two-parish district, including Plaquemines and St. Bernard, and at that time was District Attorney of the area.

Although virtually unknown outside Louisiana, Perez, from that period on, has been one of the most powerful men in the State's tempestuous politics.

He has continued the unchallenged "Czar" of the two parishes, the most backward in the State. Reputed to have an exceptional legal mind, he frequently appeared as counsel for Huey. In the weekly press of St. Bernard Parish, Perez' name is used in hushed tones when occasion arises to print it. He goes out of his way to keep out of the limelight. He has an inconspicuous office in the skyscraper American Bank Building in New Orleans, and never discusses either his private or public activities. Under his overlordship, there has been a decline in St. Bernard gambling. Most of the big operators have moved to more friendly Jefferson Parish.

But Perez' two parishes vote almost unanimously for the men he designates. One U. S. Senate investigating committee was astounded by the remarkable results achieved in St. Bernard in a Congressional election. The Perez candidate received 4,000 votes to less than a dozen for his opponent. Exclusive of the Negroes, who were not allowed to vote, the population of the parish was only 4,829, including infants in mothers' arms.

Natives of Perez-land, as the two parishes are sometimes called, shrugged at this amazing disclosure. They blandly pointed out that there were many muskrat trappers who must have been missed by the census takers, as they only came out of the swamps on election day.

In the past year, Perez has stuck his oar into national affairs. Characteristically, he has done it quietly and backstage. But the oar has been a potent one, notwithstanding. Perez was one of the principal founding fathers and money-raisers of the noisome Dixiecrat movement, and he has been very active in the pressure drives of the great oil interests to grab off the immensely rich tidelands, despite the ruling of the Supreme Court that these resources belong to the federal government.

The turning point in Huey's career was probably the abortive attempt of the silk-stocking crowd to impeach and throw him out of office. Privately, he always craved the acclaim of this hostile upper crust much more than the cheers of the masses. But after the nearly successful ouster attack, Huey realized it was a fight to the finish. He never considered as evil the many things he did dictatorially. He viewed them as necessities to shore up his defenses so he could stay on top no matter what happened.

Despite all his share-the-wealth clatter, Huey never seriously struck at the system of economic exploitation in Louisiana. Illustrative of this was his handling of the utility problem.

Most Louisiana utilities were subsidiaries of giant Electric Bond & Share Co. of New York. Parker's 1921 Constitution created a three-man elective Public Service Commission to regulate utilities. But one of the largest, New Orleans Public Service, Inc., holding monopoly franchises to supply electricity, gas, and transportation, was specifically exempted from regulation by this State agency.

Huey never made a move to remedy this extraordinary situation. In fact, when natural gas was substituted for artificial in New Orleans homes, he proved as complaisant as his political foes had been in accepting the utility's rate schedules.

After smashing the impeachment move, Huey became a complete demagogue. When he was elected to the Senate, he put in a rubber-stamp Governor and continued to rule a completely subservient Legislature. The last bulwark of opposition was crushed when he gained a fourth justice on the Louisiana Supreme Court.

There were mobilizations and marchings of the State Guard, remarkably similar to those of Hitler's storm troopers and Brown Shirts.

Louisiana's 16,000 State employees were dragooned into a Nazi-like organization and forced to contribute part of their pay to Huey's campaign chest and to subscribe to his *Voelkischer Beobachter*-type weekly, *The Louisiana Progress*. The State Highway Patrol was enlarged and transformed into a secret police, and Huey surrounded himself with a heavily armed bodyguard of plug-uglies.

Thugs beat up men still courageous enough to voice opposition. And if one of the few remaining "free" judges jailed the goons, Huey pardoned them before they left the courtroom. Similarly, on his order, the State Supreme Court would dissolve injunctions by a four-to-three vote before the ink on the injunction was dry.

Incredibly, most Louisianians were unaware of what was happening. The opposition was completely discredited. And the State press had long before lost its prestige. There had been no honest exposé of Long's regime such as the *Times-Picayune* had published about Behrman years before. Instead, there had been numerous wild and unfounded charges, which Long readily proved false and ridiculous. Also, there was not a single large paper in the State not dominated by business interests. The rural press was too dependent upon

260

public printing, dished out by the courthouse rings, to do any crusading.

Further, the lack of an intelligent and independent middle class aided powerfully to make Huey's deceptions possible. Such citizens might have been misled by him at the start, but they would not have remained so for long.

After Huey's assassination in September, 1935, Louisiana mourned him as a martyr. More than a hundred thousand passed his bier before he was interred in a concrete and steel vault on the Capitol grounds. It was a striking demonstration that many did not believe he had robbed and deluded them.

But some Louisianians were aware of what the Kingfish had done to them. On the night he died, an unidentified group appeared before his home in an exclusive residential street and erected a small wooden memorial with a wreath reading, "In memory of Dr. Carl A. Weiss"—the murderer.

Richard W. Leche, best remembered as the only Louisiana Governor to serve a term in a federal penitentiary, succeeded to the Long leadership. Leche made an open play to business interests and embarked on a program to attract new industries with tax exemptions. In a short time leading businessmen were attending a ceremony at which Leche was presented with a yacht as a testimonial for his efforts in their behalf. It turned out later that the $11,000 to buy the boat had come from the State's coffers. Leche also imposed a sales tax, sugar-coating it out of respect for Huey's following by calling it a "luxury" tax.

In brief, Leche's administration would have been a perfect Boston Club dispensation but for one thing. Leche and his pals couldn't keep their hands out of the public till.

When these thefts began to come to light, the Boston Club again raised its hands in pious horror. Indignant citizens' committees were formed and funds collected for the restoration of "reform" in Louisiana politics. After the shouting and voting was over, and the bedraggled remnants of the Long machine had been kicked out, the State was once more in the hands of the same old business crowd that had ruled it so long in years past.

The blue-stocking goons had replaced the gutter goons.

It was practically inevitable that this would happen. There is no law limiting campaign expenditures in Louisiana and elections are a big business in themselves. The only groups able to finance a state-wide campaign were the Longites and the Boston Club. Also, there is no law requiring publication of campaign contributions or accounting of funds spent. It was a perfect setup for a wide open gang battle. And that is exactly what occurred.

The Boston Club picked as its front an obscure, mediocre lawyer from Lake Charles. In addition to possessing the imposing name of Sam Houston Jones, he also had the merit of not being a Club member. Thus he would not be suspected in the rural sections of being identified with the discredited politicians who had fought Huey.

Huey's brother Earl, whose worst enemies had been unable to uncover the least indication that he was involved in the thievery under Leche, ran against Jones. With Mayor Robert Maestri driving the old Behrman machine and the Louisiana Democratic Association for Earl in New Orleans, he made a strong race in view of the machine's many handicaps. Jones won by only 19,000 votes in a run-off primary.

The whole country hailed the collapse of the Long machine and Jones became a national figure overnight.

But in Louisiana, disillusionment set in soon after he took office. Jones proved to be vacillating and indecisive. Rural Louisiana missed the lusty, hail-fellow-well-met governors to which it had become accustomed. Jones became known as "High-Hat Sam." He employed a number of top-flight newspapermen and public relations experts on his staff, but not even they could make him a colorful and popular figure.

Jones continued Leche's policy of wooing new industries with even more concessions. Also, he stripped the State sales tax of its sugar-coating and became embroiled in a squabble over the issue with Maestri. This led to the most inept of Jones's many blunders. He ordered the magnificent New Orleans Charity Hospital, a three-thousand-bed free institution serving the poor of all South Louisiana, to be closed. Public feeling at this harsh act ran high. It was widely condemned. Labor and other leaders charged Jones and Maestri with responsibility for "misery and murder."

The Young Men's Business Club of New Orleans appointed a committee to find a way to keep the hospital open. The group finally prevailed on the warring politicians to get together. Maestri agreed to call off the opposition of his bloc of legislators to the sales tax, and Jones agreed to reopen the hospital, which had been partly shut down by then. It was to be years before it got back to normal again. It is of interest to note that the next time the two ran for election, they were defeated.

The one big achievement of Jones's term was the establishment of the first state-wide civil service system. But even this reform was marred by petty partisanship. Before the law became operative, holdovers of the old Long machine were purged from their jobs. The slaughter was so terrific that the cry was raised that Jones, too, was building a machine. A State policeman, who had chauffeured Earl Long, reported that when he inquired the reason for his sudden dismissal, he was curtly told, "You drove the wrong man!"

Unfailingly inept, Jones blundered even on his one big accomplishment. He failed to include the civil service program in the list of twenty-nine amendments to the Constitution adopted during his term in office. The civil service measure was enacted merely as a statutory provision, subject to the mercies of future Legislatures.

Near the end of his term, Jones became entangled in another political jangle that disclosed that the old Long courthouse rings were quietly waiting *Der Tag*. The dispute centered in Plaquemines Parish, where Perez still ruled with an iron hand.

The Plaquemines sheriff died and Jones appointed a successor. Perez demanded that the parish coroner serve as acting sheriff. The Supreme Court upheld Jones. When Perez refused to give up the office to Jones's appointee, the Governor sent five hundred militiamen to take over by force. Perez supporters set up road blocks but fled when the guardsmen, armed with machine guns, advanced in trucks. The victors found the courthouse a shambles, with many records destroyed and others scattered. But it was only a temporary defeat for Perez. At the next election, his man won the sheriff's office overwhelmingly.

Reform *à la* Boston Club continued for four years after Jones left office. His successor was a part-time Shreveport politician and cowboy crooner named Jimmie H. Davis, composer of the juke-box hit, "You Are My Sunshine." A seven-piece hillbilly band attended all Davis's stump appearances and later found places on the State payroll.

Chief beneficiary of Davis's term was his Lieutenant Governor, J. Emile Verret. His salary was $5,000 a year except when he was Acting Governor, when it jumped to $12,000. Davis was away so often that appropriations for this contingency were twice exhausted.

The name of Louisiana's capital city, Baton Rouge, means "Red Stick." Early travelers are supposed to have so named the site because of the great red cypress trees they found

264

there. The word *baton* had been singularly appropriate ever since Standard Oil of New Jersey built its huge refinery in the city. A wave of Standard's baton usually brings a greater response from Baton Rouge officials than the most exacting conductor gets from an orchestra.

Most recent baton wave occurred after World War II, when the city settled its boundary problems. In 1940, Baton Rouge had a population of 34,719. But synthetic rubber and other plants mushroomed around the Standard refinery, and by the end of the war the area contained more than 100,000 people. It was essential that property owners pay their share of the city's tax burden.

A commission drew up a combined city-parish charter, such as existed at New Orleans. The new city limits included the Standard refinery and adjoining allied industries. But Standard did not pay the new and higher city tax rate as did the other property owners in the annexed area. A provision was inserted in the charter creating a separate "industrial zone" for Standard, with the old and lower parish tax rate.

The Boston Club clique thought it had crushed Longism forever when Maestri was thrown out of the New Orleans City Hall in 1946. A thirty-four-year-old political novice named DeLesseps S. (Chep) Morrison, whose biggest asset was the chestful of colonel's ribbons he brought back from overseas, turned this trick. The victory was all the sweeter because the blue bloods had practically abandoned hope of capturing the city.

Their first thought had been to unite behind a "man of the people." To this end they picked ex-Congressman Joachim O. (Joe) Fernandez as their nominee. As a popular ward leader in the Long regime, Fernandez had acquired the nickname "Bathtub Joe." This grew out of the strategy he employed to sift telephone callers. His wife always an·

265

swered the phone and, to inquiries for Fernandez, replied, "Joe's in the bathtub." If he wanted to talk to the caller, he answered the phone. Otherwise, Mrs. Fernandez would report she had given her husband the message and would hang up.

Fernandez pulled a fast one on the Boston Club. To its consternation, he withdrew from the race just before the expiration of the filing deadline. Socialite Morrison was the frantic last-minute substitute. His victory surprised everyone, including himself.

The new Mayor proved very energetic. He hired some of Sam Jones's publicity experts and added to his medal collection by accepting a bauble from Argentine Dictator Perón. But his idea of reforming the city government was to start building a political machine of his own, modeled after the Behrman pattern.

Morrison's blow-hard antics and the reactionary buffoonery of the Davis regime made it a cinch that Longism would return. The inevitable occurred in 1948.

The Boston Club boomed Jones again. It figured he would win easily with political New Orleans allied with instead of against him.

Earl Long again opposed Jones. In Earl's first race he was still somewhat suspect by many dyed-in-the-wool rural admirers of his brother. Had he not broken with Huey soon after the Kingfish ran for the United States Senate? Had not Earl sworn before a Senate committee that he saw his brother accept money from a representative of Electric Bond & Share Co.?

All Earl had been able to do to counter these charges was to assert that he and Huey had made up shortly before the latter's assassination. But when Earl took the stump in 1947, he had an ally calculated to stir the cockles of any Louisiana farmer's heart.

266

This ally was Huey's oldest son Russell.

Now twenty-nine and groomed for a political career, Russell took the stump with his uncle, as living proof that the Long family was united. Russell had other attributes. He bore enough of a resemblance to his father so that old-timers could slap their thighs and exclaim he was the "spittin' image." He was a graduate of his father's favorite university, and had a good war record as a Naval officer.

Russell also had studied his father's history. He assured everyone he did not consider himself a second Kingfish. There is little likelihood he ever will be, either. His upbringing and environment are very different from his father's. Huey spent much of his life in farm homes; Russell has lived mostly in better residential suburbs. He is no primitive.

The nephew and uncle won a sweeping victory. They did it by preaching the same gospel that had proved so productive as a vote-getter for Huey twenty years before. And potently aiding the Longs was the grubby eight-year rule of the Boston Club.

But the most significant thing about the campaign was the rise of an independent. He was Judge Robert Floyd Kennon, of the State Court of Appeals at Shreveport. Running wholly on his own and without a big bank roll, Kennon polled an amazing vote. He came within 20,000 of beating out Jones as a runner-up in the first primary. The count was Long 267,253; Jones 147,329; Kennon 127,569. A fourth candidate, Representative James H. Morrison, who claimed it was his introduction of a bonus bill that spurred the American Army to "victory" at Kasserine Pass, polled 101,745 ballots.

Morrison, who hails from Louisiana's strawberry belt, had run before and his vote was largely a personal following. But Kennon's vote was apparently an expression of disgust against

both the Longs and the Boston Club. It was a highly significant political development.

It was not Kennon, himself, but the independent vote
which his all-GI ticket polled that was important. Kennon
is no liberal. His views are conservative enough to please
the Boston Club. During his campaign he denounced present trends in government and asserted that the authority of
the federal government "to interfere with private business
must be curtailed and the American system of free enterprise restored." But Kennon's vote disclosed that there exists
in Louisiana a considerable body of opinion that is thoroughly
fed up with both the Longs and the Boston Club.

The Jones and Long campaigns were richly financed.
Jones's big-business backers poured out money. And one
Long supporter, William C. Feazel, was reported in a New
Orleans *Item* article to have contributed $300,000. It was
conservatively estimated by political observers that well
over $1,000,000 was spent for the two candidates.

Jones blundered throughout his campaign as he had as
Governor. He first declared Long's promises were impossible because Louisiana was not a wealthy State. Then he
switched his tune and outpromised Long.

The campaign also revealed that the State's three major
newspapers had learned nothing. They are the New Orleans *Times-Picayune*, which has a monopoly in the morning field; its afternoon edition, the *States*; and the afternoon
Item. The highly profitable *Times-Picayune* combination is
run by a board of directors, practically all of them members
of the Boston Club. The *Item* had a sordid record of weath-
ervane political switches during the 1930's, which often
had both its pro-Long and anti-Long readers gasping in
amazement. The paper was sold early in the 1940's to a
sincere and honest Quaker, originally from Indiana. He restored the *Item* to respectability and financial stability but

268

did not know where to go from there, as he was as conservative and Boston Club-minded as his opposition. Now the *Item* has been bought by the Stern interests, which formerly owned the now defunct Philadelphia *Record* and at one time published the *New York Post*.

All three papers backed Jones and in the final days of the campaign tried to torpedo Long by playing up a sensational charge of income-tax evasion. The accusation was hurled by an anti-Long Congressman under the cloak of his official immunity. Long challenged the attacker to repeat his statements off the floor of the House, a challenge that was not accepted. Similarly, the three newspapers dropped their raucous outcries immediately after the election.

Louisiana's voters responded by giving Earl a record-breaking 200,000 majority in the run-off primary.

It has cost $70,000,000 in new State taxes, but Earl has carried out most of his campaign promises. As under Huey, the chief emphasis has been on sorely needed benefits. The big hitch is that Earl hasn't had the courage to attempt a "soak-the-rich" tax program, such as proved so successful under Huey.

Earl saddled slightly more than half the new expenditures on the general public. The State sales tax was doubled; the five-cent cigarette tax was increased to eight cents, highest in the nation; the gasoline tax, already tied for highest, was boosted to nine cents; and a new tax of two and one half cents a bottle was imposed on beer. In addition, the tax on petroleum was kited from eleven cents to twenty-six cents a barrel, the highest in the country.

Curiously, there was no attempt to sugar-coat these bitter pills. The Longs merely announced that the voters had approved the tax increases by electing the Long ticket.

This had devastating effect on Long popularity. When Russell, taking advantage of the death of Senator John Overton, ran for his seat, an astounding reversal of sentiment resulted. Kennon, this time backed by the Boston Club, opposed Russell. Russell barely squeaked through in the primary by a 10,000 majority. Between February and September, 1948, the Long majority had shriveled from over 200,000 to a tiny 10,000.

It was enough to discourage any politician less thick-skinned than Huey, and Earl disclosed he was no dictator by the way he took it. At the end of his first year as Governor, he announced he would never again run for office. He appeared so soured that some of his friends said that only another tremendous flip-flop by the electorate would change his mind.

But even if Earl does retire, it will make little difference. With or without him, the Long family is back in Louisiana politics to stay. Russell is the key in all the plans for the future, with his younger brother, Palmer, considered certain to join him after he reaches twenty-nine, which apparently is considered the proper age for a Long political debut. Another Long, Dr. George S., elder brother of Earl, has indicated ambitions to seek a Congressional seat.

Enactment of his welfare program was not Earl's sole preoccupation during his first year as Governor. Under his pressure, the Legislature repealed the Civil Service Act. This opened the way for a lusty patronage grab—thanks to Jones's fatuous ineptness. Also, Earl imposed a hundred-dollar tax on an estimated ten thousand slot machines in the State, although another statute makes these devices illegal. Frank Costello, New York gambling czar, already had an interest in a Jefferson Parish gambling house. He had come to New Orleans with a bevy of slot machines in 1936 while Maestri was Mayor and liked the city so well he kept up his connections there.

If young Russell chooses a full senatorial term, the Long

270

machine may have an unexpected candidate for Governor in 1952. A dark-horse prospect is Earl's little-known Lieutenant Governor, W. H. (Bill) Dodds, a husky young newcomer who proved most adept in old-time Long oratory during the 1948 campaign.

A general belief prevails that new scandals and a dictatorship will develop under Earl. With the spoils system back, there will undoubtedly be plenty of waste. But the brazen and widespread thievery that occurred in the 1930's is unlikely. Earl is very anxious to establish the respectability of the Longs in Louisiana.

This ambition has had one curious result. Some of Huey's most violent foes have turned up as leaders in Earl's administration.

Chief among them is Francis Williams, New Orleans attorney, who fought Huey tooth-and-nail and, on one occasion, was severely mauled by some of his thugs. Earl made Williams head of a commission to investigate the Port of New Orleans, apparently in an effort to add it to the spoils-system list. The Port is nominally under "nonpartisan" control, meaning business rule. It was once a big source of patronage for Huey.

Another original Huey foe whom Earl has favored is Clem Sehrt. He was made chairman of the Louisiana Democratic Association. Similarly, Shirley G. Wimberly was named special counsel of the new Alcoholic Beverage Commission, which Earl created. The liquor business, curiously, was among the few to escape new taxes. Wimberly is an old friend of Williams and Sehrt and, like them, fought Huey.

Newcomers since Huey's day include W. H. Talbot, who became Democratic National Committeeman after serving as Earl's campaign manager; Theo Hotard, Property Commissioner and lone Longite on the New Orleans City Council; and William C. Feasel, the multimillionaire oil operator

271

from North Louisiana who made the largest single contribution to Earl's campaign. For this, Feasel got two rewards. He was appointed U. S. Senator for the few months between Overton's death and Russell's election. And Feasel's personal attorney, S. L. Digby, was made chairman of the Louisiana Conservation Commission, which determines the allocation of petroleum production in the State.

At one period during the 1948 gubernatorial campaign, doubts arose among some of the courthouse rings whether Earl could win. Reports circulated widely that Perez of Plaquemines was of this mind and was planning a break. If that had happened it would have been finis for Earl. But Perez stood fast and Earl won, thus doubly enhancing the standing of the Plaquemines boss in the esteem of the victor. When Earl was inaugurated, Perez had the honor role of master of ceremonies.

Thomas K. Griffin, staff writer of the New Orleans *Item*, after describing the scramble of the lesser politicos to get a word with the new Governor, concluded, "Since the Governor's ear is often inaccessible, the next most popular ear is that of Leander Perez, the Plaquemines Pooh-Bah, whose disarming manner belies what is possibly the shrewdest brain in Louisiana politics."

When the Legislature convened to impose the taxes necessary to carry out Earl's program, a benign influence seemed to be hovering over Plaquemines Parish.

One of its chief industries is the Freeport Sulphur Co., whose main offices are in New York City. Freeport began steaming out sulphur from a Plaquemines dome in the 1930's. While Leche was Governor, State taxes were fixed at levels slightly below those in adjoining Texas. When Earl's Legislature began boosting the tax on petroleum, similar committee action was taken on sulphur. The committees assumed that sulphur would bear its share of the increased tax load, particularly as most of the State is interested in oil and only one parish, Plaquemines, is interested in sulphur. The committees were wrong.

The proposal to increase the tax on sulphur was quietly shelved. It was not even allowed to come to a vote.

A direct example of Perez' power-behind-the-throne role was the way he made Earl stand to heel in the presidential race. In this instance, as in practically all other matters, Perez' motivation was economic. He gave rabid adherence to the Dixiecrat movement because it is the creature of the great vested interests which he serves. High among these interests is oil, violently opposed to federal ownership of the oil-rich tidelands. President Truman's unequivocal insistence on federal control was the basic reason Perez went Dixiecrat. It was also the reason why he forced Earl Long to back down on Truman.

As an orthodox Southern politician, Long is opposed to the Civil Rights program, although neither he nor his brother ever engaged in persecution of Negroes under the guise of white supremacy. Earl also opposed Truman on the tidelands issue, ostensibly because Louisiana, which had already obtained $34,000,000 in revenue from tideland leases, might lose many millions in future taxes from this source.

However, when a United Press reporter asked Earl, as he left the White House, what position he would take on Truman's nomination, Earl replied: "I don't have any position. I'm not even a delegate to the [Democratic] convention. But I will stay in the party, and whoever the Democrats nominate I will be behind as much as possible."

When the Dixiecrats set up their rump shop, their prospects did not appear very bright in Louisiana as long as Earl didn't bolt. The State law, designed to prevent Democratic splintering, provides that a new party can get on the ballot only by a petition signed by a thousand registered voters unaffiliated with existing parties. This requirement is specifically aimed at "fractionating," as a companion provision made it necessary to register as a Democrat in order to vote in the party's primary. As Democratic primaries are the actual election, most whites registered as Democrats.

A New Orleans manufacturer, John U. Barr, was wrestling with this problem as chairman of Louisiana's Dixiecrats when Perez cannily gave him the solution. The Democratic State Central Committee, top-heavy with Long machine followers, met to draw up the party ticket for the presidential election. With Perez as ringmaster, the Committee voted unanimously to throw out the Truman-Barkley ticket and substitute instead the Dixiecrat slate in the Democratic column. It was a gross and lawless act, but wholly in keeping with the temper and motivations of the Dixiecrats and their masters.

When national Democratic officials protested the outrage, Earl outwardly backtracked. He hurriedly convened a special session and passed a bill putting Truman and Barkley back on the ballot in a separate column. But he allowed the berserk Dixiecrats to appropriate the familiar (to the South) Democratic rooster and Truman had to run under a donkey emblem. Under these conditions there was little chance for him to carry Louisiana unless Long announced his support and applied pressure on his machine. Earl did neither.

Perez became a member of a permanent steering committee of the Dixiecrats, and Representative F. Edward Hebert, whose district includes Perez' two key parishes, joined him in denouncing the Democratic ticket. The Boston Club crowd, naturally, also climbed aboard the Dixiecrat van. And Sam Jones, who had announced his retirement when Earl beat him, came burping back to the hustings and toured the Midwest for the Dixiecrats.

Although Earl and Russell later claimed to have voted for Truman, neither they nor any other major politico showed up

274

when Barkley, Truman's running mate, came to New Orleans for a campaign rally. James E. Comiskey, obscure ward leader of the decrepit Behrman machine, introduced Barkley, and has been stunned by his political acumen ever since.

Among the many so-called "neutrals" was bombastic Mayor Morrison of New Orleans. He carefully lay low during the election. But after Truman's spectacular victory, Morrison strutted valiantly forth once more. He cockily boasted to reporters during a Washington visit that he had "avoided the Dixiecrat bear trap." This brought from National Committee-man Talbot, an ardent Dixiecrat, the derisive snort, "It is true Morrison did not get caught in the bear trap. But I think he should be presented with a silver-studded saddle with which to ride fences. He did not come out for Truman and rumor has it that he voted Republican."

Perez again collected his reward when the Dixiecrats carried Louisiana. He had pitched his opposition to Truman on the state's-right issue and charges of Communist influences in the national administration. But when the federal government sued Louisiana on the tidelands oil issue, Perez immediately was named Special Assistant State Attorney General to fight the case.

There was a worse shock even than Truman's victory for the Long machine in the November election. Nine of Earl's most favored amendments to the Constitution were defeated.

Study of the returns indicates that many of the 20,000 to 25,000 votes that beat these amendments may have come from Negroes. Under the Supreme Court decisions making it possible for Negroes to vote, 27,930 were eligible in Louisiana. Prejudice is still so virulent that only zealots are brave enough to register. But when they register, they vote.

It seems likely that Louisiana Negroes voted for Truman. He got about 25,000 otherwise unaccountable votes. Intelligent Louisianians knew that the neutral pose of the Longs in the presidential race was a sham. If the Longs had fought for Truman they could have carried the State for him. The Negroes who registered also most certainly saw through the pretense and voted against the Longs and their amendments. In the close fight, these votes probably made the difference.

New registration is required every four years in Louisiana. The latest registration opened in 1949 and parish registrars reported Negroes signing up in greater numbers than ever before. It is interesting to speculate what effect this will have. A comparatively small number of Negro voters could hold the balance of power in the forthcoming New Orleans mayoralty election—and in Russell Long's fight for a full six-year senatorial term.

As Louisiana enters the second half of the twentieth century, democracy in the State is still weak and puny. Neither the tweedledee of the Long machine nor the tweedledum of the Boston Club offers much hope for enlightened government. Similarly, there appears little hope at present for the development of better leaders. No matter how well intentioned they may be when they take office, Louisiana politicians soon become afraid. They all tend to build up personal political machines.

But there are a few hopeful signs.

The Supreme Court decision outlawing the basing point price system may have profound economic and political impact. The wartime expansion of Louisiana industry has already had tremendous effect. Development of the chemical empire, that got a toehold along the Gulf of Mexico during the war, will further stir new forces and leaders. So will the organizing drives of the AFL and CIO.

Finally, there is genuine hope in the Negro, both for him-

276

self and the whites. Once Negroes can make themselves felt at the polls they may help all the underprivileged to better their lot.

Democracy may yet come to full bloom for the citizenry of the Pelican State.

NEBRASKA ★ ★ ★

Norris: In Victory and Defeat

J. E. LAWRENCE

IT WAS the last campfire for three bronzed plainsmen.

In guarding the settlers from Indian attacks, they had written history in bold flourishes upon the billowy grasses.

Their job finished, they found a green valley at the head-waters of the Dismal River. It was a valley over which towering bluffs stood sentinel, lush grass flourished, a never-failing stream of clear water etched a winding silvery thread through the hills of a silent virgin country. There W. F. (Buffalo Bill) Cody, Major Frank North of the Pawnee Scouts, and his brother, Captain Luther North, brought one of the first herds of longhorns north from Texas over the old cattle trails of the Southwest. These men, who knew every foot of the vast open range from the Missouri to the foothills of the Rockies, were convinced no fairer land existed than that within the valley they had chosen.

Their own transition from the surging excitements of Indian warfare to the more prosaic routine of a budding ranching country, incorporated the outlines of one state era and

★

J. E. LAWRENCE has been editor of the *Lincoln Star* since 1922. He has had a long career in political writing. He served on the Nebraska Advisory Committee which made preliminary recommendations for the development of hydroelectric plants, and collaborated with the late Senator George Norris in writing the *Fighting Liberal*.

278

marked the beginning of another. This period is important to all understanding of Nebraska State government and the social and economic currents which molded it, because it projected a significant conflict in the exploitation of natural resources. The "cold war" between the cattle barons of the open range and the homesteaders provides even now an accurate portrait of economic, social, and political thought in Nebraska. The cattlemen came to accept fences, and the homesteader tended his fields jealously, his own little world complete and fully satisfying except in seasons of crop failure. Today Nebraska reveals the void which the absence of gold, coal, oil, forests, or great industry necessarily imposes upon the political thought of a people.

Nebraska is a land of seventy-seven thousand square miles without snow-capped mountains or tree-lined lakes. Nebraska never felt the primitive impact of a lumbering camp or knew the feverish lust for gold. For a year, prior to World War II, it tasted the intoxication of the discovery of oil. But the oil was of low grade and meager quantity and the thrill was short lived.

In Nebraska the plain rises so imperceptibly from an elevation of a thousand feet above sea level at the Missouri bluffs to the hills and tablelands of the western border as to create the perfect illusion that the earth is flat. The temperature varies kaleidoscopically from blazing summer heats of over one hundred degrees to teeth-rattling winter colds of twenty-five degrees below zero. Nebraska is also a State which, according to the 1940 census, had only one city of more than two hundred thousand people; a second, the State capital, nudging toward one hundred thousand; six ranging between ten and twenty thousand; and the remaining more than five hundred incorporated towns and villages merely rural marketing centers.

For sophistication Nebraska looks to Omaha, and Omaha

279

complies with a little gambling and a little of the aroma of the wide-open town, flaunting bold city ways at times, more discreet at others.

The early map makers had a name for this land, the "Great American Desert." The firstcomers felt only relief when they had left it behind. Those who followed were sod busters, tree planters and home builders. The task called for neither originality nor genius. Their job was to establish a predominantly agrarian democracy, and to fit it into a huge country with a complicated economy.

What have been the forces fashioned in Nebraska's State government? The result is completely agricultural in its abundance or scarcity, its wellbeing or threatened bankruptcy. And being so sensitive to drastic change, these forces have molded a smug, stubborn, conservative political philosophy which accepts established order when things go well but which breaks out in angry rebellion in times of desperation. They say out here, these Nebraskans: "Work hard, practice thrift, and find contentment. There is no quick road to riches." In State government they follow their own advice. They pay little for public service, demand and get a great deal in the form of honest handling of public affairs, especially in the expenditure of taxes. They also get a thick, sirupy type of cautious conservatism that delights in riding with the tides, and reveals no taste for disturbing the even tenor of life.

In a concerted sense they gave their first demonstration of a state-wide consciousness in the formulation of a highway program, drafted to cover a twenty-year period, at the end of which there will exist a comprehensive system of modern highways and farm-to-market roads. Although Nebraska has been building highways for more than thirty years, not until 1948 was there an attempt at a methodical

study. Then it was initiated by Governor Val Peterson, made
by a group of citizens, finally approved by the Legislature.
But this approval may be upset two years hence. Sporadic
attention has focused on farm tenancy, but is tapering off.
Thanks to the zeal of individuals, a magnificent program of
farm co-operatives has been evolved, to which every encour-
agement has been lent through legislation.

For two decades Nebraskans experienced a loss in population without alarm. This slow drift away from the State,
first interpreted as evidence of stable settlement, gained momentum in the late twenties and reached peak tide in the
early thirties. The twenties saw Nebraska lose one seat in
Congress and the thirties witnessed the loss of another. But
this took place without arousing a ripple in Nebraska political thought. Call it stupidity or indifference, no Nebraska
Governor in the last twenty years has come forward with a
clear-cut program to avert the decline in population. The
situation is reflected only in a clamor for lightened tax burdens and for cut-to-the-bone economy in State affairs.

Nebraska has reached the point where it is determining
the future largely on how little its government spends.

Three times the late Charles W. Bryan was elected Governor on a campaign of "Look at your tax receipts." When
the Democrats are in power they are spenders; when the
Republicans hold the office, the opposition turns the sharp
edge of economy upon them. In occasional bursts of unity
the leaders of the two major parties get together to undertake long-neglected developments, but that is rare. The net
result of tax domination of political thought in Nebraska has
been to blind its people to social trends throughout the
world.

It has also contributed another curious development. No
party since the eighties has remained in power for more than

ten years. Nebraska has alternated briskly between Republicans and Democrats as an effective check on spending.

The State has had honest, incorruptible government. It has missed the sensation of corruption in high places. Its officials never have given their people the opportunity to wag gossipy tongues, or to give rein to indignation against the betrayal of public trust. The Nebraska way has been to demand an exceptional degree of personal integrity in its public servants. Either exacting care in selection, fool luck, or both have been present to such a degree that eighty-two years of Statehood has failed to produce a first-class public scandal.

But that record of impeccable honesty may have denied Nebraska the sense of social responsibility—that enlightened State government is more than honest bookkeeping. It can lead to a dangerous self-satisfaction which exhausts itself when it discovers that every penny of public funds has been accounted for rigorously.

The first Governor, David Butler, was impeached shortly after the beginning of his third term on charges that he had failed to account for all the money received from the sale of public lands. The impeachment was expunged by a subsequent Legislature and Butler vindicated by subsequent election to the State Senate. There was another flurry over defalcation of public funds. In 1897, the State Treasurer, Joseph S. Bartley, was convicted of appropriating over $500,-000, sentenced to twenty years in prison and fined $303,768. Nebraska, in righteous rage, deals severely with faithless public servants. Four years later Bartley was pardoned. But not since the turn of the century has any State official been charged with dereliction of duty, abuse of power, or misuse of funds.

The ancient chivalry of the plains toward womanhood has chosen strange and devious language in which to express itself. Nebraska never has elected a woman to State office. The only concession made to women is found in the fact that nine have been permitted to serve in the State Assembly, three of them since the unicameral system became effective.

Yet the dull monotony of a pattern, deceiving in its simplicity, has borne strange political fruit in both State and national government. From out of it emerged two great liberals—the late William Jennings Bryan, and the late Senator George W. Norris. Bryan reached his peak in an era of encrusted, entrenched, national reaction. Norris, in a career covering more than forty years, successfully fought the reactionaries in his State and in the nation and enriched democratic institutions in both. Then, fantastically, Nebraska turned squarely around at the high tide of a decade of great social progress and sent to the United States Senate two of the most reactionary men on its rolls.

Young Bryan gripped the imagination of his people. He had scarcely established himself in a law office before they embraced him and sent him to Congress as their spokesman. He was molded for the classic role of a political gladiator. Well over six feet, straight as an Indian, and endowed with great physical endurance, he had overpowering eloquence and charm. But Bryan's political horizon stopped at the edge of the cities. He never understood the problems of an industrial democracy. But before embittered frustration stripped him of effectiveness, in between national crusades, the Commoner devoted much attention to Nebraska State government. He borrowed the direct primary system from "Fighting Bob" La Follette, shoving it down the throats of the regulars of both parties while they squealed in protest.

He made the direct primary a cornerstone of Nebraska State government for forty years. But he had to carry his fight directly to the voters. After he had won this battle he had to call upon boyish, tousle-headed reform Governor George L. Sheldon, a Republican, and a Legislature dominated by liberal Republicans, to uproot the old convention system of nominating candidates for State and national office. It had been the stronghold of the railroads, the liquor interests, and all privilege-seeking groups, and through it they had been able to enforce their will upon State government.

Bryan lost no time in following up this initial success. Nebraska had not adjusted itself fully to the primary before he embarked upon a new campaign, this time the bank-guarantee system, forerunner of the present Federal Bank Deposit Insurance Law. Before his death in 1925 his bank-guarantee plan had become an acknowledged failure, abandoned by the people who had approved it so eagerly. It was not adapted for a single state. The direct cause which led to early collapse, however, was a pioneer Nebraska antimonopoly measure, enacted during the Populist uprising. The law was the basis of a Nebraska Supreme Court ruling that the State Banking Department could place no limit upon the number of bank charters issued in any community. Banks sprang up like mushrooms, many in towns with only a few hundred people. The final chapter was written in scores of bank failures and estimated liabilities of from sixteen to twenty millions of dollars.

Bryan also turned his attention to prohibition and woman suffrage. He had forced himself upon his party. He made it accept him over the objections of J. Sterling Morton, Secretary of Agriculture in the Cleveland Cabinet, a fiery territorial Democrat, whose denunciation of Bryan exceeded any criticism leveled at him by Nebraska Republicans. Later Bryan split with the late Gilbert M. Hitchcock, publisher of the powerful Omaha *World-Herald,* and the late Arthur F. Mullen, who commanded a large personal following of Nebraska Democrats.

284

Little did Bryan know that in procuring passage of Nebraska's first primary law, he contributed to the election of Hitchcock to the United States Senate. Even more, Bryan could not foresee that the 1907 primary law contributed to the first Senate victory of a towering American liberal, the late George W. Norris.

Little now remains in Nebraska of the political house that Bryan built.

Senator Norris reached Nebraska ahead of Bryan, without thought of a public career. He intended to settle in Washington state. Throughout his life newness attracted him. His mother owned a small tract of land in southeastern Nebraska near Tecumseh, and on his way home to Ohio from Washington state he decided to inspect it. A few months later he was located at Beatrice, and then in the Beaver Valley to the west, where he took up the practice of law and laid the foundation for a public career.

Oddly, he had no flair for oratory. He was shy, outwardly uncertain of himself, deeply indoctrinated with the orthodox Republicanism of the Republican community where he was born and reared. He was torn between conflicting desires to practice law and to farm. Although later he was to contribute more to the independent spirit in politics and to non-partisan government than any other man of his time, in those early years Norris was a regular Republican, working through his party, supporting his party, suspicious of Populism and its leaders.

But he was deeply distressed by the misfortunes which befell the farmers, and as a judge was appalled by the flood of mortgage foreclosures brought on by ruinous commodity prices, drought, and other scourges.

Norris grew slowly but solidly.

He was in Washington when the direct-primary system

was adopted in Nebraska. He gave it his support enthusiastically. It was the fear of this stout-hearted fighting man that protected his law against the continued sabotage by the politicians in both Nebraska parties. Not until his death in the early forties did the politicians succeed in crippling the law with a partial restoration of the convention system.

Ironically, it was Norris's unicameral Legislature which accepted this scheme to appease both the politicians and the voters. Had Norris been alive, the convention endorsement law would not have slipped through the Legislature. Other states, notably Ohio, are eying this Nebraska system. In Nebraska, all but the active party workers look upon it as a backward step, curing none of the primary evils it was supposed to correct, and creating some of its own. There was an effort at the 1949 session to restore the original direct primary, but again the party organizations applied pressure and obtained a two-year reprieve.

What few recognized in the towering stature of George W. Norris was his rare sense of political timing. He lacked a gifted tongue, but he had infinite patience, unwavering resolution, and impregnable forthrightness. He spent fifteen years of grueling labor and deliberate planning, biding his opportunity in laying the foundations for Nebraska's Little TVA. In Washington he waited over eight years until he thought the temper of the American people was right for the overthrow of Speaker Joe Cannon. In Nebraska he called upon his inexhaustible pool of patience until the early thirties made it possible to realize his dream of creating a state-wide public power and irrigation system.

It was the aftermath of the first World War which laid the setting for Norris's success in establishing TVA: the combined forces of ruinous farm prices, world-wide depression, and an unbroken eight-year drought. These tragic factors gave him the opportunity for which he had long been waiting to provide his own State with one of the tools of modern living.

From the day he won the fight to overthrow Cannonism, Norris was a marked man in Nebraska politics. His Nebraska critics frequently were more savage than his enemies beyond the State's borders. They pursued him relentlessly and ruthlessly for thirty years. They fought his re-election to the Senate in 1918 in a loyalty campaign based upon his vote against war. In 1924, they attempted to exploit his friendship for Bob La Follette and his opposition to Calvin Coolidge. In 1930 they produced another George W. Norris, a grocery clerk, and attempted to put his name on the ballot without designation in order to confuse the voters. By 1936, worn and weary, he was through with party politics and wanted to retire. Friends prevailed on him at the last minute to run. He did, but as an independent and without a supporting slate. Again he won and confounded his baying foes.

That same year, against the opposition of ninety per cent of the Nebraska press and all the powers of party machinery, he made Nebraska the experimental ground of a single-house Legislature.

The politicians feared him. They feared him because gradually in Nebraska, and to a surprising degree throughout the United States, millions waited to hear what George W. Norris had to say and to see how he voted. They believed profoundly that he was utterly right and utterly honest.

Against this background the present leadership of unpredictable Senator Kenneth S. Wherry and conservative Senator Hugh Butler is a strange paradox.

When Butler looks at himself in the looking glass he sees a man with a mission. In the proper atmosphere he may tell about it, tears streaming down his ruddy cheeks. He must save America, and his own people, from present folly. He is

287

utterly honest about this. He is sincere, kindly, a successful businessman—and stuffy. Outwardly, no qualms assail him as to America's wise course in an atomic age. He believes so thoroughly in the Naughty Nineties that frequently his critics do him the injustice of crediting him with a political guile he does not possess.

Butler took a long time building up. When he got into politics he was wealthy enough to have no financial worries. He took over a moribund party organization at lowest ebb, and contributed generously when funds were hard to get. In sacrificial spirit he accepted the chairmanship of the Douglas County Republican organization. No one else would take it. He became National Committeeman, teamed up with Wherry as State Chairman, and spent unremitting years rebuilding party organization. Then he ran for the Senate, the first political office he had sought. Although now a fervent "economy" clamorer, Butler hatched a strange political chick in his campaign. To drought-ridden Nebraska farmers, he advanced a novel corn loan program, whereby those needing feed for livestock could get up to five thousand bushels from Uncle Sam's surplus stocks. Repayments would be in kind when the farmer raised corn. The idea, a modification of lend-lease, caught on and Butler won a sweeping victory.

Nature came to his rescue in the Senate. The fields produced bountifully and he was not called upon to make good his very un-Republican campaign pledge.

Six years later he was back with a new idea. He would right the wrong inflicted on wheat growers who had sold grain for European export just prior to a bonus Uncle Sam paid to encourage wheat marketing. Petitions were circulated in Nebraska wheat counties and signed by thousands. Again, Butler was elected by a handsome majority. And again he was spared from having to make good. The removal of controls in 1946, the year of his re-election, sent grain prices

288

soaring, blotting out completely the need for legislation on the no-longer-existent wheat-bonus issue.

If Senator Butler has supplied any new ideas for State government, he has kept the fact a dark secret.

Just when and where Wherry reached the decision to succeed Senator Norris is not clear. He was a little bit to the left of right when he launched himself politically at the age of thirty-five. In a restrained sense he basked on the fringes of the Norris leadership. He was elected to the Nebraska State Senate, won a second term, with Nebraska's bank-guarantee system crashing in ruins. Unpaid depositors were clamoring for their money. Wherry grabbed the bear by the tail. He introduced a bill to set aside the State's constitutional ban against bonded debt in order to permit its people to pledge the State's credit to make good those losses sustained by individual depositors in bankrupt banks. The proposal got nowhere.

But it brought down on Wherry's head the first of the two political reverses he has experienced. Bankers in his district, which embraced his home county of Pawnee and neighboring Gage, ganged up on him, and turned him out to pasture. It was only a brief dash of cold water. In 1930 Wherry emerged from obscurity to oppose Dwight Griswold, later first head of the American Mission to Greece, and Lieutenant Governor George Williams, for the Republican nomination for Governor.

It was a strange choice for an astute politician. Nebraska has a sort of fetish against promoting its Governors to Congress. Many have tried, few have succeeded. But if Wherry showed contempt for this tradition, he displayed healthy respect for doing the thing that seemed expedient. He launched his candidacy in a statement he distributed to a handful of Washington newspapermen in the outer office of

Senator Norris. If Norris knew it at the time, he regretted it later.

The campaign which followed was incredible. The shadows were growing longer and Nebraska's economic skies were crashing. Farmers were alarmed and uneasy. In that atmosphere the issue which Wherry, Griswold, and Williams took to the voters was the selection of a candidate who could beat Democrat Charles W. Bryan. Neither Wherry nor Griswold had a program of any kind.

Griswold defeated Wherry, and in turn Bryan beat him. Wherry has been given credit for an assist in Bryan's victory, although possibly undeserved. When the Democratic candidate visited the Pawnee County fair, Wherry, its barker and handyman, in a magnificent spirit of nonpartisanship, called upon his home folks to give Bryan a hand. It was apparently the beginning of a beautiful friendship between them.

Shortly after taking office, Bryan had a Republican vacancy on the Board of Control. He named Wherry, who after a brief hesitation declined.

Soon thereafter, Wherry was exercising his showmanship to bring the Republican Party back to life. His reward for a most intense county-by-county revival was the senatorship, in a campaign in which he made the New Deal and all of its works his target. Now he fondly eyes the White House.

There has been little stability in Nebraska political thought other than that of inherent caution. In the absence of marked contrast between dire poverty and great wealth, social consciousness is apt to nap. Even the aging land, the basis of Nebraska economy, inspired no concern over soil depletion until Roosevelt came on the scene. The farmers today, schooled in conservation, still rebel against the slightest taint of compulsion or regimentation.

A fabulous empire, with no strings attached, was given to

290

the railroads, to encourage the construction of transportation facilities. Through federal grants, in one expansive gesture the Union Pacific, the Burlington and Missouri, the Sioux City and Pacific, and the St. Joe and Denver obtained a princely subsidy of 7,879,241 acres, much of it the choicest and most productive land in the fertile Platte valley. Based on present values it would more than cover the original cost of construction. The Union Pacific alone got 4,800,000 acres. The State itself distributed an additional half million acres among nine railroads. That, and some of the earlier homesteading practices in Nebraska, inspired the distinguished historian, Dr. A. E. Sheldon, to write that it was "the speculator, not the cultivator of the soil" who reaped the benefits of early settlement.

Nebraska got the railroads, for which she clamored to connect her farms with the primary markets, at a heavy price. Almost from the beginning her people became convinced they were the victims of discriminatory freight rates which exacted an undue share of the returns from the land, and which stifled industrial development. The railroads entered politics and became the most powerful force in State affairs until their yoke was thrown off. They played a dominant role in the election of Governors, legislators, and even got around in municipal affairs.

Nebraska has long dreamed of a flourishing industry to complement the basic agricultural economy.

Originally the State did not build its tax structure with that in mind. But in recent years it has extolled the virtues of the simple tax base, resting almost exclusively upon levies against real and personal property, in the hope of attracting manufacturing. That was one of the two objectives of a national "White Spot" campaign ten years ago when neighboring commonwealths, and the seaboards, were bombarded with propaganda that was truthful only to the extent that Ne-

291

braska was without bonded debt, had no general sales tax, and no State income tax. In 1939, Nebraska manufacturing institutions employed only twenty-five thousand workers. Ten years later the number had doubled, but there was only a handful of manufacturing plants employing more than one thousand, and the bright expectations inspired by the "White Spot" drive and later by the war boom, had faded.

Paternity of the phrase "Nebraska White Spot" is clouded. It is said to have been conceived in the plush offices of an Omaha advertising agency, employed by a group of businessmen to formulate a campaign to head off mounting demands for broadening the State's tax base. No debutante could have been presented with more tender, loving care. The White Spot was showered with the most gorgeous flowers, the most carefully chosen bons mots.

Actually, at the time, Nebraska tax solvency was attributable in a large measure to the vast sums of federal funds poured into the State in the form of farm subsidies, a broad-gauged public works program, and river developments. Delinquent taxes were wiped out through funds from federal farm benefits, and in scores of Nebraska communities by federal home loans. In its hours of glory, the Nebraska White Spot became the toast of a wide circle of cynical admirers, outwardly smitten with the fresh young charm of no bonded indebtedness, no State sales tax, no State income tax. Politicians in the two major parties fell over themselves in paying court. They hovered around like bees gathering in the sweetness of a delicate bloom. But less than ten years later the popular idol had lost much of its sheen.

The State government found itself the victim of its own hoax. The small home owner and the farmer were in rebellion against carrying the major burden of the tax load. State agencies were starved for adequate operating funds. From the rocking chair of his front porch in Emporia the late William

Allen White described Nebraska's White Spot as "a shameless little hussy, walking the street, painted cheeks, bold eyes."

Nebraska needs industry. But no leadership has appeared to encourage it. The bulk of the raw products of the soil go out of the State for processing.

Nebraska ships small grain to be manufactured into chicken feed, pays the freight coming and going to produce millions of pounds of poultry, and with a few notable exceptions ships the live poultry East. Nebraska saw one of its largest food products concerns leave the State for a crowded metropolis, and the loss provoked little thought.

Of late, a new spirit has been budding. There has been much questioning as to the cause of the steady loss in population, why young people leave and newcomers move on. The young people supply an answer which at least to them is sufficient. Their exodus, they say, is the result of a blighting conservatism reflecting itself in social outlook, in economic practice, and finally in political policies.

The absence of industry has had marked influence in shaping labor policy. Nebraska was one of the states that in 1947 adopted the so-called "right to work" amendment. It became a part of the State Constitution. Petitions placed it on the ballot, and the hulking figure of John L. Lewis was hauled out to arouse voters to ban the closed shop.

The feeling on labor runs deeply, surprisingly, because Nebraska's view necessarily is shaped by labor-management conflict beyond her borders. Outside the railroad brotherhoods, packing industry, and a few isolated plants, there are no large labor payrolls. Generally, relationships of employer and worker in Nebraska have been harmonious. Strikes have been few. Years ago, employer and labor met on common ground and without difficulty reached agreement upon a compensation law. An industrial court to serve as a conciliation agency in differences affecting utilities inspired labor's opposition, but at the end of two years it has been called upon in remarkably few cases. Nebraska has had an anti-picketing law for nearly two decades, but it has rarely been invoked. In the few cases which have arisen the State has deftly shifted responsibility to local authorities.

If nature penalized Nebraska in natural resources, the State was exceedingly fortunate in the character of those who settled it.

They buried racial hatreds when they left the Old World.

They came into Nebraska by the thousands, seeking land, hungry for homes. Germans, Swedes, Danes, Bohemians, Poles, Italians, with the Germans predominant, the Swedes next, and the Bohemians third. They established their own communities in the beginning, founded their own churches and schools, and spoke their native tongues. That did not last long. It disintegrated in the melting pot. Even before the second generation reached maturity, it was disappearing.

They were good farmers, thrifty, industrious, neighborly. They had a love for land, and they lavished a tender affection upon it. They were free from bigotry and racial prejudices. They did fear government, a strong government. Their European heritage made them wary and resentful of attempts at regulation. The dominant German in Nebraska practiced temperance rigidly, but it was his voting strength which on two occasions rejected prohibition proposals.

In State government, the dominant strain has been the bulwark of the demand for simplicity, thrift, and individual freedom. The farmer relied so completely upon himself, his land had made him so self-sufficient, his character was so marked by integrity and law obedience, that he felt the greatest contribution government could make was to grant him complete freedom of action. The less government, the

294

more certain he was of happiness. He resented change at first but when first Bryan and then Norris captured his imagination, he became a loyal and devoted follower. He accepted the State primary, he was ardent in his support of the initiative and the referendum, he fell in behind the ill-fated experiment of the Nebraska State bank-guarantee law, and against the party bosses his vote approved the one-house Legislature.

Similarly, he came by his isolation understandably. He or his parents had fled Europe with its militarism and its wars. He had sympathized with Bryan's campaign against imperialism in 1900, and has been chary of foreign entanglements ever since.

It was out of this background that the composite Nebraskan has emerged. The German boy married the French, the Swedish, or the Bohemian girl who lived down the road. That composite Nebraskan represents the second or the third generation. His government must be free from intolerance, racial persecution, or religious bigotry.

But the record is not entirely free of racial tensions. In 1919 an Omaha mob battered its way to the Douglas County jail, seized a Negro being held on suspicion, set fire to the building, entailing thousands of dollars of loss, and nearly hanged Mayor Ed P. Smith, a capable, brave official, who attempted to restrain the mob. The episode is still a tender spot in Nebraska history, and had a sobering effect upon the people. Nebraska has handled its racial tensions largely without legislative action.

In the 1949 legislative session, and in its predecessor, there were demands for a constitutional convention. Speaker Earl J. Lee introduced a bill for a constitutional convention, but the proposal died in committee. The present Constitution was drafted and approved in 1920.

Nebraskans have shown the greatest reluctance to alter the

basic conceptions with which they embarked upon Statehood. The changes that have come do not represent the work of any of the three constitutional conventions which have been held since Nebraska entered the Union. Every basic change in constitutional government has been brought about by amendments, submitted either by the Legislature or through the initiative.

The first Nebraska Constitution was the curious product of poverty and ignorance of constitutional processes. In 1864, three years before Statehood, territorial delegates met for a constitutional convention in Omaha, but adjourned immediately without putting a scratch on paper. Two years later a handful of men, without official commission, gathered in the office of a lawyer, Experience Estabrook, and with the Iowa code as a working model drafted a fragmentary Constitution. It was submitted to a territorial Legislature under the most amazing conditions. No amendments could be offered from the floor, and the Legislature was not provided with copies of the document. In a literal sense, the Constitution was voted sight unseen.

One of its provisions, restricting voting rights to whites, cast a cloud of uncertainty on Statehood until the limitation was removed on the demand of President Andrew Johnson.

By 1871 Nebraska thought it was again ready to try its hand at drawing a Constitution. The Illinois Constitution of 1870, embodying agrarian wisdom, was lifted bodily. But when submitted to the people, the draft was rejected, along with separate proposals to give women the ballot, prohibition, compulsory education, and municipal aid to corporations. The chief factor contributing to the defeat was a provision taxing church property which exceeded five thousand dollars in value.

Four years later another constitutional convention convened. It utilized largely the draft of 1871 but incorporated one idea unique in state government: a flat prohibition against bonded debt and limitation of the borrowing power of the State for temporary purposes to one hundred thousand dollars. That provision is in effect today. It has held fast against all attacks and there have been times when it has pinched cruelly. It has excited wonder in other states.

Its virtues, especially in recent years of modern highways, mounting educational costs, social security, and other financial burdens, have been loudly extolled and proclaimed. The main penalties it has imposed upon Nebraska's progress have been carefully ignored or obscured.

This bonded-debt ban owes its place in the Nebraska Constitution largely to a handsome, eloquent, dark-eyed leader, Arthur J. Weaver, Sr. A member of the convention, he beat off determinedly all attempts to increase borrowing authority and to authorize bonded debt. As a result Nebraska is the only State which throughout its existence has been on a pay-as-you-go basis—a source of great pride to its people. Twice, however, Nebraska's general fund has been overdrawn, its warrants discounted, and claimants either waited for their money or discounted their warrants in order to get the cash due. The most notable example began in November, 1926, and continued until March, 1928, when all warrants in excess of ten dollars were registered. For nearly eighteen months Nebraska was not on a pay-as-you-go basis in the full sense; the State Treasurer registered 66,070 warrants, aggregating $10,219,022.19, which cost the State $174,415.68 interest.

Under its debt limitation Nebraska built a magnificent Capitol costing ten millions, an outstanding architectural achievement, and it was paid for upon completion. The State has spent nearly three hundred million dollars for highways without issuing a bond, through gas tax revenues and federal funds. That is on the bright side. On the other side, the pay-as-you-go policy has penalized educational institutions and institutions housing unfortunates. Over a twenty-year period, Nebraska's policy of no bonded debt limited expenditures for additions to the physical plant of the State University, now boasting an enrollment of over ten thousand, to three buildings costing approximately three-quarters of a million dollars.

A more distressing sign of shortsighted frugality was apparent throughout debates in the 1949 Legislature. Two years before, at the crest of agricultural prosperity, Nebraska decided to do something about a long-neglected task. It set up a modest special levy for building purposes, to be divided among the Board of Control in charge of the institutions housing the State's wards, the University of Nebraska, the four State Normal Colleges, and the National Guard armories. But the succeeding Legislature decided to tighten the purse strings, although it was not denied that more than five hundred insane patients, whose only crime was loss of reason, were being housed in jails, crowded in corridors and wards, parceled out to makeshift homes, without skilled treatment or proper care. In one Nebraska county a feeble-minded teenaged child was held in a county jail for over a year because of lack of accommodations.

Nebraska faces a painful decision. Its pay-as-you-go policy, its prohibition against bonded debt, its limited tax structure—kept inviolate while its neighbors were resorting to an income tax or general sales tax, or both, to supply necessary revenue—has created a crushing burden on real and personal property.

Outwardly no state has condemned more vehemently the federal policy of allocating tax dollars to the states for highway construction, for Social Security, for school lunches, and for other federal programs. But thrifty Nebraska has never turned down any federal money. It has taken every cent and cried for more. It has become politically fashionable to denounce dollar matching. Yet when unprecedented blizzards blocked hundreds of miles of Nebraska highways in 1949, Nebraska's State government appealed to Washington for help. Army Engineers opened Nebraska's blocked highways at a cost to Uncle Sam of more than eight million dollars. The State itself spent a little over one hundred thousand dollars of its own funds. Nebraska sought and got more federal help than three of her hard-pressed neighbors.

Members of the 1949 unicameral Legislature tried to outdo one another in denouncing federal dollar matching. An $800,000 allotment of funds in the school-lunch program called for a showdown. Nebraska took the money.

There continues a deep resentment against old-age assistance. One of the very first steps which the Legislature took was to pass a law providing for a poverty affidavit. It requires the relatives of the aged to swear that they are unable to support the applicant, setting forth in detail any property they may possess. In 1947, the Legislature adopted a lien law, establishing the State's claim to any property an old-age pensioner may possess at the time of death. "Cost of Nebraska old-age aid multiplies tenfold in thirteen years," a headline in the Omaha *World-Herald* thundered. "In depression-time March, 1936, cost to the taxpayers was $91,779 as 8,310 persons got old-age assistance. In March of prosperous 1949, cost had zoomed to $939,397—more than $32,000 a day as old-age assistance rolls totaled 23,840, almost three times as many as in 1936."

Nebraska's acceptance of old-age assistance has been with tongue in cheek. It growls while it mulls over the possibility that the financial burdens of the system may become a fixed, permanent pattern of State government. Since the inception of Social Security no state administration has been bold enough to project old-age assistance as a continuing respon-

299

sibility of the people, necessitating a definite tax base for its support. First, at the expense of highway construction, the State gasoline tax was tapped for one-half cent a gallon. To this was added revenue from liquor taxes. When more funds were needed a head tax of two dollars was approved. Finally the raid on highway funds led to the substitution of a cigarette tax for gasoline revenue.

Tax support for old-age assistance, for the blind, and for dependent children still remains on an emergency basis.

The tax blight extends to other fields.

Two years ago a sales-tax proposal to provide funds for State aid to weak school districts was rejected emphatically. At the same time the school redistricting bill to usher in a program of consolidation met defeat in the Legislature because of opposition to some of its compulsory features. At the 1949 session a more moderate bill, for voluntary consolidation, was adopted.

There are more than seven thousand school districts, urban and rural, in Nebraska's system of public education. Hundreds of them in the more sparsely settled rural areas are housed in ancient, poorly ventilated, unsanitary buildings. Scores of them have fewer than five pupils. More are one-teacher schools with a single instructor for children of all ages. Teachers in these smaller districts are notoriously underpaid; the prevailing teacher shortage has been felt acutely but no early relief appears in sight.

An attempt to broaden the tax base failed. Both a sales tax and an income-tax plan were slaughtered in the 1949 Legislature.

Nebraska still refuses to face a thorough overhauling of the tax machinery.

As a final salute to economy the Legislature passed a reso-

300

lution, with only a scattered handful of opposition, calling upon Congress to reduce all appropriations by ten per cent.

The most useful tool of Nebraska State government did not spring from native seed.

It was imported.

Timid in viewing change, limited in growth by early limitations in its Constitution, intended to serve as a curb against impetuous action, Nebraska has utilized the initiative and referendum more than any other instrument of government.

All of its constitutional changes, one at a time, have come about this way. Without the initiative and the referendum there would be no unicameral Legislature. Without the initiative Nebraska would not have experimented with prohibition two years in advance of federal action, and without it the "drys" could not have tested public sentiment again, unsuccessfully, in recent years. The initiative paved the way for the submission of seven constitutional amendments, four of which were approved, three defeated. Among those approved was one for a pure-food department, another for nonpartisan election of nonpolitical officials (judicial and educational), the third legalized pari-mutuel betting on races, the fourth created the Nebraska unicameral Legislature. Those defeated included woman suffrage, an attempt by the gasoline interests to block diversion of gasoline tax funds, and a proposal to legalize slot machines. The initiative has been drawn upon to propose laws on thirteen separate occasions. It was the means of giving Nebraska an employer's liability law. It established the principle of public convenience in the issuance of bank charters, and it was the basis of Nebraska's antipicketing law.

In 1930, the initiative was the springboard for one of the most unusual steps taken by the people of Nebraska. Twice Senator Norris and others had attempted through legislative action to permit municipally operated light plants to serve rural homes beyond their corporate limits. Twice they lost to a conference committee, where a powerful private-utility lobby succeeded in doing what it could not accomplish on the floor. By the initiative, public power forces proposed a law granting cities and towns owning electric-light plants the right to extend their lines. The voters were called upon to choose between two proposals which, except for the titles, contained precisely the same language except in the closing paragraphs. One granted authority to the municipal stations to build lines beyond the corporate limits; the other, submitted by the private power companies, refused permission, leaving the situation in status quo. Senator Norris then was in the center of the TVA fight in Washington, after a successful struggle for the Lame Duck amendment.

His participation was limited to a letter of endorsement, a plea to his fellow Nebraskans to approve action permitting municipal light plants to serve farm families and nearby villages. The vote was an amazing demonstration of the power of his name. The law carried: 204,579 for, 89,205 against. In a fine test of discrimination the proposal by the private utility companies was defeated in the same election: 118,617 for, and 162,050 against.

The initiative and the referendum came to Nebraska through an organization known as the Nebraska Direct Legislation League. Its ranks were drawn largely from devoted Norris followers. The foundations for a campaign in its behalf in Nebraska—one of the thirteen states to adopt it—were begun shortly after the overthrow of Cannonism in Washington. Again the people were ripe for a change. Party organization, with the railroad hold finally broken, continued to block popular measures in the Legislature. The mood of the Nebraska voter was demonstrated strikingly when finally the 1911 legislative session did submit a constitutional

302

amendment for the initiative and referendum. It was approved: 189,200 for, to only 15,515 against.

The Nebraska Direct Legislation League knew its way around. The party bosses were sulky, fearful to attempt direct public attack, confident that they could win their fight in the Legislature itself. The League got a plank in the Democratic State program approving submission of the initiative and referendum. It made no effort at a Republican convention, held on the same day, to write a similar plank in that platform. That did it. The Democrats were committed, and Republican legislators generally had to go along.

There has been uniform approval of the initiative and the referendum. Not only has it contributed tremendously by the adoption of major constructive laws but has been equally effective in rejecting undesirable measures.

Drums beat angrily when the 1949 Nebraska Unicameral swept the litter from its cluttered desk. The sixth regular session had brought the skeptics out of hiding. The Legislature had passed an appropriation bill calling for one hundred and fifty-one million dollars, largest in Nebraska history. Taxpayers muttered angrily. Two measures had served to fan criticism of the unicameral system. One, which decontrolled rents, was passed over Governor Val Peterson's veto, in carnival spirit. The other was a bitterly controversial measure, authorizing the four Teachers Colleges to grant liberal arts degrees.

Both bills aroused hot cries of lobbying. The limited size of the Unicameral, forty-three members, has inspired critics to say it is a lobbyists' paradise. The Teachers College measure brought additional charges of an orgy of vote trading.

The rent-decontrol bill more truthfully could have been attributed to Nebraska's hatred of controls, its opposition to regimentation, especially in the rural areas which furnished the votes for decontrol. Only five of the more populous Nebraska communities were troubled by housing shortages. But the 1949 Unicameral did contribute to its own unpopularity by the tone of the debate on rent control. One member reminded his colleagues of the publicity Nebraska would receive as the first state in the Union to abandon controls.

A petition campaign seeks to increase the membership of the Unicameral from forty-three to seventy-five, with some support both in rural and urban areas. Another proposal, submitted by the Legislature itself, goes to the voters in 1950. It would extend the legislative term from two to four years, with staggered elections. The measure would also fix annual instead of biannual sessions and would increase salaries. There is an undertone, chiefly from old irreconcilables, in favor of abolishing the nonpartisan election requirement and putting the Unicameral on a straight party basis. The demand is for party responsibility. It is claimed that the fact that Unicameral members are not responsible to party control or leadership induces incoherence and discrimination. But beyond talking about this, no one has undertaken to do anything about it.

With one exception, the Unicameral is the late Senator Norris's most distinctive contribution to Nebraska State government. It was based on his own legislative experience. He came to the conclusion that the conference committee of the two-house legislature was the source of evil, the lobby's paradise, the final refuge for powerful, selfish interests in thwarting public will. Much of the legislation of vital concern to the people is actually written in conference committees, and in the eleventh hour rushed through without opportunity for change or a corrective fight.

After the spadework was finished at a meeting in Lincoln, largely attended, petitions were put in circulation for a constitutional amendment. The summer of 1936 was one of punishing temperatures. It appeared that the effort to procure the required number of signers would fail. Finally the petitions were completed. Although an independent candidate for re-election to the United States Senate in a three-cornered race, with regular Republican and Democratic candidates opposing him, Norris, in a whirlwind campaign covering nearly a month, devoted virtually all of his time to the Unicameral proposal.

He was seventy-six. The distances were great, and he was constantly on the go from early morning until late at night, speaking a number of times every day. Everywhere he was getting a type of audience rarely seen in American political life —undemonstrative but eager, thoughtful, ready with questions, hungry to learn. Only two of the daily newspapers in Nebraska supported the Unicameral amendment, only a few of the weekly press. Both major party organizations were vigorously opposed to it. Yet while the other candidates were drawing only handfuls, Norris was attracting throngs, particularly young people, educators, and independents.

The amendment carried: 286,086 to 193,152. Of the ninety-three counties in the State, eighty-five provided majorities and only eight were against.

New Year's Day, 1937, Senator Norris stopped briefly in Lincoln for the opening session of the Unicameral. It was a crowded week for him. In Washington his Lame Duck amendment was taking effect simultaneously.

The rules under which the one-house Legislature operates were drawn by its members. The pattern has been to devote the afternoons and evenings to committee hearings until the docket is cleared, the mornings to floor deliberations and action. Executive sessions of the committees are rare, although there is no provision in the rules against working behind closed doors. Any member can procure a roll call upon any measure by demand voiced from the floor.

Procedure is simplicity itself. After the introduction of a bill, it is assigned to a committee for public hearing. If approved, it is sent to the general file. If killed in the committee a bill can be revived by majority vote of the Unicameral. The first step on general file sends a measure to enrollment and review, for needed corrections. It is then placed on select file where review amendments are considered. On second passage it goes to the enrollment committee for engrossment. It is then reported for final reading. There is no debate on final reading but a day must elapse before final action. The Governor has five days in which to approve or veto.

Nebraska has not been reapportioned since it was organized into forty-three districts on a population basis. The attempt was to equalize representation between the urban eastern half of the State and the rural west. The largest district has 38,245 people, the smallest 26,016.

Forty years in Congress had given Norris full insight into the blighting effects of misguided partisanship. In the closing years of his life he came to look upon its evil as second only to lobby pressures. Frequently he expressed the opinion that more sins were committed in the name of party regularity than by any other force affecting legislation.

In developing the Unicameral plan, there was only one point upon which Norris would not yield. He insisted that election to the Unicameral must be upon a nonpartisan basis; that its members be chosen on individual merit and without party label. He thought a body of twenty-five men could function better than a larger group but in no sense was he insistent in fixing the number of legislative districts.

Norris could have avoided much of the opposition to the Unicameral plan had he been willing to go along with party demands for election of members on a partisan basis. Yet his rare political intuition seems to have been vindicated as the Unicameral has moved from experimental stages to the status of an accepted institution of State government.

It offers an amazing political paradox.

In 1949, a Republican, Val Peterson, was Governor; Republican Senator Earl J. Lee, of Fremont, was chosen Speaker; and a Democrat, Senator John S. Callan, of O'Dell, became chairman of the all-powerful appropriations committee. Such an unorthodox political setup normally would be expected to spell trouble. It did not. Party differences have been buried in the Unicameral to a very large extent. Speaker Lee was elected over a fellow Republican by a Legislature made up of men affiliated with the Republican Party. Throughout the session Governor Peterson and Chairman Callan worked in closest harmony on budget matters. At the close of the session Peterson extolled Callan's work.

That is a paradox to be found in the political history of few states. It is no accident in Nebraska, where it has been the pattern for four years.

Two years before, in a similar atmosphere, with Republicans filling every State office, Senator Walter R. Raecke of Central City, a Democrat, was made Speaker—the deserved, overwhelming choice of his colleagues, a majority of them Republicans. A man of scholarly bearing, quietly effective, Raecke was one of the pillars of that session. He had an extraordinary capacity to keep deliberations free of partisanship. Similarly, two years earlier, Senator Callan, heading the Appropriations Committee, kept out of party politics the issues of how much money should be spent by the various agencies.

The Unicameral system owes a great deal to the leadership of Senator C. Petrus Peterson, of Lincoln, a Republican, who served in it half the period of its existence. As a legislator he revealed great intellectual capacity and a curiously enchanting, impelling personality. He would command respect in any parliamentary body. Big physically, well over six feet, massive head and shoulders, eloquent and persuasive, Peterson did much to root Unicameral in the esteem of Nebraska people.

Another who contributed much was the late Senator Charles Dafoe, of Tecumseh. Able, vigorous, and a born leader, he left a successful law practice to enter the Service at the outbreak of World War II, dying in a flaming plane while completing training as a combat pilot. There were others, including one of Senator Norris's close friends, John N. Norton, of Polk, a member of the first Unicameral, who had much to do with drafting the rules under which it now functions.

The system has succeeded in drawing to legislative service unusual numbers of young men, vigorous, capable, liberal in outlook. It has blended youthful enthusiasm with mature, seasoned experience. It has seen more women serve in the time that it has been in effect than in all the preceding years of Statehood. It has seemed to encourage individual members to visit the State institutions, to pry into State problems, and to keep in touch with State affairs the year around.

The Unicameral has markedly improved the quality of legislative membership. A recent survey revealed that a very large proportion, more than eighty per cent of the membership, had been active in community and civic affairs before election. It is generally recognized that the small membership does impose heavy committee burdens upon each member, each generally serving on at least two committees.

Nebraska's legislative experiment has attracted the attention of other states near and far, notably Colorado and Ohio. Its place in the State is best demonstrated, perhaps, by the fact that no one has dared launch a campaign aimed at wiping it out.

The melting snows and the rains washing the face of the granite eastern slopes of the Rockies come to rest, in the upper valley of the North Platte river at Keystone, against a huge earthen dam. It is more than one hundred and fifty feet in height and completely dams the canyon, forming a crystal blue lake over three miles in width, thirty-five miles in length, and approximately one hundred and forty feet in depth.

There is a new surging vitality in Nebraska representing many years of planning, a classic struggle against heavy odds, a dream come true in the form of a rich, stable irrigation empire that embraces more than a million acres of the most productive land. It is the only state-wide system of public power generation and distribution in the United States.

Back of it is a Homeric tale.

It represents the fruits of homespun Nebraska thought at its finest. The federal government lent the bulk of the funds, more than sixty million dollars, under a long term plan of amortization, for construction of key projects. But from the start the actual direction and operation of Nebraska's TVA has been under the sympathetic guidance of the State government.

It was State legislation that created the foundation for all this. The great hydroelectric districts were organized under its provisions; the chief distributing agency, too, serving more than three hundred and fifty cities and towns with electricity, looks to it for legal existence. The rural electrification districts, thirty-eight of them, now serving more than forty thousand modern farm homes, equipped with modern conveniences, are organized under its provisions. Finally Omaha organized under it, took over the facilities of the private utility concern serving it, became a vital unit of a State grid system, and now lights its home and business institutions and turns the wheels of its factories with electricity generated by the power plants at Columbus, and on the Upper Platte, more than three hundred miles away.

The crown which this legislation wears is incorporated in a single sentence, dedicating these facilities forever to public ownership and operation.

Through it, the lakes and their waters, the power plants and their throbbing turbines, the vast network of transmission lines belong to the people of Nebraska, to use as they will, and to contribute to their happiness.

It could be changed, but with Nebraska on guard, it is doubtful it will. The system reports annually to the Governor and the State Auditor. It is responsible to the Legislature.

The private power companies fought the legislation with everything in their book. When the usual arguments failed they set in motion a wave of fear to stampede the tax-conscious people. It is a tribute to the intelligence of Nebraska voters that the utilities failed. They claimed a debt would be created which never would be paid, huge reservoirs erected which never would be filled, a colossal Frankenstein set in motion that would devour the State. Well, the reservoirs are full and working. The system itself pays to all political subdivisions—city, county, school, and State—every penny of tax revenue formerly received from the private utilities. And rates for electricity have been slashed substantially even during the period that debt retirement has been in progress.

When the utilities lost their fight in Nebraska, they transferred and redoubled their efforts in Washington to block construction of the three state hydros by opposing allocation of funds to them. But, again, the power interests lost, thanks to the persistence, skill, and indomitable will of George Norris.

In fifteen years Nebraska has been reborn.

310

Its soil has a new vitality, its fields a new abundance, its people a new perspective.

Its farm homes, in the majority substantial two-story, modern, sanitary dwellings, are bright in new coats of paint, well-kept lawns, flowers, and shrubs; and at night in the gathering darkness the lights come on. In the Yuletide season thousands of living Christmas trees shed their radiance and the spirit of good will. The sleek herds graze on the range not far from the shining waters of the lake. The waters sing a merry tune as they move through hundreds of miles of canals and laterals to thirsty acres. A State has found new freedom in the planning and the labor of its people, through a responsive State government inspired by the grandeur of its own vision.

In the torment of the thirties Nebraska found a new, mighty strength through emancipation from age-old prejudices.

There are three main developments on the Nebraska streams, the largest of which is the Tri-County. It owes its beginnings to C. W. McConnaughey of Holdrege, George P. Kingsley of Minden, and the late J. S. Canaday of Minden. There were others but these three were the most persistent throughout a twenty-two-year struggle. The Tri-County built the great dam and its power plants. Not far away on the same stream, the Platte, the Sutherland sprang up. Over on the Loup, homeland of a friendly Pawnee tribe, the Columbus plant was built. In the Upper Loup valleys, the North and Middle tributaries of the main stream, irrigation developments were completed. Then all were knit into a compact system of generation and transmission. The final step saw the purchase of every private-utility property in Nebraska through a loan privately floated, and now substantially reduced from the profits of the sale of electricity.

It is oversimplification to say that there was a master plan in the beginning. Originally the Loup planned to market its electricity through the private power companies. The Tri-County looked to rural electrification, and to small towns with costly steam municipal plants as an outlet for its current.

Senator Norris provided the master plan, even under the weight of his duties in Washington, and devoted months to Nebraska's Little TVA.

It has brought new crops. It has increased farm population. Its cheap power has doubled industrial employment.

Last year a half billion kilowatt hours of electricity came from the turbines of the hydroelectric plants, and another two hundred million kilowatt hours from steam generation by the facilities obtained from the private utilities. In prophetic words, Senator Norris answered his critics on their charges that there was no market for electricity. The Little TVA was no sooner in operation than its output was taken. Electric consumption has steadily increased in the city and on the farm. The margin is thin now between available current and actual requirements. Nebraska looks eagerly forward to a Missouri basin development, now hamstrung by the struggle between an MVA and the Pick-Sloan plan, while once again the old battle fills the air with noise.

High in the mountains the eagle builds his nest. Above him are the ice fields, the accumulation of snow and sleet, freezing and thawing. In the summer the glistening rivulets of snow water dance down the mountainside, rushing to the sea, sometimes boisterously and destructively.

They have been put to work in Nebraska.

Far to the east on the rolling plains they gather in concert to give voice to the anthem of human aspirations.

In the white moonlight of a summer's night old hills reflect the mysteries of the ages. They look down upon the embers of the campfires of hunters, trappers, and gold seekers. The rumble of covered caravans long has been stilled, and after eighty-two years of Statehood the people of Nebraska have found the "gold" others scorned. Year after year they have mined it in courage and decent purpose, in humility and industry.

It remained for one of their own, George W. Norris, to school them in guarding the soil against the ravages of erosion and impoverishment, and to control the waters of their rivers against flood and drought. He led them into the electrical age, lighting their homes, their farms, and their industries.

They have been so eager to learn.

Before their eyes appear new vistas of a more stable economy, a better rural life, more prosperous, attractive, neighborly towns and cities.

There in the moonlight the soft breezes blow. Over the stretches from the Missouri to the high hills of the Nebraska panhandle they say that the best is still ahead.

Norris sleeps in his beloved valley. Eighty miles away on the Frenchman another great dam is taking shape, and up and down the valley engineers are constructing other works. Norris's people have seen the glory of a reborn land.

There is much to be done. Yet in all it has done, and in all that it has failed to do, Nebraska is beautiful.

TEXAS ★ ★ ★

Owned by Oil and Interlocking Directorates

HART STILWELL

ONE hundred and fifteen years ago, William B. Travis drew a line with his sword on the ground inside the Alamo, and asked all willing to join him in fighting to the death for the freedom of Texas to cross it. All crossed.

In the spring of 1949, State Senator Fred Harris drew an imaginary line down the center of the chamber and asked all willing to stand up for the rights of Texas children against the Humble Oil Company to "step across" the line by voting for a bill he was sponsoring.

Fourteen Senators stepped across. Fifteen did not.

Texas has gone far since Travis and his men died at the Alamo. But the direction is doubtful in the light of the principles for which those early Texans fought. For Texas today is the largest and most profitable colony in the world—a distinction that became hers automatically the day India achieved independence. Wall Street has done with money what men with swords and guns could not do.

It has been a long battle, one that is still raging. The issues were clearly drawn in 1946 when Dr. Homer P. Rainey, deposed president of the University of Texas, sought the gov-

★

HART STILWELL is a native Texan. He was graduated from the University of Texas and is the author of a number of books, including *Border City* and *Uncovered Wagon*. His latest book, *State College*, dealing with life in a state university, will be published in January, 1950.

ernorship. He lost. But others carry on, and the outcome of their struggle will determine the path that Texas, and much of the rest of the Southwest, will follow during the next generation—a people's path or a colonial path.

Oil is the master of present-day Texas. And as Texas oil is owned by Wall Street, Wall Street dominates Texas. Most Texans know this, but few care to discuss it. When R. W. Calvert slipped and admitted it at a luncheon in 1947, when he was chairman of the Democratic State Executive Committee, the cry of anguish could be heard from the Gulf of Mexico to the Rocky Mountains—that is, across Texas.

Calvert said, "It may not be a wholesome thing to say, but the oil industry today is in complete control of State politics and State government."

This foreign ownership is admitted in other quarters. In *State and Local Government in Texas*, a textbook used in some colleges, appears this statement: "The grip of foreign-controlled monopolies upon much of the State's basic resources will become a potent issue as the people generally awaken to the realization of the facts."

Seventy-five per cent of Texas oil is owned by Wall Street, in the broad sense of that term. Owners of the other twenty-five per cent must sell to the owners of the seventy-five per cent, who possess the pipelines and refineries. And the ease with which the oil industry exercises its rule of Texas is demonstrated by the fact that one and one-half per cent of the oil companies operating in Texas own ninety-eight per cent of the oil production. Getting oil interests together in Texas amounts to little more than getting representatives of the various long arms of Standard Oil (Humble, Magnolia, etc.) into conference.

The controlling pressure may be exerted in circuitous and unexpected ways. For example: Humble Oil and Refining Co. (Standard of New Jersey), largest in Texas, doesn't even

315

have a lobbyist at Austin. But Humble is a dominant factor in the Texas Mid-Continent Oil & Gas Association, which keeps two lobbyists at Austin during legislative sessions.

The result? In the "line-drawing" episode, the bill under consideration would have moved venue in a tidewater land suit from Kenedy County, where three-fourths of the county's 180 qualified jurors are employed by or otherwise connected with the Kenedy Ranch, to Travis County, in which Austin, the State capital, is located. Oil leases amounting to more than $2,000,000 are at stake, and the chances of the State winning (the revenue would go into the school fund) might reasonably be considered slightly better in Travis than Kenedy County.

But Humble held the lease on the Kenedy Ranch. So the Senators did not cross the line.

It is easy to bring powerful pressures to bear in Texas because the industrial and financial structure of the State is actually one huge maze of interlocking directorates. If unraveled and put in a straight line, the ramifications of these corporate tentacles would reach to Mars and back.

Here is a graphic example:

Jesse Jones's National Bank of Commerce in Houston is linked, through outright ownership or through interlocking directorates, with the Houston *Chronicle*, Radio Station KTRH, the Rice Hotel and several others, the Houston Deep Water Land Company, and the Gulf Oil Corp., which is owned by the Mellons, who also hold a big slice of Texas Gulf Sulphur, which is under Morgan management.

Continuing through the maze (hold your hat), Texas Gulf Sulphur is tied up with The Texas Company, and through it with The Freeport Sulphur Co.,* the other half of the sulphur monopoly and one in which the Rockefellers are heavily

* See Ralph O'Leary's *Louisiana: The Pelican State.*

interested. Connections extend on to The Neches Butane Products Co., the First National Bank of Dallas, the Frost National Bank of San Antonio, American General Life Insurance Company, Seaboard Life Insurance Company, the Dr. Pepper Company of Dallas, and the Houston Lighting & Power Co., which in turn was controlled until recently by the National Power & Light Co., a subsidiary of giant Electric Bond & Share.

That still isn't all. Through directorates extending in other directions, Jesse Jones's bank is linked with Houston's big law firms, and through them with Dillon, Reed & Co., the Missouri Pacific System and other railroads, Anderson, Clayton & Co., world's largest cotton brokers, and Wesson Oil & Snowdrift Company, which owns the South Texas Cotton Oil Company, with mills and refineries all over the State. Through these ties, the connections extend to Oriental Textile Mills, the Great Southern Life Insurance Company, Kirby Petroleum Company, and Carr P. Collins of Dallas, the man who started "Pass-the-biscuits Pappy" O'Daniel on his way.

The list is almost endless. A few other connections are Hughes Tool Company, Transcontinental & Western Air, Gulf Bitulithic Company, Longhorn Portland Cement Company, Union Producing Company, and United Gas Corp.

The above is just a segment of the intricate and complex story of who owns and rules Texas.

More light was shed on this all-powerful control during the progress of a bill introduced by Representative Charles McLellan in the 1949 Legislature. The measure proposed increasing the tax on natural gas from one mill per thousand cubic feet to one cent. This would have produced close to twenty million dollars' revenue a year, instead of the two-million-dollar pittance the State now gets from this great natural resource. But McLellan's bill did not pass.

Texas could perform near miracles in developments if the State would adequately tax the exploiters of its fabulous natural resources. A forthright income tax would perform wonders. Examination of the income of one Texan illustrates the point.

According to *Life* magazine, which certainly cannot be accused of unfairness to the rich, Haralson Hunt of Dallas has an oil income of $1,000,000 *a week*—$52,000,000 *a year*. The total revenue the State of Texas gets from oil flowing from its soil is less than $80,000,000 a year.

It is a simple fact that the combined incomes of the twenty richest oilmen in Texas would pay the State's total operating cost, around $350,000,000 a year. The Constitution of Texas empowers the Legislature to levy an income tax. But such a tax is not even mentioned at legislative sessions. In 1949, Representative Marshall Bell of San Antonio sought to make such a tax impossible by introducing a constitutional amendment forever barring it. He quickly lost interest when his bill was amended so that its provisions applied only to incomes up to $5,000 a year.

Texas taxes oil at the rate of 4.5 per cent of the market value at the well, gas at the rate of 5.25 per cent, and sulphur at the rate of $1.27 a ton. A high official of Texas Gulf Sulphur once said, "We're prepared to pay as much as $5 a ton if we must." When he said this, he was talking privately to a friend. For public consumption, the business tycoon screams confiscation at the suggestion of a higher tax.

Immense as oil and gas income is (sixty per cent of the State's total wealth), it might not be such a dominant factor except for a provision of the federal income-tax law exempting twenty-seven and one-half per cent of oil income from taxation as depletion of capital assets. This gravy-train provision was put into the law largely through the efforts of that

318

pompous Major Hoople of the U.S. Senate, Tom Connally. Many Texans draw amusement from the fact that Speaker Sam Rayburn has repeatedly scared the oil, gas, and utility boys out of trying to defeat him, as they would dearly love to do, by threatening to plug up this loophole if they so much as "put one dime in my district against me."

Under this provision Haralson Hunt, as one example, can charge off $14,300,000 of his annual income as depletion of capital assets. Since there is no State income tax, he thus pays no tax on that at all. Also, Texas oilmen are not slow when it comes to taking advantage of other loopholes. Fewer things eat up profits, if managed properly, and whittle down income tax quicker than a big ranch. It has become the practice for Texas oil millionaires to acquire large ranches, stock them with expensive cattle, and parade around in handmade cowboy attire. Strangely, the wealthy cattlemen are still the socially elite of Texas. They look disdainfully down their sunburned noses at the Johnny-come-lately oil rich.

Because of these tax loopholes, it is possible for oilmen to spread large sums of money among candidates for public office as freely as low-grade mash is spread among hogs. Almost any candidate can get some oil money. As an illustration: In the 1946 Democratic primary, four of the five leading gubernatorial contenders were acceptable to the oilmen. But they hesitated choosing among the four for fear of making an enemy who might win. The situation became critical when Dr. Rainey, who definitely was not acceptable, began forging ahead. The oilmen decided to settle on one man and shoot the works.

They selected the late Beauford Jester, former attorney for Magnolia Oil (Standard of New York) and State Railroad Commissioner. The Railroad Commission regulates the oil industry. Two weeks before election, Jester started gaining.

He finished like Citation, leading in the first primary and defeating Rainey almost two to one in the run-off.

At least $100,000 is necessary to make even a modest race for Governor in Texas. It is generally agreed that a minimum of $300,000 is necessary to assure election. Obviously, few candidates not backed by oil have a chance.

Texans are becoming aware of this brutal fact, as well as others. Change is in the air. Since the day blatant Representative Martin Dies took one good look at the way union labor was prepared to knock the props out from under him and quit without a fight, the "other side" of industrialization is being heard from. Texas is in a period of transition. Its economy has forged rapidly ahead, but, as so often happens, its legislative and social progress has lagged. Today the State might well be compared to the East during the latter days of the Robber Barons.

Like the Robber Barons, most of the Oil Barons are uncouth, domineering, and repulsively ostentatious. Their attitude toward educators, scientists, writers, artists, musicians, etc., is, "If you're so damn smart, why aren't you rich?" A Houston newspaperman, weary of the ancient wheeze, turned it on one Oil Baron by asking, "If you're so damn rich, why aren't you smart?"

Of course the answer to that is, "If you are as rich as an oilman, you don't have to be smart."

Insatiable craving for conspicuous display has led to startling exhibitions in the U. S., but few surpass the potlatches staged by Texas Oil Barons. The widely fanfared opening of Glenn McCarthy's Shamrock Hotel in Houston in 1949 is a graphic example. A onetime oil-well rigger, McCarthy determined to show the world he was as good as anybody else, maybe a little better. He practically moved Hollywood to the Shamrock for the occasion. All was splendor, down to

320

the newsboys in full dress. Also all was confusion, including a drunken orgy that stopped a national radio show, and a mob at the door that barred the way to a courier who had flown all the way from Ireland with shamrocks.

Three weeks before the opening, five newspapermen were fired from the chain of suburban weeklies owned by McCarthy—in the interest of economy.

That is the gaudy, material side of the transition. The human side may not be too far off.

Texas is switching from an agricultural to an industrial economy, and the confusion is almost as great as it was at the Shamrock opening. The political life is changing from that of a small town ruled by a banker to that of a big city ruled by corporations. The economic life is changing from that of the frontier—dog eat dog—to that of an industrial system where the sheer concentration of labor compels recognition of conditions that the isolated farm worker endures in solitude.

Many factors are working toward these changes. To understand them clearly, it is necessary to grasp what Texas is today and how it got that way.

The State contains 169,000,000 acres of land and 2,000,000 acres of water surface. Roughly, it is 800 miles across in any direction. It spans almost the entire range of climate in the nation, and most of the range of agriculture, from wheat in the Panhandle to citrus fruit in the Lower Rio Grande Valley.

Texas takes in more than $1,000,000,000 a year from farm and ranch produce, with livestock income slightly ahead. Cotton is still king, although no longer reigning in solitude; less than half of farm income is from cotton.

Oil production is usually held to around 750,000,000 barrels a year, or 44 per cent of the nation's total. The State's oil reserves are estimated at 12 billion barrels, 55 per cent of the nation's total. Gas production approximates 1,700,000 million cubic feet, 44 per cent of the nation's total. Sulphur production is slightly more than 3,000,000 long tons.

Approximately 250,000 wells have been drilled in Texas, more than 70 per cent producers. Of the 254 counties, 172 are producing oil or gas, and land in every county is under lease for oil exploration.

Development of the oil industry on a large scale began in 1901, with the discovery of oil in the Spindletop Field, near Beaumont. Chaos reigned during much of the development, and a prolonged battle between independents and the big corporations drove prices down to as little as six cents a barrel. In 1938, there were 155 refineries in the great East Texas field, most of them independently owned. By 1941, there were only three refineries, owned by the majors. They had won the fight and now control Texas oil.

Texas is first in so many fields of production the mere listing becomes monotonous—oil, cotton, beef, gas, goats, mules, turkeys, sulphur, grain sorghum, and so on and so on. Most of the firsts are due to the immense size of the State. But in the spheres relating to advancement in the art of living comfortably and happily, Texas does not rank so high. Most Texans prefer to ignore this. Some data reflecting unfavorably on the State are not to be found in *The Texas Almanac,* published by the Dallas *News.* However, comparisons are made at times, such as the following, compiled several years ago by Dr. Dan R. Davis of the Texas Agricultural and Mechanical College:

First in cotton ......48th in pellagra control
First in beef ....45th in control of infant mortality
First in wool ....38th in school systems
First in mules ......47th in library service
First in turkeys .....declining rural church facilities

322

First in goats ....inadequate rural recreation
First in grain
   sorghums ....inadequate rural medical facilities

Not all the figures on the right are now correct. For instance, Texas ranks 24th in school systems, and will soon rank still higher. But the figures are accurate enough to shed a new light on all those "firsts" of the State.

Texas was settled in the early days of the past century, won her independence from Mexico in 1836, came into the Union in 1846, and fought with the Confederacy in the Civil War, enduring the trying ordeal of Reconstruction.

The Reconstruction Era ended with the adoption of a new Constitution in 1876. Records of the constitutional convention make fascinating reading. Judging from some of the speeches, public education was viewed as dangerous a threat to democracy as medical insurance is today. As finally adopted, the Constitution, in the words of a present-day Texas editor, "is a document that it is difficult to revere." In addition to a Bill of Rights and provisions for a State government, the Constitution embodies a tremendous mass of material that rightfully belongs in the field of statutory law.

Texans were afraid of strong men then. They still are. There is not a strong man in the public life of Texas today. The Constitution specifically sets out the powers of all officials, down to Hide and Animal Inspector. If the Hide and Animal Inspector wants to inspect goat hides when the Constitution provides only for inspecting cowhides, a constitutional amendment is required. Ninety-five have been enacted so far, and each Legislature submits a batch of new ones.

Part of the Constitution deals with public lands. On entering the Union, Texas offered her public lands, sixty per cent of the total acreage, to the federal government in exchange for assumption of the State's debt of $10,000,000.

Washington declined. So the State gave 32,000,000 acres to railroads in the form of subsidies, traded another 3,500,000 acres for a Capitol building, and set aside 52,000,000 acres for the public schools, with 2,329,000 acres allotted to the University of Texas.

From the sale of school lands, and from oil leases and royalties on lands still held, a school fund of $100,000,000 has been created. In addition, the University of Texas has about the same amount from lease and royalty money, with an income of $15,000,000 annually.

Railroads and insurance trusts were the first to make a bid for Texas. A champion equal to the occasion came to the front and fought the State's battles. He was James Stephen Hogg. Governor from 1891 to 1895, he put through laws curbing the power of monopolies, reducing interest rates, regulating the issue of stocks and bonds, and establishing a Railroad Commission to regulate the carriers.

But there was also a dark side to the Hogg administration. A Jim Crow law was spread on the statute books.

Hogg was almost a man-mountain in size. Huge and rotund, he swept Texans off their feet when he hefted his bulk into a farm wagon and drove through the streets behind six white oxen to ridicule an opponent in a fancy carriage drawn by six white horses. Hogg was a rich man. Yet he fought the people's battle (except the downtrodden Negro's), and won.

The fight Hogg started lasted for years. Suits against the Waters-Pierce Oil Co., charging monopoly in kerosene oil distribution, were finally settled in 1906 in favor of the State, which recovered $1,623,000. Before the Waters-Pierce case ended, the first gusher at Spindletop blew in, inaugurating the era of oil in Texas.

Twice since the days of Jim Hogg, Texans have flocked to the standards of men promising to fight the battle against vested interest. One of these men was undoubtedly sincere

in much that he said and tried to do. The other was pure
phony. The sincere man was James E. Ferguson. The phony
was W. Lee O'Daniel.

Ferguson promised to help the tenant farmer and other
poor. He proposed regulating by law the amount a landlord
could take from a tenant's crop. Ferguson also advocated
limiting dispossession and providing State warehouses. Similarly, he was going to do great things for the "little red
schoolhouse at the forks of the creek." Ferguson was an ora-
tor of the old school, and a good one. He swept the poor off
their feet with his rousing speeches, concluding one with
the astounding pronouncement, "I'm for the HOME. If that
be treason, make the most of it!"

In sharp contrast to "Pappy" O'Daniel, Ferguson earnestly
tried to make good his promises. He did get attention focused on rural schools and improved conditions somewhat.
He also passed some laws to help tenant farmers, although
reactionary courts later invalidated parts of them. He did
other things. He fought prohibition tooth and nail, at a time
when it was becoming a power. And in his fight for the
"little red schoolhouse" he slashed funds for other institutions on the ground that "too many people are going hog-
wild over higher education."

Ferguson became Governor in 1915. In 1917, the bitter
conflict between him and the Legislature came to a climax
when he vetoed the appropriation for the University of
Texas. He was impeached and barred from ever holding
State office again. Many charges of misconduct were hurled
against him, but the chief basis for his removal was a $156,-
000 loan from breweries. Ferguson claimed he had repaid
the money.

A decade later his wife, Mrs. Miriam A. Ferguson, served
two terms as Governor and another term from 1933 to 1935.
Texans elected her the first time rather than stomach a man

with Ku Klux Klan backing. They elected her in 1932 when the State was in the grip of the Hoover depression. The poor figured "Ma" would give them bread. She did. The State issued $20,000,000 in "bread bonds."

Throughout all of Mrs. Ferguson's terms, her husband was the real Governor.

All the terms were distinguished by fierce conflict, wholesale convict pardoning, and by threatened and real investigations and suits. Dan Moody, Attorney General during Ma's first administration, recovered several hundred thousand dollars from highway contractors in overpayments, and rode into office as Governor on that record.

Nothing was done about wholesale pardoning (except to tell jokes about it) until the Fergusons were out of office. Then a constitutional amendment was voted prohibiting the Governor from issuing pardons except on the recommendation of a Board of Pardons and Paroles.

Most of the New Deal-type legislation now on the Texas statutes, old-age pensions, child welfare, unemployment assistance, etc., was enacted during the administration of James Allred, 1935 to 1939. Allred was not an outstanding Governor, but he was a towering giant compared to what followed him.

"Pappy" O'Daniel came out of Fort Worth waving a flour sack in one hand and a copy of the Decalogue in the other. He promised to give pensions to all old people, drive the politicians out of Austin, industrialize Texas, and perform other miracles—all, apparently, without increasing taxes. He swore he would fight a sales tax to the bitter end.

From the beginning, O'Daniel had big money behind him, some of the most reactionary big money in the State. Carr P. Collins, millionaire Dallas insurance man, was his sponsor. Soon other rich men lined up behind him, after Collins convinced them they had nothing to fear from O'Daniel. He had the solid backing of those who later were active in supporting the Christian Americans, a Jew-baiting, Negro-baiting, New Deal-baiting, labor-baiting organization.

To watch O'Daniel and listen to him was an extraordinary experience. In a completely toneless voice, and his strangely staring, coldly expressionless eyes fixing the audience, he would attribute the most despicable motives and practices to opponents and critics. It was weird. Seldom has so much terrifying venom been evinced by one human being. And seldom were so many so cruelly deceived as were the poor and the aged of Texas by O'Daniel.

Almost immediately after he was elected, he tried to ram a sales tax through the Legislature, calling it a "transactions" tax. A group in the House, who came to be called "The Immortal Fifty-six," headed by Price Daniel, later Attorney General, blocked the measure.

Using the prestige he acquired by his feat of sweeping to victory in the first primary, O'Daniel did wangle through a labor law making picket-line violence a felony. The law lists shouting "scab" as an act of violence.

Under O'Daniel, old-age pensions went down instead of up. He blamed the Legislature and was re-elected. With O'Daniel having generated so much heat for increased old-age assistance, the Legislature tossed him the ball. An omnibus bill was adopted taxing gas, sulphur, and oil, and imposing a sales tax on cosmetics, automobiles, radio sets, and playing cards. There was nothing for O'Daniel to do but sign.

Shortly thereafter he was elected to the Senate in a special election and was re-elected in 1942. The belief was general in Texas that big money backed him for the Senate to get him out of the State. It is certain O'Daniel still had big money behind him. But when he came back to Texas in 1947, to check on the prospects for re-election, even his

327

stanchest backers wanted no more of him. He didn't even attempt to run.

Coke Stevenson, O'Daniel's successor as Governor, followed almost the same path. Stevenson was considered a more enlightened man, partly because he seldom said anything. But he loaded up State agencies with the same type O'Daniel had named, the most reactionary millionaires and their lawyers. However, there is one basic difference between Stevenson and O'Daniel. Stevenson is a reactionary with a rural background, probably the last of the cracker-barrel philosophers to play a dominant part in Texas life. O'Daniel is a reactionary with a background of industrial strife. Stevenson's conservatism stems from affection for a way of life —the poor boy who worked hard and became rich. He was never filled with bitter hatreds and urges to punish. O'Daniel evinced almost hysterical hatreds and driving punitive urges.

But despite their disparate motivations, the results of their regimes were the same. Stevenson completed what O'Daniel began, putting Texas in the hands of the interlocking directorates. Under O'Daniel and Stevenson, the major oil companies took over Texas.

This policy was continued by Jester. But he got such a shock when two relatively unknown candidates polled forty-eight per cent of the vote in the 1948 primary that he worriedly set about to regain his prestige. Jester was a different type from both his predecessors. He wanted profoundly to be liked. He gloried in friendship, good will and praise. There was nothing petty or mean about him. But unfortunately he lacked the understanding to grasp the full meaning of such intangibles as academic freedom. Also, the advice of friends and his staff, who made most of his decisions, was often bad. Jester was influenced by public opinion, but his advisers

328

were able to convince him that the wishes of the Real Estate Board of Texas were the wishes of all Texans.

On the whole, his administration represented an advance, especially after he set out to regain his prestige. His appointments, with the exception of some on educational boards, were markedly better than those of O'Daniel and Stevenson. Jester picked conservatives, but many of them were enlightened and reasonable men. Also, in his second term, he worked hard for a halfway liberal civil rights bill, for improvement in State hospitals, and for other progressive legislation.

Before Jester's sudden death in July, 1949, the Legislature voted a $5,000,000 appropriation for soil conservation, established a retirement system for judges, and put committees to work on a revision of the criminal code. Also, a constitutional amendment for annual legislative sessions was submitted to popular vote.

Jester's death was probably a setback to liberalism in Texas. By no stretch of the imagination could he be called a liberal. But he was sensitive to public opinion, and he was a kindly man. There was nothing of the power-hungry schemer about him. His successor, Lieutenant Governor Allan Shivers, is a distinctly different type.

Forty-one years old, and married to one of the multimillionaire fortunes of Texas, he is acutely ambitious, ultraconservative, and aggressive.

As presiding officer of the State Senate in the last two Legislatures, Shivers' record is one to give Texans much food for thought. Among other things, he showed himself a smooth and agile operator who was aiming for the governorship as a stepping-stone to the United States Senate. Even before Jester's death, Shivers was already a leading candidate for Governor.

His appointments in the Senate were uniformly loaded on

the side of vested interests. Similarly, he exerted himself constantly to block legislation opposed by these interests. An example of this was his frustration of an effort to raise the $35,000,000 constitutional limitation on the amount the State can spend on its needy aged. Similarly, he played a leading role in forcing through legislation that requires old people who receive a pension to give the State a lien on their few remaining possessions.

As presiding officer of the Senate, he came much nearer to being the boss of the chamber than any other Lieutenant Governor in many years. As Governor, there is every reason to anticipate he will attempt to make himself the boss of Texas. One thing is certain: The cause of liberalism can expect nothing from him.

While Texas Governors have given direction to the State government, powerfully influencing policy through their proposals and appointments, it is the Legislature that actually runs the machinery.

The Texas Legislature consists of two chambers: a Senate with thirty-one members and a House of a hundred and fifty members. Senators are elected for four years, House members for two. The Legislature meets in January of each odd-numbered year, and a regular session is one hundred and twenty days, during which members receive ten dollars a day. If the Legislature remains in session longer, the pay drops to five dollars a day.

There have been numerous attempts, the last in 1949, to amend the Constitution and increase legislator salaries. Big-business interests vigorously oppose that. It is much easier to pressure poorly paid legislators than well-paid ones. And the people are not sure they're getting their money's worth as it is. They raised the Governor's salary from $4,000 to $12,000, and look what they got.

Twenty-five of the thirty-one Senators are lawyers. Usually, about seventy-five per cent of the House members are lawyers. Young lawyers seek the office for prestige; older lawyers, because clients want them to. Many members of both chambers have among their clients sulphur, oil, gas, and other big corporations. There is no way of knowing the extent of such representation, as the information is not required for public record.

But aside from this, the Legislature does not truly represent Texas, as there has been no redistricting since 1920. The Constitution requires this every ten years, and there have been tremendous population shifts in the past three decades. But every move to redistrict has been defeated, with the result that the big cities are denied fair representation.

The rural Representatives, with big-business backing, have not only blocked redistricting, but they put through an amendment providing that no county could ever have more than seven Representatives. Houston, Dallas, San Antonio, and Fort Worth now have twenty members in the House, whereas they should have about forty. Under the Constitution they can never have more than twenty-eight.

Whether redistricting, now guaranteed by a new amendment, will bring an improvement is a moot question. As things stand now, the Representatives from the four cities make up a solid bloc of reaction, particularly on labor legislation. That may seem strange, but a study of the situation explains it. It is in the cities that organized labor is making its strongest bid for representation, and the fiercest resistance centers there. So far big business has been able to defeat labor. However, some rural Representatives are beginning to realize that they have much in common with labor. Representative Don A. Lewis of Midlothian, which has little organized labor, supported a fair labor bill in the 1949 session.

Marshall Bell of San Antonio and four Dallas Representatives have led the battle against labor in recent years. With

the exception of Carlton Moore of Houston, practically all
the other big-city Representatives have gone along with
these five leaders.

The four antilabor leaders from Dallas are Sam Hannah,
W. O. Reed, George Parkhouse, and Douglas Bergman.
Parkhouse, Hannah, Reed, and Bell were the ramrods behind nine highly restrictive and punitive labor bills passed
in 1947. With Bergman, they formed the bloc that defeated
the Timmons bill in 1949. This measure, sponsored by Blake
Timmons of Amarillo, would have repealed the 1947 acts
and substituted a reasonable labor law.

The operations of the antilabor clique have been simpli-
fied by the fact that most of the Speakers of the House in
recent years have been union foes. Speaker Durwood Manford, of the 1949 Legislature, authored the Manford Law of
1943, which required, among other things, that labor organizers be licensed. He named sixteen antilabor men to the
twenty-one-man House Labor Committee in 1949.

Yet, labor put up a surprisingly effective fight in the last
session. The showing was indicative of changing times. Led
by Otis Lee of Port Arthur (a CIO member), labor mustered
sixty-three votes, against sixty-six for the Timmons bill. The
best count in 1947 was thirty-three votes. Among those who
aided Lee were John B. Rogers of Austin, Miller Walker and
Jack Brooks of Beaumont, Don A. Lewis of Midlothian, and
Deno Tufares of Wichita Falls.

In the Senate, labor has no hope at present. A few members try to be fair if it doesn't cost them too much. But labor
has no outspoken champion as it has in the House. The list
of bitter labor foes is headed by Jim Taylor—most influential
man in the Senate until his resignation recently—R. A. Weinert
of Seguin, Carlos Ashley of Travis County (elected over a
liberal partly through furious efforts of the Medical Association), Walter Tynan of San Antonio, James Phillips of Angle-

ton, A. M. Aikin, Jr., of Paris, and Fred Harris, the Senator who made the dramatic line-drawing gesture for the children of Texas.

The attitude of a Texas official on labor, or on any other issue, cannot always be taken as a complete indication of his over-all attitude toward progress. Some men who have voted consistently against labor have been leaders in efforts to better education and State hospitals, to improve the treatment of Texas-Mexicans, increase pensions, and raise corporation taxes on natural resources. An official may fight valiantly for the rights of Texas-Mexicans, then turn around and strenuously oppose granting the same rights to Negroes. Attorney General Price Daniel has done exactly that. Yet, when in the Legislature, he was fair to labor.

Actually, the word "liberal" has little concrete meaning in Texas.

On the whole, the 1949 Legislature was much better than any other in recent years. It faced issues and did things, some good, some questionable, others unfortunate. It faced the need for reform of the prison system and passed a bill to overhaul the physical plant. It approved a constitutional amendment giving women the right to serve on juries. It adopted an effective secret-ballot law. It killed a proposal to remove franchise tax exemptions for co-operatives. And in a far-reaching step, the Legislature reorganized the public school setup.

The new plan is complex. It transfers control from an elected State Superintendent to an elected twenty-one-man board, and grants increased State aid with the use of an economic index to determine the amount to be allotted each county. This will mean heavier taxes in some rural areas, but in the past many counties levied no school tax at all. The bill also raised the salary minimum for teachers from $2,000 to $2,400.

The reorganization shifts control of education from rural areas to the cities, part of the industrial swing. And it definitely increases the amount to be spent on education.

The Legislature also accepted in part the challenge presented by Jester in his diluted civil rights bill (there was no mention of fair employment or removal of segregation laws). It passed an antilynch bill and agreed to submit a constitutional amendment eliminating the poll tax. Also, additional funds were granted Texas State University for Negroes, a practical step in the fight to keep Negroes out of the University of Texas.

On the other hand, a bill was passed wiping out Jim Hogg's antitrust law as it applied to oil fields, under the trick heading of "unitization," and the real-estate lobby put through a measure to decontrol rents.

In the closing days of the session the lawmakers battled frantically over revenue, and once more put off the inevitable—new taxes. If the major part of the 1949 program is carried out, the State will wind up $150,000,000 in the red. That means there must either be economizing, new taxes, or a constitutional amendment, as the State now operates on a cash basis.

A fair, sound, and permanent solution is an income tax. But the pressures are too great against that. Meanwhile, the big-business interests are setting the stage to ram through a sales tax, thus piling a major share of the burden on the shoulders of the poor.

Many of these decisions, as well as those resulting in the passage or defeat of other measures, were influenced by special interests. High on the list of those exerting these pressures was Ed Clark, Austin attorney. Clark represents Herman Brown, several utilities companies, and Southwestern Bell Telephone. Brown is a millionaire contractor, owner of the "Big Inch" pipeline and other properties, and the largest employer of nonunion labor in Texas. He began to loom large when he got the contract to build the huge Naval Air Base at Corpus Christi. Brown has continued to loom larger each year. He was a big backer of U. S. Senator Lyndon Johnson, and of State Representative Pearce Johnson of Austin. He was a moving force behind the vicious labor laws passed in 1947. Ed Clark was the brains that directed the job.

Clark also was a guiding hand in determining the destiny of much vital legislation in 1949. Texas lobbyists do not confine their efforts to their own pet bills. They pitch in and help other lobbyists with similar objectives.

Next to Clark, D. F. Strickland and Ike Ashburn are probably the most influential lobbyists in Austin. Strickland, a lawyer, represents Karl Hoblitzelle, owner of Interstate Theatres (spread throughout much of the State) and leader in the fight to blot out academic freedom in Texas. Yet, amazingly, Strickland worked hard for the school reorganization program at the 1949 Legislature. Strange things happen in Texas politics.

Ike Ashburn has spent much of his life as a Chamber of Commerce man. He represents the Texas Good Roads Association, which represents Texas cement interests and some oil interests. Ashburn lobbies for big highways requiring lots of concrete construction. At the 1949 session, he and his friends succeeded in diverting attention from a real rural road bill to a so-called "farm-to-market" highway program. Little concrete is used in rural roads.

Another potent lobbyist is Charles Simons, formerly with the Good Roads Association and now publicity director of the Texas Mid-Continent Oil & Gas Association. Regular lobbyist for the Association, controlled by Standard Oil, is Andrew Howley. Simons was a lobbyist for Texas cement interests while secretary of the Executive Committee of the

Democratic Party, at the time the so-called Texas Regulars tried to steal the State's electoral vote from Roosevelt.

Two other lobbyists much in evidence are Ed Burris, secretary of the Texas Manufacturers' Association, and Jack Harris, representing utilities companies.

Most of the other lobbyists are "one-shotters." They come to Austin to work for a bill, then go home. Many are former members of the Legislature, such as Claude Gilmer, a member of the committee that drafted the school reorganization plan. He returned to Austin as lobbyist for Karl Hoblitzelle and worked for the legislation.

There are also a few lobbyists on the "other side."

Robert Eckhardt, attorney for the Communications Workers Association, lobbies for labor and liberal causes. So do Jeff Hickman of the CIO, Harry Acreman and Paul C. Sparks of the AFL, and Mrs. Marion Storm of the Texas Social and Legislative Conference. Their lobbying consists largely in rounding up witnesses to testify at hearings. It is not of the beefsteak variety. They have no money.

During the heat of a session, the lawmakers are pampered like prize cattle, and *with* prize beef. On their lean ten dollars a day, which drops to five dollars late in every session, they can eat juicy steaks, at the expense of lobbyists, as long as "steak bills" are up for consideration. The extent to which this beefsteak business goes is unknown to the public. One reason is that a corporation can retain a lawyer without explaining the nature of the service. A majority of the Representatives are lawyers. Another factor that makes "beefsteak" legislation quite simple has to do with oil. An oil company can lease a man's land for exploration and the rate of pay is their own business.

Much of the administration of the government of Texas is transacted by boards. Texans love to shout derision at federal bureaus. But there are more than one hundred separate boards in Texas. In the words of the authors of that text-book, *State & Local Government in Texas*, ". . . the State's administrative machinery, taken as a whole, is a sort of historic museum. It consists of vast collections of agencies floating around loose, with responsibility running in all directions, with endless duplications and overlapping of functions, and with no means of working in unison."

Still, practically every Legislature creates new boards.

In 1933, during the lean years, the firm of Griffenhagen and Associates was employed to study the State government and recommend reorganization in the interest of efficiency and economy. In its report the firm said, ". . . the financial condition of the State as a whole is not known; there is no way of establishing the amounts owed either to or by the State; future estimates are but guesses; the first principles of expenditure control are not even understood, much less applied."

That condition remains unchanged. In 1949, there was a difference of $38,000,000 in estimates of the Speaker of the House and the State Auditor on anticipated revenue.

On the basis of the Griffenhagen report, a bill to streamline the State government was introduced and passed by the House. The measure proposed to merge the boards under nineteen State departments, with the heads of fifteen of the departments to be appointed by the Governor, constituting a sort of cabinet over which he had control. But the Senate, stronghold of the Blue Chip Boys, killed the bill.

The Texas judicial system functions independently. All judges are elected. The greatest need is a sweeping over-hauling of procedure in trial courts and improvement in the caliber of judges. Criminal cases involving wealthy defendants sometimes are dragged out for years, ending with acquittal in a different jurisdiction. Similarly, civil cases are protracted indefinitely, depending on the money involved.

Members of the bar usually select the judge. Lawyers in Texas are extremely conservative and, naturally, they pick conservative judges. They also incline strongly to mediocre choices, as few able lawyers care to go on the bench—except on the higher courts for prestige—at the salary Texas pays.

But in this field, too, there has been a change in recent years. The two highest tribunals, the Supreme Court and the Court of Criminal Appeals, have been enlarged, with the result that they now keep abreast of their calendars. A decade ago, the Supreme Court was four years behind in its work.

Also, despite the underlying conservatism of the nine Supreme Court justices, they have displayed an increasing awareness of the importance of human rights as against property rights—with one exception. This is the right of Negroes.

This generally broadened viewpoint may be due to reluctance of the Court to continue making decisions it knows will be thrown out by the U. S. Supreme Court. There is no question that that tribunal's edicts have had profound effect. However, some of the Texas justices are broad-gauged men. It is a fact that a number of Texas tycoons have been astounded at decisions handed down by Justices St. John Garwood and James Hart. Garwood is the son-in-law of cotton multimillionaire Will Clayton; and shortly before Hart went on the bench, he was attorney for the AFL in its court battle against the 1947 labor laws. Both jurists are conservative, but enlightened and fair.

Significant of the trend in the Court was its invalidation of some of the worst features of the labor laws. The anti-picketing clause and the requirement that labor organizers obtain licenses were ruled unconstitutional. Recently, the Court rocked the oil moguls by upholding an order of the State Railroad Commission that oil companies end the wasteful practice of flaring gas at wells.

This was a tremendous departure from the past.

The press of Texas must bear its share of the blame for the evils in the State government.

Texas newspapers run the gamut from conservative to reactionary. They are far behind the people, yet look down on them. The average Texan is neither a yokel nor a hidebound reactionary. The press assumes he is or tries to make him that way.

The Bible of many Texans is the Dallas *News*. For reasons highly amusing to literate Texans, the *News* is sometimes likened to the New York *Herald Tribune*. This may stem from a similarity in typography, or from the *News's* excellent book and music departments. Otherwise, the paper is the most reactionary in Texas, and that is saying a lot. The *News* is violently against organized labor, State and federal power developments, co-operatives, academic freedom at the University of Texas, and freedom of the press for *The Daily Texan*, a student newspaper of the University.

Not only does the *News* voice its virulent opposition editorially, but it does so in its news columns. There are frequent instances of biased and "angled" news handling.

Most of the other large Texas newspapers follow the *News* in their political, economic, and social thinking. Some, such as the Houston *Post*, are equally venomous, although not quite so articulate. But few carry their editorial opinions over into their news pages as does the *News*. The Houston *Chronicle* and Houston *Post* are notably fair in their labor reporting.

Another serious charge against Texas newspapers is that they are dull and mediocre. Much of this is due to the low salaries paid editorial staffs. There is little inducement for quality newsmen to remain in Texas.

There is practically no behind-the-scenes reporting of consequence in the State press, even by columnists. It is almost impossible to get an accurate picture of what occurs in the State Capitol, though the Associated Press Bureau in Austin is scrupulously fair and thorough. It is simply that reporting is deadpan and "straight." As that sparkling little publication, *The Texas Spectator,* once put it, "If O'Daniel says it is raining and Allred says it is not, the reporter is not supposed to have enough sense to look out the window and see for himself."

There is no probing for motives and pressures. Lobbyists and their operations are seldom mentioned, unless they represent such groups as labor and school teachers. The business connections and holdings of public officials are rarely reported. And if a pathetic delegation of deaf children calls on the Governor to complain about being beaten and mistreated, the Texas press makes no effort to expose the shocking situation.

About the only way it is at all possible to learn what is going on behind the scenes in State affairs is to read the weekly confidential letter issued by Stuart Long and John McCully, liberal free-lance newsmen in the Capitol.

Some of the smaller papers are moderately liberal. Among them are the Corpus Christi *Caller-Times,* Wichita Falls *Wichita Times* and *Record-News,* San Angelo *Standard-Times,* Gladewater *Times-Tribune,* Temple *Telegram,* the Sherman *Democrat,* and the McAllen *Valley Evening Monitor.*

The only papers in the State that are consistently and aggressively liberal are two little weeklies, the *State Observer* and the Houston *Informer.* The *State Observer* is published in Austin by Paul Holcomb, one of the truly great men in Texas life. The Houston *Informer,* a Negro paper, is published by Carter Wesley, an able and fearless American.

The Texas Spectator made its appearance in 1945, and it was a tremendous shot in the arm to Texas newspapermen. A weekly published in Austin by C. Badger Reed, Harold

340

Young, and Hubert Mewhinney, the *Spectator* was lively and stimulating. It ribbed the great and near-great, the Oil Barons and other tycoons. "Fear no more the frown o' the great" was the slogan that flew bravely from its masthead. But the little paper got no advertising and folded in three years.

At present the most interesting newspaper is *The Daily Texan* at the University of Texas. It has been consistently liberal, facing issues intelligently and courageously. But the paper is frowned on by University officials, and its days of freedom may be numbered.

One of the great forces for progress in Texas was being forged at the University before it was taken over by the Blue Chip Boys in 1944.

Decision to do this was made at a secret meeting of a half-dozen multimillionaires in Houston in 1940. It is generally believed O'Daniel, then Governor, took part in the meeting. It is a fact that he carried out the conspiracy, and Coke Stevenson, his successor, finished the job.

In a remarkably short time an interlocking directorate came into existence that took control of education in Texas.

Maco Stewart, Galveston multimillionaire, became chairman of the State Board of Education. His attorney, Lewis Valentine Ulrey, head of Christian Americans, became adviser in the selection of textbooks. Karl Hoblitzelle, of Interstate Theatres, became a director and eventually boss of Texas Tech. Hoblitzelle's lobbyist, Strickland, became a regent of the University of Texas, along with Orville Bullington, multimillionaire and onetime Republican candidate for Governor, and Dan Harrison, oil multimillionaire and Republican. Lon C. Hill, Jr., president of Central Power & Light, became a regent of Texas A. & I., as did H. E. Butt, wealthy chain-store operator with oil holdings. Robert Briggs, millionaire contractor, was made a regent of Texas

341

A. & M., and Gibb Gilchrist, State Highway Engineer and friend of Briggs, became president of A. & M.

Thus the interlocking directorate of wealth and reaction took over.

Never did the newspapers of Texas look shoddier than when they permitted all this to happen, including the discharge of Dr. Rainey as head of the State University, without making any effort to inform the people what was going on. The fight came into the open when Strickland, Bullington, Harrison, *et al,* set out to "get" Rainey. He brought their attack out into the open, and, finally, a Senate investigation aired a part of the plot.

Dr. Rainey ran for Governor and was defeated.

Today in his place at the University of Texas sits Dr. T. S. Painter. When he took over, he gave the faculty his solemn word that his only intent was to "hold things together" until the conflict was resolved. But as soon as he was sure of the backing of the regents, Painter inaugurated a "get tough" policy. Under his petty and deadening hand, the lusty spirit of the University began to wither. The University is on the blacklist of the American Association of University Professors, and many of its best young teachers have left. Painter and the regents changed the University's rules on leaves especially to get rid of J. Frank Dobie, one of Texas's most eminent literary figures.

The University of Texas has ceased to be the center of a free and aggressive spirit of progress.

What makes political advance so difficult in Texas is the one-party system. There is a Republican Party, but it belongs to R. B. Creager, ultraconservative Brownsville lawyer. Few in Texas know anything about the Party, except when the time arrives to select delegates to the national convention. Then Creager picks them.

He has headed the Party for more than a quarter century,

and he must look back with longing to those plush Harding-Coolidge-Hoover days when he cut a wide swath. Then he made federal judges, postmasters, customs collectors, U. S. district attorneys, U. S. marshals, and other officials. During the days of his glory Creager's prestige was such that many corporations, particularly those seeking to build bridges across the Rio Grande, were eager to have him as counsel. He was for years active head of the Gateway Bridge Company at Brownsville.

Most Texas Republicans are in the Democratic Party.

Extent of this Republican participation was strikingly displayed by the violent opposition of big-city legislators to a bill passed by the 1949 Legislature requiring voters to register and confine their voting to their own party in the primary. One San Antonio Representative said the bill would cost him fifteen thousand Republican votes and he would be defeated.

The encouraging feature of the struggle for progress in Texas is that minority groups are, at last, organizing and working together.

Union labor is becoming politically alert, even though many members were completely baffled when labor backed Coke Stevenson for the U. S. Senate. Admittedly, in view of Lyndon Johnson's Taft-Hartley record, there wasn't much choice. But, still, there is an underlying world of difference between the two men. There are 380,000 union members in Texas, and now that the AFL and CIO have stopped fighting each other, they are becoming a factor in political affairs.

The Texas-Mexican is also waking up to realities. He is breaking away from domination by Anglo-American bosses and, under the dynamic leadership of such young men as Gus Garcia of San Antonio and Dr. Hector Garcia of Corpus Christi, is becoming an active and progressive political force.

Similarly, the Negro offers high hope. Negroes can now vote in primaries, and the politicians are becoming very con-

343

scious of them. The Negroes have established their own Democratic organization and are beginning to move forward.

In the past there was no medium through which the efforts of these groups, and the efforts of the independent liberals generally, could be co-ordinated. Now there is. It is the Texas Social and Legislative Conference, which came into being largely through the efforts of Mrs. Minnie Fisher Cunningham, probably the outstanding liberal in Texas today, the late Dr. A. Caswell Ellis, and Mrs. Marion Storm.

This organization operates realistically, pinning its hopes on educational work and electioneering on the precinct level. If it can win the support of such groups as rural mail carriers, tenant farmers, teachers, and the like, it may prove a big factor in turning the tide. Already labor, Negro, and Texas-Mexican elements are affiliated with the organization.

There *is* hope for a better day in Texas. But the power and greed of oil cannot be underestimated. It operates in devious and unceasing ways, polluting and discoloring many things it touches. The grim struggle to free Texas from control by oil is not an easy one.

UTAH ★ ★ ★

Contrary State

ERNEST H. LINFORD

WHEN Harry Truman's campaign train rolled into Salt Lake City, a slight, goateed man was first to extend the hand of welcome. The amiable greeter was also in the car with the President and Governor Maw in the parade from the depot to the beehive-crowned Hotel Utah. As the auto drove away, a tourist, craning his neck, asked, "Who's the old guy with the beard?"

"That is George Albert Smith," answered a woman, belligerently.

The tourist lost himself in the crowd, a puzzled expression on his face. Unwittingly he had shown disrespect for the leader, prophet, seer, and revelator of the Church of Jesus Christ of Latter-Day Saints.

Devout President Smith was discharging one of his many duties as the head of Utah's dominant Church, which numbers more than a million members throughout the world and comprises about 65 per cent of Utah's population. Concentrated mostly in the intermountain West, they call themselves Latter-Day Saints. But to the public they are

★

ERNEST H. LINFORD has been a newspaperman for twenty years in the Rocky Mountain West. He has twice received national citations for distinguished presswork. He is a former Nieman Fellow at Harvard University.

"Mormons" because they use the Book of Mormon as a supplement to the Bible.

That evening Smith sat with President Truman in the great egg-shaped Mormon Tabernacle. Smith chuckled good-naturedly when Mr. Truman alluded facetiously to his home county of Jackson, Missouri. Though the "Saints" were expelled from Jackson County in the early 1830's, by prophecy of their founder, Joseph Smith, they will one day return to re-establish Zion, "a land of promise, a land flowing with milk and honey, upon which there shall be no curse when the Lord cometh." The prophecy is not discussed much these days. Salt Lake City is now the Mormon Zion and the land of promise.

Some weeks later President Smith was again on hand when another campaign train rolled in. This time he greeted Governor Thomas E. Dewey. Later, Church and Republican dignitaries mingled on the Tabernacle platform when Dewey made his address. It was an important speech on foreign policy. Next day the leading papers of the area gave the story second position to another, bannered, "Thousands Convene Today for LDS Conference." Probably only the perplexed tourist questioned this strange evaluation of news.

"Conference" is top news in Utah. "Conference" is the semiannual gathering of the Saints from the far corners. A recharging of the spiritual batteries of the faithful, it is also an important business event for the ecclesiastical, trading, and social capital of the intermountain region. "Conference" is bigger news than the Legislature, the Supreme Court, or conventions of the livestock association and the mining congress. It is a tremendous sounding board. Although Church leaders now restrict most of their utterances to matters pertaining to the soul, Mormon and Gentile (non-Mormon) alike listen attentively.

Utah, the home ranch of Mormonism, is the center of a

group of "public land" states, but in tradition and culture it differs extensively from its neighbors. "Utahns," says the State's official guidebook, "contributed to the book of Western history the most stubbornly cross-grained chapter it contains. All the conventions of Western life went haywire in Utah." A State of striking contrasts and contradictions in people, scenery, and climate, Utah's anomalies are reflected in its government.

The federal government owns 74 per cent of Utah's terrain. Federal land is to be found within ten miles of practically every community. Utah warred with the federal government, was victimized by "carpetbaggers," and was denied statehood for almost half a century. Even without this background, Utahns would be touchy about "encroachment" and "interference." The State's heavy dependence upon federal assistance adds to the resentment. Yet federal payroll and grants-in-aid are all-important to Utah's economy, and its welfare fluctuates with changes in Washington's political climate.

Characteristically, though they suffer when federal spending is slashed, Utahns are sharply critical of openhanded Congressional budgets. For years Senator Elbert D. Thomas has sponsored federal-aid-to-education legislation. When the measure came before the Eighty-first Congress, he received a scorching letter from the Salt Lake Board of Education branding it "an additional infringement of the federal government on individual rights and one more step in the socialization of the American way of life." The outburst did not, however, deter him. He took a leading part in the fight that put the measure through the Senate.

Contrasts are legion in Utah. It is illegal to influence a voter, but not a legislator. Clean, orderly towns are offset by haphazard mining camps. Magnificent mountain peaks top blistering salt flats. Prehistoric dinosaur graves are neighbors

347

to oil rigs and uranium workings. Sparkling water from Wa-satch snowbanks flows into a dead sea forty miles wide and seventy miles long—the Great Salt Lake that is 27.2 per cent salt.

Utah was the only western state to be settled by blue-print. The Mormon pioneers brought their stern, righteous, theocratic government with them. Utah had law and order before it had anything else. Every detail of the early settle-ment was carefully planned and its execution rigidly super-vised. Every person was hand-picked and assigned to a job. Brigham Young, prophet and ruler, did the planning and enforced the orders if need be. His lieutenants were of the priesthood, with authority according to their rank.

The Mormons hoped to isolate themselves in the desolate land they thought nobody else wanted. But by one of fate's sardonic tricks, the region lay across the path of the empire. It was a "halfway" provisioning point for forty-niners and immigrant trains headed for California and Oregon.

Also, when the brush-covered Salt Lake valley became sanctuary for this oppressed people, it was Mexican territory. But before the settlement was a year old, it was ceded to the United States, whose bounds the Mormons had fled. They continued their colonization of the State of Deseret, and for a time it extended from the Rockies to the Sierra Nevada and from Oregon to Mexico, embracing a part of the south-ern California seacoast. Six applications for admission to the Union were rejected. When the greatly shrunken State was finally accepted in 1896, it was not under the Book of Mor-mon name its settlers chose, but one honoring the indolent, cricket-eating Ute Indians.

Founder Joseph Smith drew up Zion's blueprint, even to the mile-square cities, wide straight streets, and large lots. The plan prevails throughout Mormonland today, but specu-lation has reared its head in the newer subdivisions, which

348

have narrow streets and small lots. Change has also come to "old town" sections. Large gardens and barnyards have been replaced with crowded, blighted, slumlike areas.

The "intruding" Gentiles resented ecclesiastical rule, but it was the ultimate in efficiency. It was a mixture of authoritarianism and town-hall government. Church authorities served in civil capacities; bishops of the wards administered the laws, with the Quorum of the Twelve Apostles serving as the court of appeals. Even after the establishment of civil government, these bishops' courts continued to function, especially in rural sections. Today the bishop is still the most important person in a Mormon ward, but his role has become primarily advisory.

At the outset there were no real political parties in Utah. Early-day Mormons were Democrats because Joseph Smith had sought nomination for the presidency on that ticket. Today most of the Church hierarchy is conservative Republican. At first, candidates for public office were named by Church leaders and "sustained" by the people. Political divisions began in 1870 when a group of "rebels" joined non-Mormons and formed the Liberal Party. It became aggressively anti-Mormon. The "Saints" formed the People's Party. Except in the turbulent mining camps, this party held control until the Church's political power was crushed, with the help of the federal government. Liberal Party ascendency in 1890 was marked by a series of bond issues for public improvements and the establishment of the first nonsectarian school system.

The Mormons gave up the People's Party and in 1891 the Church presidency published a statement that henceforth it would not control members' votes. Strange as it may seem today, members were asked to volunteer to vote Republican to counter the charge of a regimented electorate.

There are no political bosses in Utah. While Mormons

number from 27 to 92 per cent of the voting population in the counties, many non-Mormons are elected to office. Also, in Utah, voter participation in elections is considerably higher than the national average.

Brigham Young's informal manner of conducting legislative sessions, with both houses and the county judges meeting together, shocked an early federal jurist. During a reformation movement in 1856-57, members of the territorial legislature took a recess and were rebaptized for the remission of their sins. Today legislative proceedings are no different than in other states. The members are generally inexperienced and poorly paid, and the sessions are too short. The Legislature meets biennially for sixty days and does most of its work in the last week. As the pay is only $300 annually, regardless of the number of sessions, membership is limited largely to the well to do, the retired or jobless, and those supported by outside funds. A high rate of turnover is usual. In 1949, two-thirds of the House were newcomers. Periodic efforts to amend the Constitution to increase legislator pay have never gotten anywhere.

The Legislature is strongly rural-dominated. The "Big Three" counties—Salt Lake, Utah, and Weber—have 69 per cent of the population, but only 48 per cent of legislative representation. Also, while the Constitution specifies regular reapportionment, the mandate has long been ignored. A Salt Lake City district with 30,000 residents has the same representation as Daggett County with only 564 residents.

Notwithstanding such gross inequalities, powerful urban interests are strongly opposed to a change. Explained a leading Salt Lake businessman, "It's better the way it is. People from the country are less radical."

Mayor Glade, however, doesn't see it that way. To him it is shocking that a city with one-third of the State's population should be the "creature of a Legislature" ruled by

350

farmers who have no interest in or knowledge of municipal problems. "We are bound hand and foot by State laws and our every act is by their sufferance," Glade protests. He should know. From finances to parking problems, Salt Lake has to go to the rural-controlled Legislature.

But the cities are increasingly asserting their independence. Through the Utah Municipal League, they are pressuring and battling for a greater measure of home rule. A council appointed by the 1947 Legislature to study the problem made a number of enlightened recommendations. The 1949 Legislature ignored them, but a new council is now functioning and there is fair prospect it may have better luck.

Practically all forms of government-by-pressure are to be found in the Utah Legislature. Large interests and small are represented, each usually exerting influence in direct proportion to the size of its bank roll. Many of the lobbies operate on a year-round basis, with permanent offices, staffs, and high-powered press agents. Regardless of which party is in power, these lobbies have close ties in them. The 1949 Legislature was Democratic, but none of the major party planks was passed.

Strikingly illustrative of the standing of lobbyists was the dinner given by the Legislature for the lobbyist of the mining industry.

Other elements also wield potent lobbyist pressure. The Daughters of Utah Pioneers, local version of the D.A.R., wangled a $460,000 appropriation for a memorial building. Over the outraged protests of architects and other authorities, the structure was located on a small plot in the center of a traffic bottleneck in Salt Lake City. Similarly, the Legislature voted a costly Pioneer Centennial Memorial Highway from Salt Lake to Henefer. After $420,000 had been spent and funds had run short, a belated effort was made to drop the project. The Chamber of Commerce of Ogden, which is by-passed by the route, denounced it as a "transportation monstrosity, clothed in the lambskin of religious sentimentalism, shrouded in intrigue, and fed by pressure groups." Notwithstanding, few doubt that the "road to nowhere" will be completed.

The Utah Legislature currently suffers from lack of effective liberal leadership, of the kind provided by Herbert B. Maw when he was a member of the body. The Democrats control the Legislature, but owing to want of strong and purposeful leadership they have done little of a constructive nature. What little they have accomplished has been in the House, where the Democratic majority displays a greater degree of liberalism and party responsibility than its colleagues in the Senate. That chamber consists chiefly of pleaders for special interests. Comprising twelve Democrats —a number of them ultraconservative—and eleven Republicans, the Senate has stifled practically all liberal legislation.

President Pro Tempore Alonzo F. Hopkin, cattleman and old-line Democrat, characterizes the Senate. He went along agreeably with Republican Governor Lee and after the session ended he became chairman of the legislative council and was named by Lee head of a special committee to investigate the State prison. Similarly Senator Marl D. Gibson, Carbon County Democrat, teamed up with Republican Senator Mitchell Melich of Moab as a fighting spearhead for "economy" and the Old Guard line.

What liberal effort was made in the Senate came from P. S. Marthakis, Salt Lake schoolteacher, L. E. Elggren, Salt Lake businessman and founder and leader of the Consumers Welfare League, and J. E. Burns, who had served more than twenty years on the Highway Commission.

Democratic leadership in the House was like a green football team: it showed promise for next season. Speaker Ed J. McPolin and Floor Leader Maurice Anderson performed

352

moderately well, but it was freshman Justin C. Stewart and A. I. Tippetts, junior college professor, who supplied the real liberal leadership. It was Stewart who put through the bill to enable Utah communities to participate in the national low-cost housing program. The Senate, with Old Guard Democratic votes, later killed it. Another liberal legislator was Frank Bonacci, scrappy regional director of the CIO. The conservative leadership had the advantage of being more experienced. It was exemplified by Clifton G. M. Kerr, Tremonton businessman, and Dilworth Woolley, executive of three Salt Lake corporations.

Despite the Democratic majority, the Senate went along with Lee as agreeably as if the Republicans had been in control. This led to a bitter feud with the House over the general appropriations bill which Lee demanded be cut drastically. A deadlock resulted and Lee was handed a measure which he forthrightly slashed.

The struggle of the United States Forest Service to restore and conserve ranges and watersheds has been going on since 1907. But it is still touch and go. At least twenty Utah watersheds are wide open for floods, but little concern is displayed in the State Capitol. Funds have been voted for debris dams and flood channels, but the lawmakers are cold to proposals for reseeding and grazing control. Five million acres of sagebrush could be reclaimed if planted in grass. Yet a piddling conservation appropriation was vetoed by Governor Lee. He also wiped out funds for an agency engaged in the vital work of constructing small dams. Lee did this in the face of the fact that flood damage has cost one hundred and fifty Utah communities more than $10,000,000.

Rugged old-timers and general antipathy to "bureaucrats" are gradually disappearing, but loud protests are still heard against curtailment of grazing in the National Forests. The big livestock interests still wield a mean bull whip.

A movement to establish a State Conservation Department has made no headway. The 1948 legislative council rejected it as "impractical at this time." The State government openly balks at coming to grips with the crucial conservation problem.

Organized sportsmen wield more power than even the stockmen. Their "sacred cows" are deer. During hard winters deer roam city streets, raid orchards and farmyards. The State Fish and Game Department, supported by licenses and fines, is completely dominated by sportsman elements. The agency permits deer and other game herds far in excess of the limitations of the depleted ranges. Utah now has thirty times as many deer as it had in 1917.

As urbanization expands, Utah's government finds itself increasingly confronted with new and more complex problems. An illustration is water pollution.

Major departments suffer from the weaknesses of the commission form of government. Three bosses, usually laymen, compete for funds, public attention, and patronage. The legislative council and other organizations are urging a return to the board and professional director type of departmental administration.

Three-fourths of the State's population is concentrated at the base of the Wasatch. Every community has delightful, verdant canyons which, with the growth of winter sports, have become year-round playgrounds. But pollution of streams and lakes is seriously threatening these canyons. So far, the State has done practically nothing about the matter. Salt Lake City's sewage flows untreated into the Great Salt Lake, through an open canal that in one place is less than a mile from the city limits.

Utah has the initiative and referendum but has used them rarely. The latest occasion was to nullify a tax on chain stores. Voted by the Legislature, the tax was junked by the voters by a four-to-one majority. Liquor interests have made a number of efforts to liberalize the liquor laws by this process, but have gotten nowhere.

Utah's major economic problem is capital to develop its vast natural resources. The State goes to great lengths to bring in outside capital. As a result, Utah is a happy hunting ground of both big business and big government. Monopolies call the tune on industries, prices, and freight rates, while land and water developments, essential to agricultural as well as industrial expansion, depend on the pleasure of Congress. The evils of absentee rule are frequently assailed, but Professor Elroy Nelson of the University of Utah expressed the general attitude when he observed, "We don't care where the capital comes from just so it comes to develop our resources."

Similarly, the State government, under constant pressure for expanded services, frantically probes about for new revenues. But in this search great care is exercised not to kill the goose that lays the golden egg, or even to frighten the bird lest it go elsewhere. Small businessmen complain bitterly that big interests are escaping their share of the tax burden.

The Utah Foundation, a research outfit financed by big taxpayers, claims that all the taxes collected annually in Utah come to more than half the new wealth produced, and that the percentage of taxes to total income is greater than in any other western state. These contentions are subject to challenge, on the basis of what constitutes a tax. But it is fact that taxes are high in Utah.

Forty-two cents of Utah's tax dollar goes for education. The State has more children per adult taxpayer than other states, and most are in school. A recent survey showed Utah thirty-second in "ability to support" education, yet it "outclassed" other states in over-all performance. The public-instruction superintendent is second in importance to the Governor in State government.

The Mormon Church, through varied and extensive business interests, plays a major role in Utah's economy. Official figures are unavailable, but the business holdings of the Church are estimated at more than $200,000,000.

No key industry is wholly controlled, but Church-owned enterprises hold intensely competitive positions in a number of fields. The Church controls, among other things in Salt Lake City, two leading hotels, three large banks, the largest department store, the largest radio and television station, the largest bookstore, a daily newspaper, the largest commercial printing plant, a life insurance company, and a fire insurance company. Church interests also own and operate the Utah-Idaho Sugar Company, which made a net profit of $2,032,914 in 1948, a gain of more than one hundred per cent over the previous year. And the realty holdings of the Church are the largest in Utah.

Through its newspaper, the Church violently opposes government spending and is vehemently anti-New Deal. Leading policymaker of the Church is J. Reuben Clark. A rock-ribbed Republican, he was Ambassador to Mexico and Undersecretary of State in the Hoover administration. Clark's views have changed little since then. Of twenty-four former ambassadors, he was the only one against the North Atlantic Pact.

The numerous prohibitions in Utah reflect the Church's sober, strait-laced influence and this, in turn, has a direct effect on the tourist industry. Estimated at $75,000,000 in 1948, it was surpassed only by agriculture, mining, and manufacturing. The big problem is how to persuade the tourist, so often on his way elsewhere, to stay longer. Utah boasts practically everything for the pleasure seeker—except sin. That can be had, of course, but it isn't prominently displayed. It has to be sought out. Scenery is the great attraction. No state has more bizarre, more incredible, or more contrasting wonderlands. But most tourists demand more than scenery. They seek the kind of lusty entertainment to be found in Nevada or Idaho, where transgressions are legal, or in Wyoming, where they are enticingly illegal.

For all its neighborliness and over-the-fence amenities, Utah is unexciting. One-armed bandits are few and bordellos rare. There are no famous rodeos. Taverns and roadhouses make a pretense of western gaiety, but they are obvious mild imitations of the boisterous pleasure houses across the State line. The red tape and high cost of getting a drink and the practice of rolling up the sidewalks early keep many well-heeled tourists away.

Attempts to liberalize the drastic liquor and gambling laws are made regularly, but without success. Utah boasts a low crime and juvenile delinquency record, attributable in part to the ban against saloons and rackets. Home training and the strict moral discipline also are important factors. The Mormon Church has law-enforcement committees that scan all candidates for office and nudge lax officials. Though seemingly preoccupied at times with minor offenses, they are a force which discourages more serious violations. Vice squads do not hesitate to descend on private clubs suspected of harboring slot machines and other illicit gewgaws. Also, Church insistence upon Sabbath observance has a pronounced effect on Sunday business. Youth organizations are especially active in the enforcement of Sunday closing laws.

The Church's "Word of Wisdom" ban on liquor, tea, coffee, and tobacco, is reflected in the State's laws. It is illegal, for example, to portray on a billboard a woman smoking. For a short period, cigarettes were outlawed entirely. In 1948, only Arkansas had a lower cigarette consumption rate.

357

At a Church Conference that year, one high authority said, "Tobacco, tea, and coffee are not the worst things in the world, and we must not cast aside a man because he uses those things." But this did not mean letting down the bars. At a later Conference, the same authority severely denounced violators of the "Word of Wisdom."

Zion lays constant stress on the sanctity of the home and the evil of divorce. But Sociologist Henry H. Frost, Jr., found the rate of divorce in Utah little different from the rest of the country. It was one divorce to three marriages in 1946, and the State has the same seven permissible grounds for divorce as neighboring Nevada.

Utah has few racial problems, as its population is ninety-eight per cent white and Anglo-Scandinavian. Orientals and American Indians are fairly treated on the whole. The Negro encounters most discrimination. Under the laws of the State, all children receive the same educational privileges. But Negro graduates, as elsewhere, encounter difficulties in obtaining employment. Similarly, while the law makes it a misdemeanor to discriminate in "public inns," such discrimination is quite common, particularly against Negroes. Indians generally receive better treatment.

According to the Book of Mormon, American Indians (Lamanites) are descendants of white people who came from the Near East and settled in Central America in Old Testament times. This belief led to an early paternalism toward the red men, much of which still lingers. The "Curse of Ham" prevents Negroes from holding Mormon priesthood, though they may join the Church. Civil Rights bills make periodic appearances in the Legislature, but are invariably pigeonholed in spite of the efforts of small but vocal groups to get action on them.

Two separate welfare programs function in Utah, contrarily rivaling and supplementing each other.

358

One is the Mormon Church's "we-take-care-of-our-own" program, with $7,600,000 resources at the end of 1948. The other is the State-federal welfare system. More than one-third of the State's revenue goes for this purpose. Utah's public assistance payments are among the highest in the country.

Born in the depression, the Church welfare program is bold and vigorous. Each Church community established a welfare project to which all the faithful contribute. Turning back the clock to Brigham Young's concept of communal self-sufficiency, the projects swap goods and services and maintain large reserves of food and materials as insurance against hard times. Many carloads have been shipped to needy "Saints" in Europe. The ward bishops certify Church welfare clients, thereby closely allying temporal and spiritual needs. The Church claims that 2,029 persons have been removed from public relief rolls in six years and that of these, 1,291 are now self-supporting.

Yet Utah has received huge sums from the federal government for welfare purposes. The question constantly asked is why the State's welfare outlay is so considerable when the Church is presumably carrying part of the burden. There are several answers. The Church's welfare recipients work for their goods and services, while public welfare clients are paid in cash. Also, the Church plan is for members; thirty-five per cent of Utah's population is non-Mormon.

The Church's welfare program is a unique social experiment. It is a present-day version of the old Mormon United Order. The nearest thing to collectivism on a large scale in American history, this pious, benevolent, communal society was far more significant than Brook Farm, New Harmony, and other Fourier-type ventures. In the United Order, members pooled their resources and labor, receiving only subsistence for themselves and their families. Contrasted with godless russian Communism, this type of collectivism was voluntary and based on religious concepts. The law of tithing, which requires Mormons to give ten per cent of their earnings to "The Work of the Lord," is another manifestation of the co-operative spirit. Some members estimate that their tithing, welfare, and fast-offering outlays amount to twenty per cent of their incomes. Yet nowhere is there more violent opposition to socialism than in Utah, and the most vociferous critics are Church leaders.

Liquor rivals welfare as a Utah dilemma.

A reluctant merchant, the State has a complete monopoly on the sale of alcoholic beverages and the profits are the principal source of the general revenue fund. Yet there is more legislative oratory about liquor than any other subject. Despite Church resistance, Utah was the thirty-sixth state to ratify the Twenty-first Amendment. But prohibition is not dead. Said Church Apostle Henry D. Moyle at the April, 1949, Conference, "It is bad enough to traffic in liquor at all. If prohibition is the only way to end the evil of liquor let's start fighting for it to preserve the doctrine of righteousness. . . ."

Utah needs liquor revenue, but officially frowns on drinking and has a number of legal obstacles to discourage it. Liquor is sold at State package stores, but only to those who have obtained permits to buy it. Beer (3.2 per cent) is dispensed in grocery and drugstores under license. As a result, Utah has a very low rate of liquor consumption, less than a gallon per capita per year. Yet liquor is a constant issue. It was the only one on which the Mormon Church took a public stand in the 1948 campaign.

Road building and maintenance are by expediency and political pressure. A stretch of road is built here, another there, with no over-all plan or co-ordination. Thousands of cars travel daily between Salt Lake and Ogden, yet part of the thirty-seven-mile route is a narrow two-lane death strip, and more than half of Utah's roads are less than the twenty-foot minimum width specified for traffic safety. In 1949, the Highway Department was a full year behind in matching federal grants.

In the early days, federal judges carried the non-Mormon banner in the fierce territorial conflicts. On occasion, hand-picked juries were used to convict Mormons, and tension was not uncommon between bishops' courts and the civil courts. These conditions exist no longer.

Utah's judiciary is able and generally liberal, particularly the Supreme Court. Judges are elected on a partisan basis, but for many years efforts have been made to take the courts out of politics. The 1949 Legislature passed a bill designed to do this, but it was vetoed by Governor Lee. The Republicans' argument was that the measure would remove the courts from close contact with the people.

Decisions in workmen's compensation cases, interpretation of fair labor standards, and some phases of constitutional law have put Utah's Supreme Court in the liberal column. The tribunal has long evinced an enlightened and sympathetic attitude toward social change and civil rights. Though few cases are spectacular, the court strongly favors the "little fellow."

Justice James H. Wolfe, whose learned decisions have wide recognition, is a veteran liberal and the best-member of the tribunal. He has served on nation finding and mediation boards, and in earlier day sailed by conservatives as a "parlor socialist." And liberal is Justice Roger I. McDonough, who ha on mediation boards and won recognition out

A tempest in a teapot exploded early in Supreme Court upheld the Legislature's a priate funds for a memorial museum for

Utah Pioneers, an auxiliary of the Mormon Church. The outlay was attacked as State funds appropriated for Church purposes. Catholic McDonough led the majority in holding the appropriation legal, while Justice E. E. Pratt, descendant of an early Mormon leader, and Unitarian Wolfe dissented on grounds that it violated Utah's strict Church-State division.

Justice G. W. Latimer is the only Republican on the bench and one of the few currently serving on a State court. The fifth member is Justice L. A. Wade, of Mormon descent, like Latimer.

Utah's district judges are fairly liberal and though their "mediocrity" has been criticized as an argument for reform in the mode of election, their records compare favorably with judges in other states. Critics say Utah's court system has no real over-all control or integration and that judges are sometimes absent when needed. Also, with no really outstanding figures among the district judges, Utah courts lack the color of earlier days when Orlando Powers, Arthur Brown, and Samuel Thurman exhibited their showmanship as trial attorneys.

Penal and other institutions are sadly overcrowded and understaffed. In addition, they are constantly subjected to political meddling. For years the State prison has been in he process of being rebuilt, and while the State mental hos- al at Provo is not exactly a "Snake Pit," it is far from a mendable institution. In 1948, the staff consisted of two rs and four nurses for more than 1,200 patients. The n improved somewhat after being publicized. Even to -minded Governor Lee relaxed his no-building rule d State institutions.

T cize o yearn for crusading journalism sometimes criti-
Four ress as timid and on occasion subservient. The has become ultrarespectable and invectives

Utah Pioneers, an auxiliary of the Mormon Church. The outlay was attacked as State funds appropriated for Church purposes. Catholic McDonough led the majority in holding the appropriation legal, while Justice E. E. Pratt, descendant of an early Mormon leader, and Unitarian Wolfe dissented on grounds that it violated Utah's strict Church-State division.

Justice G. W. Latimer is the only Republican on the bench and one of the few currently serving on a State court. The fifth member is Justice L. A. Wade, of Mormon descent, like Latimer.

Utah's district judges are fairly liberal and though their "mediocrity" has been criticized as an argument for reform in the mode of election, their records compare favorably with judges in other states. Critics say Utah's court system has no real over-all control or integration and that judges are sometimes absent when needed. Also, with no really outstanding figures among the district judges, Utah courts lack the color of earlier days when Orlando Powers, Arthur Brown, and Samuel Thurman exhibited their showmanship as trial attorneys.

Penal and other institutions are sadly overcrowded and understaffed. In addition, they are constantly subjected to political meddling. For years the State prison has been in the process of being rebuilt, and while the State mental hospital at Provo is not exactly a "Snake Pit," it is far from a commendable institution. In 1948, the staff consisted of two doctors and four nurses for more than 1,200 patients. The situation improved somewhat after being publicized. Even economy-minded Governor Lee relaxed his no-building rule to expand State institutions.

Those who yearn for crusading journalism sometimes criticize Utah's press as timid and on occasion subservient. The Fourth Estate has become ultrarespectable and invectives the thirty-seven-mile route is a narrow two-lane death strip, and more than half of Utah's roads are less than the twenty-foot minimum width specified for traffic safety. In 1949, the Highway Department was a full year behind in matching federal grants.

In the early days, federal judges carried the non-Mormon banner in the fierce territorial conflicts. On occasion, hand-picked juries were used to convict Mormons, and tension was not uncommon between bishops' courts and the civil courts. These conditions exist no longer.

Utah's judiciary is able and generally liberal, particularly the Supreme Court. Judges are elected on a partisan basis, but for many years efforts have been made to take the courts out of politics. The 1949 Legislature passed a bill designed to do this, but it was vetoed by Governor Lee. The Republicans' argument was that the measure would remove the courts from close contact with the people.

Decisions in workmen's compensation cases, interpretation of fair labor standards, and some phases of constitutional law have put Utah's Supreme Court in the liberal column. The tribunal has long evinced an enlightened and sympathetic attitude toward social change and civil rights. Though few cases are spectacular, the court strongly favors the "little fellow."

Justice James H. Wolfe, whose learned decisions have won wide recognition, is a veteran liberal and the best-known member of the tribunal. He has served on national fact-finding and mediation boards, and in earlier days was assailed by conservatives as a "parlor socialist." Another stanch liberal is Justice Roger I. McDonough, who has also served on mediation boards and won recognition outside the State.

A tempest in a teapot exploded early in 1949 when the Supreme Court upheld the Legislature's authority to appropriate funds for a memorial museum for the Daughters of are no longer in the style books. Of the State's six dailies, four are owned locally. But only the capital city has a competitive press. The Salt Lake *Tribune* and Salt Lake *Telegram* are owned by non-Mormons. They are friendly to Mormon interests, as are all Utah papers, but maintain an independent viewpoint. The official Church paper, the *Deseret News*, is indistinguishable from other dailies, even to its Sunday issues. The only exception is its weekly Church News supplement. The *Deseret News* is the most conservative in Utah. The Ogden *Standard-Examiner* is the only paper that accepts liquor advertising. The Provo and Logan dailies are owned by the Scripps chain. The sixty weeklies in the State range from good to poor.

Perhaps the non-Mormon press's greatest service has been the promotion of better Mormon and non-Mormon relations.

While Utah's politics are at times tinged with religious differences, old antagonisms have mellowed. In a typical Utah anomaly, the third non-Mormon Governor, Republican J. Bracken Lee, won with the support of Mormons, Masons, liquor interests, and prohibitionists.

In recent years, politics was overshadowed by one name—Maw. From 1940 to 1949, Governor Herbert B. Maw epitomized the great Utah paradox. He took office as a promising liberal and eight years later was turned out in a wave of disillusion and anger. Some appointees let him down by misconduct and inefficiency. Whether he knew of their shortcomings and loyally stood by them or was unaware of what went on remains a moot question.

A faithful Mormon, Maw was a Chaplain in World War I and served on the boards of the Deseret Sunday School Union and the Young Men's Mutual Improvement Association. But he split with Church leadership early in his regime and this feud was featured by his requested retirement from his ecclesiastical positions and, in turn, his failure to appoint apostles to important educational boards.

Amiable and articulate, the former speech professor successfully fought the powerful Utah Power & Light Company as a State Senator. He championed the cause of the "common man," and his ambitious plans for industrialization, attracting tourists, and otherwise arousing the State from its long sleep won him repute for vision and courage. Liberals of both parties flocked to his banner.

Maw fulfilled his pledges at the outset. He established the direct primary, and shook up the Statehouse from top to bottom. Among those ousted were appointees of the previous Old Guard Democratic regime. But after having made this resounding start, Maw then turned around and packed vacancies with his political henchmen—disgruntled party-fringers, free-lancers, and nincompoops. The hopes that had run high for abler and more liberal government began to falter and fade.

Some claimed Maw merely exploited discontent and championed popular causes for personal advancement. They said his "common man" was Maw, and subsequent events seemed to support the charge. He was re-elected only by a narrow margin over an upstart political maverick, "Brack" Lee. All the forces of conservatism and orthodox political rule were arrayed against Maw.

His political empire was already crumbling when the clang of a burglar alarm in Salt Lake City the night of March 1, 1948, signaled the final breakup. The burglary was a fake staged in a State liquor agency to cover up defalcations. A grand jury indicted Cyrus V. Lack, the operator of the store, and Robert S. Harries, head of the enforcement bureau of the State Liquor Department. Both were subsequently convicted of embezzlement and bribery. The head of the Tavern Owners' Association also was indicted, but his case was dismissed. Lack and Harries appealed.

On the witness stand, Lack told of friendships with numerous prominent figures and claimed Maw knew about his activities. The Governor issued an immediate and emphatic denial.

The grand jury continued in session more than nine months, a record. Innumerable rumors were sifted and three hundred and fifty persons interviewed. Another Maw appointee, Ray H. Leavitt, chairman of the State Road Commission, was indicted. He was convicted on a perjury count for denying he had received $500 from a rock asphalt salesman.

The jury also staged some gambling raids in which several hundred pinball and other devices were seized and smashed. In a pronouncement the jury declared it could not understand why Maw had allowed Lack to operate the liquor store after disclosures of "open violations." The jury flailed auditing procedures and urged separation of liquor and politics. Then, turning its attention to other matters, the jury denounced the "hopelessly antiquated" State prison in the heart of Salt Lake City, censured the policy of allowing policemen to have other jobs, and blasted county and city commissioners for "careless" practices.

But after all this furor, no other indictments were returned. The mountain had brought forth a mouse. There were loud outcries that the $70,000 dragnet had brought in only minnows. Others pointed out the highly interesting fact that the major witnesses who had appeared before the jury were from Price, where Brack Lee, again running for Governor, had been Mayor.

The final weeks of Maw's campaign were desperate. His lieutenants tried to turn the campaign into a moral-religious issue. Lee was branded an ally of liquor and gambling inter-

365

ests, and in a now famous "Dear Brother" letter, Maw appealed to Mormon priesthood members to help stem a "drive of the underworld to make Utah an open State." Warning that the "people are in danger of losing the results of a hundred years of effort," he thundered that "the underworld seeks to eliminate State control of the liquor traffic by doing away with the law-enforcement division."

Lee's camp saw to it that the letter found its way into the press, which reacted with vigor. The Mt. Pleasant *Pyramid* proclaimed, "Any man who attempts to create political division among free American citizens on the basis of church affiliation is a bigot. Governor Maw has done just that in his letter. Waving the white banner of virtue is an obvious attempt to obscure fumbling of proven bribery . . . The letter is a ludicrous example of political double talk. Governor Maw's record doesn't jibe with Brother Maw's letter."

The Church also voiced stern reproof. President Smith said, "No one can speak for the Church except over the signatures of the first presidency. . . . Action by a committee of Church workers does not imply action by the Church itself."

Maw created the Publicity and Industrial Development (PID) office to industrialize Utah and attract tourists and investors, but he used its talents to his political advantage with abandon. The PID served in the field for which it was created, notably surveying and publicizing Utah's fabulous raw-materials wealth. In addition to the routine chamber-of-commerce activities, it set up and operated factories and museums. (One project turned out to be completion of a high-school where Maw votes were needed.) It built roads for the motion picture industry and built the controversial Centennial Highway, independently of the road commission. Its employees also wrote Maw campaign literature.

Maw's welfare machine was unique too. A special "investigation and rehabilitation" staff operated from his office in the Capitol, independently of the State and county welfare commissions. Its ostensible aim was to remove "chiselers" from the rolls. But it worked to keep old folks in the Maw camp. Robert Siddoway, chief welfare investigator for Maw, was also head of the organized pensioners.

Maw was one of two Democratic Governors defeated in 1948. The other was Monrad C. Wallgren of Washington. Their cases were strikingly similar. Wallgren also had "liquor trouble," and in his state, as in Utah, every other Democratic candidate for state office was elected.

As Governor, Lee has swung a lusty ax, raising cries of pain and dismay throughout the State. He has particularly outraged labor, agriculture, veterans, and teachers. But the big, organized taxpayers have shouted huzzas and with ecstatic satisfaction noted that "for the first time in twenty years the upward trend of the State budget had been reversed."

Fulfilling Maw's "Dear Brother" prophecy, but ostensibly for nobler purpose, Lee has abolished the enforcement bureau of the Liquor Department and told reluctant sheriffs and police chiefs their duty was clear. When his veto quashed a $40,000 appropriation for the Attorney General, $25,000 of which was for "special investigations," critics roared that the open saloon was just around the corner.

After reorganizing the Liquor Department, Lee notified liquor companies that their local representatives were no longer needed. He suggested that the fees and commissions they had received be paid to the State. His proposal that all states buy direct from distillers received a cold shoulder from the National Alcoholic Beverage Control Association. But Lee was undaunted. His argument that taxpayers should be saved the sums paid to liquor salesmen was answered by the now jobless representatives by pointing out that his only

367

accomplishment was to wipe out a tidy $170,000 "free enter-prise" payroll in Utah.

Lee also cracked down on the Publicity and Industrial Development (PID) office so vigorously that the Legislature refused to appropriate funds for State promotion and adver-tising. As a result, the eight-year-old agency is dolefully liquidating its operations.

Through his economy axing, Lee has almost outdone his predecessor in lopping off State jobs. He rejected ten per cent of the one hundred and nineteen legislative bills that reached his desk, and hacked twenty-five items totaling $4,000,000 from appropriations. Lee also applied a razing hatchet to educational institutions on all levels. Chief among his victims were the Salt Lake area vocational school and extension funds for the State University and the Agricultural College.

The extension fund veto proved explosive and led to a fierce feud with Democratic officials. Attorney General Clin-ton Vernon caustically branded as unconstitutional Lee's proposal to use the State Agricultural College funds to pay county agents.

A tense deadlock ensued, and a court decision invalidated the veto of extension service funds. The row was finally dis-solved in a compromise that saved face for both Lee and Ver-non. The arrangement avoided the necessity of calling a special session or of further litigation. Lee, in effect, conceded that his vetoes had been invalid, and department heads prom-ised to operate within the budgets he fixed. Also, the State Uni-versity and Department of Education received additional funds. These gains made it possible for the University and the Agricultural College finally to get in motion important functions that had been halted by the months of uncertainty and tension. But while Lee and Vernon were saved political embarrassment, several questions remained unsettled, notably the legality of transferring appropriated funds, and the powers of the Maw-created State Finance Commission over University funds.

Brack Lee isn't the "vetoingest" Governor in Utah's history, but he chalked up an impressive record of thirteen rejections out of the one hundred and nineteen bills.

He angered Utah bar leaders when he killed a bill to take the courts out of politics, and war veterans when he refused to extend their income-tax exemption. Other Lee vetoes were a bill to increase hunting and fishing licenses to create a fund to pay landowners for damages done by wild game; an appropriation to make up a $40,000 deficit of the Utah symphony, a private organization; a measure to legalize bigamous marriages contracted in good faith; and exemption of Utah law-school graduates from State bar examinations.

To the outcries that he had set the State back thirty years, Lee reiterated his oft-voiced contention that Utah had to learn to operate within its income.

He also charged the Maw administration with "irregularities" and demanded investigation and reimbursement. He billed tire companies $10,000 for alleged overcharges, and assailed payments to architects on the ground that the $500,-000 they had received was unauthorized. Others, also, were blasted on various grounds, but Lee produced no documentary evidence to support his accusations.

Lee's violent attacks on the previous administration aroused hopes that he would surround himself with outstanding appointees. He had boasted that he was under obligation to no one. But a number of his selections have left much to be desired. Government-by-crony is still rampant in Utah.

To the Board of Regents of the State University he named a Salt Lake doctor known to be hostile to the highly regarded medical school. Senate refusal to confirm blocked this deed.

As State Engineer, a position calling for expert knowledge of complex irrigation and other technical problems, Lee appointed a retired construction foreman with little engineering training and no experience in many of the duties he was to perform. Similarly, a merchant was made head of the Board of Agriculture, and labor protested bitterly that it was disregarded on the State Industrial Commission.

A small-town insurance man, Brack Lee is an Elk and a thirty-second degree Mason. Though of Mormon ancestry, he is not a member of the Church. However, he has given a number of leading Mormons important posts in his administration. During his six terms as Mayor of Price, he put through some excellent civic improvements.

Lee's outstanding characteristic is stand-patism. He is against government spending and for tax reductions to attract industry to Utah. He is vehemently against what he calls "socialistic trends," and for removal of rent controls. Similarly, he assailed low-cost public housing and public power projects. Yet Utah's industrial future depends largely on cheap electricity.

All the men behind Lee are archconservatives. P. H. Mulcahy, Ogden businessman and former railroad official, was made chairman of the powerful State Finance Commission and immediately began expanding his authority. J. A. Theobald, former secretary of the Price Chamber of Commerce, was given the juicy plum of chairman of the State Fair Board. In every key spot, Lee has planted a tried and proven fellow Old Guarder.

Who rules Utah?

The dominant Church cannot be overlooked, of course, though its influence is often overrated. Direct political power of the Mormon hierarchy has not been great the last twenty years. Church influence is stronger, however, where moral or sectarian issues are involved. A directive from, or a con-

370

ference at 47 East South Temple Street has undoubtedly changed many an official mind on questions such as the sale of liquor by the drink. But on economic and political issues this influence would have considerably less weight. Legislators and party leaders are respectful to Church officials, but they go their own political ways.

The influence of the Mormon Church is difficult to isolate and evaluate, outside the moral and ecclesiastical fields. On tax and similar issues the view of the Church hierarchy is so close to that of the Utah Manufacturers Association and the Salt Lake City Chamber of Commerce that it is impossible to differentiate among them.

With its large payroll and the area it controls, the federal government partially rules Utah through far-flung agencies. Around 40,200 persons are on national, State, county, and city payrolls in Utah. These public employees compare with a total of 14,000 working in mines, 26,200 in industry, and 40,000 in agriculture.

The schools have the most potent pressure organization in Utah. The know-how, ability, and persistence of the teachers is bolstered by the support of parent-teacher associations and other allied organizations. The extent of this influence is reflected in the liberal school program for which Utah is noted.

Certain Salt Lake City law firms have influential members of both political parties and reputedly wield great power behind the scenes regardless of whether Republicans or Democrats are in the saddle. But Utah is not machine ruled and has no Kelleys, Curleys, or Hagues. Labor had a heyday during the New Deal era but its influence has waned considerably. Livestock and farm organizations are consistently strong, though they did not fare so well in the 1949 Legislature. Their most distinguished member is Secretary of State

371

Heber Bennion, Jr., who is Acting Governor during the absence of the chief executive.

Once outstandingly distinctive for individuality, Utah's government today is comparatively colorless, ordinary, and mediocre. Pressure groups jockey and manipulate against rival special interests to get their way.

Yet for all its unspectacular mediocrity, for all the compromises and the leveling-off in the last half century, Utah still clings to some of its ancient contrariness and inconsistency. Socialism and nonconformance are abominations, but as late as 1949 a resolute splinter sect isolated itself in the sagebrush wastelands to set up a new Utopia.

Brack Lee graphically represents the Utah anomaly. At the 1949 Governors' Conference he boasted that his State led in government economy and fought extravagance by rejecting federal grants-in-aid. Then Lee hurried home and wired Congress demanding prompt and vigorous action by the federal government to relieve "critical conditions in Utah mines."

CALIFORNIA ★ ★ ★

The First Hundred Years

RICHARD V. HYER

IN THE Year of Our Lord, 1948, California began observing a series of centennials; the discovery of gold, the forty-niner migration, admission to Statehood, and other historic events. The State could view with justifiable pride the many achievements of its first hundred years, for it has grown swiftly to great economic and political stature. But amid all the parades, pageants, fiestas, books, and oratory there was one thing that found no place on the official agenda.

This was an outsized political and legislative mess of national as well as local significance.

Its origins go back to the governorship of the late Hiram Johnson, who was better known for the bedrock isolationism of his career as a United States Senator. Its probabilities reach at least as far into the future as the 1952 presidential election. Its elements, only loosely related at first glance, include Johnson's reforms of the State's political processes, the events of the 1947 and 1949 Legislatures, the coming 1950 census and State elections, the reapportionment of congres-

★

RICHARD HYER was born and educated in Illinois. He has been a newspaperman for twenty-five years, chiefly in San Francisco, where he is now a member of the *San Francisco Chronicle* staff. His specialty is investigating and reporting organized crime, and its attendant corruption in high places.

373

sional districts to follow, and, finally, what is known as the Third House, made up of lobbyists and other pressure manipulators.

The Johnson reforms included, among other features, a system of election cross-filing. The practical effect of this has been to neutralize partisan politics by permitting a candidate for State office to run as both a Republican and a Democrat. As a result, normal political processes have been supplanted to a considerable extent by the machinations of the Third House, a fact graphically demonstrated in State elections and recent sessions of the Legislature.

Barring a public explosion, there seems little likelihood of any diminution of lobbyist activities and powers in the foreseeable future. That future includes the 1950 elections in which the voters will choose a new Legislature and new State officers. In 1950 there will also be a new national census.

Experts estimate conservatively that this census will increase California's congressional delegation from twenty-three members to at least thirty, and possibly to as many as thirty-five. The State's electoral college ballot will go up correspondingly, making California an even greater prize in the 1952 presidential election.

With California's registration predominantly Democratic, it would appear that the State would go Democratic. That is not necessarily so.

In the first place, the Legislature elected in 1950 will have the job of carving up the State to create the new congressional districts. It is a political axiom that reapportionment inevitably involves a certain amount of gerrymandering in which the party in control endeavors to strengthen its position still further. It is also axiomatic in California that the Third House will have a profound effect on the election and on what subsequently happens in the new Legislature. And the Third House owes allegiance to no party; it flies no flag but the beautiful green banner of the United States currency.

California's Third House has become probably the strongest and most arrogant aggregation of lobbyists extant in any state. Their archetype is an enormous man who wields enormous power. He sows, reaps, and controls a dense tangle of internal issues that smother and do violence to partisan politics and constitutional government alike.

When he blows the whistle half the State jumps without knowing the source of the command. He is the uncrowned King of Confusion so far as the bemused electorate is concerned. In more knowledgeable circles he is the Khan of California, and no Oriental potentate ever ruled with more effectiveness. With quite becoming modesty, he bills himself simply as a public relations counsel. Privately, he lays claim to more power than the Governor and refers affectionately to the Legislature as "my baby."

His name is Arthur H. Samish. There are, of course, a great many other lobbyists in California; the State Capital at Sacramento swarms with them. Some are entirely reputable in their activities and the interests they represent. But none compares with Samish in power, influence, prestige, command of resources, personal wealth, and a sort of clandestine prestige amassed in the more than thirty years of his activities.

An accurate gauge of his strength may be found in the fact that most of his colleagues, no matter how pure their objectives, discover it is more expedient and effective to lobby Samish than to lobby the Legislature.

He is reaching out, now, for respectability. Occasionally he uses his organization to kill a bad piece of legislation. He has been known of late to scold venerable lawmakers for unseemly conduct or a too tolerant attitude toward a questionable bill. For several years he has also conducted a quiet campaign to establish himself with the "right people"—

375

bankers, lawyers, executives, merchants, industrialists, publishers and the like—as a useful friend and wise counselor. He has even taken to making speeches, although these occasionally backfire because he is apt to indulge in florid boasts.

When discussing the varied life and times of Arthur Samish, he emphasizes his many gifts to charities and how he has established small but profitable businesses for deserving chambermaids, bellhops and newsboys. In short, he has been busy lobbying the entire State to portray himself as a sort of benign elder statesman and warmhearted benefactor.

As he sums it up: "I'm riding a white horse now." Notwithstanding this latter-day assertion of saintliness, Samish's career has all the earmarks of political dictatorship, however ostentatious its benevolence. This domination epitomizes the development and use of hitherto unheard of controls to the point where they usurp the prerogatives of the electorate and make representative government a travesty.

The logical question arises: Why hasn't something been done about it?

An attempt was made in 1937 when Frank F. Merriam was governor. Samish emerged stronger than ever, while Merriam and other Samish adversaries of that period have, for the most part, sunk into political oblivion. If the investigation served any purpose at all, it was to teach the lobbies how to protect themselves better in the future.

The Third House is now so formidably entrenched that any full-scale inquiry into its leading members would probably leave the scene littered with maimed casualties of every political stripe.

But there are men of integrity in both major parties who are angered and aghast at the arrogant, contemptuous, and apparently well-founded presumption of power by the Third House. They have excellent reason for their dismay. In the

1949 Legislature, the lobbies blocked practically every progressive bill and spent much time hand-picking their selections for the 1950 election handicaps.

The potency of the lobbies in elections is corollary to their strength in the Legislature. Samish, for instance, takes a bow for a prominent part in the election not only of Mayor Elmer E. Robinson of San Francisco, but in that of Mayor William O'Dwyer of New York as well. He also admits that he brought about the election of Attorney General Fred N. Howser in 1946.

In a way, this is a remarkable confession. Howser has proved to be a veritable political Pandora.

Almost from the moment he lifted the lid of his desk, California has been swept by a series of racket and graft scandals over gang killings, bookmaking, the nationwide horse-racing wire service, slot machines and punchboards, with the end not yet in sight. The turmoil has reached into many counties, and as far east as New York to involve the notorious Frankie Costello, the country's No. 1 mobster.

Samish now publicly disowns Howser, a disclaimer viewed with skepticism in many quarters.

But whatever their current relationship, the Samish-Howser affair remains a dramatic illustration of the overweening influence of the Third House. It exemplifies the sinister power of lobbyist rule.

California always has been an unruly and unpredictable mass of extremes. Within its boundaries are such violent contrasts as the lowest place in the country, Death Valley, 276 feet below sea level; Mount Whitney, the highest, with its 14,500-foot peak; Mount Lassen, the nation's most recently active volcano; the vast, flat, fertile Central Valley plains; the snow-capped Sierra Nevada; blighted deserts; the giant redwoods, oldest living things on earth; Los Angeles and San Francisco.

The State's history is comparable in its vagaries.

The Spaniards took California away from the Indian aborigines as an offshoot of the conquest of Mexico. In 1825, four years after Mexico got rid of the Spaniards, it became a Mexican Territory, and in 1836 a Mexican Free State. Ten years later, during the United States' peculiar war with Mexico, California seceded and proclaimed itself the independent Grizzly Bear Republic. That state of affairs lasted just twenty-four days. In 1847, following Mexico's surrender, California became an American possession. In 1848, James Marshall discovered gold and precipitated the celebrated '49 gold rush. In 1850 the newly rich, brash, lusty, brawling political adolescent was taken into the Union. It had experienced no sobering probationary period as a Territory. It remained a juvenile delinquent among the states for quite some time.

During the next sixty years California went through two major phases of political development. The first ended in 1879 when a new Constitution was ratified after some of the worst disorders in the nation's history.

Most of this astonishing uproar occurred in San Francisco. It produced such phenomena as a reign of terror under a hoodlum mob known as The Hounds; more than a thousand killings between 1849 and 1856; and the Vigilantes, who had their own artillery-armed police, conducted their own courts, hanged five men, and restored a semblance of law and order. This violent period was followed, in the 1870's, by certain political reforms. Farmers, small businessmen, and labor joined forces to combat unbridled plundering by special interests. One of the factions of the coalition was the Workingman's Party of California, formed by an Irish demagogue named Dennis Kearney, and as radical for that period as any labor group in the country.

In 1878, when a constitutional convention was called,

Kearney's party, known popularly as the Sand-lotters, was strong enough to control one-third of the convention's votes.

The Constitution ratified in 1879 contained remarkably progressive changes in the State's organic law. It established the eight-hour day; cut deeply at the powers of the great corporations by imposing the beginnings of regulation by government; and created a State Board of Equalization to eliminate tax inequities. It also contained a prophetic passage concerning the Third House. One of its provisions defined "improper" lobbying and made it a felony. But so far as is known, this law has never been successfully invoked.

Good as it was for its era, the new Constitution could not and did not halt the grandiose exploitation achieved by the railroads from 1869 to 1910. In 1869 the Central (now Southern) Pacific joined the Union Pacific in Utah to form the nation's first transcontinental railway. The historic event heralded forty years of economic conquest in California and all the West. The larceny included wholesale land-grabbing by the railroads under government grants. It is of note that Leland Stanford, for whom the great University at Palo Alto is named, was variously President of Central Pacific, Governor of California, and United States Senator.

But in 1910 the freebooting era came to an end in California, for the railroads at least. Hiram W. Johnson became Governor.

His political career began in 1908 during the San Francisco graft trials. In a dramatic courtroom fracas, the special prosecutor, Francis J. Heney, was shot in the neck by a psychopathic talesman who had been disqualified from jury service. Johnson took Heney's place and concluded the trial by convicting Abe Ruef, then the political boss of the city. Ruef was freed later.

The great scandals plummeted Johnson into prominence. Reform elements saw in him a potentially great banner

379

bearer. Among his early supporters was the late Chester Rowell, at that time editor of the Fresno *Republican* and later editor of the *San Francisco Chronicle*. Johnson was persuaded to run for Governor on a platform that pledged the Southern Pacific would be driven out of politics. It was a reform movement that received indirect impetus from the national reform wave that elected Woodrow Wilson President.

Johnson's campaign was made tremendously colorful and complicated by the fact that his father, Grove L. Johnson, was the Southern Pacific's chief lobbyist. Father and son fought each other bitterly.

Johnson won. He did drive the Southern Pacific out of politics (although one school of thought contends the railroad had everything it wanted by then). He also squelched a Democratic resurgence in the State. And California politics moved into a pattern, the general outlines of which still exist.

Johnson enacted the most progressive program ever adopted by a single session of the California Legislature. The new laws were aimed primarily at destruction of the political machinery constructed and employed through the years by the railroads and other special interests, and did an excellent job of it.

Johnson substituted the direct primary election with cross-filings, for the old party convention system with its political ward heeling and bossism. He also instituted the initiative and referendum, the recall, workmen's compensation, and regulation of railroads and utilities under a State Commission.

But unique and outstanding as his record was, Johnson's reforms proved to be not wholly an unmixed blessing. Also, they were won at the cost of quite a little tarnish on the bright halo of the Governor's political purity. He found it necessary to make a major compromise that is known to

380

only a few of the surviving participants but which had far-reaching effect.

Johnson had to submit his reforms to the State for approval before they could become law. To get them on the ballot he needed a two-thirds majority in both houses of the Legislature. He did not have it. San Francisco at that time was by far the most powerful community in California and had the largest delegation in the Senate and Assembly. The undisputed boss of both delegations was Tom Finn, member of the Senate and one of the shrewdest politicians California ever produced. Johnson made a deal with Finn.

In return for support of the reform program, Johnson gave Finn control of the juicy patronage accruing to the State's management of the teeming San Francisco waterfront. Both men kept the bargain.

As to the mixed blessings of the reforms, as time passed the new laws created a sort of vacuum in the political structure of the State, a void into which filtered the inimical forces of the Third House. It is of interest to note that at the time of the deal with Johnson, one of Finn's casual protégés was a tall youngster named Arthur H. Samish, who now refers to "Tom Finn of the Hiram Johnson organization" as one of his earliest mentors in the science of political and legislative manipulation.

From the events that followed Hiram Johnson's first administration came the outlines of what was to develop into a pattern of right-wing Republican conservatism that has dominated politics in California for a long time. Even now, in the face of the State's preponderantly Democratic registration, there are shrewd observers who will wager that it "remains in the hands of the original owners."

Johnson detested the very conservative *Los Angeles Times* and all its works, especially Harrison Gray Otis, then the publisher. This sentiment was shared by Tom Finn. The result was a north-south rift in the Republican ranks, but it did not last very long.

Johnson was re-elected Governor in 1914, the first man to win a second four-year term. In the middle of his second term, he ran for the United States Senate. His victory produced a unique situation. Lieutenant Governor John Eshelman had died and there was nobody to succeed Johnson. He solved the problem by appointing a Southern California Congressman, Republican William D. Stephens, to fill Eshelman's vacancy as Lieutenant Governor. Then, on March 15, 1917, Johnson resigned to become Senator and Stephens stepped in as Governor.

Stephens served out Johnson's unexpired term, won a second term in 1918, and tried for a third in 1922. This time he was defeated in a coup engineered by Kyle Palmer, political editor of the *Los Angeles Times,* who still remains the bellwether of the Republican right wing.

The *Times* candidate was Friend W. Richardson, who had been State Treasurer for seven years. To his support the *Times* rallied the powerful backing of the *San Francisco Chronicle* and *Oakland Tribune.* The alliance brought into prominence a Republican hierarchy that has become known as the Chandler-Cameron-Knowland Axis, so named for the publishers of the three giants of the State's Republican press: Harry Chandler, then of the *Times,* now deceased and succeeded by his son, Norman; George T. Cameron of the *Chronicle;* Joseph R. Knowland of the *Tribune.*

Of this triumvirate the *Times* was long the dominant member, although of late there has been a shift of influence to the north. Paul Smith, red-haired editor and general manager of the *Chronicle* under Publisher Cameron, has exerted a strong liberalizing influence on the standpat conservatism of the so-called Axis. Also, the shift of power from the south to the north has been made easier by the fact that Norman Chand-

382

ler does not take as much personal interest in political issues and candidates as did his father. Norman is said to rely largely on the advice of Palmer and Chester Hanson, who heads the *Times'* bureau in Sacramento.

But whatever the ebbs and flows of power within the Republican hierarchy, it has been defeated only once since the days of Hiram Johnson.

Richardson's administration was followed by a resounding intramural Republican squabble in which the still strong progressive elements managed to swing the Party leads over to a liberal candidate, C. C. Young.

He was elected in 1926, and many Californians believe he was the most competent Governor the State ever had. But he made several powerful enemies who cut short his career. One was Tom Finn, the San Francisco political boss, the other ex-Governor Richardson.

Young ignored the patronage arrangements Finn had enjoyed since his original deal with Johnson. Finn retaliated when Young came up for re-election by joining forces with the *Times,* which materially aided a consolidation of the north-south Republican forces. Richardson meanwhile had been very busy undercutting Young. He convinced the *Times,* with no difficulty, that Young, regarded as the last California leaf on the extinct Bull Moose tree, was too radical to hold an office that made him titular head of the Republican Party in California. Richardson persuaded the *Times* to support, instead, Buron Fitts, newly elected District Attorney of Los Angeles.

Not content with these arrangements, Richardson, aided by others, then persuaded James Rolph, Jr., San Francisco's colorful mayor, to enter the race as a third candidate for the Republican nomination, which was tantamount at that time to victory in the general election. There had not been a Democratic Governor since James H. Budd won in 1894.

The three Republican candidates stacked up this way: Young was a dry and had nominal Republican Axis support in the north; Fitts was a reformer and a dry, and had the *Times* support in the south; Rolph was frankly and joyously wet, had some support from the *Chronicle,* and was riding the rising tide of prohibition repeal.

The result was inevitable, although it came as a shock to portions of the Republican hierarchy. Fitts got the Southern California dry vote. Young got the Northern California dry vote. Rolph beat them both with the State's entire wet vote.

Rolph died during his fourth year in office, and was succeeded by Lieutenant Governor Frank F. Merriam.

The advent of Franklin D. Roosevelt started a Republican debacle in California, as elsewhere, although it did not immediately affect the Party's control of the major State offices.

For years the indulgent Republicans had regarded Democratic antics as little more than the political exercises of a curious sect. But in 1932 a lot of Democrats, riding on Roosevelt's coattails, won election to the State Legislature. They took over a number of seats the happy Republicans had created in carving up the State for reapportionment. They were an impecunious lot, many of them so broke they did not have the railroad fare to Sacramento and had to hitch-hike. One disgruntled Republican wit dubbed them "our oversexed and underprivileged legislators."

By 1934 the situation had changed still more. The Democratic nomination for Governor was won by a man who scared the Republicans and big business almost out of their wits. He was Upton Sinclair, reformer-novelist and father of an ingenious version of the more abundant life known as EPIC (End Poverty in California). His major plank was a $50-a-month pension for every needy person over sixty.

Even the orthodox Democrats wanted no part of Sinclair. Senator William G. McAdoo, as head of the Democratic

384

forces, stumped for George Creel, aging journalist who had been propaganda chief during World War I. The Republican candidate, logically, was Merriam, who had succeeded Rolph when the latter died in office.

In the runoff, Merriam defeated Sinclair. But the strength of the EPIC movement had asserted itself unmistakably. Sinclair polled nearly a million votes, losing by only a narrow margin. And more than thirty EPIC candidates won seats in the Legislature. Most prominent among them was a State Senator from Los Angeles named Culbert L. Olson. But while the Democrats had finally achieved a strong position in both houses, they failed to make effective use of their new power because of a fatal cleavage. Olson and his forces never forgave McAdoo and his faction for deserting Sinclair.

In 1936 more Democrats got into the Legislature. In the lower house they managed, for the first time, to elect the Speaker.

The year 1938 brought the first of the Republican Axis defeats, although lack of party discipline, a traditional ailment, nearly cost the Democrats their first Governor since 1894. Riding high, they came up with a large assortment of candidates in their own primary. The list included Raymond Haight, John Dockweiler, Herbert Legg, Sheriff Dan Murphy of San Francisco, Federal Judge J. F. T. O'Connor, William Neblett, and State Senator Olson.

Neblett was McAdoo's viceroy in the Democratic Party. Dockweiler was the candidate of the pension elements which by then had enlarged the EPIC program into a grandiose affair—"Thirty Dollars Every Thursday" for every needy person over fifty. Haight, Legg, and Judge O'Connor were more or less maverick candidates. Olson and Sheriff Murphy fought it out as rivals in the Democratic left-wing camp.

When they picked up the primary pieces, Olson was the Democratic candidate for Governor.

In the Republican ranks, Merriam again was the choice after a sharp battle with Lieutenant Governor George J. (The Hat) Hatfield. Hatfield's candidacy was engineered by Arthur H. Samish, by then a great power, presumably in revenge for a lobby investigation that started during the Merriam regime.

In the election, Olson defeated Merriam, the choice of the Chandler-Cameron-Knowland hierachy. But they regained control in 1942 with the election of Earl Warren as Governor and retained it through his re-election in 1946. What 1950 has in store is anybody's guess.

Olson's short-lived success was almost foreordained by an illusion and by his badly mixed political complexion.

Olson's illusion was aptly described by Democratic Attorney General Robert Kenny as "a belief that he, like Roosevelt, had a mandate to create a millennium in the biennium." The governorship had come to Olson too late for that. With World War II approaching, economic conditions were rapidly improving and his ideas for social legislation collided with the worst of adversaries—good times. Also, his political coloring became so confused that he looked like a radical to the conservatives, and like a conservative to the radicals.

His handling of a single State issue—relief—was sufficient to create this odd dilemma. Upon taking office Olson tried to pay off a welter of campaign debts with the meager resources at his command by putting some leftists into State relief administration jobs. Immediately, from within his own ranks, rose a great hue and cry, "get rid of the Reds." Whereupon Olson launched a "Red purge," threw out a number of people who had done much to elect him, and went so far as to make a burnt offering of Relief Administrator Dewey Anderson. He was a member of the Stanford University faculty, author of a definitive work on State taxes, and was highly regarded by many right-wing Democrats and Republicans alike.

The combined effect was to put Olson in bad with virtually all political groups. On top of this, he didn't help himself with the Third House. Having inherited the lobby scandals touched off by Merriam's investigation of the Third House, Olson tried to continue it for his own purposes and came to grief there, too.

In 1942 Olson managed to obtain the Democratic nomination for Governor again. But he was badly defeated by the Republican Earl Warren.

In theory, California has a political system of such purity as to delight the student of political science. But the question remains: How has a Republican hierarchy held so much power for so long?

The answer has several elements. In general, the Republicans have resisted, better than the Democrats, the processes that have dulled the sharp edge of partisan politics. By and large, the Democrats do not have as much money as the Republicans, have far less discipline, and are apt to squander their resources, like a man betting on eight horses in a single race. Witness 1938, when they had seven candidates for Governor in their own primary.

In contrast, the Republicans may squabble bitterly over the selection of a candidate, but once the choice is made he usually gets solid backing. Even dissident Party members would rather vote for a bad Republican than a good Democrat.

The matter of a final choice, however, is something over which the *Tribune-Chronicle-Times* Axis exercises great influence. When they act in concert, the three newspapers comprise the most powerful publicity organ in the State. Because of this, and of their record of successes, "smart" Republican money invariably goes to the candidate they endorse. Also, the Axis is canny in its strategy against numerically superior forces. It employs the time-tested tactics of adding fuel to the Democrats' own fiery quarrels over issues and candidates,

387

as a means of breaking a solid front into ineffectual fragments.

Even when they lose, the Republican leaders can sit back and wait philosophically for a reversion to the status quo ante. A case in point was Olson's election as Governor.

He and his supporters probably envisioned the overthrow of the Republican regime and establishment of a new political dynasty in California. What Olson didn't understand is that a Governor is politically insolvent the moment he takes office. He has few assets and thousands of liabilities. He can reward only a small group of his principal creditors. Ninety-eight per cent of all city, county, and State employees are under civil service. It is this technical purity of California's political system that has created the political vacuum into which the Third House has filtered. Lobby influences and lobby finances frequently take over the functions nominally performed by a party machine. The more powerful lobbies command almost unlimited money and have a virtual monopoly on key media of advertising, such as billboards and trade journals. Sometimes lobby interests coincide with those of one party or the other, more often with the Republicans.

As a result, the lobbies are sought out and consulted by political leaders to determine their attitude on a given issue or a potential candidate. On occasion the lobby influences take the initiative, to the point of dictating the selection of a major candidate.

There is no rule of thumb on this aspect of California politics, but there are some striking examples of it. A notable instance was the influence of Arthur H. Samish on the choice of Fred N. Howser as the Republican candidate for Attorney General in 1946.

Arthur Samish attributes the origin of his lobbying career to Jesse Steinhart, now considered the "elder statesman of Republican politics in California." Samish states he was an employee of the State Division of Markets when Steinhart was lobbyist for the United Cigar and S. & H. Green Trading Stamp interests.

"Steinhart called me in," Samish recalls, "and said, 'Art, I don't want this kind of work any more. You take it over.' That was my lobby start, my first good big job. From there on it's been whoopee, to the point where I won't take any more business now, except as a personal favor. From then on, I've always been known in my line as the highest-priced in the business. The results, I'll leave to you, but the pay—that's mine. I like to work on a contingent basis. That's when results pay off.

"I don't want any more business now. It would just cost me money. I'd rather have $20,000 tax free than $120,000 subject to taxes. In fact, I have just (May, 1949) turned down a proposition that would mean a fee of $200,000 a year for the next five years."

After taking over from Steinhart, Samish moved in with Buck Travis of the California Motor Carriers Association and became secretary-manager, a title he still retains, along with the emoluments of the job. The Motor Carriers now include all the State's bus lines, among them the huge Pacific Greyhound Company. Samish made his first tour de force in behalf of his bus clients and, incidentally, established in his own mind a completely cynical approach to the business of lobbying and politics.

He undertook a fight with the railroads, handling campaigns and directing legislation that brought the bus lines finally to full status as public utilities. He forced the railroads to buy into the bus companies. In establishing the companies as public utilities, he suffered one major defeat but came back to win a much greater victory. It was in this triumph that he acquired convincing proof of the incorrigible gullibility of the voting public.

389

"The problem," he says, "was to get the buses out from under a load of county and municipal taxes by making them public utilities subject only to a State tax, like the railroads. The first time we went out honestly and spent huge sums trying to educate the people on the fairness of the proposition. We got licked by 70,000 votes. I think that was in 1923. In 1925 I went to Sacramento and put an amendment for this through the Legislature. It had to be approved by the voters. So we uncorked a new campaign.

"In this one I figured the hell with education. That hadn't worked before. Instead, this time we plastered the State with billboards that had a picture of a big ugly hog's head and said, 'Drive This Hog Off the Road—Vote Yes on Number . . .' whatever number it was.

"It carried by more than 600,000 votes, the biggest majority a proposition ever got before or since, and it was the same damn thing we took a dumping on before. What does it prove? It proves people are suckers for a picture and a slogan. Trying to educate them is a waste of time and money."

By 1939, while Young was still Governor, Samish had emerged as a force at Sacramento. In that year he flexed the muscles of his developing legislative controls and took on Frank F. Merriam in a fight over the speakership of the Assembly. Merriam won by a single vote, but the photo finish demonstrated Samish's rising power and gave him a new prominence, accompanied by a more thoughtful respect, in legislative circles.

By the time prohibition ended and the State began the laborious construction of liquor controls, he was in a position to capitalize in an important manner on the situation.

Beer lobby accounts flowed into his office. The same channels later brought him major whisky and wine accounts. His organization expanded. He formed the California State Brewers' Institute as a starter, and followed up with various

390

liquor distribution associations. At the same time California's Alcoholic Beverage Control Act came into being. Samish asserts he had nothing to do with this, but the statement has always been taken with a large dosage of salt because the ABC Act, as the liquor-control measure is called, goes straight to the core of his operations.

The law put liquor licensing and policing in the hands of the State Board of Equalization. This agency was created by the State Constitution of 1879 for the purpose of tax administration, chiefly to remove inequalities. The underlying intent was to put the all-important matter of taxes directly under the jurisdiction of elected rather than appointed officials. SBE is made up of four members, one from each of the State's four Board of Equalization districts, with the State Controller, also elective, the fifth member.

What creation of the Board actually accomplished was to put taxes in the hands of political factions strong enough to elect the members. There are many arguments pro and con over whether this is good or bad. But when the taxation powers of SBE are combined with control of liquor traffic, they reach dizzy heights. Many authorities on government regard California's Board of Equalization as it functions today as one of the most outrageous bureaucracies ever foisted on a commonwealth.

It is a government both within and without the major governmental structure and nothing short of state-wide upheaval can unseat it.

Concerning its liquor-licensing and police powers, SBE states in one of its brochures: "These licenses, issued only to applicants and establishments complying with the strict requirements of the Alcoholic Beverage Control Act, may be revoked or suspended by the Board for any violation of the law."

The brief statement is very revealing regarding the Board's

enormous powers. Also it is in reference to the use of these powers that Samish enters the picture. For when the powers of the SBE are combined with his command of liquor money and advertising media for political campaigns and legislative pressures, they give Samish more political and economic strength than any other individual or organization in California.

This may seem an extravagant statement, but the facts bear it out. On the surface it would appear that the Board of Equalization, with its great authority over the liquor industry, would have the whip hand and could perpetuate itself into a sort of political dynasty. Actually, there have been many changes in Board personnel. If a Board member becomes too aggressive and evinces a disposition to impose new taxes and costly regulations, his career is apt to be cut short. This can be accomplished by the industry's political organization headed by Samish.

His methods are bluntly simple.

Samish is said to exercise final approval of candidates who are to receive liquor industry support in campaigns for election to SBE. There are no details, of course, on the conferences between him and his principal clients leading to such decisions. But "the word" is passed up and down the State to all licensees by whisky, beer, and wine salesmen, through trade journals, and in other ways. Campaign funds pour in in big chunks from the big companies, in smaller but fairly standardized amounts from the bars, taverns, and package stores.

The Samish candidate usually wins. For years the lobbyist has thus maintained, a position of great influence with the Board of Equalization although individual members deny they are subject to it. But it cannot be denied that the Board has been very kind to the liquor interests. In fact, it has been estimated that although only ten per cent of the tax revenue handled by the Board comes from liquor, it nevertheless devotes about ninety per cent of its efforts to liquor matters. These efforts are sometimes very strange.

For example: Although the Board "may revoke or suspend a liquor license for any violation of the law," its agents blandly ignore bookmaking, slot machines, and even gambling operations. It is a matter of record, in statements issued by the Board, that the agency has set itself above and beyond the laws of the State. It has asserted that it retains the authority to determine whether a license should be suspended or revoked even when the licensee has been convicted of a felony.

On the other hand, the Board's enforcement of liquor trade regulations is phenomenally efficient. Let a licensee sell a drink or a bottle below the established price and he is jerked up for discipline so fast he hardly knows what hit him.

Virtually all the Board's publicity concerns the liquor industry, with the result that the public has no real understanding of its vast powers in other tax fields. As Samish has remained largely anonymous except among the political cognoscenti, the electorate has even less understanding of his immense influence with the Board.

Samish does not like to talk about this and brushes it aside. It is a matter of record, however, that all manner of big corporations and big individuals have found it necessary either to employ him directly as a "legislative advocate," to use the polite term, or to hire other lobbyists who have discovered it was better to work with him rather than without or against him.

Concerning the list of his clients, only Samish and God are informed. He will admit that "you'd be surprised at all the top people who come to me for help," but does not proceed with any surprising revelations. Those that are known include the whisky, beer, wine, bottle, bus, trucking, race-track, milk, tobacco, and labor interests—even the World Federalists—to name a few.

Of late years Samish's pre-eminence as a lobbyist and mastermind of campaigns has attained such heights that he has even gone into business against his clients with impunity. He will admit that during the war he opened a string of retail liquor stores. He says he is no longer in the retail business, but does concede that he organized a big distributing company called Better Brands, Inc., which competes with the wholesale end of the whisky industry he represents. Early in 1949, Better Brands acquired the Northern California agency for Budweiser beer, which also put him into competition with his beer clients.

Samish was put under the microscope in 1937, while Frank F. Merriam was Governor. A charge of attempted bribery was made in the Senate. The Legislature passed a joint resolution calling on District Attorney Otis D. Babcock of Sacramento to investigate. Governor Merriam provided the money.

Although the original charges were leveled at Gene Flint, Assemblyman from Los Angeles, the inquiry soon focused on Samish and legislators suspected of being under his influence. Subpoenaed to appear before a grand jury with his bank accounts and income-tax returns, Samish resisted mightily, but eventually did so.

The investigative firm of Edwin N. Atherton and Associates conducted the exploration into corruption, with Howard R. Philbrick in charge. Atherton, now dead, had made the famous 1935-37 San Francisco police graft investigation, in which sixteen high-ranking officers were fired from the force for refusing to disclose the source of wealth far above their known incomes.

Throughout, the probe was hamstrung to the point of being unable to undertake any prosecutions directly. But it nevertheless produced some astonishing information. Phil-

394

brick's final report made a series of findings that are probably even more applicable today than they were then. None of his recommendations for control of lobbying has been carried out.

Excerpts from the findings follow:

"Ample evidence has been produced by this investigation to show that corruption, direct and indirect, has influenced the course of legislation . . . Corruption is not necessarily bribery. The term is a general one suggesting loss of integrity—a taint. The instances of bribery encountered in this investigation were relatively few. They were, also, relatively unimportant in the light of more widespread methods of corruption. A detailed dollars and cents record has been produced . . . to show that huge sums of money have been spent to influence legislation. The principal source of corruption has been money pressure. The principal methods of exercising money pressure have been through fees paid to lawyer-legislators and through expenditures of lobbyists.

"The principal offender among lobbyists has been Arthur H. Samish of San Francisco, through whose accounts has been traced a total of $496,138.62 during the years 1935-38. All of this money was provided by individuals, businesses, and organizations directly interested in legislation.

"As long as lobbying of the type and on the scale practiced by Samish is countenanced there will be corruption in the Legislature. For he seeks to establish, and the evidence shows he has in some instances established, a secretive 'fourth branch' of the government—in effect a super-government overriding the legislative, executive, and judicial branches. Such a system breeds corruption, for its single standard is not merit, nor responsibility to the public, but the size of the fee paid to the lobbyist, and expended in part by him—directly or indirectly—with members of the Legislature to perpetuate his influence.

395

"While the public, when encountering a corrupt member of the Legislature, has the recourse of repudiating him at the next ensuing election, the public, when encountering a corrupt or corrupting lobbyist, has no recourse under present law unless he carelessly trespasses into the field of open and shut bribery."

Since the Philbrick report was submitted in December of 1938, lobbying has markedly increased in Sacramento. It has produced, in addition to lawyer-legislators with fat fees from clients interested in legislation, insurance agent–legislators, real-estate broker–legislators and public-relations counsel–legislators—with similar fees. It has also produced, along with pre-election campaign contributions, the trick of cozening up to a successful but neglected candidate by paying his campaign deficits.

And despite the coldly factual Philbrick report, which remains unchallenged, Samish is more than ever the ruler of the Third House.

His defense during the investigation was typical. First publication of the sensational fact that Samish was involved, was a news beat scored by John C. Lee, an intelligent, bitter young man on Hearst's *San Francisco Examiner*. For a while the *Examiner* devoted its considerable editorial and make-up abilities to giving the story a tremendous and righteous play. Then Samish acquired a new attorney.

He was John Francis Neylan, a firebrand liberal close to Hiram Johnson twenty years before but who now had settled down into more respectable Republican ways as Hearst's counsel and fiscal adviser. When Neylan entered the case, the *Examiner* completely reversed its stand and overnight plumped for Samish. Young Lee, enraged, quit his job and has since become a leading publicist.

What manner of man is Samish?

He is six feet two inches tall and weighs around three

hundred pounds. He has a fringe of gray-white hair, friar-fashion, around a pink bald pate. Little keen blue eyes peer shrewdly over a broad, squat nose, a wide mouth, and heavy jowls. His complexion is rosy clear. For the street, he usually drapes his tremendous bulk with carelessly immaculate sports clothes and wears a soft-brimmed hat turned up in front, like an elderly, obese sophomore.

He can be as disarming as a child, hard as Bessemer steel, and shrewd as the devil himself. His twin gods are money and power. He may bestow the former on friends with a lavish hand, but none of the latter slips through his fingers.

An audience (the term is advised) with him between 10 A.M. and noon usually finds him padding around his hotel suite in Sacramento in broken-down leather mules, a blue and red polka-dotted silk robe, and nothing else. The visitor enters Room 428, where a brace of secretaries is at work. He is escorted to an adjoining conference room furnished with a big round table, comfortable chairs, davenport, radio, phonograph, stacks of record albums, a bathroom converted into a full-rigged kitchen, and a buffet table lined with a choice assortment of liquors. Samish's personal quarters are in a third room.

His conferences are interrupted by repeated telephone calls in which the parties on the other end do all the talking except for grunts or monosyllabic "yeah's" and "no's" from Samish. The telephone, he is convinced, is "man's worst enemy."

The Samish headquarters, on the fourth floor of the Senator Hotel, are known as "Samish Alley." When the Legislature is not in session he circulates among the permanent headquarters he maintains in San Francisco, Los Angeles, and New York City. All are ceaselessly busy conducting probably the greatest privately operated intelligence system in existence.

Nobody, not even his closest associates, knows the identities of all the people on the Samish payroll, or who are under sufficient obligation to him to serve as agents to furnish information. The annotation of that information for Samish's purposes is complete.

At Sacramento no important committee hearing or social function takes place that is not attended by a Samish informer, known or otherwise. All this material is summarized, catalogued, and filed. By absorbing it, and applying to it his profound knowledge of legislative processes, Samish has the unique ability to predict with uncanny accuracy how a given legislator will react to a given bill, if allowed to follow his own devices, or if subjected to pressure.

This intelligence system also provides a more subtle and damaging type of information that can be applied to bring a rebellious lawmaker to heel, or to put an overly ambitious one back in line. Astutely, Samish does not exercise these controls unless absolutely necessary. He prefers to use the genuinely charming and convincing manner he possesses. As a result, he has a remarkable number of close friends and admirers who include some of the most respected members of many branches of both State and federal government. They include, too, innumerable employees who can be exceedingly useful.

Samish has several titles that might be called honorary. In five minutes he can break down the formality of a visitor to the point where the latter is calling him Artie. Those who have grown old in his service or under his domination respectfully address him as "Colonel." Among the more raucous members of the Third House he may be referred to (out of his hearing) as "Mr. Big Me," because of his vanity, or "The Goose," a term reminiscent of his earlier and less discreet lobbyist days when golden eggs were laid.

Samish's personal vanity is colossal but under control; it

398

seldom if ever interferes with his sound judgment. In his younger days he dressed like a horse-player who had parlayed two bucks into a million. His attire included a belt set with diamonds that spelled out "Arthur." But after meeting men of greater and more established wealth and observing their quiet dress, Samish abandoned gaudy furbelows.

He is given to boasting, up to a point. He will remark, for instance: "Every branch of the alcohol industry consults me. I'm the daddy of the whole thing. Men on my staff represent various branches, including labor. But it's a one-man show, and don't forget it. I control the purse strings, and sweetheart, there's a lot of dough in that purse."

But if he is asked how much money he controls, or what he is worth personally, he will smile and reply: "None of your damn business."

In recent years Samish has seldom crossed the street from the Senator Hotel to the Capitol. Once in a while he will do so, and will suddenly walk into a committee hearing where he probably has no interest whatsoever. He knows that no matter what the committee does, then, it will be credited to him. He enjoys hugely this sort of reputation-pyramiding.

Concerning his organization, he brags that his people are the highest paid in the world, and it is a fact that his top aides have become or are becoming rich in his service. They include Frank X. (Porky) Flynn, William (Shovelnose) Jasper, Dorothy Ready—buxom confidential secretary who knows more about Samish than anyone else—and a host of lawyers, among them Sandy Quattron, B. P. Calhoun, Emil J. Hoerschner, and Anthony J. Kennedy.

In asserting they are the highest paid in the world, Samish thoughtfully explains: "I want them to make a career out of it, not a racket."

Samish admits he makes an annual trek to Hot Springs, Arkansas, where the so-called Big Mob of national gangsters

399

are supposed to hold a sort of directors' meeting for the purpose of splitting up racket concessions. But he vigorously denies he has any part of that. He goes there after the season has closed, he says, "just for the baths and to take off a little weight."

He admits also he has had contact with some of the underworld's leading characters, particularly Mickey Cohen, reputed to be the Big Mob's West Coast man since Benjamin (Bugsy) Siegel was murdered in Beverly Hills in 1947. As to that, Samish explains: "Some of these guys like Cohen call me up and give me tips on races and things. That's all there is to it."

Samish lives and entertains sybaritically. At the end of each legislative session he gives a party that is the social event of the Sacramento season. Everyone who counts, frequently including governors, attends. In years past he was famous also for Christmas parties he gave at San Quentin, one of the State prisons, for a selected list of convicts. Entertainment at these soirees was very earthy, and the Yule cheer he provided included fine cigars and fine whisky, notwithstanding prohibitory prison regulations. But these affairs were stopped by new State Director of Corrections Richard A. McGee.

He loves a lavish gag. In the spring of 1949, he made a bet with Murray Stravers, investigator for State Senator Jack Tenney when the latter headed a committee on un-American activities, that Tenney would run no better than fourth in the Los Angeles mayoralty race.

The terms were $200, wagered by Stravers, against 200 laps around the Senator Hotel lobby in a costume designed by Samish. Stravers lost. The night of the pay-off Samish took a throne chair at one end of the lobby. His minions, Porky Flynn and Shovelnose Jasper, staked out the course with pennants. A miniature hospital layout was installed, complete with real doctor, nurse, bed, and stretcher, for ministrations to Stravers, should he collapse. Clowns in costume, hired from a circus, added to the festivities. The hilarious audience had paper hats, horns, and popcorn. Finally, Stravers appeared for his marathon attired in bright red trunks emblazoned with a hammer and sickle on the seat. Stimulated at the rate of one snort per lap, he managed to make ten rounds.

No sketch of Arthur H. Samish would be complete without a brief digest of his views on State and national affairs. He may have no more party coloration than a political chameleon, but his broad approach is revealing.

"Mass psychology," he says, "is running the show, and if you want to stay in it you've got to help those who can't help themselves." What he apparently means is that the less privileged classes are coming into power and he (Samish) will use the trend rather than fight it.

He blames lack of understanding of this factor for "those bum polls." "They don't talk to the people who can't afford cars or telephones," he explains. "My organization does and we haven't taken a bum poll yet."

He is convinced, also, that the State and country are in a condition of flux which should be thoroughly examined as a required preface to establishment of new legislative or administrative policies. He believes that legislatures should declare a moratorium on all but the most essential measures "until we find out whether we're in a recession, transition, or depression, and if we didn't have the cold war in Europe it would be a hell of a depression."

As to his efforts in his own backyard—California—Samish jovially concedes: "I'm doing all right."

That is the understatement of the decade. He has evolved an organization and a system which make it possible for him to sway legislators to enact into law—which the courts must uphold—the special privileges of his very special clients.

In short, Samish has a basic patent on legal methods of doing things in California which would be impossible in other States of the Union.

One of the most aggravated examples of Third House interference in California's political processes is Samish's admitted influence in the 1946 election of Fred N. Howser as Attorney General, the State's highest law-enforcement officer.

Samish's story is this:

"One day in 1946 Sam Collins (Speaker of the Assembly) came in to talk about the Attorney General race. He was interested in running and he was the *Los Angeles Times'* choice. (The *Times* denies it.) Howser was being talked about, too. I've known him since he was an Assemblyman. I advised him then; in fact, had him made chairman of the public morals committee. We decided on Howser because his name sounded like the Fred Houser who had been a great Lieutenant Governor. Also, because he would get the support of liberal elements and because he was pretty well known, being head of the biggest District Attorney layout in the country.

"Well, I got him elected. I didn't know he had all the funny money behind him. I was looking to the future, thinking maybe I might have me a U.S. Senator or a Governor some day. But when I came up to the '47 Legislature I heard all those rumblings. I called him in and told him he'd have to cut it out and give the autonomy back to the counties. But he didn't do it.

"I'm off him now. I've had to go back and unsell everybody I got to go for him, including the big publishers. That's the Howser story, as far as I'm concerned."

Samish's account is naive. The idea that he did not know about the torrential flow of "funny money" into the Howser campaign is sheer nonsense; that kind of money follows Samish's lead.

Within a month or two after Howser took office in January of 1947, rumors of gambling-racket shakedowns and organization attempts began to pop up all over the State. Although Governor Warren denies the rumors were the cause, he nevertheless obtained legislative authority to establish a commission to study organized crime.

This commission is headed by Admiral William H. Standley, U.S.N. retired, former United States Ambassador to Russia. Its counsel is Warren Olney III, distinguished young lawyer who served under Warren when the latter was Attorney General. The commission did not go into action until November of 1947. By then some of the racket uproar had broken into the open.

The first barrage came out of Jackson, county seat of Amador County which has had wide-open gambling—craps, roulette, blackjack, chuckaluck, and slot machines—since its earliest days. Attorneys General have simply let it alone as though it were in neighboring Nevada. Gambling is an integral part of the business community. Any sheriff or district attorney who tried to stop it would be recalled, if not ridden out of town on a rail.

From this county came the story that men representing themselves as Howser agents had first ordered gambling closed, then had been followed by emissaries who said they could "fix" the Attorney General's office—for a big cut of the gambling take. The county closed down of its own accord, on the principle of "millions for defense but not one cent for tribute." It remained closed for a year until Howser's office was so deeply involved as to be virtually helpless.

Next came a story from Nevada County that followed the same pattern. This furor involved Speaker Sam Collins, whom

403

Samish says he persuaded to withdraw from the Attorney General contest.

An Appellate Court Judge accused Collins of political chicanery in promoting a bill to take away police powers from State parole officers. They had raided a bookie parlor where parolees were patrons. The affair was serious enough to compel the Assembly to go through the motions of an investigation. Testimony included a digression into an account that Collins and a brother, a legislative employee, had called on the District Attorney and offered to contact Howser in connection with the slot-machine situation. Collins denied it. The investigation ended with exoneration by the Assembly, which put the Judge on trial rather than Collins.

The next scandal was an offshoot of the Crime Commission's attack on the bookmaking racket. The Commission's initial objective was to ban the wire service that supplies racing data to illegal handbooks. This wire service had passed into the hands of the big-time Eastern and Middle Western racketeers. It gave them over-all organizational control of bookmaking throughout the country, since a bookie without the service could not compete with one who had it.

The Crime Commission found that gangster control of bookmaking led to inevitable corruption, which in turn made possible the organization of other rackets.

The Commission asked Howser to investigate wire service "drops" from which the racing data were distributed to handbooks. One of these was in Palm Springs, California's famous desert spa. Two Howser subordinates, Wiley H. (Buck) Caddel and John Riggs went there. Caddel was in charge, it developed later, but Riggs was ordered to sign an altered and negative report from which Caddel's name was deleted. The Commission sent in its own investigator, who uncovered perfect evidence; the "drop" had a direct wire connection with a big horse parlor and both were operated by the same man.

With this and other evidence on the illegal use of telephone and telegraph facilities leased by the wire service, the Commission went before the State Public Utilities Commission and asked for corrective measures.

This agency issued a rule that telephone and telegraph companies, when informed by law-enforcement agencies of illegal use of their facilities, must cancel the leases involved. District Attorney Edmund G. Brown of San Francisco immediately had the wire service "drop" and numerous subsidiary teletypes cut off in his jurisdiction. The District Attorney of Kern County followed suit. The Crime Commission then "suggested" that Howser request severance of the wire service's main leased trunk into California, via Western Union. He did so, and wire-service operations since then have been of the costly bootlegged variety, with serious effect on the bookmaking racket.

The wire service, known as Continental Press Service, brought suit in federal court at Los Angeles for reinstatement of its main leased telegraph line. From there on Howser, despite his embarrassment over the Palm Springs incident, refused to take any part in the fight. Governor Warren eventually was compelled to ask the Public Utilities Commission to assign its own counsel to represent the State. Continental lost the suit.

While this affair was in progress other scandals involving Howser's staff came to light. They all followed the same basic pattern: men who said they represented the Attorney General appeared in counties and demanded a cut of gambling proceeds, chiefly from slot machines and punchboards, in return for protection against raids by Howser agents. This sort of racket occurred in Kern, Santa Cruz, Mendocino, San Luis Obispo, Yuba, San Mateo, Contra Costa, Placer, Fresno, San Bernardino, Tuolumne, Imperial, Napa, San Joaquin, and Los Angeles counties.

In two of these—Mendocino and San Luis Obispo counties —the Crime Commission and local authorities developed enough evidence to obtain grand jury indictments. The San Luis Obispo case ended in acquittal. But in Mendocino the jury convicted Wiley Caddel, the Howser subordinate who had figured in the Palm Springs matter, and two others on charges of bribery and conspiracy to violate the gambling laws. In late 1949 the case was still on appeal.

When caught, it was charged, they had partly organized the county's slot-machine operations for an initial pay-off of $4 per week per machine, boosted later to $10 a week, for the alleged protection of the Attorney General's office.

Before Caddel and his co-defendants were indicted, Howser sent a swarm of agents into the county, he announced, to determine if Caddel was being framed. Caddel, himself, was part of the investigating crew. After the convictions, Howser publicly quarreled with the verdict, strongly indicating he believed Caddel innocent. Trial Judge Lilburn Gibson excoriated Caddel as a criminal of the worst type, one who betrays the public trust inherent in an official position by consorting and conspiring with gangsters and attempting to corrupt other officials.

It is interesting to note that Howser's official attitude in the Caddel case was typical of his attitude in the other scandals that received enough official attention to compel an inquiry. Time and again agents who were named in charges were assigned to investigate themselves. Similarly, Howser repeatedly announced that the charges were without merit; that there was no evidence involving him or his staff.

But as the reports of racket shakedowns in the Attorney General's name spread up and down the State, Howser realized his political standing was crumbling. He fought back violently with a series of attacks on the Crime Commission and Governor Warren, accusing them of a vague but monstrous plot to create a "police state" and to destroy him (Howser) politically. He pictured himself as Warren's most dangerous foe for leadership of the Republican Party. He called the Crime Commission a "tumorous growth on the body politic, conceived in Warren's political ambitions." The outbursts reached a point of hysterical silliness before Howser's friends and advisers managed to quiet him.

The response he drew was rude.

The California Peace Officers' Association, after listening to one of his tirades, adopted a resolution vigorously commending Governor Warren and the Crime Commission. Olney, the Commission's attorney, also addressed the Association. He asked approval of a resolution calling on the Federal Communications Commission to investigate the bookie wire service for the purpose of destroying it everywhere. This resolution was passed, too, and gave strong support to similar action already taken by the State Public Utilities Commission.

The FCC phase of the wire service fight was based, in large part, on remarkable disclosures during the Utilities Commission hearings which led to the wire service ban in California. Olney had discovered that the FCC had already made an inquiry to determine the impact of organized gambling on the nation's communications facilities during World War II. The report of the FCC findings, labeled "confidential," had never been made public. But Olney managed to obtain a photostatic copy that was not marked "confidential" and put it into the record of the Utilities Commission proceedings.

It contained astonishing data: documented evidence showing that the wire service and the gambling interests it served enjoyed the status of customers favored over even the most essential of wartime operations. Also, that when an airplane crashed near Bakersfield, California, and tore down Western Union trunk lines, the wire leased by the bookie service was

407

restored in half an hour. But several hours elapsed before the wire leased by the Army's Western Defense Command, which serviced strategic military posts from Acapulco to Alaska, was restored.

To this writing, there has been no response from the FCC concerning the California petitions for a national investigation of the race-track wire service. Howser meanwhile emphasized his attacks on Warren and the Crime Commission by making personal appearances before 1949 legislative committees in attempts to kill a $102,000 appropriation to finance the Commission for another year. He failed. His furious statements, however, compelled Warren to reply and to bring into the open, at last, the bitter enmity between the State's two highest constitutional officers.

At a press conference, the Governor bluntly charged that Howser, in his refusal to act for the State in the wire-service litigation, and by his attitude in general, had left California practically helpless before the attempts of the crime syndicates to move in and exploit the huge postwar growth. In the face of Howser's strange administration of the State's highest law-enforcement agency, the Governor said, to kill off the Crime Commission would be a "surrender to the underworld."

Frankie Costello, big-time gangster, stuck his long nose into the picture all the way from New York, when he read that the Commission had referred to him as the "reputed head of the national slot-machine racket," and probably deeply interested in California. Costello wrote an open letter to Warren, denying all and complaining that he was so bereft of official influence anywhere that he could not fix a traffic tag in his home town of New York.

In its detailed discussion of the slot-machine racket, the Commission reported some astonishing discoveries made by its undercover men at the national convention of the Coin

Machine Institute in Chicago early in 1949. They found that the CMI is the master organization for slot-machine interests all over the country; that its legal staff conducts "seminars in graft" to instruct on the best methods of corrupting public officials; that CMI collects and spends huge sums to influence legislation and court decisions in many states.

They also heard a California operator make a speech in which he demanded allocation of more money for CMI efforts in California to remove from office public officials who were hindering the "industry."

Named as specific targets by the speaker were Governor Warren and Mayor Fletcher Bowron of Los Angeles. There was no mention of Fred N. Howser, California's chief law-enforcement officer.

The Commission's report was submitted in March, 1949. In May the *San Francisco Chronicle,* originally a Howser supporter but finally one of his severest critics, broke a sensational story that revealed a few more dim outlines of the state-wide pattern. The locale was San Bernardino County, where a grand jury had investigated the organized vice rackets and recommended the ouster of the sheriff.

The *Chronicle* obtained secret testimony before the grand jury by a Mrs. Earl Wilson, who flatly accused State Senator Ralph E. Swing of soliciting a fifteen per cent "under the-table" cut for using his influence in obtaining a midget auto racing concession from the county's National Orange Show. Swing is a director of the Orange Show. Mrs. Wilson testified also that W. C. Shay, chief agent for the Board of Equalization in the county, had demanded a five per cent cut of the racing concession; that the negotiations involving Swing were originated by Edward J. Seeman, notorious as the county's slot-machine king.

The Swing-Seeman connections were developed further when the *Chronicle* found Division of Corporation records showing they had been partners in an extremely lucrative liquor business known as the Alfred Hart Distributing Company of San Bernardino and Riverside. A third partner in the firm was a Miss E. Mack, identified as a friend of Samish, who had a hand in setting up half a dozen or more of the Hart liquor companies. For a capital investment of less than $2,000, Senator Swing, slot-machine operator Seeman, and Miss Mack had split net profits of more than $100,000.

By way of a filip, the *Chronicle* disclosed further that Mrs Wilson testified she was told by Seeman (in 1946) that Howser had to be elected if the slot-machine racket was to continue in operation, and that Seeman's office at the time was stacked with Howser literature, cards, and placards.

Howser was in the grand jury room when the testimony was given. He was offered a chance to speak but had nothing to say. There have been only negative aftermaths so far from the whole affair, although a thorough investigation has been made by the Crime Commission that may produce developments later.

At Sacramento the staid Senate was severely jarred by the Swing disclosures. He denied them, of course, as did Shay. Swing's colleagues, after many sub rosa conferences, decided to try to ride out the trouble with no formal investigation.

Howser, meantime, had made another of his so-called inquiries into San Bernardino County. His office duly announced there was no evidence of organized rackets or corruption.

"L'affaire Howser" reached such proportions that early in 1949 recall movements were tentatively started against him in both San Francisco and Los Angeles. But they were dropped as inexpedient and too costly; the voters could decide the issue, if necessary, in the 1950 State elections. They may have to.

Howser has announced that he will be a candidate for re-election. His friends contend he has "rehabilitated himself and cleaned up his office." Several of his key appointees have "resigned." They include Wiley Caddel, the agent convicted in Mendocino County; Charles Hoy, another agent who got out shortly after the scandals started exploding; Walter H. Lentz, Howser's chief investigator and superior of Caddel and Hoy.

By mid-June, 1949, Howser's campaign had begun, in an atmosphere of sweetness and light. He abandoned his attacks on the Crime Commission, reversed his field, and was publicly declaring the Commission was a fine thing. He was also pledging, again, that he would respect the autonomy of counties. But his private plans called for a series of personal raids on racket operations here and there, with the aim of emerging as a sort of marked-down Tom Dewey. In addition, a state-wide propaganda drive was launched to make Howser appear the victim of political persecution by the Warren-led Republican elements.

Samish, who had announced with great emphasis that he was through with Howser, gave signs of a change of mind. In May, 1949, one of his most trusted aides, Porky Flynn, let it be known that the "Colonel" believed Howser should run again for Attorney General because he had cleaned up his office, and that further attacks on him would indeed be political persecution.

What these antics might mean caused a lot of speculation. But Howser as a potential candidate came a severe cropper on July 20, 1949. He had complained many times about his "bad press." On that day his press was simply awful. Three events occurred:

1. District Attorney Chester Watson of San Joaquin County publicly charged that Howser was trying to get out of prison a millionaire who had been convicted of vast frauds.

Sixteen District Attorneys promptly joined in an appeal to the State Supreme Court to circumvent Howser's efforts.

2. Howser's $300,000 libel suit against Columnist Drew Pearson backfired mightily. The Attorney General's "private eye," Walter H. Lentz (formerly Howser's chief special agent) was arrested by the Federal Bureau of Investigation on charges of causing money to be passed to James T. Mulloy, one of Pearson's major witnesses, in an attempt to have Mulloy change his testimony.

3. Gangsters mowed down Mobster Mickey Cohen and three companions in a night ambush on Los Angeles's notorious "Sunset Strip." One of the victims was Harry Cooper, a special agent on Howser's staff. Cooper had been assigned as Cohen's personal bodyguard. The fact that Cohen, reputed boss of the Los Angeles County underworld, had been given a bodyguard by the State's highest law-enforcement officer, touched off widespread public indignation. Howser left July 29 on a vacation trip to Mexico City, without coherent explanation.

The situation produced by the Cohen shooting simmered for seventeen days, then blew high, wide and very ugly.

A San Francisco Chronicle reporter, who had aided in the preliminary investigation of the Lentz case, was sent from Fresno to Los Angeles to dig into the attempt on the gangster's life.

The reporter unearthed a transcript of sound recordings made by Los Angeles police at Cohen's home between April 13, 1947 and March 17, 1948, and kept hidden ever since.

He took the highly secret document back to his office, where it was photostated. At the direction of Editor Paul Smith, this treasure trove of astonishing information was made available to the Los Angeles Times and both papers published spectacu-

lar accounts of it the night of August 15, and ran subsequent
stories for several days.

The disclosures included frank discussions of graft and corruption in high places for the protection of crime syndicate
racket operations, with ramifications extending into other sections of the State and beyond its borders to the Middle West,
East and South.

As of this writing, The Chronicle's enterprising bit of journalism had touched off a complicated set of interlocking investigations in which six Federal agencies and the authorities
of four cities and four counties were participating.

California, take it away!